MW00857164

Gerald lectures passionately oɪ
eagerly grouped around him in the

"Gravity is bullshit, a lie we believe collectively. If we could release ourselves from this illusion, we would be able to fly around the room like they did in the movie, *Mary Poppins*. Remember when they floated up and had a tea party on the ceiling?"

An unanticipated surge of rage rises from deep inside my chest, reddening my cheeks. I tilt my face downwards to hide, but Gerald catches my reaction and makes an example of me.

"Elizabeth, do you have a problem with what I just said?" He glares, rising from his seat and approaching me threateningly.

"Yyyyyes," I stammer, cursing myself for wearing my emotions on my sleeve, as usual . . . now forced to admit my lack of faith publicly.

"See everybody," he turns to face the rest of my comrades, "this proves my point. Elizabeth is defending the lie that we can't fly, and that lie is precisely what holds us all on the ground."

I recede into my chair in humiliation. His accusations make me feel personally responsible for keeping the entire human race weighted down on the Earth's surface . . . Another surge of rage passes through me, commanding me to jump up and argue, even attack him for what he has just claimed, but I hold myself back, suppressing my reaction, keeping my butt glued to my seat. Nonetheless, Gerald senses my continued opposition and turns, raising his voice, filling me with terror . . .

"I thank the authors for illuminating the subtleties of cult involvement along with the agonizing struggle to break the spell. An incredible story."
Frederick J. Berle, Ph.D., Clinical Psychologist
Author of "Cults and Abusive Religions"

"*Torn From the Arms of Satan* is a testimony to human weakness and the ability of love to conquer evil."
Al Sullivan
Senior Staff Writer, The Hudson Reporter

"An intriguing story . . . reveals how devious individuals can take advantage of good people in a vulnerable moment. Bottom line — a book everyone should read!"
David R. Cole, Vice President
Leo J. Ryan Education Foundation for Cult Awareness

"Burchard and Carlone, in the revelatory *Torn From the Arms of Satan*, have rendered an invaluable service. All of us <u>must</u> be alerted to the consummate devastation which may be perpetrated by an enslaving, malevolent predator. Wake up America! Read this book!"

Evelyn Ortner
Executive Director, The Unity Group, Inc.
A non-profit advocacy group for battered women & their children

"A painstaking, sometimes painful, insightful case study — the surprising part of this tale is that despite two decades of mind control, the author was able to be deprogrammed by a dedicated individual. The grit, patience and determination displayed by Judith Carlone (the "deprogrammer") had me mixing metaphors — describing her as an avatar of St. Michael."

Dayn DeRose,
Adjunct Instructor, Drew University

"This story clearly reveals how currently popular spiritual principles can be manipulated by a power-hungry individual concealed behind a benevolent facade; how the lives of innocent people can be utterly destroyed — entirely permissible within the bounds of our legal system. A testimony to true friendship and the resilience of the human spirit."

Judy Chapman
Editor and Founder, Garden State Woman Magazine

"*Torn From the Arms of Satan* is a wake-up call to the harsh realities of deception and extreme emotional and spiritual abuse. It could happen to anyone!"

Ann Rubino, Hoboken, N.J.

"A fascinating account; I couldn't put it down. The authors brilliantly expose the faulty logic and manipulative masterminding of the cult leader, a malevolent genius. I found myself rising from my seat to cheer for Carlone's courage and Burchard's escape."

Barbara Girafalo, Union Beach, N.J.

Torn
From The
Arms
of
Satan

A True Story of
Seduction and Escape
from a
Contemporary New Age Cult

*Elizabeth R. Burchard
and Judith L. Carlone*

Ace Academics Inc., New Jersey

This is a true story.
Some of the names have been changed to protect
the privacy of the people involved.
Conversations were composed from memory
and presented to reflect the intention of the speakers
with the greatest possible accuracy.

TORN FROM THE ARMS OF SATAN
©2000 by Elizabeth R. Burchard & Judith L. Carlone

ISBN 1-881374-05-X

cover design by Judith L. Carlone
cover art by Jared Phillips ©1998
title by Michael P. Carlone

Published by Ace Academics Inc.
253 Closter Dock Road, Suite 6
Closter, N.J. 07624
1-888-3-STUDY-3
fax: 1-800-FLASH-45
e-mail: acepub2@aol.com
www.EXAMBUSTERS.com

In gratitude to each of my great teachers, Rachael, George, Mike, Matt, Cynthia, amidst your opposition, I found the strength to survive.

To the memory of the two men I lost, both taken too young and too soon.

To the friends I left behind — I pray for their eyes to open, that someday they will reach for the light . . .

To the two women who left "The Group" before me, thank you for your support and the healing we shared together.

To Christina, my editor, for her invaluable comments.

To those generous of spirit, who knowingly or unknowingly helped me find my freedom. Addy R., Melissa G., Preston, Nestor, Bob D., Hal D., Val, Robert C., Tony D., Tom P., and Lee G.

To Michael, who trusted me enough to share the person closest to his heart.

. . .and finally, to my Angel, Judy, there are no words . . .

Elizabeth R. Burchard

To my mother who protected me and taught me how to love.

To my father, Eugene F. and Lucy C. for challenging my weaknesses.

To Michael, my husband, for enduring with boundless love, since the moment we met.

To Leslie S. for helping me to overcome my personal battles.

To all my animals for their unconditional love.

To God, for selecting me to carry out His extraordinary mission.

Judith Lynn Carlone

I don't believe in secrets. Secrets cover shame, and shame poisons the soul. With the assistance and encouragement of others, combined with my own naivete, I have committed terrible crimes in my life — crimes mostly against myself. My sins lie within these pages — a story of persecution, betrayal and miracles, of finding the strength to overcome.

I was a vulnerable and needy young woman, searching for guidance in all the wrong places. Perhaps, despite the strange circumstances, you will see some of yourself in me . . .

Introduction

The word "cult" elicits a variety of responses from people: fear, anger, disgust, fascination; thoughts like — *It would never happen to me*, or *I don't understand how the members can embrace such ridiculous doctrines; it's obvious that they are simply weak, stupid people.* Yet, after my own arduous journey, an experience which robbed me of half of my forty years, I have come to view the ordeal as a sort of bizarre addiction, sustained by those who had much to gain from my enslavement, people who were initially able to convince me that I could trust them. The cost was heavy; I lost a sizable inheritance from my father, threw away childhood plans of becoming a doctor, ruined my health and severed ties to everyone from my past. Nonetheless, I began like most; I developed hobbies, attended college, planned my future and fell in love. Every day I tried to make the most sensible choices I could, and yet, despite my most conscientious efforts, I eventually came to find myself entangled in a world of evil beyond anything I ever could have imagined. Low self-esteem, youthful idealism, gullibility and loneliness all led to my entrapment . . . and as a basically isolated person with few friends or family, once I had succumbed, there was no one there to protest or try to rescue me from the quicksand. I now realize that I am not unique. Most people possess at least some of the weaknesses which permitted my seduction; and these shortcomings emerge to foster human miseries besides cult involvement: failed relationships and businesses, self-destructive habits like overeating and work-a-holism, or obsession with the wrong lover.

It was indeed my weaker self — insecure, unassertive and demanding recognition — which led me to my seat and strapped me down. From there I endured the evolution of "The Group" which began as "Stress Reduction" sessions in the office of a Manhattan psychologist, but soon developed into an incestuous cultic religion — a small group of primarily women who served every whim of their idolized leader, a pathological liar and a malevolent, exploitative genius.

It was my higher self, the part which knows love and humility, that eventually helped me find freedom. This self relentlessly sent out an SOS, even as my totally brainwashed and obsessed mind patently ignored its desperate pleas. But although I didn't know it, God was listening; and when I reached my breaking point, He sent assistance.

Cults like mine meet every day, all around us, even in our own backyards. In the past several months, I have discovered three similar groups within five miles of my home. They share common characteristics: a charismatic guru who controls the minds and lives of his followers and a worshipful assembly who willingly (or unwillingly) donates its allegiance, energy, time and money to their fraudulent spiritual leader. The members might surprise you: a neighbor, mayor, physician or rabbi; even your child's school teacher.

Search for Spirituality

"All of us have a sense of spiritual destiny, a deep longing for eternity."
(Dr. David Jeremiah, *What The Bible Says About Angels*)

Many of us believe in the existence of a separate world, a higher truth beyond this secular carnal existence. Despite faithful attempts to govern our personal lives, unanticipated events occur, often for incomprehensible reasons. Gut instincts, coincidences and ultimately, the keys to our destiny seem to originate from this invisible realm which terrifies and yet fascinates us, our connection to eternity. Sometimes, especially during crisis, we seek comfort in the knowledge that a higher intelligence exists, a God who loves and protects us. We strive to understand this divine presence with whom, when our fleeting physical journeys are complete, we will ultimately find happiness, peace and a home for our souls.

Frequently, as a part of raising us, our parents transmit a set of instructions, both verbal and non-verbal — a personal rule book on which to base future decisions. If we don't like what we see and renounce our parents' way of life, how do we know where to begin to find our way? At the dawning of this new century, more than ever before, humanity seems to crave spiritual knowledge. Those not fortunate enough to discern a path through upbringing or organized religion become seekers. I was an only child and my mother, a single parent. We were all each other had, yet we never got along. Emotional conflict was perpetual and resolution hopeless. As a small child I rejected her as my role-model. Thus I spent my youth longing for an adult mentor — a source of strength, wisdom and truth from which I could draw when I felt insecure or lost.

Gerald Sharkman, a man I met as a college freshman in 1977, seemed to be the answer to my prayers. He was merely a biofeedback therapist, assistant to an Upper East Side psychologist, but he clearly had a calling; I had never heard anyone speak that passionately about higher truth. His conviction was so powerful that my yearning for spiritual wisdom awoke screaming for nourishment. His charisma captivated me and my intensely aroused emotions supplied irrevocable evidence that through him must lie the keys to all of the unanswered questions in the universe. He seemed to have uncovered a magical recipe for the perfect life, and I sincerely believed that mastering his way of thinking would afford me anything I could ever want. I took him at face value, assuming he truly was the person I needed him to be. Thus, I gave my allegiance to Gerald and embraced him as my personal teacher and guide. I glued myself to him, drinking in his every word. With the goal of absorbing all that was in his mind and making it my own, I became his most avid and faithful student. The furious desire for his knowledge overwhelmed me and immediately took priority over everything else. Every single one of Gerald's lessons was taken to heart and I carried his precious jewels of supernatural wisdom out into the world where I eagerly sought to verify them.

In the search for happiness, prosperity and peace, many find New Age spirituality extremely attractive. This is evident at Gerald's *Barnes and Noble* author signings for his self-help book, *Biofeedback Without Machines*, where the audience absorbs his concepts willingly — professed formulas for personal fulfillment, shedding lies and illusions, or removing blockage and unlocking infinite potential. These concepts are the cornerstones of many popular self-help and New Age books. Although Gerald's assertions are attractive, very much in line with Neale Donald Walsch — author of *Conversations with God*, James Redfield — author of *The Celestine Prophesy* and Dr. Deepak Chopra, in contrast, Gerald possesses a personal hidden agenda. Many of those exposed to his rhetoric, or that of other cult leaders — Jim Jones (The People's Temple), Marshall Applewhite (Heaven's Gate) — respond just as I did; they trust his pretense — a passionate instructor whose heart is focused on your greatest good and who will share your joy as you grow spiritually. They have no idea what danger lies ahead, should they choose to take that fateful step toward his inner circle.

Elizabeth R. Burchard — July 2000

I visit my mother's apartment on Manhattan's Upper West Side for the first time since the breakup. As I enter the dimly lit hallway, ghosts of neglect and decay rush through me like disembodied spirits crying plaintively of unfulfilled dreams, a wasted life now almost concluded. The place is beyond dirty, it is filthy. I am appalled by the sight and can't imagine how it was possible to ever get this bad. The kitchen floor, tiled black and white, is almost completely black. Splotches of some unidentifiable brown substance stain the sides of the freestanding white metal cabinet — a dented off balance monstrosity which holds her treasured collection of plastic wonton soup containers and marred brown plastic vitamin bottles, some dating back to my pre-teen years. The face of the dish cabinet displays a large circle of grimy dirt which originates at the knobs and fans outward, covering much of the white painted wooden doors. A nauseating stench emanates from a hopelessly scorched pot which sits at the back of the stove filled with brackish water. My mother admits that the smell is repugnant but she has "gotten used to it". I suggest gently that she throw it out and she looks bewildered, as if the idea never occurred to her. The build-up of frost in the freezer leaves little room for her food; most of it carelessly wrapped in wax paper and rubber bands, severely freezer-burned, some of it more than a few years old. Large balls of dust scatter on the living-room floor as my steps disturb them. There are two rolled up room-sized Persian rugs which once graced the floors of my father's ten-room Park Avenue apartment when he was alive. They are still in brown paper, wrapped from a visit to the dry cleaners a decade ago. My mother's cocktail party lifestyle, with designer clothes and carefully applied make-up, has long faded. Now she reigns, the Queen of Polyester, over a kingdom of overstuffed closets. $10 pants and $3 shirts spill onto the floor, treasures she has purchased at 14th Street discount stores. My childhood bookcases are filled with $5 slippers, up to six pairs of identical styles in various neon colors. Her short hair, burnt brittle from too many coloring sessions, is almost orange, with an inch of grey root forming the part on top of her head. She has a slight cold and a bead of fluid glistens, clinging tenuously to the tip of her nose, but she seems oblivious to its presence. Her red polyester pants don't quite reach her ankles or the green slippers she wears with them, and her thermal underwear peeks out from under a partially buttoned orange shirt. The fabric barely covers her extended belly, extra weight she has gathered from lack of exercise and "eating too much chocolate cake, my favorite". She walks the rooms in a trance-like state, wearing the keys to her apartment on a thick green cord around her neck. They jostle below the undershirt and bounce on her belly button in rhythm to her step. On the street she has sometimes been mistaken for a bag-lady, despite the fact that at seventy-five years old, she still holds a full-time job as research economist for the Department of Consumer Affairs to which she dutifully commutes by subway daily.

She discontinued the weekly maid soon after I moved out; it has been fifteen years since the house was properly cleaned. Not that she can't afford the cost, it is just no longer a priority. I offer to help her at least vacuum a bit, but she cuts me off defensively,

"No Liz, you would just take over and boss me around. I don't trust you. You don't treat me well."

The shower curtain is green from algae growth and I am afraid to sit on the toilet seat. There is dust on every surface including the bathroom sink which has been unusable for over two years, requiring some minor repair that she never got around to arranging with the building superintendent. This beautiful pre-war co-op apartment is huge for one person — three bedrooms, two baths, eat-in kitchen, parlor and large living room; yet she has collected so many things that it is difficult to move about. Even my childhood toys still rest on a shelf in the third bedroom, her "storage room". There are piles of paper everywhere — fascinating newspaper articles, the past fifteen years' tax returns, Ross Perot's *United We Stand America* propaganda and devotedly safeguarded manila folders filled with appetizing tidbits of material that once touched our former life together — "apple-picking", "Liz's school report cards", "summer camp", "vitamins and health".

I am struck by the profusion of small slips of paper strewn everywhere on which my mother has preserved choice morsels of her thought and personal affirmations. On top of the TV, dated two years ago, one states boldly, "I do exist; I must learn to assert this." Next to the telephone lies another, "My daughter is a separate person from me." Under that one I discover yet another which lists my former Hackensack, N.J. apartment phone number, disconnected eight years ago. Her bed is entirely covered with piles of additional, unattended folders which she believes she will someday need. To avoid spending the several necessary minutes to move them each night, she has been sleeping on the couch for the past five years.

I realize that being surrounded by these thoughts fills her emptiness, that she has no life other than to bury herself in the senseless logic which springs forth from her mind. Sadly, I see an old woman who has thrown away her self-respect, dignity and her only child for a life of rubbish and denial.

Amidst this disarray my mother has three havens: her computer, her microwave oven and her television. I visualize her filling lonely days rotating her attention from one machine to the next, deriving a cherished sense of vitality from her interactions with these inanimate offspring of our modern technology. My heart breaks for the barrenness of her soul. How did this ever happen to her? Always at the head of the class, my mother skipped three grades and graduated college at the age of nineteen. She obtained a master's degree in the early 1940's, a time when many of her peers had left school after the eighth grade. If only I could rent a Dumpster, park it on 85th Street and throw all of her papers and dust out of that third story apartment's front windows. *How did I ever come from a place like this?* I wonder. I yearn desperately to pluck her out of the decay and sweep her away on my white horse who soars on wings of love, courage and passion, but I know she will not reach for my extended hand . . . that although momentarily I can force her with my stronger will, when I let go she will inevitably return, like an over-stretched rubber band which regains its natural shape as soon as the tension is released.

My Past — January 1939 to September 1977

In 1940, my mother, Grace, married her professor of psychology, Edward Burchard, upon graduating State College. She was nineteen and he was thirty-one. She went on to earn her Master's Degree in Sociology at the University of Pennsylvania. My father, a magna cum laude graduate of the University of Pittsburgh with a Ph.D. in psychology, was a quiet intellectual with an unusually high I.Q. and numerous professional awards to his credit. They spent the first years of their marriage, the early 1940's, in Washington, D.C. There, my father served in the World War II United States Navy, decoding enemy intelligence. Eventually they ended up in New York City, my father accepting the position of psychology professor at Queens College.

My father in the early 1940's.

After nineteen years of marriage, on December 29, 1959, their only child, Elizabeth R. Burchard, was born at Mount Sinai Hospital on the Upper East Side. Why did they wait so long? According to my mother, my father did not want any children. Their marriage was empty and passionless; they slept in separate beds. Grace, always obsessed with improving herself, had a string of therapists over a thirty-year period who gladly took her money and yet accomplished nothing. One of these mentors counseled her thus,

"If you want to have a baby, you have the right demand it of your husband."

My mother about 1959.

Somehow she managed to maneuver him into a sexual encounter and conceived.

I don't remember much about my first three years, but according to my mother, my parents fought all the time. One day, just after my third birthday, there were big men moving things out of our 96th Street, Park Avenue apartment. Wandering around confused, I bumped into my mother who informed me without explanation, "We are moving away from your father."

That day we moved directly across town to West End Avenue. Many years later my mother explained her decision; my father ignored her and she could no longer tolerate feeling unappreciated. Another reason for the breakup was "Uncle Keith", a man she had been introduced to a year or so earlier at one of those Upper East Side cocktail parties my parents so often attended with other members of the intellectual set. She was totally enthralled with Mr. Brace, a prominent lawyer with a fancy Park Avenue duplex, a quintessential Manhattan playboy who was separated but conveniently not divorced. Keith was happy to keep her on his arm and in his bed, but had no intention of making any commitment. Grace chased him for many years, trying to use all of her feminine will and manipulations to convince him to cut the cord with his wife and marry her. Every so often he would throw her a bone and transform into Mr. Sincere, journeying to his wife's Virginia residence to plead for a divorce. Days later he would return with the report that she had refused him again and sadly, there was nothing more he could do.

Me at the time of the divorce.

With my father out of the way, I became the center of my mother's life. However, the roles she required me to play were not those of a toddler. In a sense, we reversed the positions of parent and child. Her unspoken message demanded that I, at age four, be decision maker, confidante and even father. Grace, in turn, often acted like a helpless little girl, endlessly seeking recognition; she had never resolved the pain of her own childhood where both of her parents, especially my grandfather, ignored her. Ensnared in her web of insecurity and emotional dysfunction, I felt no strength, protection or support.

I found myself perpetually frustrated by her lack of common sense and frequent displays of unreasonable antisocial behavior. She threw impulsive tantrums in public, shrieking irrationally at innocent restaurant waiters to complain about food which had not been prepared to meet her expectations. I experienced intense mortification, desiring to crawl under the table, wanting to reassure all of the shocked onlookers that I didn't know this woman; she was no relation of mine. In addition, we began to fight regularly. Suddenly, for no apparent reason, she would become enraged. She focused her anger on me, accusing me of bad intentions and misbehavior that she seemed to have invented and that I never understood. "You are rude and defiant. You never listen to me. You don't respect me." Without warning, she would react to something I had innocently said and slap me full in the face, in public, sometimes in front of one of my little friends. Her scorn and humiliation stung much worse than the blow.

One day while walking up 96th Street, I began skipping over pavement seams and chanting something we had been singing at recess, "Step on a crack and break your mother's back." My mother responded immediately, slapping me fiercely several times. Frightened tears ran down my face as I struggled to defend myself, to make her understand that it was simply a song I had learned in school. Apparently she had taken the rhyme personally, thinking I was insulting her and wishing her dead. After several desperate minutes I finally reached her and she dropped the issue, but I observed that she experienced no remorse over the abuse I had just been forced to swallow as a result of her mistaken interpretation. Instead, she simply changed the subject. On another day this scene would be repeated over some other imagined transgression as I found myself trapped in a perpetual loop where she would accuse unreasonably and I would defend to no avail . . . and then there times when it was worse . . . like the time we were riding a bus up Broadway (I was about four) and I said something she didn't approve of. She offered me the choice of being spanked right there in front of all of the other bus-riders, or else waiting until we got home. I chose the less shameful option. For the rest of our journey my stomach twisted in terror of anticipation. As we entered our building I looked up at the doorman with pleading eyes, imploring him to rescue me, *As soon as our apartment door closes behind us, my mommy is going to hurt me. Could you please stop her?* And once inside, my mother dragged me immediately into the back bedroom where she commanded me to pull down my underpants so that when she delivered my punishment, I would be sure to learn my lesson really well.

When I learned to write, she disciplined me frequently with the assignment of writing two hundred times, "I will not be rude to my mother". I spent many evenings, pencil in hand, studiously forcing myself through this drudgery, and occasionally glancing wistfully out the window as my friends played in the courtyard below. Occasionally my mother's demon took residence in me. We had this dog, a stupid yappy black miniature poodle named "Napoleon" after his obnoxious personality. Every afternoon I was responsible for walking him and he always took his time, frequently making me wait twenty minutes to empty himself. I wasn't allowed to return upstairs until he "did number two" and one day he just wouldn't. He squatted several times, teasing me, but nothing came out, and finally I dragged him back into the lobby where I suddenly lost control and began punching him furiously. He couldn't have weighed more than six pounds and my blows threatened to seriously injure him, but overpowering waves of pent up frustration over my own oppression poured out in those moments, venting their fury on this poor innocent animal. In the midst of this tantrum another tenant entered the lobby, a woman who ran over yelling, "What are you doing? Stop it now!" I instantly came to my senses and toxicity flooded my body and soul, causing me to drop my head in shame, whimpering internally, probably suffering much more than my pet. I ran for the elevator, jumped inside and pushed the button to close it quickly, before the woman could make it through the doors. I couldn't have endured the ride up to the fifteenth floor with my sin so freshly written all over me for her to read. I told no one about the incident but paid extra special attention to Napoleon for several days after, until I was sure he was fine and my guilty feelings had faded. During my sleep I relived my conflict-ridden days and sometimes nightmares brought an ugly cruel witch to persecute me. From beneath her black hat my mother's face sneered with contempt and the sadistic pleasure she took in keeping me prisoner. And to this day, I still honestly do not understand how Grace found me to be so continually terrible.

To compensate for the lack of love and support in my home, I became fascinated with some of my female teachers and baby sitters, in fact, anyone who was nice to me. When my mother sensed my allegiance to this new person, she would go crazy with jealousy, discrediting the object of my affection and my feelings as well.

"How can you look up to that woman? She is so unsophisticated, downright dumb. Besides, you are rude and bossy. No one could stand spending too much time around you. You'll never be able to keep friends for very long."

There was a silent and unnegotiable message that she would not tolerate emotional commitments to any other person but herself, ever. In fact, I felt that if she were permitted to fulfill her plans, I would never leave home and we would remain each other's sole companion for our entire lives. I struggled against this mostly invisible and unspoken pressure, feeling too powerless to ever hope to overcome it. An awareness of her intentions for my future filled me with horrible dread. As if trapped in quicksand, I feared that no matter how hard I struggled, my efforts would be futile. Living with Grace, I felt totally alone.

Where was my father during all of this? Keeping his head in the sand like an ostrich. My father's fear of confrontation prevented him from ever rushing to my defense. He was an avoider who preferred burying his nose in a book, memorizing trivia that he could impress people with at cocktail parties, instead of facing his problems and taking responsibility for his child's well-being. One day when I was about eight, I discovered that he was not my ally. I was sitting on his lap in his apartment, speaking to mother on the phone. As usual, she was attacking me for some crime she had cooked up in her head. The injustice and hurt cut right though me, but when I hung up the phone I realized that my father was insensitive to my pain. Despite my tearful face, he neither attempted to acknowledge my mother's abuse, nor to comfort me. Furthermore, when I tried to share it with him, he blocked me and changed the subject.

In third grade I took an I.Q. test in order to gain entrance into an Upper West Side private school. The psychologist who administered the exam told my mother that my intelligence far exceeded my current grade level but unfortunately, I also had serious emotional problems. Grace decided to send me to a child psychologist. (I remained on the couch until I was ready to go to college.) My father protested, "Don't bother putting her into therapy; she is the child of a broken home and will never be happy." He didn't intend for me to suffer; he just couldn't deal with his own shame over the fact that his daughter was disturbed.

Despite my father's inability to help me cope with my mother, the precious Saturdays spent with him every weekend were my only break from her. With him I felt free to be myself. We had a subscription to the *Lincoln Center Ballet* and visited museums and restaurants all over Manhattan. Our trips to *FAO Schwartz* were frequent and my father bought me almost anything I asked for. He also stashed several *Beatles'* records in his phonograph cabinet especially for me. In my happiest memories I am whirling around his living room in a spontaneous dance inspired by *The Magical Mystery Tour* or *White Album*. Frequently we visited his well-heeled Westchester colleagues and spent lazy summer afternoons on their luxurious manicured lawns, sipping lemonade or swimming in a nearby lake. The world was sweet and gentle with my oppressor miles away from plaguing me. Edward bragged about me to his friends, who lavished attention on me; he was always so proud of his smart vivacious daughter. Most Augusts we vacationed in Provincetown, on Massachusetts' Cape Cod. Alone with my father I felt safe, loved and happy. At the age of eight I knew in my heart that I wanted to follow in his footsteps, so I selected a future career similar to his. I decided to become a psychiatrist and set my heart on getting into medical school someday.

December 7, 1971 was three weeks before my twelfth birthday. It was the day of the seventh grade Christmas PTA Bazaar and I spent my lunch hour buying handmade gifts for my mother, my father and numerous cousins, aunts and uncles on my mother's side. When the school bus dropped me off I rushed into the apartment to find my mother sitting on the couch. I grabbed my school bag, about to pull out the little treasures I had obtained just a few hours earlier. Christmas gift buying for our large extended family was one of the few ventures we enjoyed together. However, just as I was about to display my first item, she stopped me in mid-sentence. Suddenly I connected with her emotions and perceived that something was tragically wrong. My stomach fell to my shoes seconds before she gave me news of an event I would never have imagined could possibly happen.

"Elizabeth, your father died today."

All in one profound moment the significance of this reality ripped through me. My life force felt as if it was being sucked out of my body as I stared at her in shock, not willing to believe, unable to understand, refusing to accept. My mother seemed to feel genuinely sorry for me, but she was now a distant entity in another universe of experience; in this moment I was totally alone and completely destroyed. My sadness and loss were beyond infinite as I immediately awoke to the realization that my father had abandoned me, dooming me to the unsupervised jurisdiction of my mother, my enemy. Our maid, Annabelle, a warm and wonderful Black woman from Brooklyn who had cleaned for our family for more than twenty years, had found him that morning in his bed. He had died during the night of a completely unexpected heart attack. He was almost sixty-four. An hour later I found myself pacing the hallway outside her bedroom door while she telephoned my father's two half-sisters in northwestern Oil City, Pennsylvania, and her two brothers outside of Philadelphia. She repeated the same short sentence to all of them,

"I just wanted to let you know that Ed died today."

Those words were a gong ringing sadness into my soul, and from that day forward a shadow of grief accompanied me everywhere, throbbing loneliness as if my heart had been ripped out of my chest. Life no longer held importance and I became cut off from everyone and everything. In addition, my father's death left me with a crushing demand to replace him. That need established a stronghold inside my chest, and from the walls of that mighty fortress it screamed mercilessly, demanding satisfaction at any cost. An addiction as

My father as I knew him.

powerful as any to food, drugs or alcohol ever could be, it afflicted me with its impossible demand every day, for years to come. When my father passed away, I inherited $183,000. In 1972, this was a small fortune, but I really didn't care, I just wanted my father back.

Two years before my father's death, my mother had established herself as inflexible dictator in the isolated realm of her private mind where she obsessively pursued self-help strategies. It all started when a busybody neighbor from down the hall approached her by the elevators. While gossiping casually, this woman glanced down and commented on my complexion.

"Your daughter looks a little peaked. I suggest that you give her some wheat-germ. If you wait here for a moment, I'll fetch you my extra jar."

She sprinted to her apartment and returned a few minutes later, handing my mother an ample container of this, according to her, miraculous substance. On that fateful day Grace developed an obsession for health foods, and soon she had turned Adele Davis' book, *Let's Eat Right to Keep Fit*, into her personal bible. It was filled with bookmarks, underlining and paper clips, and she could quote the vitamin or mineral solution to any ailment; she spoke of nothing else. Her mania was annoying and embarrassing. She started shoving health foods down my throat, and her ideas down the throats of our friends and relatives.

The following fall, we moved to Riverdale, a middle-class section of the Bronx. That first winter, despite her health food diet, my mother's symptoms of hypoglycemia (low blood sugar) began. The frigid December air would hit her lungs, causing them to spasm into an asthma attack. A two-block walk took thirty minutes. She would take a few steps and then stop to clutch a lamppost for several minutes, bent over, gasping for breath. To me she looked as feeble as a ninety-year-old. Concerned passers-by would stop and ask if she needed help. My mother would turn to look up at them with pale face and feeble gaze murmuring, "I'm just having a little trouble breathing. I'll be OK in a bit after I rest some more."

I didn't understand what was happening to her. Without even seeking to pinpoint the source of her symptoms, Grace clung tenaciously to the belief that her faith in Adele Davis' theories would cure her. She never sought a professional who might diagnose and teach her to control her disorder. Meanwhile, her symptoms continued to worsen, almost completely disabling her for days at a time, obliging me to care for her and myself as well.

Organic foods and vitamins filled my mother's thoughts and our kitchen, and they drained her wallet. After her start with Adele Davis, she decided to seek out a guru with whom she could interact in person. Dr. Seidler was a Manhattan chiropractor-nutritionist. He prescribed "living vitamins", which came from Ohio, and enchanted her with detailed narratives of the vitamin factory where they "pull the carrot out of the ground and immediately grind it into a capsule for you to swallow". These garden stories justified in Grace's mind the exorbitant costs, in 1972, of more than $250 a month for those pill-shaped carrots. Twice a week she dutifully visited his office where he put her on a weird machine with a small wheel that went up and down her back. After leaving the room for fifteen minutes he would return, stating encouragingly, "You're doing very well; you can add more oranges to your diet."

His sage advice offered, he would hand her a bill for $55. Dr. Seidler's consummate answer to good health was the potato. He claimed they were nature's perfect food because "they were starch when raw, but when you baked them they turned into protein". This logic felt wrong to me, but I was only twelve and had not yet learned introductory biology in school. However Grace, despite her master's degree, viewed his word as scripture. Everywhere we went, my mother's potatoes, packed lovingly in a plastic container, accompanied her. She ate at least four per day, cold, with the skin on, holding one up and biting into it as if it was an apple, even while seated on a bus or subway; she had no shame. In addition, we were both required to begin each day with an ample glassful of the doctor's special concoction — tomato and lemon juices, living vitamins, lecithin, brewer's yeast and tiger's milk — a blender cocktail. My mother jokingly referred to it as "Witches Brew", and it tasted so vile that I literally gagged every time, holding my nose to choke it down. I begged her repeatedly not to force me to drink it, that my health was fine, but my pleas fell on deaf ears. Grace had no mercy and I resorted to pouring it down the sink behind her back whenever I could. At meals a small saucer rested next to my plate containing my vitamin pills, at least twenty. To get past this distasteful ritual as swiftly as possible, I learned to down them all in one gulp. Dr. Seidler told her that the vitamins would be more effectively absorbed into her bloodstream if she actually chewed them, so she spent every meal painstakingly wrapping each of her thirty individual pills in a piece of food. She said they tasted so awful that she "wouldn't wish it on a horse", yet she persisted. However, after three years of faithful attendance, the good doc was no longer satisfied with his $110 per week plus $3000 per year in vitamin sales. In the sanctuary of his office, safely concealed from his wife's watchful eye, he began slipping his hands toward my mother's breasts. He even tried to steal a kiss while she was lying on the table with that strange wheel machine rolling up and down her back. After a few such incidents, although she definitely seemed flattered by his interest, my mother concluded analytically that he was "probably not acting in her best interest". Therefore, she decided to abandon Dr. Seidler, his potatoes and his living vitamins.

With the onset of my mother's nutrition obsession and her insistence that I participate, our fights became more frequent. One day, during a particularly heated encounter, I received yet another slap in the face for my defiant attitude. At the age of thirteen I had grown close to her height, and that day for the first time, an unexpected power rose up inside of me, a rage at the injustice of her unreasonable and domineering attitude. Instead of complaining and defending, I took action and slapped her back with conviction, just once. I didn't say a word but she got the message. After that day, she never laid a hand on me again.

Almost immediately upon the exit of Dr. Seidler, Grace found a new guru, Dr. Max Winston, a chiropractor who had written a book on nutrition, destined to become my mother's next bible. She purchased a couple dozen copies to distribute among friends and family, and every month we made our two-hour pilgrimage to Stamford, Connecticut. The doctor's strategy for better health confused me. During each $125 visit, I sat under a red lamp for fifteen minutes, and then a blue one for another ten. After the light show, Dr. Winston pulled a little on my arms, legs and neck (but not too much, he was a doddering eighty-year-old and what little strength he had was budgeted to writing a deposit slip for the bank). At the end of the session he evaluated our current diets and added a few choice items. "This month you may eat ten grapes twice a week and next month we'll add half a cantaloupe every other day."

His prescription delivered, Grace would look up at him adoringly, her eyes shining with gratitude and excitement. On the drive home she would chatter ecstatically about her new permitted foods, like a kindergartner anticipating milk and cookies. After the first visit, where I observed his methods and heard his fee, I hit the roof. When we returned to our apartment I confronted her, trying to wake her up to the truth, that Dr. Winston was taking advantage of us, that his diet was just a ridiculous excuse to collect large sums of money. In my heart, I knew he was exploiting her; my innate instinct of common sense and fairness clamored to be heard. However, as usual, my efforts were wasted. I screamed and begged, crying in frustration for a long time that day, but I could not break down her brick wall. She was convinced that she knew what she was doing and was going to follow every single instruction of Dr. Winston's, no matter what . . .

Her new doctor's miracle foods were lemons and grapefruits, and he prescribed the "grapefruit fast" (twenty-four hours of exclusively grapefruit) to my mother, three days a week, to detoxify her system. The rest of the week she was to drink the juice of two lemons, three times a day, and eat nothing but fruit until dinner. (During this period, my mother squeezed more than sixty lemons per week, by hand, for the two of us) For her only real meal of the day, she could select a fowl or fish protein, steamed vegetables and more fruit. No fat or dairy was permitted. Grace followed this regime religiously for over a year, a diet that was perfect poison for a hypoglycemic, the equivalent of feeding sugar to a diabetic and taking away their insulin. Her post nasal drip (a symptom of hypoglycemia) was constant, and by bedtime, her lungs had become so filled with mucus that she spent more than two hours in the middle of each night coughing it up. Her asthma was perpetual and she had no energy. For several weeks at a time she was bedridden. In this state she couldn't hold a job and we lived off my father's Social Security benefits. Soon she started losing weight, eventually going down to eighty-nine pounds. With a medium build and a height of 5'6" she looked emaciated. Two of her girlfriends, Judy, a teacher, and Stella, a psychologist, begged her to stop.

They knew enough about proper diet to advise her with confidence that this extreme regime was endangering her well-being. My mother was oblivious; her allegiance to the doctor was overpowering. He had cast a spell over her and she followed him like a zombie, completely ignoring the extreme symptoms that she was suffering as a result. Then it got worse. Her blood sugar was crashing so low from this devastating diet that she began to have seizures. She fell in the hall outside my room in the middle of the night and I rushed from my bed, terrified to see her convulsing on the floor. She was so thin that, now a ninth grader, I was able to pick her up and carry her back to bed. During these seizures she would froth at the mouth and let go of her bladder and bowels. I thought she was going to die.

My only emotional support came from Addy, a Manhattan social worker my mother and I started seeing during my early teen years. Every Saturday my mother pulled up to the front of our building in our turquoise and white 1966 Rambler, and we drove down the West Side Highway to Addy's East 81st street apartment-office off Lexington Ave. Addy, a genuinely empathetic woman with a healthy dose of common sense, developed a special place in her heart for me. This weekly three-hour therapy session was supposed to assist mother and daughter in building a better relationship. Much to my relief, after a few years with Addy, all of a sudden, without explanation, almost as if she had become bored with one hobby and had decided to focus on another, my mother gave up Dr. Winston. Apparently, just like his predecessor, he had made a pass at her one day while she sunned herself under his precious red lamp. Grace changed her diet which quickly reversed many of her hypoglycemia symptoms. Addy had become her new guru. Under Addy's tutelage, she mounted a xerox of Dr. Winston's face on a cardboard carton. This creation sat on the floor next to her bed, a sacred altar representing my mother's commitment to her personal growth. As a nightly exercise she stabbed the paper with an ice pick, uttering obscenities to vent her hostility toward her former mentor whose negligence had almost killed her. (Dr. Winston died of cancer a few years later.) In addition, my mother woke herself up several times during each night to write down her dreams. Cardboard cartons overflowing with paper covered her bedroom floor, scribbled records of her involuntary thoughts and analyses of her personal problems. Like a diligent doctorate student, she delivered

In ninth grade with braces

numerous pages of her insightful revelations to Addy every Saturday, hundreds of words that our therapist could never have possibly had enough spare time to read. My mother also took notes on our daily fights so that she could report my transgressions as well. She scrutinized and analyzed my behavior with friends. She pointed out that I was dysfunctional and self-destructive and she didn't approve of my choice of boyfriends. Instead of shoving vitamins down my throat, my diet now consisted of perpetual therapy. "Elizabeth said this; Elizabeth did that; I don't think Elizabeth should like this boy or have that friend . . . " She analyzed me to death. She drove me insane.

Addy labeled my mother as "socially defiant", a woman who did and said whatever she felt like, regardless of how distasteful it was to others. During this time, the early seventies, short skirts were in and Addy was horrified to hear my mother's description of a job interview where she wore no underwear, shamelessly offering the office manager a full view of her private parts. Addy spent several sessions trying to convince Grace that this and some of her other behavior, such as leaving the bathroom door open while using it, was my mother's attempt to control people by upsetting and offending them. Unfortunately, Addy really couldn't do anything for Grace because deep down, my mother really didn't want to change; she simply craved the distraction and the self-importance she experienced from her dedicated involvement with a health professional. Eventually my mother became aware that our therapist disagreed with many of her actions, and that Addy also felt genuinely sorry for me. Grace accused her of unprofessionally taking my side against her and began to view Addy as an enemy who was influencing daughter against mother. She analyzed Addy and concluded that she had "very serious problems" and therefore had nothing to offer us. Grace ended their relationship by running up a bill of close to $2000 and then quitting without paying her, an action she justified because "Addy's priority was to serve herself".

I made valedictorian in junior high school and my mother scheduled me to take the entrance exam for the Bronx High School of Science. I passed and began my sophomore year. Early that first semester, I noticed a handsome blond boy with glasses seated two desks in front of me in French class. One day, while he turned to pass back some papers, I suddenly found myself intensely drawn to him. This sensation was not a typical teenage hormonal response, instead a feeling of white light burst from inside and tickled me, as if my body was filled with seltzer, as if a sense level higher than emotion or intellect had suddenly awakened. This intense, new and strange feeling of love and destiny was so overpowering that it actually terrified me. My classmate's name was Joe Radic, and apparently, he felt the same as I did. During our senior year we finally began dating, and for those twelve short months we were together constantly, one life force, one being. As if a bubble surrounded and protected us, we felt totally comfortable and safe, a sameness of souls. We trusted and loved each other completely and knew we would always be together. For the first time since before my father died, I experienced an oasis of happiness.

I graduated high school in June of 1977 and moved that fall into a Swarthmore College dorm to begin my freshman year. I was forced to leave Joe behind, but I knew that this separation was only temporary. Joe had his sights set on becoming a mechanical engineer and continued to live at home, in the Bronx, where he attended Manhattan College. I was terribly lonely without him; as if a part of me was missing. In spite of the distance between us our feelings toward each other never changed. Although our phone calls were infrequent I was constantly aware of my total commitment to him and the future we had planned. We would finish college, each become a professional, get married and have kids. Our lives would be wonderful . . .

During those first few months of college a friend recommended biofeedback therapy to my mother as an innovative method of stress reduction. My mother yearned to fill the void which had formerly been occupied by Addy, and eagerly pursued this fresh path toward self-improvement, starting weekly sessions at St. Vincent's Hospital downtown. Soon she found her way to Dr. David Rogers, Ph.D., a psychologist who specialized in biofeedback and breathing relaxation exercises. Twice a week my mother reported to his office on 86th between Park and Lexington. To begin the therapy, she was seated in a comfortable brown leather chair while the doctor strapped three electrodes mounted to a nylon band onto her forehead. For the next half hour she sat in a darkened room and listened with headphones as the biofeedback machine translated the degree of her muscular stress into a low buzzing sound. As she relaxed the sound slowed down, and in this way she could learn to loosen those tight muscles which were causing her discomfort. The doctor had an assistant, Gerald Sharkman, a licensed biofeedback technician, and one summer day Gerald substituted for Dr. Rogers, who was on vacation. My mother expected the same instructions as Dr. Rogers, but when she asked him, "What exercise should I do while I am on the machine?" He replied to her surprise, "None, just leave yourself alone." For some reason, this permission to "do nothing" impressed my mother tremendously. It triggered a rare and special lift, a sense of delicious freedom which she associated with the man who had delivered the suggestion. Over the next several weeks, Gerald became my mother's favorite topic and she insisted that I must have a session with him during my Thanksgiving visit home. Instinctively, I was suspicious. In fact, I had a bad feeling about Gerald. All my life Grace had worshipfully paraded what seemed like an endless stream of self-serving male creeps in front of me, and now it looked as if Gerald was the next in line. However, at the same time I really needed to relate with my mother, she was all I had, and sharing her obsessions was the only way I could feel some kind of connection with her. Although I really didn't want to meet Gerald, I decided to give it a try.

My Present — November 1977

I am one month shy of my eighteenth birthday on the day Dr. Rogers conducts my orientation interview. He asks me why I have come and I describe the demons that torment me. Despite the joy I experience with Joe, I have frequent bouts of suicidal depression. A year ago I locked myself in my room during a three-day internal battle. The conflict was so intense that I couldn't go to school. As if something was literally sitting on my chest, crushing it, I couldn't even speak to tell my mother what was wrong. During those few days a voice in my mind screamed relentlessly, commanding me to consume the entire bottle of my mother's sleeping pills and end my life. However, another part of me wouldn't permit that destructive impulse to be acted out. I snuck out to her medicine cabinet, but only swallowed three pills and slept eighteen hours until mercifully, the misery finally lifted.

In addition, I am obsessed with food. I can't stop eating carbohydrates, even when I am so full that I feel as if I would throw up if I ate another bite. As a result, after having been slim for most of my life, I am terribly distressed over a recent gain of thirty pounds which has forced me into size 12-13 clothing. Unbeknownst to me, Gerald is eavesdropping from the adjacent office. Suddenly, he enters unannounced and interrupts our conversation. Barely introducing himself, already a self-elected expert about my life, he informs me with assurance that I am exaggerating my problems. They really aren't such a big deal, hardly worth the air time. The message I perceive behind his transparent facade of diplomacy is that he thinks I am making things up to get people to feel sorry for me. Immediately, my gut feelings respond; I practically detest him. First impressions are often correct, but at seventeen I am vulnerable and confused and my emotional priority is to somehow please my mother. Therefore, with tremendous willpower, I push my instincts aside, and not for the last time . . .

Soon Gerald puts me on the biofeedback machine. Dimming the light he exits, advising me to "have a good time". Half an hour later he returns and slips into an armchair facing me. Together again, I give him the once over. Gerald Ezra Sharkman is a six-foot, slim, rather handsome, thirty-eight year old man with curly brown hair. Some of his Jewish heritage shows through in his selection and pronunciation of various words. Aside from his abrupt introduction earlier, his demeanor is easy on the eye. Gerald asks me what I have experienced on the machine and I reply that after several minutes I dozed off. I anticipate forthcoming advice about relaxing during the coming holiday week, but instead, from this moment on, the unexpected is destined to become routine. Sitting at the edge of his chair he leans toward me and delivers my first dose of his true nature. Completely intent on reaching for and discovering some "new information" through his conversation with me, he lectures, referring to incredible feelings, spiritual love and uncovering the ultimate truth in a sea of confused thoughts. His passion for this "truth-talk" fascinates me. I have never heard such rhetoric and I am immediately captivated. What really attracts me as much as what he seems to be saying, is the passion and energy of his performance, his charisma. After spending my last seventeen years watching Grace chase one quack doctor after another, paying thousands of dollars, making a fool of herself, alienating friends and relatives with her obsessions and never gaining anything of value, I am starving for a person who can deliver confidence and commitment. I yearn for a sense of purpose and I am desperate for a role model. I crave a mentor who will help me develop a stronger personality and a more fulfilling life than my mother's. I want to accomplish big things, to be a mover and a shaker, to help people and make a difference in this world. Gerald juggles his interpretations of life like balls in the air. He weaves together universal truths he has absorbed from books on Eastern religion, self-help and popular psychology into a patchwork quilt that compels me into a state a veritable, intellectual ecstasy, a feeling which sweeps me away.

Gerald explains his working concept for achieving personal growth, overcoming the "Fight or Flight" reaction. "Animals operate by instinct alone. They are totally controlled by this reaction. We start out like animals too. For example, when someone insults you, you either want to punch their lights out in retaliation — fight, or run away with hurt feelings — flight. Either way, their insult affects your physiology. Our bodies react as if we are afraid of being eaten by a saber-toothed tiger. This is all a lie because we no longer live in the jungle where a challenge from another means that our survival is at stake. There is only one way to get rid of these useless reactions. When you are triggered, sit through them, neither fight nor run. It will be painful at first; you must endure the uncomfortable adrenalin rushes and a burning desire to take action to diffuse these sensations. However, it gets easier, and when you finally triumph, you will be a bigger, more grown up person and closer to your true spiritual life. Pursuing personal growth consists of seeking situations which will trigger you to react, facing your fears. I call this 'search and destroy'. Every time you confront the programming you absorbed from your parents and society, and refuse to let it control you, you break a barrier in yourself; you reclaim another small piece of your freedom. The more reactions you break, the happier you'll be. These reactions also separate us from our true potential, locked inside our brain. Scientists have proven that we only use <u>three percent of half the brain</u>. Imagine what a wonderful life we are missing out on! This is our mission, to merge into oneness with each other and the universe, to realize our genuine, inborn capacities. Instead of each of us being separate, <u>alone</u>, we will become <u>all one</u>."

He ends our session with these fervent words, "I don't care if it's a book or a chair, but we relate to everything and everyone as if it was mother. We have never matured beyond our first and most significant relationship, the person who gave birth to us. Everything is mother!"

I am impressed by the simplicity of this statement. It seems to cut through all the possible entangled, intellectual analyses right to the core nature of all relationships. To me these words hold great meaning and I am determined to go out into the world and verify them. My mind becomes ablaze with abstractions, contemplations, and seemingly logical conclusions. After this short conversation with Gerald, I am hooked. That poignant, first impression I experienced just one short hour ago is completely forgotten. It is incredible how such fleeting moments can drastically alter the entire course of your life . . .

By the time my boyfriend, Joe, meets me in front of Dr. Rogers' office to drive me to my mother's apartment, my mouth is a river of ideas and theories. Sitting there in the front seat of his older brother's yellow *Sebring*, my mouth goes into automatic pilot; I can't shut up. Making no sense at all, nevertheless, I am overwhelmingly excited and speak unceasingly about this incredible man I have just met. I have been infected with the virus of motor-mouth babble. However to me, every word which springs from my lips is terribly significant, and I know that I have a future ally, Gerald, with whom to share this babble. I beg Joe to find a way to meet him. He just has to be able to share this exhilaration I feel!

I return to college and remain there until Christmas vacation. I think about Gerald a lot. From that short one-hour session he has quickly become larger than life. I do not question my feelings but instead reinforce them by spending hours filling the ears of one of my roommates, Pauline from Roanoke, Virginia, with the things Gerald has said. My mouth races to keep up with my mind as I strive for new heights of creative thinking, stemming from the seeds planted during my first meeting with Gerald. As I attempt to make discoveries about "truth" myself, I anticipate seeing him again in order to run my ideas by him.

In the interim, Joe takes my advice and schedules an appointment with Gerald. Because Joe has no money and no physical problems either, Gerald concocts some phony ailment so that they can bill his insurance company. With Joe he is "man to man", and he starts educating his new student about the "Female Game" or "Female Program", as Gerald refers to it. According to him, all females have the same intention, to manipulate men. They do it through sex and emotional control. "All females" includes me who was, up until that moment, the love of Joe's life and his best friend. Joe begins to question our relationship. I don't understand what is happening, but when I return for winter break, the man I love so much, to whom I have totally committed myself, rebuffs me coldly. Sitting in Gerald's waiting room, listening to him joking with Joe on the other side of the wall, I endure painful spurts of rage, but using Gerald's logic, that negative reactions, hostility and anger are all lies stemming from the "Fight or Flight Reaction", I struggle to explain away these feelings . . . *This must be evidence of my immaturity, possessive insecurity that I must conquer. After all, Joe has the right to enjoy a relationship with someone other than me.* However, in spite of my attempts to squash my reaction, my conflict remains, primarily because Gerald seems to have won Joe's allegiance away from me. During that vacation Joe and I are estranged from each other for the first time. He accuses me of playing childish games and manipulating him, and finally he refuses to see or talk to me until I grow up. He has absorbed the prejudices of Gerald's mind like a sponge and is projecting them onto me, and worse, Gerald is encouraging him to do so. I am hurt and confused. I have done nothing to earn this rejection and I feel powerless to repair the rift between us. Since the first day Joe set eyes on me, he has loved me more than anyone. Now I have lost my most precious friend and I can't comprehend why . . .

January 1978

In mid-January I return to Swarthmore to begin my second semester of freshman year. About a week later I go to bed early, about 8:00 P.M. At the end of the previous semester I had joined the swimming team and tonight we have just returned from a swim meet. Feeling exhausted, depressed and strangely empty, I welcome an escape into the safe cocoon of sleep. The communal hall phone rings and a few moments later, a neighbor knocks on the door and calls my name. I walk to the phone half asleep. My mother's voice speaks from the other end of the line and she sounds upset. I ask her what's going on. She sighs, takes a deep breath and forces these terrible words past her lips,

"I'm sorry Liz, but Joe is dead."

Anguished thoughts fly through my mind. *It can't be . . . We had plans, we were going to get married . . .*

Joe was not happy living with his parents and sought a school with a better engineering program. Two months ago he was accepted as a midyear transfer student at the State University of New York (SUNY - Stony Brook), on Long Island. On his first day at the new college he was walking next to the train tracks. It was a windy, frigid January day and he kept his jacket hood securely fastened to protect his head from the cold. He didn't hear the train coming. In an instant he was killed. He had just turned nineteen. My friend Jeannie, (my mother's girlfriend Judy's daughter) who was also attending Stony Brook, read about his death in the school paper. She called my mother with the news. My mother immediately consulted Gerald about how to break it to me. He delivered his advice like a command from a general to a private,

"Don't procrastinate; call her and get it over with. Then tell her to move past it right away."

I just absolutely can't believe it. Joe was not suicidal and he wasn't stupid. He neither drank nor took drugs. He was intelligent, sweet and alive with a bright future ahead of him. What was going on in his head that day? How did he get so distracted that he put himself in mortal danger? How could he not have sensed the rumble and heard the noise of an approaching train? Now I will never know.

The last time I saw him we were standing on the corner of Fifth Avenue and 80th Street after one of Gerald's sessions. I remember us parting, he walking South and me, North. I looked back over my shoulder, watching him retreat. We had just had another fight about the "games" I was playing, games with which Gerald had poisoned his mind. I hadn't known how dangerous it was for us to be trapped and controlled in that ugly place. If only I could have reached his higher self so that he could once again feel the love and commitment we had shared so completely before he ever set foot in Gerald's office. If only I could have made a stand about the lies that Gerald was filling his head with and won back his allegiance. If only I could have reestablished the connection of love that God had given us so that he would not have felt so lost, alone and distracted on that fateful day. Maybe things would have been different . . .

I return to New York for the funeral. That first night my mother lends me a black dress and takes me to the viewing. I am a sleepwalker, moving my body automatically, too numb to feel. Joe's parents greet me without emotion and then drift away. I can't understand this strange detached behavior until one of their relatives explains that the family doctor has put them on drugs; the pain of losing their favorite son is too much to bear. As I enter the room, despite the presence of Joe's family, I still hope that this is all a big mistake, that when I finally make it to the coffin it won't be him . . . Joe is dressed in a brown suit. Funny, I have never seen him like that; I can only remember his casual clothing — jeans, corduroys, sneakers, tee-shirts, and his smiling face drinking me in, sharing his innermost feelings with me. Joe is not here, if he was I would feel him connect with me. This empty shell no longer holds my best friend and I wonder where he is. I hope that he knows how much I loved him, how devastated I am by his loss. I pray that somehow, from the other world, he will be able to help me go on with my life. The face is unscathed because the blow that took Joe's life was to the back of the head. I stroke his cold, lifeless hand and cheek, thinking of all the warm and wonderful times we spent together, touching, sharing, making love and planning our future. I think of how perfectly he understood and accepted me as no one else ever had, how we both believed that we were destined for each other alone. Harsh reality sinks in, crushing my heart; what I have lost today, I can never replace. I am alone again, truly alone . . .

My mother schedules a "therapy session" with Gerald for the day following the funeral. I arrive at his office hoping he can help me, and sink down into the big leather chair next to the biofeedback machine staring at the floor, my throat suffocating with emotion. I can't even speak, so I wait for him to start the dialogue, to help me cope with this unbearable sadness and loss. Gerald throws an opening line at me, "What's going on?"

He is matter-of-fact, unemotional. In fact, he acts as if this day is just like any other and I look up at him, shocked. Although his face expresses nothing, it almost seems that he is content with the outcome of these events, as if some mission has been accomplished. This confuses and terrifies me. I had expected Gerald to empathize with me as Addy would have, perhaps to even break the professional barrier in this moment of tragedy and consolingly put his arm around

me, one human to another. Instead, he is cold and composed. Responding to his question, I stammer, "Well, I feel so terrible, you know . . . "
My voice falls off as tears fill my eyes and my head drops again. His response comes quickly and falls like a blunt instrument, "Well that's all over now. It's time to move on. What else is going on?"
I feel as if I have just been kicked in the stomach. This man not only does not grieve over the untimely loss of his new friend, a young life so needlessly snuffed out, but he has no empathy for my grief either! For his unforgivable insensitivity I despise him. In this moment, in light of the true inner nature Gerald has just exposed, I want to walk out of the office never to return, but I haven't the emotional resources to assert myself. It requires all of my strength just to make it through each moment. Therefore, I find a way to contain my hurt, and try to follow the professional advice given by the authority figure chosen and respected by my mother; the man whose direction must have more validity than my personal feelings because he works in the office of Dr. Rogers, psychologist on the Upper East Side, a man who has worked many long years to gain his Ph.D. and many more helping patients. This doctor must surely know how to select the assistant in whose hands he entrusts the well-being of his patients, people who consult him because they, by their own admission, have weaknesses to address and improvements to make. I ask Gerald why he didn't attend the funeral, since Joe was his friend too, and he replies with authority,
"I don't need to go to those things to impress other people. My feelings live in here." He points to his chest. "I know what I feel and that is all that is important."
Leaving the office, drowning in sadness, I realize that I must try to get past this, as Gerald has advised. What choice do I have anyway? Living in this present is too painful. *Gerald knows how to help me do this*, I conclude, *I must see him again and learn how to cope.*
Joe's passing is even worse than my father's. This man was my intimate partner, my complement, my other half. With the stream of my life force choked to a bare trickle, I can no longer think straight. My chest is so swollen from mourning that I can't even cry. Nothing in this world holds any importance. I return to college in deep depression and roam the campus as if drugged, mechanically fulfilling the demands of my scheduled courses, praying for night when I can escape this dreadful reality in sleep's temporary solace. I interact with no one; in fact, my three roommates generally avoid me now; my grief is so enormous and I make them uncomfortable. I lose interest in my future plans and my grades suffer. A voice screams relentlessly in my head, *I want to leave this Earth.* I would do anything to take this pain away, yet, I can't lift a finger to hurt myself. So from my feelings I find no relief. The only hope I can embrace is that my participation in Gerald's mission for higher truth will lift me out of my despair. This premise begins to serve as an emotional anchor.

March 1978 to December 1979

Apathetically dragging myself though lectures and term papers, I am haunted by the specter of Joe's memory and search for him daily in the crowded cafeteria. The back of a blond head turns, powerful male thighs bulge in familiar corduroy pants with a tiny "Gap" label on the back pocket. Mentally, I reconstruct him from the parts of other young men. During the evenings I gaze dejectedly at embracing couples between the library stacks, or downstairs in the student center, and I think to myself, *If only they knew how lucky they are* . . . In my brain his voice still calls my name, or laughs at some silly joke. Yet with each day these images fade just a tiny bit more. Resolutely, I clutch at the vanishing shreds of my dearest friend as if by sheer willpower I could pull him back to Earth, back into my arms to soothe me, to stroke my face and tell me it's all OK now.

To relieve myself of this perpetual sorrow, I anticipate another meeting with Gerald, wondering, *Where will the next phase lead us?* Naturally, when I return to the city for Spring Break, my mother has scheduled appointments with him already, in fact, twice a week. Gerald acts as if Joe never existed and does not inquire about my feelings. However, he is very friendly and enthusiastically shares his latest revelations. His positive energy supplies a welcome distraction from my misery and solitude on campus. Gerald introduces the concept of "love" which now manages to appear in all of his conversations. It is not the type of emotion exchanged between two soul-mates or lovers, but a generalized sort of caring which to the experienced practitioner, he claims, may escalate into an intense sensation of oneness and unity. He declares that our goal is to reach this state. In fact, that first day back, just as I am about to leave the office Gerald approaches, and without explanation, kisses me lightly on the cheek; the first semblance of affection I have received since before Joe died. I experience a seemingly intimate connection between the two of us and joy floods me spontaneously; I float from the waiting room out onto East 86th Street with clouds under my feet. My emotions catapult me upwards into instant ecstasy; I am surely in love . . . and I do not descend for at least forty-eight hours.

The following week, after my thirty-minute stint on the biofeedback machine, Gerald inquires lightly, with childlike innocence,

"Would you like to try an experiment?"

"What do you want to do?" I return with genuine curiosity.

"I wonder how it would be if you took your shirt off, you know, to break a social barrier. In Europe the women go topless on the beach and it's no big deal; they are much freer over there. We uptight Americans were trained to be ashamed of ourselves and it's all a big lie. We must learn to accept our bodies. After all, everyone has one and we are not born wearing clothing!"

A surge of adrenalin flushes my face with heated embarrassment, a sensation I misinterpret as excitement. I feel trapped, as if he has just ever so politely forced me into a corner, but mentally, I do see validity in his logic. Inside myself, I squirm and panic because I have never been put on the spot like this before. I should not feel that I am required to follow his instructions if they make me uncomfortable; I could just simply walk out and ask his boss, Dr. Rogers, why his assistant requires me to do this exercise. However, I am terrified of asserting myself or of opposing another's opinion, especially someone in an authority position. I fear rejection and disapproval, so instead I comply. I remove my shirt and sit bare-chested in the big brown leather chair next to the biofeedback machine, giggling like a little girl, nervous and ashamed and yet somehow fulfilled by the attention Gerald rewards me with for my cooperation. In fact, I crave this attention so much, that I convince myself it is genuine love. Within a few minutes, Gerald invites me to sit on his lap. After I calm down, he gently places a hand on my breast.

"See Elizabeth, it's not really such a big deal. Just a new experience to adjust to," he reassures me.

Soon the hour session is over and I am gratefully released. When I leave his office I never tell a soul, but then again, who do I have to tell? I am an isolated person. I have no close family except my mother and she always seems eager to go along with anything Gerald might suggest. In fact if I tell her, I fear that she might react jealously, disappointed that he didn't select her for the experiment first. There is no person whom I trust or depend upon for advice and I lack the fortitude to stand up for myself. Two short months ago I lost my best friend in a horrible accident, and these days I still endure almost perpetual depression. My self-esteem is on the floor.

A couple of sessions later, Gerald pushes at the envelope, asking me if I would like to take another step into the unknown.

"How about if you try to masturbate in front of me?" He suggests with sweet caress and curiosity in his tone.

My adrenalin surges instantly from fear. Again I feel trapped, and again I misinterpret this sensation as excitement, triggered from the anticipation of this forbidden and taboo activity. I follow his suggestion and remove my panties. He positions himself in an armchair across the room, a voyeur, studying my every motion. I am nervous. I hate what I am doing, yet somehow I push through it, relieved when it is finally over. When I have dressed again, Gerald offers to train me to "focus".

"Just look directly into my eyes and try not to blink . . . No, don't move your eyes back and forth, just straight ahead. Look at one point only and soon the whole room will come into view . . . "

After about ten minutes, he asks me what I feel.

"Well, I was nervous at first but that passed and now I feel like I'm floating. I have no more thoughts; I feel calm, as if the room around us, all the sights and sounds, have receded into a distant background. Now this is really weird, but I see white and green light around your head and it keeps getting more intense. What is that?"

Gerald grins proudly, "Very good, you are really coming along. That light is the energy that flows through everything. It is all around us but most people are too distracted to notice it. When you connect with the light, you get in touch with your real, living self, not the programmed robot self. You connect to the universe, and everything in it."

"I see light around the chair too, why is that?"

"You see, all things are alive, not just people and animals; everything is made of energy; it is all one interconnected mass. Only our minds break things into parts. Actually, you could interpret that the chair is more alive than we are because it doesn't have controlling, know-it-all thoughts which get in the way of just yielding and existing."

"I've never tried it, but this must be like meditation . . . ?"

"Not at all; this is way beyond. People who meditate put themselves into a state of stagnation by repeating a mantra. They make themselves even more dead than they already are. Focusing makes you alive and advances you spiritually."

My mind races from his explanations. I would never have believed that a chair was alive, my biology textbook certainly has a different viewpoint, but I didn't imagine this light I just saw for several minutes, so although this doesn't feel right, I must keep an open mind; maybe I have more to learn.

As I am leaving, Gerald tells me that I was courageous to have been willing to break today's barrier, and I will be rewarded with personal growth from our session. He also warns me that "the others", (Dr. Rogers, my mother, and his other patients), aren't advanced enough to understand.

"This must be our secret until they can grow to our level. You understand?"

I agree to comply.

These barrier-breaking episodes bond us and I soon become Gerald's protege, his partner in discovery. Among all of his patients, he has selected me and I feel special. I finally have a mentor who knows where he is going, a man I can emulate. More than anything I want to be just like him, to possess his passion, purpose and confidence. In my own mind I give birth to the new me, "Little Gerald", and my commitment solidifies. There is another bonus as well, a partnership with my mother, (as long as I keep the secrets from her). Over the next several months, Gerald, my mother and I become the pioneers of a new and exciting mission, the originators of what is to come, and still continues today. Although I am only able to see him on vacations, when I am home he usually shares any new information with me first. Gerald reads copiously, and the authors' ideas from those myriad books become the seeds of his personal discoveries. However, he convinces us that this pastime just gives his mind "something to play with", that his true information is delivered directly from some higher, spiritual source. Therefore, he becomes divine and specially chosen in our eyes. My mother soon claims to friends and relatives that he is a "gifted and unique genius". By the end of the year he has self-published his own book. It's plain, brown cover sports the title *Biofeedback Without Machines*. All of his innovative ideas for assisting people to attain personal growth lie between its covers. My mother buys twenty copies to distribute to friends, relatives and co-workers, people she is sure would benefit from Gerald's wisdom.

As Gerald continues to break subsequent "social barriers", the biofeedback machine frequently remains untouched during our sessions and instead, we find ourselves lying on the office floor locked in sexual embrace. He directs our activities with such conviction that I now comply unhesitatingly with every suggestion. It feels good to have someone guiding me, especially because I believe that Gerald is interested in my well-being and wants to watch over for me. Naturally, the possibility of being caught is ever-present, but our fear from shared risk only fuses us even more. Gerald seems to trust me to keep his secrets and he begins to let me in on just about everything. For example, Jackie, the office receptionist, is attracted to him, so one day after work they release their passions — writhing on the carpet under Dr. Rogers' desk while he is across town meeting with patients. He is also sitting naked with some of the other female patients. I am not jealous. I don't need to be the only one. I just want him to pay attention to me. Anything to fill the emptiness from Joe's absence.

"Elizabeth, how about if I stop by your apartment this afternoon before your mother comes home?" Gerald suggests after one of our sessions.

His gently delivered "How about if . . . ?" the preface to all of his propositions, leaves me with a sense of personal choice every time. In my mind this is merely another innocent, curious experiment. So, later that day, his professional commitments complete, he heads uptown to visit. I am so excited . . . I can't wait to give him the grand tour of my home, especially my room — to share another piece of myself with him. My favorite hobby is photography and I have set up my darkroom in a spare bedroom. However, Gerald has his own plans and immediately upon crossing the apartment's threshold, he strides swiftly down the long hallway, past the livingroom's French doors and finally into my bedroom. Uncannily, as if reading my mind, he plops down on my bed and abruptly states,

"And don't show me any photographs; I <u>don't</u> want to see them."

Instantaneously, he squashes my spirit with a giant invisible fist. I don't understand why he won't let me express myself to him naturally in my own home. Most people enjoy viewing my images; why wouldn't he want to as well . . .? Command delivered, Gerald moves on, soon noticing a baby picture on my bureau — an appealing image of a vivacious one-year-old. He disapproves and begins lecturing,

"This whole stupid society is lost. Everyone is living in the past, hanging onto memories instead of experiencing the now. How can we ever understand what's going on in the moment with all of those irrelevant thoughts distracting us? Whatever we live through should be enjoyed and then let go. We don't need photographs, home movies, diaries and old letters to bring back experiences which are dead now. People only save those mementoes from insecurity. They don't have the courage to feel valid from just being alive. I don't hold onto anything. I travel light and live each moment to the fullest; then, onto the next. My home is under my hat. I threw out all of my old photographs years ago and I feel much freer."

Seating myself next to him I reflect on his words for a moment and then deliberately make a sacred commitment — From now on I will find the means to drag myself out of the oppressive, stagnant thinking patterns into which I was conditioned. I embrace his controversial, yet exhilarating perspective. Gerald is clearly a man ahead of his time. It will take hard work and dedication on my part to attain the lofty, enlightened station he now occupies, but I intend to give it everything I've got. We remain on my bed a while

My first birthday portrait

longer, chatting. Today we have crossed another barrier from professional to personal together. Our relationship is maturing and Gerald E. Sharkman is beginning to play a most significant role in my life. On this day, I am more convinced than ever that I am terribly important, even indispensable to Gerald. If I remain cooperative and continue to please him, I am sure he will return the favor and I can enjoy relating with him in the role of the daddy and mentor I have been so desperately searching for. My fabricated system of emotional barter is unconscious, its invisibility making it all that much more powerful. Of course the visit must remain another secret from my mother and Dr. Rogers . . .

A week later I force myself past my resistence and take the necessary action to prove my new commitment. While my mother visits the local grocery, I place two treasured albums of my baby pictures and more than 100 rolls of black and white negatives, pictures I've developed in my darkroom since high school, into a brown grocery bag. Exiting our apartment, I walk halfway down the hall. Taking a deep breath, I resolutely open the door and wince as the heavy books bang against the incinerator walls while they make their final journey into a pile of ashes four stories below. Hating to give it all up, the hundreds of hours of heartfelt dedication to my craft, the irreplaceable mementos of my childhood, I attempt to reassure myself, *Now I am one step closer to the freedom that Gerald is leading us toward. I must expect this personal growth to be difficult, but the rewards will be worth the pain and Gerald will certainly be proud of me!*

Within a few weeks, Gerald informs my mother of his visit to our home, and trips to our apartment become a regular event. My mother is thrilled. It is company, something she doesn't have much of. She feeds him hamburgers and he talks, and talks and talks . . . He entertains us. His presence fills our empty lives. We learn more about his family, his past, his personal philosophies and his dreams for the future. Through these hours in our living room the three of us solidify our relationship. We feel as if we possess the seeds of some special intellectual and spiritual gift that we are going to sow and water in order to harvest something unimaginably wonderful together in the future. Like intimate friends, hungry for details about each other, we share our personal histories. Among many other things, my mother gives him the particulars of my father's death and the money I inherited.

Gerald also tells us about his past. He was the middle of three boys. His father was a nice, although weak-willed, man who developed a lucrative family business selling lung equipment to physicians. In fact he invented some of the breathing apparatus that is used in hospitals today. In contrast, his mother, he claims, was the most evil woman in existence. She was abusive and nasty. Once when Gerald was a baby in his high chair he vomited, and his enraged mother fed it back to him. She emasculated him constantly and threw irrational tantrums without warning, often chasing him around the house with a butcher's knife. Gerald adds that he found it amusing when she went crazy and often laughed at her, escalating her reaction to even higher levels. In addition, he sometimes said things on purpose just to "heat her up". He brags that his mother was so good at manipulating others that she could intimidate and control anyone on the planet, using her personality to bring them to their knees in terror whenever she wanted.

However, Gerald would never let her control him. No way. While the other kids were outside playing, at three years old he was sitting in the kitchen scrutinizing his mother and her female friends while they interacted. He analyzed their behavior so that he could learn how to avoid the psychological traps they set. At that tender age, he began to intensively study "The Female Game". Now he insists that no woman will ever get over on him with any type of seduction or control. He is an expert at spotting all female manipulation.

As a child Gerald developed "grand mal" seizures. A frequent occurrence, they prevented him from being a successful student or holding down a regular job when he got older. One day, as a man in his early twenties, he decided to use his willpower to force himself to remain conscious during a seizure. At one spectacular moment within this experience he perceived a new path of total bliss. He knew what he would dedicate his life to, reaching for more of that feeling. Soon after that incident his seizures ceased. In college he mastered the art of hypnosis. He claims that he could hypnotize an entire room full of people. One time he put himself and two other boys under. All three wandered around the school for a few days doing and saying strange things until the dean finally found out and demanded that Gerald remove the post-hypnotic suggestions holding them captive. During his undergraduate years he also discovered that his body put out an inordinate amount of energy, so much so that when he carried batteries in his pocket, they discharged themselves. Gerald never graduated from college. A psychology major, he quit school just three weeks before he was due to earn his diploma. He did this on purpose because he wanted to prove to himself and the world that he does not need "society's approval" to succeed in life. After that, he earned only one professional credential, a biofeedback technician's license.

At the time of these intimate meetings in our apartment Gerald is in financial straits. He earns $18 per hour assisting Dr. Rogers part time and drives a beat up white *V.W. Beetle*. He has two children, Samantha, age ten, and Martin, age eight. His family is crammed into a two-bedroom apartment on the Upper West Side. His wife, Doris, adds what little she can to the family income with part-time bookkeeping jobs. Up until recently, Gerald worked in sales for his father's business. However, he, by his own admission, was lazy, and would often slip into rated-X, porno movie theaters during the afternoons rather than making the rounds to his father's customers. Eventually, a breakup occurred and his spiteful mother cut him out of the family fortune. For some unfathomable reason, he seems to be proud of the fact that he is now the black sheep of the family. Nonetheless, he is left to his own devices and although he acts cocky and confident, my mother and I both sense that his money problems terrify him . . .

One day Gerald invites me to sit in on a session with a new person. Sara is a heavyset thirty-something African-American who lives on the Upper West Side near Central Park, about fifteen blocks south of us. She is very jolly and positive about everything and Gerald finds her weird and fascinating. In fact, he soon becomes obsessed with her and starts visiting her apartment several evenings a week, bringing me back stories of tarot cards, incense, strange homemade wine, and occult relics she has collected from all over the world. Apparently Sara claims to be a spirit channel and the two of them spend hours together immersed in her special powers, meditating, focusing and brainstorming. Gerald seems to want to suck all of the knowledge out of her head. Unexpectedly, during one of those intimate sessions, something miraculous occurs. According to him,

"My head just started shaking side to side on it's own!"

Gerald is out of his mind with excitement and head shaking immediately becomes his personal obsession. Almost at once, he trades his interest in Sara for the head shaking, and she soon disappears from the scene.

The three of us are engaged in an evening session at my mother's apartment when Gerald first introduces us to his new found skill. Seating himself in one of our high-backed living room chairs, he commences his routine, shaking his head slowly and purposely from side to side. Faster and faster he goes until it looks like he must be hurting his neck. Soon both of his legs begin levitating, and after that, his arms rise as well. What a bizarre creature he appears, all four limbs suspended in the air as if on the end of a puppeteer's strings, now throwing his head back and forth violently. As my mother and I continue to concentrate on his head movements, we feel somehow mesmerized by the motion and I slip into a state of relaxation. My thoughts float away, rendering me mentally and emotionally sluggish. Pausing after several minutes, Gerald explains,

"You know how a dog shakes his head to change his mood, well now we can do it too. We can control and change our emotions."

After several more minutes of shaking, Gerald asks us what we are experiencing. I tell him that I am calmer and he explains why,

"The energy pouring out of my body can relax and even heal any person who is willing to give in to it. Soon we won't need to use the biofeedback machine as a tool anymore. We'll be able to release our stress just from the head shaking. When I shake, I feel a switch turn on in the back of my head which releases my special energy, 'The Energy'. Others don't need to shake, all they have to do is sit near me and experience what I am putting out."

His eyes glow and his passion increases as he feeds to us, and back to himself, the incredible significance of what he is just now discovering about his special powers.

"For some reason, I have been chosen to pass The Energy through my body. I can see now that it is the answer to every problem ever made. It can heal our bodies and minds; it will get us to freedom, out of 'The Program' forever."

"What's The Program?" I ask.

"It is a universal rule book that they handed us at birth. All people in society follow it like dead robots and because they are too stupid to realize what they are doing and break their habits, they never get to live their real lives. Look at everyone around you. People celebrate holidays which don't mean anything and give gifts to family members they hate because they were trained to feel obligated. I never bring a gift when I pay someone a visit, holiday, birthday or otherwise, I am the gift, not some stupid, meaningless object that the person probably won't appreciate anyway. And funerals — look at how ridiculous a coffin is, fancy satin and mahogany; useless speeches to a lifeless body which couldn't care less; if my mother died I wouldn't even waste my time with any of that; I'd just stick her in a pine box; she won't know the difference . . . And men; I don't care which house you pick, the husband is controlled by his wife, but he acts macho to cover it up and then defies and punishes her behind her back. Now take the woman, she constantly puts her husband down and then denies him sex to make sure she gets what she wants. Every interaction between people is no more than a parent-child game, *Mommy, I will perform so you can approve of me.* This starts when we are children but we never grow out of it. No one has the courage to go for themselves, to mature and become their own person. Instead they are constantly focused on Mommy. I broke The Program in myself years ago when I started observing my mother's games and I want to teach others to do the same. Feeling The Energy forces people out of The Program temporarily. Then they must make a decision to work toward their freedom. It is all about breaking distractions, resistance, reactions and fears which like strong wires, connect you to The Program. This is an essential part of our mission; it is why we are all together."

My mother is all applause, but I am not. I sense his obsession with the head shaking, and this strikes me as very unnatural. I don't like the fact that he is doing it several hours a day. He is completely consumed and worshipful of this bizarre manifestation in himself and talks unceasingly about 'feelings'.

"When I shake my head, I have wonderful feelings," he tells us.

I get the message that Gerald perceives these feelings as the ultimate, which surpass all possible others, that they are now the goal and the answer. He also tells us that the shaking evolves his brain and propels him into another dimension. In fact, it makes him invisible to the people in The Program. Once in this place, he claims, he could even walk down 42nd Street stark naked, and no one would pay any attention to him . . . I find this declaration outrageous, but I am rapidly developing a powerful internal coach which always reminds me at times like these to *Keep an open mind; you never know what could happen. We are on a journey of discovery. There are amazing and unbelievable things waiting for us in the future if we can find the courage to challenge our programmed thinking patterns.*

I try the shaking myself because I have an intense curiosity about everything Gerald does. I always want to know exactly what he is feeling and what it means.

The resulting calm from the exertion feels the same as when I exercise. This peace separates me from my stress. These physical feelings are enjoyable, but nothing compared to the aliveness and fulfillment I experienced being in love with Joe. I refuse to believe that these head shaking feelings are the ultimate; they are certainly not my goal. I yearn for more of the feelings I had with Joe. In fact, as if Gerald had just been swindled by a con-man, my instincts scream to wake him up to this dangerous seduction — the formidable lies which I am convinced have engulfed him, but I am only nineteen years old and have little life experience on which to base this conclusion. I do not understand consciously what is happening; only my intuition leads me to react as I do. I am unable to oppress the powerful feelings running through me. Uncharacteristically, I confront him angrily, my face reddening in frustration as I exclaim,

"No. This is not the way. It is wrong. You can't get to great feelings like that. The head shaking feelings are only physical. There is something else out there, something real that I want very much and it is not this. You are believing lies!"

I expect that my passionately delivered opinion will affect them, but I am sadly mistaken. Instead, my words fall on the deaf ears of Gerald and my mother as they continue to praise this wonderful new discovery. I try harder, yelling for over an hour, begging to be heard, until my voice is hoarse and my throat sore.

"I hate you; this is all wrong; I despise you for not listening to me."

I cry, scream, plead . . . but my efforts are futile and Gerald just stares at the wall, cutting himself off from my emotional outburst. When I have finally given up from pure exhaustion, he thanks me sincerely,

"Elizabeth, I really appreciate what you have just done. You have helped me to become even more sure than before that I am right . . . "

A few days later, I return home from work to discover that my mother is seated on the floor of her bedroom closet. She has been there for eight hours, only taking a break to use the bathroom. A sense of disgust and outrage floods me and I immediately know who is behind this ridiculous behavior.

"Gerald has given us an exercise to break our resistance. He says that our lives are filled with distractions: working, watching TV, talking on the telephone, cooking, shopping, etc. We must learn to put these things out of our minds in order to be open to his special knowledge. Sitting in this small, dark place will force us to drop our thoughts and make room for new information."

My mother is aglow, a model student who has completed her assignment with flying colors. My disdain holds no validity for her, and she repeats this action several more times during the next few weeks. Although I despise the idea, I begin to feel like a traitor for not following suit. One day I finally give in and spend five hours in her closet while she is out doing errands. After a period of irritated boredom I slip into a deep sleep. I wake up feeling refreshed, but otherwise untransformed from the experience. When my mother returns home and discovers me there, she is very proud. I smile weakly with relief. Her acceptance supplies a perverted form of emotional fulfillment. Sometimes it is easier to give in rather than fight.

In the months which follow Gerald's head shaking becomes his trademark. He shamelessly performs his act in restaurants, on airplanes, at movies, parties and family dinners. In public places, embarrassed strangers try not to look at him. Not understanding what they are witnessing, they usually conclude that he has an affliction to his nervous system, some sort of palsy. His wife is mortified. She calls him a weirdo and begs him to stop. Defiantly, he responds to her frustration with pride,

"Hey, I'm a weirdo. That's pretty cool. I like that label."

Gerald seems to relish the attention people pay to him, and the discomfort it causes them as well. He likes the fact that they don't understand what he is doing and why, that the true explanation behind the shaking is his coveted secret, only to be shared with his carefully selected inner circle. His visits to our apartment after office sessions continue to be frequent, and we spend hours simply staring at him shaking, trying to feel some shift in our physiology and mood. His movements are so drastic that the window panes rattle and the chair joints squeak painfully, threatening to become unglued. The irritating repetitive sound drives me crazy and I sit there hating him, wishing he would stop. However, Gerald doesn't care; nothing else in this world exists for him but that shaking.

January to December 1980

I spend the spring semester of my junior year living in France and attending the University of Grenoble. On the first day I meet a young woman named Lisa, a Swarthmore sophomore. We are drawn to each other and soon become inseparable. During the time that I am on another continent, Gerald seduces my mother (twenty years his senior). I don't know how it first happened but I am sure that she gave him no resistance. When I return to the United States after six months, it doesn't take me long to figure out what is going on. My mother is acting like his wife, as if she owns him and he has made a commitment to her. My common sense fills in the rest. Within a week Gerald tells me anyway. However, he explains that he obtains no pleasure from these sexual encounters.

"It's just an experiment for growth. I find her body repulsive and I want to break this barrier, to free myself from my reactions of disgust to an old woman."

He justifies his liaison with her by referring again to the concept of personal growth he introduced me to at our very first meeting.

"You see, all people are filled with reactions. Because they are cowards and don't want to experience discomfort, they avoid situations which will trigger them. Therefore, they only live ten degrees out of a possible three hundred sixty-degree life. To grow, we must sit in the environment that causes us anxiety until the reactions pass. I know that my methods work because I have trained my body not to need a coat in winter. I used to stand outside and shiver until my body adjusted and made more heat. It is like letting your body become infected by the chicken pox so that it will build up immunity, only now we are building up our emotional and spiritual immune systems."

I understand the logic behind his theories although I am terribly distressed by their application to his relationship with my mother. Since I cannot force them to terminate their affair, I convince myself that in time I may come to understand and accept the larger truth which Gerald is always alluding to. In regard to his reaction to cold temperatures, even today you may see Gerald striding confidently in mid-town Manhattan in twenty-degree weather without a jacket; he does not shiver in the slightest.

At about this time, Dr. Rogers receives a complaint from a female patient who reports that Gerald has invited her to sit naked with him during her biofeedback session. Gerald denies it, claiming that she is insecure and hostile and only wants to persecute him to make herself feel empowered. Nonetheless, his boss threatens to let him go if there are any more incidents. Gerald complains to us resentfully that despite the fact that he has single-handedly saved Dr. Rogers' business from going under by tackling his most difficult clients, the doctor is clearly too small to appreciate him and the unique things he is capable of accomplishing. Gerald always sounds so sure of himself so as usual, we believe him. A few months later, Dr. Rogers does let him go. Gerald does not give us the specifics of the breakup, but simply explains that the doctor was an asshole and that this change is a blessing in disguise. My mother feels sorry for him; she knows he is scared because he has just lost his source of income, and she volunteers to leave Dr. Rogers' office and follow him. They can continue private sessions in our apartment.

Three other patients also quit the doctor to remain with Gerald. Beatrice Friedman, like my mother, is in her late fifties. A short, dark-haired woman of average height and looks, she is married to a wealthy Manhattan financial manager. She has four grown children who live in other states and three grandchildren. Her relationship with her husband has never extended beyond the superficial, and behind his back, she puts him down mercilessly. A former librarian with a Master's Degree in Library Science, she has not worked for many years and these days, she has nothing but time on her hands. Her husband foots the bill for her "stress reduction therapy" to satisfy her need to fill her calendar.

Next, there is Bess. Quite pretty and petite with straight long dark hair and complexion, her European Jewish features almost resemble those of a Native American Indian. Bess is about thirty and manages the office of a Manhattan lawyer. She is single, friendless and mistrusts men because she has been badly burnt in a recently ended long-term relationship. Over the last decade she has floated in and out of country-western bands and is currently trying to develop a demo tape so that she can obtain a record deal.

Finally, there is Laura. A never married thirty-something registered nurse at Manhattan's Columbia Presbyterian Hospital, she is tall and could be attractive if she chose to emphasize her female attributes, which she doesn't. Instead she makes herself as unappealing as possible. Prone to immature childish outbursts, she is generally hostile. Although she proudly states that she "hates everyone", she especially despises men. Her nasty expressions push people away, and it is virtually impossible to relate with her.

Gerald convinces his five new clients to see him for $25 per hour wherever and whenever they can. He might meet one of us in a downtown diner during a lunch hour where he'll talk and shake his head over hamburgers. My mother and I receive him at our apartment a few times a week and he implores us to recruit others. In my Swarthmore dorm room I have been singing Gerald's praises to my roommates Lisa and Pauline and my passion sways them. In fact, they can't wait to meet him. My mother invites her girlfriend of seventeen years, Judy, and her two daughters — Jeannie, age twenty-two, and Brigette, age thirteen. They live on

Long Island and can only come during the evening. To accommodate them, Gerald starts a Wednesday night group meeting from 7:00 to 9:00 P.M. and my mother generously agrees to lend him our living room. It is there that I first meet Laura, Beatrice and Bess, the previous patients of Dr. Rogers. Although Gerald seems relieved to have my mother's support, he wants to keep all of his patients on an equal level, so my mother and I still pay $10 each for the session along with the rest. A sense of kinship develops among all of us and we soon begin to refer to ourselves as "The Group".

Gerald is a phenomenon to this small circle of women, a sort of spiritual harem, and having him as our personal enlightened master makes us feel exclusive and specially chosen. His personality is completely different from anyone we have ever known; he has one goal only, to always "talk truth". At parties, to strangers in the street, waitresses who serve him in restaurants, to wife, relatives, children and patients, his ambition and willpower are the tools he employs to turn the conversation in a direction where he can use the responses of the other person to "get to more truth". He is not always polite about it either and enjoys confronting Moonies, Jehovah's Witnesses and Christians who hand out pamphlets on the streets of Manhattan. Engaging them in lengthy discourse , sometimes over an hour, he attempts to interrogate and corner them into revealing contradictions within their belief systems. Once he has succeeded in maneuvering them into a position where they are stammering from his intense rapid battering questions, he severs the conversation abruptly, informing them that they are a "waste of time". He walks away feeling victorious, bragging about how he has just used these "stupid fools" to get himself to the next level of growth.

Gerald tells us that we must work every moment of every day toward our personal growth. Our goal is to arrive at a point where we will need no other person, nor any activity to keep us feeling alive and happy. Each individual will revel in his own universe of happiness, a shining star with its own source of fuel. In fact, one day in the future we will be able to "sit in a rocking chair <u>doing absolutely nothing</u> for eternity" and feel totally content. With our mission always in mind, any time and energy invested in work, a hobby, or a personal interaction will always yield a dividend, "laying another brick on the foundation of our future home". In fact, any action is permissible as long as you can find a way to grow from it. To this effect, Gerald coaches us heartily,

"We are trained to focus on the outside, to put other people first and deny ourselves to satisfy them. But, do you know who the most important person in this world is? It's you, of course! That is the only person you need to pay attention to and improve. You are responsible for everything that happens to you, both good and bad. However, you don't owe anything to anyone but yourself. We must learn to stop caring what others think or if they approve. After all, we come into and leave this world alone." He always includes a hearty and encouraging, "Your only job is to go for yourself . . . Just learn to be selfish."

Although I try as always to follow his logic, secretly inside myself I despise the "Rocking Chair Theory" with everything I've got . . . and I have no idea why.

In December, my mother throws my twenty-first birthday party in our apartment. Of course Gerald, our newly adopted head of the family, is invited. My mother also invites Stella, a psychologist, her close friend since they were college roommates together in the late thirties. Stella has two sons, Jack and Grant, who are about the same age as me. Jack, about to graduate from Swarthmore College, is planning on becoming a rabbi. The brothers are intellectual and love to debate on most topics. At the party, Gerald corners them and embarks on a loud discourse about religion. Despite the fact that he himself is Jewish, he begins to make controversial remarks about the Jewish people. At the height of what has now become an argument he declares,

"The Jews heated up Hitler, antagonized him with their lousy personalities. You know they controlled all the money, the German economy, and the Germans were oppressed by their greed. In reality, their obnoxious behavior actually drove him to destroy them. The Holocaust is really their fault. Hitler was just giving them what they asked for. They were just as stupid as Jesus Christ. Now there was a real dumbo! Christ defied the authorities and they just said 'Fuck you!' and hung him on the cross. What an asshole! He deserved what he got."

These pronouncements delivered, his eyes roll toward the ceiling and his upper lip curls as he sneers with contemptuous self-righteousness. Jack and Grant go nuts as they try to convince him to take back what he has just said or change his opinion. Stella observes from the couch, clearly outraged, a stern look frozen on her face. Even my mother is very angry at Gerald because he has taken center stage at my birthday party and affronted our guests, and worse, he seems to enjoy the fact that all of these people are indignant and upset. The week after the party, Stella tells my mother in no uncertain terms that she does not like Gerald, and not only for his remarks about the Holocaust. In response, my mother gives her friend's feelings no validity. Soon, the steady forty-year friendship between Grace and Stella begins to cool down.

January 1981 to September 1984

I return to finish my final two semesters of college, bringing a biofeedback machine with me so that I can continue to practice stress reduction. I publicly declare my allegiance to my new way of life by mounting a photograph on my dorm room door where I sport the machine's headphones on my head. Its caption reads, *Do not disturb. Biofeedback in session.* For reasons that I can't identify, I begin to experience miserable, physical symptoms. My brain fog is so extreme that sometimes I can hardly read the blackboard. Frequently, intolerable fatigue drives me to sleep more than fifteen hours a day. I am nervous and anxious; I speed when I talk, my hands flying in front of me as I struggle to express my ideas. I also continue to have frequent bouts of suicidal depression. My mother's hypoglycemia symptoms have chosen me as their next victim, but I am too uninformed to identify their source. I never seek help to relieve myself because Gerald has told us that your body will probably react to resist the spiritual changes we are moving toward. This resistance is expected, part of the price we must pay to ultimately achieve our goals. In fact, the worse you feel, the faster you are growing. Therefore, I endure the symptoms and press on with my life, believing that eventually the resistance will give up and release me from this oppressive bondage. However, despite my belief in his powers, my feelings for Gerald cause me terrible conflict. I despise him for seducing both my mother and me. Yet, at the same time, I am totally entranced by his passionate drive to discover truth. My participation in his mission gives meaning to my otherwise empty life. I am split in half, alternating between fury and fascination as if there are two separate opposite beings simultaneously inhabiting my body. When I adore Gerald he is larger than life, greater than God . . . but then, sometimes, the memory of my visit to his office the day after Joe's funeral grips me and I loathe him. Acidic, violent, vengeful passions inundate me, threatening to explode. I must stifle them; neither their perpetrator, nor my mother, would ever allow me to express them, and I know that restitution is hopeless. These thoughts arrive frequently, and yet, once the adrenalin surges have calmed, I experience amnesia. Blind to my schizophrenia, I live only in the moment, believing whichever part of me happens to be out at the time, never comprehending that I am a profound and total contradiction to myself.

In June of 1982, I earn a Bachelor's degree in biochemistry with a minor in French. True to my career plans I have taken the MCAT exam and applied to twenty medical schools. Unfortunately, my GPA is in the mid-threes, miles away from a 4.0, and after numerous interviews, I fail to gain admission. Instead, I am wait-listed at three schools. My roommate Pauline, an English major, has been applying for teaching jobs, so I decide to do the same. My plan is to teach science for a year and then reapply to medical school. What careful and perfect plans I have laid since I was a little girl, to build a respectable and fulfilling life for myself. After several meetings I finally obtain a position at Fieldston School, Riverdale, N.Y., as high school chemistry and eighth grade physical science teacher, starting in September. The school is located only few blocks from one of the apartments my mother and I shared about ten years ago. Private schools pay less than public schools and that first year, my salary is only $10,500. I move back into my mother's apartment and each morning, I drive North on the Henry Hudson Parkway to my new job.

My two college roommates, Lisa (a history major from Spokane, Washington), and Pauline, decide to move to New York City after we all graduate together. They have no immediate plans nor job offers but prefer to settle in some large city where well-paying employment is more readily available. They share an apartment about five blocks from my mother's, on 96h Street off Broadway. Because they have no roots in New York, they mostly rely on me for guidance and companionship. My enthusiasm has infected them and after hearing so much about Gerald they anticipate their first meeting with him. When the day finally arrives, they are star struck. Pauline tells him reverently, as if grateful to simply be breathing the same air as him,

"I feel so honored to meet you; I have been waiting so long and have heard so many wonderful things about you."

I am glad that they are going to join us in our exciting mission . . . My mother offers the use of our apartment for their semiweekly sessions. My friends arrive together and Gerald sees them in my bedroom; he always closes the door. One night they emerge after their hour looking terrified, as if in shock. After Gerald leaves, I ask Lisa what's wrong. Her mouth trembles in a face white with anguish.

"He forced us to kiss each other on the lips to break a barrier . . . I'm not a lesbian and I am not attracted to Pauline. I didn't want to do it and I hope I never have to again!"

I know how she feels and I am sorry for her . . .

Gerald also teaches them the Spiritual "Law of Reciprocity",

"You must be willing to sacrifice everything for the mission. Only by letting go of all that is safe and familiar, only with total commitment will you arrive at your desired destination. The more hours you spend with me, the faster you will grow, and if you are willing to release your money and trust in the future, it will come back to you and then some."

Lisa has some financial resources from her family, but Pauline is always broke. She is so terrified from her lack of money that when we go to a restaurant together, she feels compelled to calculate her portion of the tab down to the closest nickel. Paying for groceries is difficult and the two roommates fight over splitting the $1.50 cost of a box of brownie mix because Pauline claims she eats fewer than Lisa does. Yet, Lisa frequently covers Pauline's portion of the rent until payday. My own life away from my teaching job is filled with Gerald. Every Saturday and Sunday morning at 7:00 A.M. he arrives for "therapy" sessions. On Saturday morning the doorbell rings, our Schnauzer barks and I hear my mother running past my bedroom, down the long hallway toward the front door. She doesn't bother getting dressed but greets him naked, covered only with a half-opened bathrobe. From my bed I hear Gerald enter our home. His long confident strides echo in the corridor as if he owns our apartment and our lives. I detest his attitude. They immediately head back down the hall together, past my closed door and further on into my mother's bedroom where they both quickly disrobe and then Gerald mounts her missionary style. I sense that my mother gets no pleasure out of their sex, that she is simply complying because he has asked. In my mind I hear hers speaking. *Sure Gerald, you can have anything I own; take it all — my money, my dignity, my daughter, my soul; just keep coming back to fill my life with your presence* . . . They don't even bother closing her door. I am outraged, trapped in my own home. I can't go to the bathroom without passing her doorway and witnessing this degrading scene so I hold it in, hiding my head under my pillow so that I won't hear their movements. I pray that I can sleep through this but I never do. The minutes drag by as I grit my teeth, pleading with the hands of the clock to please hurry up, for him to leave her bedroom so that I can breathe a sigh of relief, until tomorrow, Sunday, when it will all start again. Sometimes I throw on my clothes and run out of the apartment, walking the streets until I am sure that he is gone. Rage rises in my chest until I feel my heart will explode as I fantasize about calling the police or blowing his head off with a gun. He senses this wrath and lectures me; my reaction is a personal dysfunction that I must overcome.

"That's too bad. You'll have to get over it. I don't follow any of society's bullshit superficial rules. I don't have to. I have more important things to do; you should realize and respect that."

I complain to my mother. I beg her to stop but she does not respond to my frustrated misery. Somehow this sick twisted drama is fulfilling her needs and they take priority over my feelings and any sense of human decency. After Gerald has taken what he desires in the bedroom they retire to the living room where he sits on the sofa partially dressed, shaking his head for awhile, interrupting his exercise only to pontificate about his latest discoveries. When the two hours are up she pays him, often serving him breakfast as well.

Soon I am commanded to participate in these morning meetings. They spend their bedroom hour together and then I must join them. My mother remains in her skimpy night clothes as we all settle on the couch and I must carefully avoid looking directly at her, lest I gain an unsolicited view of her partially exposed genitalia. Gerald seats himself between us. Putting his arms around both, he begins the head shaking ritual. His entire body quakes so violently that I must relax mine and yield to his movements so that he doesn't bang into me and hurt me. Sometimes, out of my mother's line of vision, he slips his hand between the buttons of my pajama top or under my panties to fondle me. I am terrified and confused and yet the adrenalin released from my fear causes excitement as well. I can't tell him to stop, because this will expose my shame and arouse my mother's jealous wrath. Besides, I have the same weakness as my mother, a need to have someone pay attention to me, an emptiness so deep that I am willing to tolerate this outrageous behavior despite my conflict. Since I am working now, I must pay for this time that I have been obliged to spend with him. My mother schedules so many hours that one day, when I decide to calculate the annual bill, I discover it to be $5000 a year, half of my salary! I scream at her, begging her to open her eyes to the severity of her obsession.

"This is not fair. I **won't** give him half of my salary. I work too hard for that money!"

If only she would see what I am saying. Together we could alter the situation to our own best interest. Unfortunately, I have neither the strength or skill to go against both of them and wake them up, nor the courage to throw myself out of the nest and abandon them. I have no other anchor to hang on to. If only I had gotten into medical school; I wouldn't even be here . . .

One night there is a snow storm. Gerald is seeing people in Manhattan and he calls my mother to ask if he can stop by our apartment until it passes. However by 10:00 P.M. it is much worse and she offers him the couch for the night. Before going to bed he whispers to me subversively, "Come and visit me after your mother retires."

At midnight I creep furtively to the couch, in nervous conflict as usual. We kiss and fondle. When he touches me my skin crawls; I want to run away. Gerald senses my feelings and explains gently that they are simply resistence to growth. It is like exercise — no pain, no gain. I must learn to sit through them until they break. Finally he releases me and I gratefully return to my bed. Several minutes later Grace's door opens. I hear her tip-toeing ever so softly down the hall toward the living room. Apparently she is paying Gerald a visit too. I am nervous and sick to my stomach. I bury my head under my pillow so I don't have to hear any more. The next day Gerald laughingly describes his nocturnal adventure,

"Your mother visited me in the middle of the night too, even though I didn't invite her. She wants to be my next wife." His smirk reveals his unspoken thoughts. *Fat chance Grace. Why would I ever want a disgusting, old, dried-up fool like you? What good would you be to me?*

With his new paying entourage, Gerald manages to save a down-payment and decides to move his family out of Manhattan. He purchases a small, three-bedroom home in Westwood, N.J., about fifteen minutes from the George Washington Bridge. After settling in, his wife, Doris, opens a small gift shop, and Gerald seeks new avenues for delivering his message of truth and gathering interested participants. He begins by teaching an adult education course in "Stress Reduction" at the Northern Valley, Demarest High School, close to his home. Here he connects with new people. Soon, the Wednesday night group at my mother's place ends, replaced by a Thursday night group, from 7:30 to 9:30 P.M., in the den of his N.J. house. My mother, Lisa, Pauline and I drive out once a week to participate. Grace is very excited to see that Gerald is progressing so quickly.

Quickly I become acquainted with these new participants. There is Caroline, a forty-something heavyset Italian housewife with two teenage children. Blond, attractive and passionate, she lacks self-confidence and is looking for answers. Nora, an intensely intellectual grade school librarian has an empty childless marriage. She puts down her husband constantly. In her late thirties, she has short dark hair and a muscular, almost masculine physique. I soon discover that her favorite hobby is photography, something we have in common. Harriet, a sweet but naive retired school secretary is in her seventies. Plagued with severe migraines, she hopes that Gerald's classes will help her. Harriet has been widowed for the past ten years and lives alone in a tiny Cape Cod down the block from the high school.

Finally there is Mitchell Stavos. Unlike the women, he isn't a recruit from the adult education class. His parents live just a few blocks from Gerald's new home, next door to Doris' sister Joanne. Mitchell first meets Gerald at a Halloween party given by his neighbors. Gerald, dressed like a "Cone-head" from the Dan Akroyd movie, pulls Mitchell to the side and immediately captivates him with his rhetoric. Mitchell is of average height with a body that reminds me of a chimpanzee, large head, small gut, long arms and torso. His face is hidden behind a dark beard and mustache, and at twenty-nine, his hairline is beginning to recede significantly.

As the sessions with Gerald continue, my friends Lisa and Pauline, having become deeply involved, drop any previous plans of obtaining advanced degrees. After their expensive Swarthmore educations, they soon take jobs as legal secretaries to pay the rent. They do everything together and begin to dress, walk and talk alike. In our circle they are referred to as "The Girls". Lisa confesses with anguish that she feels like she has lost her identity and that she and Pauline have become the same person. After renting a series of studio apartments, they eventually purchase a two-bedroom co-op in Queens and commute by subway to their Manhattan jobs. Lisa purchases a 1983 Honda Civic and twice a week they make the grueling three-hour round trip drive, frequently fighting heavy traffic, to Gerald's New Jersey home. Gerald also opens a small office in Manhattan where he receives them, and several others, as well.

Gerald gains more and more influence in all of our lives. He teaches the rest of his patients how to "focus" and soon everyone has developed the skill of seeing light or auras around each other and various objects. Often, after focusing for several minutes, arms, legs or heads begin jolting spontaneously and Gerald explains that we are becoming "electrified with The Energy". This is proof that we are "making progress". This physical manifestation is evidence enough, convincing us that there is indeed a real transition occurring in his room, and in our bodies and lives.

Gerald seems to have the answers to our present struggles and a prophetic view of our futures too, all of which he connects to his shaking — The Energy, the light we see and the electrical pulses we feel. One day, after he has just finished shaking his head for over an hour, he advances into uncharted territory with Mitchell faithfully by his side.

"It's time to start practicing relating in a new way. You can have any of the women who come here; which one do you want?"

Mitchell rubs his chin thoughtfully, "Well that girl, Elizabeth, the young teacher, she intrigues me."

Gerald says nothing and begins shaking again for a few minutes. Then he stops abruptly.

"Done. She's yours in the other place."

Mitchell believes him . . .

With a hectic teaching schedule, sessions with Gerald and free time spent with Lisa and Pauline, I am still lonely and lost. I have spent the last three years looking for someone to love, hoping to find a person to replace Joe's position in my life. Being immeasurably needy, I do not realize that this kind of love does not come very often, and certainly not when you're trying to force it to happen. Gerald decides to put me together with Mitchell. He whets my appetite by informing me that "the man in The Group with the beard" is interested in me.

Excitement and hope seize my mind. Perhaps I will finally be able to fill my aching inner void. I know almost nothing about Mitchell, but I feel terribly lucky to have been chosen as a prospective partner by the only man in The Group. Gerald tells me further that I might end up having a relationship with him. A relationship! That sounds just wonderful. I am starved for intimacy. Since I lost Joe, in my desperation, I have dated about twenty men — mostly one-night stands which left me feeling cheated and used. I can find no one who has a genuine interest in me — the person, and I feel like Diane Keaton in the movie *Looking for Mr. Goodbar*. So, after the next Thursday group, Mitchell and I end up walking and talking outside of Gerald's house. The hopeful lift from meeting a new person is a welcome relief after months of fruitless searching for Mr. Right. I want so much to finally find "the one" that I don't even attempt to get to know Mitchell as a person. I don't consider whether or not I like him; I just hope; this time it will work; it has to. We decide to experiment, to try a date, to "see what will happen", and Gerald approves.

Mitchell is the only child of Corinne, a Greek fur saleswoman, and Dick, an Irish-German printer. He has just recently earned his college degree, a few years later than his classmates he claims, due to a personal battle with dyslexia. After college his girlfriend dumped him in order to marry a doctor (she wanted a man with a secure financial future) and since that betrayal, he has retreated from the apartment they both shared back to his childhood bedroom in his parents' Westwood home. There he hides, filling his days with TV movies, unable to leave the house due to agoraphobia and seizures. He has made the rounds of most of the major psychiatric hospitals in the tri-state area, attempting to get himself committed. However, he has had no luck — the doctors claim that there is nothing significantly wrong with him. Thanks to meeting Gerald he has finally decided to turn his life around, and for the past few months he has been diligently sheet-rocking his parents' basement in order to build the office suite of *Artmarketing Advertising*. Between hammering and painting he invests countless hours pasting up typesetting for his new business cards and brochures, but he has no viable clients and no steady source of income. Mitchell views himself as very spiritual, frequently pausing from his business stationery design tasks to connect with the balls of light and energy he sees floating around him in the air as he practices the focusing exercises we have learned in The Group. Gerald praises him for investing so much time in this additional "homework".

Mitchell and I have been put together to experiment with having a relationship. Like choosing a lab partner in chemistry class, it doesn't really matter who was selected for me because, as Gerald has told us,

"Everyone is interchangeable. Your goal is to discover your weaknesses so you can eliminate them and grow."

However, my agenda is different; I want love. My need is so powerful that regardless of what I learn about Mitchell's past, I have faith that, with some encouragement and support from me, he will eventually change for the better. On our first date, Mitchell escorts me to *Beefsteak Charlie's* on Route 4 in Paramus. (It turns out to be the one and only time he is willing to pay for my restaurant meal for the unforeseeable future.) During dinner an argument erupts. Because I refuse to agree with him, Mitchell is offended and concludes that I have not given him the respect he deserves. The next morning he calls Gerald and complains that I am too opinionated and he wants no further part of me. Father Gerald tells him to give me another chance. Mitchell agrees and we date again the following week.

A month or so later we spend New Year's Eve with Lisa and Pauline at their Queens apartment. The Girls lend us a bedroom for the night and a little after midnight we retire. Mitchell and I lie down together and he rubs my back. Unexpectedly an odd feeling overcomes me. For a few fleeting moments I am propelled into another dimension of perception. Through a set of eyes I never knew I possessed, I discern beneath Mitchell's surface behavior. It is not like ESP; I don't pick up thoughts. Instead the intentions of his soul are revealed to me. In my vision Mitchell is trapping me with his willful personality and possessing me as his property. I realize that if he has his way, he will control me totally and I will never be able to escape. The sensation is creepy and I do not know what to do with the information, so when the moment passes, I forget all about it.

Gerald shows The Group something new. As he shakes, his arms float up over his head as if he was a marionette. They undulate in a languid manner and then slowly descend back to his lap. Soon he rises from his chair to wander aimlessly around the room, eyes closed, waving his arms and swaying like a drunkard. Leaning against a wall, he lets his body slide slowly and laboriously to the floor. Regaining his seat again a few moments later, he recommences his head shaking and his legs rise slowly until they are both sticking straight out in front of him, in midair, totally parallel to the floor. He explains his bizarre performance thus,

"I am being moved by energy from the 'other place' we are all working to get to. My mind is not doing this. Although my legs are straight in the air, there is no tension in my muscles holding them up. They are totally slack; it feels as if there is invisible *Jell-O* underneath them, supporting them. People, you know we have to be loose and mushy to go to the other place. All the crazy people out there are obsessed with exercise but they are really breaking down their bodies from the stress of tensing their muscles; it just makes them old fast. Exercise is a total waste of time."

I peer at his thighs to see the outline of his bulging muscles. They look tight to me. However, I do not dare contradict him. Gerald encourages us to seek this experience ourselves. During The Group, as his head shaking intensifies, several others join him. Harriet frequently rises from the couch, slowly crossing the room to eventually intersect with Gerald where they share a sort of impersonal embrace. Nora's arms sway proudly in an invisible breeze. Pauline leans slowly forward as if pulled by some unseen cord, until she actually falls gently off her chair. She remains on the floor, face down in a heap, for several minutes, continuing to allow The Energy to navigate her jolting limbs in a strange modern dance. Mitchell rolls from the couch to the floor and drags me with him. He hovers his body over mine, rubbing against me suggestively and I am mortified beyond description, yet unable to oppose him. This would cause an interruption in the holy atmosphere of this sanctuary where no matter what The Energy commands, you acquiesce without objection. Choked by my rebellious feelings, I am immeasurably and secretly guilty.

In the evenings my mother often voyages through our apartment. She waves her arms rhythmically, eyes tightly closed, bumping into doors and furniture, to duplicate the experiences we have in The Group. One night at about 2:00 A.M., I am jolted out of my sleep for some unexplained reason. I hear my mother just down the hall, a few steps from my almost closed door. To my horror, in the next few moments the handle turns and I feel her applying the necessary force to push it open. Soon she has gained entrance and is approaching my bed in her skimpy sheer nightgown like a sleepwalker, arms floating, barely a few feet from me. Absolutely spooked, I say nothing, but lie stock still, waiting to see what she is up to. Slowly she approaches my prone body and then makes her way toward my head. Her arms continue to wave carelessly as she bends down closer. Now my fear paralyzes me as her arms move toward my body. Finally one of her hands comes to rest, with seemingly arbitrary intent, on my breast. I am frozen from shock, unable to speak, as a violent desire to throw her off of me and slam her into the wall threatens to break my paralysis. I endure in silence until she withdraws her hand a little while later, and after this brief action she withdraws from the room. She immediately returns to her bedroom. It is as if some shadowy specter has just paid me a visit; if I didn't feel so devastated, I would almost wonder if I had made the whole thing up . . .

The next day, as I teach my students, I am close to a breakdown. My chest is swollen and tears well in my eyes continually. I push them back, turning my head so the kids won't see. I have no one to talk to about this, except Gerald. After the last class I rush from the Bronx to his office in Manhattan, seeking relief from my terrible feelings of betrayal. Lisa and Pauline are in the middle of a session with him. I can't even wait for them to finish, but burst into the room and plead to see him alone. They are kind enough to leave, and as soon as they do I totally lose it, sobbing on him, "My mother made a pass at me in the middle of the night."

Not expecting this drama and not knowing what to do with my reaction, he looks at me knowingly and comments analytically and removed, "Oh, that is big."

I want him to put his arms around me and comfort me, to hold me until the pain passes, but he makes no move to do this. He simply allows me to finish my story and then throws out his typical, "Let's see if we can get past this."

His advice stated, he focuses into my eyes and begins shaking his head.

Having used him as a sounding board, I have released my emotion, so I feel better. That night I confront Grace and ask her why she did this to me. Clearly insensitive to the agonizing emotions I have endured all day, she replies lightly in a singsong voice,

"Oh, no reason, I just wanted to see what it would be like. It doesn't really mean anything. You know what Gery-Wery says," her voice chirps, "It's what's inside that counts; the outside is meaningless, just flesh against flesh."

After that, I don't want to live with her anymore . . .

I try to rent an apartment with Lisa and Pauline but we just can't agree on a suitable location. Finally, we are forced to give up and I escape from my mother a few nights every week by sleeping at Mitchell's parents' house in New Jersey. He has a single bed; I am crammed against the wall and wake up stiff. In addition, his parents do not really welcome our presence and there are frequent fights. I realize that this arrangement must end soon and I decide to find my own place.

To make matters more uncomfortable, Mitchell has been sharing my car for several months. His ten-year-old burgundy *Fiat* has been sitting in the driveway for close to a year because he can't afford the repair. He keeps promising that he'll "bring it to the shop next week", but he never does. I hate the restriction of my freedom but I feel obligated to help him because he is my boyfriend. Finally, he asks me to lend him $600 for car repairs. I resist, but with conflict; maybe if I give him the money, I will finally have my car to myself.

"Come on," he encourages me, trying to push me over the edge, "Gerald says we have to learn to let go of money. Hanging onto it only keeps you small. This is an opportunity for you to grow."

On the way to the bank to get him the cash, my mind repeats Mitchell's logic over and over to drown out my reluctance. I escalate my thoughts hyperactively, intent on convincing myself that breaking this barrier of possessiveness over money will be good for me. I am sure that even before Mitchell is able to pay me back, The "Law of Reciprocity" will reward me for my action, and Gerald would definitely approve!

As the weeks pass rapidly during my second year at Fieldston, I begin to lose touch with my passion to be a psychiatrist. I have never reapplied to medical school as I had planned, and my motivation to do so has slipped away unnoticed. My symptoms of brain fog and fatigue are ever-present and my emotional conflict only aggravates them. It takes everything I've got just to make it through each day. As much as I hate to admit it, I know that I would never be able to survive the rigorous schedule of a medical student. Over the past two years the path I have followed so diligently since I was a little girl has gradually evaporated, and there is nothing to replace it. I do realize, however, that I don't want to commit my life to teaching, as much as I enjoy it. I couldn't support myself on such a salary. So, by the end of that second year, I decide to leave my teaching job. In addition, I look for an apartment in earnest. Rentals in New York City are unaffordable so I scan the listings in the North Jersey papers. After three months of careful searching, I finally rent the upstairs of a Hackensack Cape Cod. With three hundred square feet of living space and seven foot ceilings, it is a tiny hotbox which costs me $400 per month. Without viable employment to cover basic living expenses, I cannot justify using my inheritance to pay more than this minimal rent. Mitchell and I have been seeing each other for about nine months now, and the relationship, although far from ideal, has become my primary emotional anchor. Therefore, I take Mitchell with me to this new apartment with little hesitation. There is no discussion about splitting expenses. In fact it is never stated, but mutually understood that I will pay the bills until he can recover from his emotional phobias and "get himself on his feet financially". He and Gerald both reassure me frequently that with Mitchell's dedicated focus on The Energy, this will happen very soon.

Fall 1984 to Summer 1987

Mitchell and I begin our life as a couple. I am relieved not to have a regular work schedule because the only thing I want to do is sleep; I have very few hours of normal energy. Most days I count the time until I can lie down and gain a few hours of blessed relief from the stress of constantly forcing my body to stay awake. In between sleeping I worry about what to do with my life. I have no direction. To make some money, I take a job with an agency tutoring high school students. For the next three years, I visit several homes each week teaching chemistry, biology, math and French. In addition, I take part-time jobs in photography: at *Sears Portrait Studio*, as a wedding photographer's assistant and finally as a wedding studio manager. I pick photographers' brains about equipment, posing and pricing. I live moment to moment, always struggling to walk through the deep water of my confused emotions and physical fatigue. Migraine headaches which compel me to vomit are frequent too — "all part of your resistence to personal growth," Gerald reassures me, "The more pain, the more gain." The months turn into years, and much to my distress, no solid plan of action for my future emerges. I try to convince myself to enroll in a graduate program in biochemistry but I can't find the energy to motivate these well-meant thoughts into action. Each day I float farther away from my original career plans toward . . . I don't know what.

I make the best home that I can for us, furnishing it with the bare essentials. I shop, cook and clean. Mitchell follows me in the supermarket like a toddler. He lights up like a Christmas tree each night when I make dinner, oohing and aahing over my choice of spice for the side dishes and beaming down contentedly upon our freshly ground coffee and dessert. Occasionally he takes out the garbage . . . I keep asking when he will pay back the $600 I lent him for auto repairs.

"I have just started to make a little money; I can't do it yet," he retorts, annoyed that I won't just get off his back and trust him.

Soon the *Fiat* breaks down again and Mitchell realizes that a more expensive car is necessary anyway to impress the important advertising clients he is sure he will be courting very soon. He finds a two-year-old light blue 1983 *Honda Accord* sedan in the paper, so we take a drive to inspect it one evening. Mitchell makes a $4000 deal on the spot and then turns to me for a $2000 loan. We are standing in front of the seller. I feel obligated to support him in his efforts to improve his life; I don't want to appear controversial and embarrass us, so I write the check with a trembling hand, fervently pushing away my doubts once again.

The following week, Mitchell applies for a part-time job at a Formica furniture store, *Room Plus*, in Paramus. He works eight hours per week and his pay check is typically $55. After a few "beginner's luck" sales which yield additional commissions, the rest of his deals fall through. He blames the customers for not appreciating his intelligence and dedication. I entreat him to ask for more hours and to try to learn from his manager, a top salesman who is worthy of his regard and study. He claims that he doesn't like the manager's personality, too egotistical, and besides, he is not strong enough yet to throw himself in; his agoraphobia still plagues him from time to time. However, he acknowledges that Gerald is really helping him, and he hopes that soon he will be able to work full time. Unfortunately, he can only afford the $25 session fee once a week.

"If only I could pay for additional sessions with Gerald," Mitchell complains.

In the hope that my investment will yield fruit in the form of Mitchell finding some serious work, I offer to pay for two additional hours per week.

In spite of my intentions for Mitchell's advancement, our life is anything but improving, and I begin to feel helpless to change my predicament. As if trapped in a nightmare, miserable vignettes repeat themselves over and over, such as: Mitchell is on his way to the Bank — "I am going to cash a $15 check. That is all I have in my account," he complains, "When I go to buy a coffee and donut I feel I can't afford it . . . " or, Mitchell looks up at me like a lost, helpless puppy. "I'm a little tapped out today, would you lend me $5 for breakfast?" I hand him the bill and drop him at the diner. Driving away, I wish I could dump him there forever.

I hate my life; I deserve better than this. Yet, I try so hard to make us work, writing checks to fill in for his lack of contribution, promising myself that this is the last time, that next month I will make sure that things are different. I believe his promises, that it will all change soon. I believe Gerald's promises, that this is the rough part of the relationship and that if I am willing to survive it, there will be rewards later on.

Life in the bedroom is no better.

"Elizabeth," Mitchell demands sternly, "I want some sex. You don't give me enough."

Having jolted me with his command, he changes to a softer, more convincing tone,

"Come on, I'll make you feel good too. You don't know how to let yourself go and let me please you. You are too rigid."

Immediately my skin begins to crawl. I want to be anywhere but next to him. I grope for excuses.

"I'm too tired. I have to work tomorrow."

I try to change the subject, to distract him with the proposal that we rent a video and then go out for ice cream. This cozy suggestion works for that evening, but a few days later the demand returns again with additional intensity. This time, slipping away is more difficult. Unwilling to allow my escape, Mitchell grabs me by the collar, throwing me onto the floor, declaring that I am an ungrateful bitch.

"You have such an intelligent talented man, a person who sees Gerald and is 'going for himself'. You won't find another man out there courageous enough to last on the mission. You are so lucky, and this is how you show your appreciation!"

His eyes bug out in anger as he raises his voice and approaches me again. I fear that he is on the edge of hitting me. He outweighs me significantly; I won't be able to protect myself, so I must give in. Repressing the injustice I comply and enter the bedroom, quickly removing my clothes. I lie down, retreating inside of myself to a safe place where I can pretend that this isn't really happening.

Nevertheless, in The Group, Gerald touts us as "the couple that is staying together and making it work". The approval from the rest makes me forget what our home life is really like. Safe inside their familiar bosom, I feel hopeful that we can indeed work it out. I must continue trying to reach Mitchell, to convince him to change. Behind the scenes I complain to him that he has to be fair and take on his share of the financial load. When I'm not complaining, I try to explain it all to him like a patient teacher. He assures me that he is well aware of the problem and just needs a little more time, that our happiness is "just around the corner".

"Elizabeth, I know I haven't always been able to pay half of the bills, but I have been trying to play catchup football for all the years I lost when I was ill. I was talking to some clients last week and they told me they're seriously considering my proposal. This deal really looks good. You know that I always give you money when I have it. Don't be too hard on me. I had a very rough childhood and it's taken me so many years to get back into the real world. All my friends from high school have families and houses by now and I don't have anything. Don't forget, Gerald says to be patient. I am getting so much better every day."

I feel guilty about being so demanding. He is right. We are learning about having more patience in The Group and I am not being a good student. The Energy will bring all things in time to its faithful followers. However, things that come from the right place, from The Energy's infinite wisdom, take longer. Once again, for the time being, I leave him alone.

Occasionally, however, the emotions stemming from my sense of injustice rise from deep inside of me like a geyser. A rage like this can empower you to make essential changes in your life, and like a child who knows he has finally pushed his mother too far, Mitchell senses that I am getting to that point. The next few weeks are filled with constant affection and attentiveness from him. He transforms into a gourmet chef, filling my plate with all of my favorite foods. Under my pillow I find little gifts with loving notes attached; he throws me his warmest looks and biggest smiles; he entertains me with long drives through the Saddle River countryside and amusing joke and anecdotes; he hugs and squeezes me, satisfying my starvation for affection. His efforts court me right back into my familiar comfort zone until I forget that I was ever unhappy. That mighty voice of truth which had temporarily opened a window to the true desires of my soul is slowly silenced. My feelings of injustice fly back into their locked trunk in the basement for another long vacation.

By the mid-1980's Gerald's inner circle consists of thirteen members, eleven women and two men. In addition to my mother, Lisa, Pauline, Bess, Laura, Nora, Harriet, Mitchell, Beatrice, Caroline and myself, there are two new members: Jane is a divorced, forty-something, eighth-grade, special education teacher from Manhattan. Short and thin, she has black hair and an easy-going personality. Carl, referred by Jane, is short, almost bald and in his early forties. His attitude is generally selfish, nasty and critical. After a stint in the *Peace Corps* fifteen years ago, he has failed to select a career and instead lives off a monthly allowance donated by his mother. Gerald asks Lisa and Pauline which one of them would like to try a relationship with Carl. Lisa says she would prefer not to. Pauline, by default, is left to begin the experiment. Gerald also gains additional "outer-circle" people from the classes he continues to teach at the Demarest adult school or through referrals from other group members. At any one time, there are a dozen or so of these short term clients. Each of us feels terribly fortunate to have acquired a coveted position of membership in the clan of "chosen people" who have found The Man with the ultimate answers to it all. We know we will travel the entire journey because a big reward is guaranteed and a dreadful fate threatened if we do not. Gerald reminds us frequently,

"I have been chosen and gifted with special knowledge. You need me to find the way. I am the pioneer on the frontier and if you support me, I will cut the path. All you have to do is follow right behind me. If you leave this group, you will be lost. You can't make it without me so don't try to do this on your own."

He encourages us to socialize together.

"Because you all have the mission in common, you will get more out of spending free time together on weekends and vacations than with others not in The Group who don't know anything. You should only spend time with your family and friends from your past in order to learn how you do **not** want to live."

Bess responds with zeal, "I am the luckiest person on the Earth to have met you. There is no hope for the billions of people on the planet unless they one day learn of your knowledge and follow you too like I do. When I spend time with other people outside The Group, I realize how smart I am, and how far beyond them. They could never understand this unless they put in all the time and do all the difficult work that I have done."

Gerald nods his head up and down, absorbing her adoration, smiling with pride at his brood of devoted seekers.

All of us in the inner circle have increased the frequency of our sessions. The more time we spend, the faster we'll learn, and when we enter Gerald's den, we seat ourselves purposefully, looking up expectantly like baby birds waiting for mother to place life-giving food into our mouths. With a craving for Gerald's input that increases daily, instead of "feed me" we say, "lead me, fill me with your ideas and motivations". By relying on his presumed strength, it feels as if he is taking responsibility for our lives, carrying our burdens for us. Our nourishment is derived from his enlightened ideas. Each day he presents "new information" which we hungrily seek to ingest and compete with each other to cultivate. Our discussions based on Gerald's revelations are lively and stimulating as we revel in an orgy of intellectual abstractions, "wisdom" which fills us with a marvelous sense of empowerment. The Group is evolving into a family and a community. We have become actors in a long running play with distinct roles and a growing interdependency on one another. Our collective and singular mind is developing, characterized by unique and distinctive philosophies about life, work, relationships and the world around us. By constantly reinforcing our evolving ideology with each other, we become more and more isolated from the rest of the world. We seek Gerald's attention and praise with increasing desperation as this steadily evolves into our only source of any sense of value, well-being or emotional and spiritual sustenance. As we struggle to fill ourselves, Gerald begins slowly, almost unnoticeably, to withdraw what little recognition he has been willing to give. It is as if, a little at a time, he is pinching the air hose which contains our only source of oxygen, leaving us on the edge of suffocation where we can just barely function. Thus, our obsession with his approval increases until we have become ravenous emotional beggars with no other goal in life than to obtain this coveted prize.

The reality created in Gerald's den obliterates the outside world, the "crazy world", as Gerald refers to it, inhabited by "crazy people" or "dead robots". The Energy, which comes solely from Gerald, is the only frame of reference against which we can measure our feelings and thoughts. In its role of absolute power, The Energy begins to form its own independent personality. The Energy brings you good fortune. If you get a raise at your job, The Energy made it happen. If people smile at you on the subway, they feel The Energy. If your cat slept next to you last night, The Energy attracted her to you. Good weather means The Energy is strong, while bad weather means we are resisting The Energy. When the stock market goes up, the world is feeling and yielding to Gerald's Energy. In a bad economy, the world is afraid of "the good stuff" he is creating. If you get caught in a long line at the supermarket check out, you must be opposing The Energy. If another secretary in Pauline's office offers to do her xeroxing, this is proof that The Energy is using people to do her work for her. After all, because of our mission, we have a more important job to do. In fact according to Gerald, when we break all of our resistance we won't have to work anymore at all. Others will be attracted to give us all that we need, the same way Jesus Christ was taken care of as he journeyed, spreading the word of truth.

Enthusiasm about our stupendous discovery explodes exponentially and we zealously seek to spread the word. Our recruitment efforts hold no bounds and like Jehovah's Witnesses handing out bible tracts we focus our attention everywhere: family and friends of course, but also co-workers, old boyfriends, bus drivers, repairmen, librarians, etc., literally anyone with whom we come in contact. We hunger greedily to enlist new members, and our passion and willpower frequently ignites the interest of some polite stranger as we explain that "It's something special and unique, but you have to experience it to understand". A steady flow of "visitors" begins at the Thursday night groups. Gerald generally spends the entire evening focusing with the newcomer, explaining the wonders of The Energy with misty-eyed awe. Sometimes they "get it" and begin to attend sessions. Mitchell receives high compliments from Gerald when he brings his friend Rich Barton. A local computer operator fascinated by spiritual development and psychic powers, Rich seems to fit right in. Soon his girlfriend, Janet, joins too. She merges her mastery of Transcendental Meditation with Gerald's Energy, and while assuming the lotus position, floats in blissful dissociation for hours. Our group is growing in just the way we know it must and our leader's delicious praise for each new recruit fuels us to try even harder.

Sometimes Gerald gives me a ride home after our sessions in his city office. Crawling up the FDR Drive North in rush hour traffic, he shakes his head for a few minutes and then asks if I see the congestion loosening. Encouraged by our shared goal, I do believe that I see The Energy affecting the cars around us. This is my evidence that The Energy really works . . . Gerald even tells us that he has tried driving with his eyes closed on the Palisades Parkway, to test the inherent talents of "his friend". True to its nature, The Energy navigated the car for him, keeping him in his lane and safe from harm.

We begin to regard The Energy as an invisible friend, a constant companion who will never abandon us, and in addition, will give us everything we could ever want, provided we trust it, have patience and let it be the authority in our lives. Of course, since Gerald is the keeper of The Energy, and "The Energy is his partner", and "he and The Energy are one and the same", and with it,"he has gone beyond being just a human man" — therefore, The Energy must speak to us through Gerald. He is the source and we must consult him about everything. Should I look for a new job? Should I attend this family dinner? Should I read this book? Should I buy this dress? Should I take my dog to the vet? Should I try to go to bed earlier? Should I purchase health insurance? Anything and everything that is relevant to our lives is discussed in The Group. We know more intimacies about each other than we ever could have wanted to . . .

"The Energy enters me in a raw form which I must refine so that it will be palatable to the people I am trying to help. I am being used to channel it through my body."

Gerald never says who or what is using him for this purpose. In fact he doesn't know. He only knows that someone, a long time ago, made a big mess out of the whole human race by creating resistance and a universal crazy thought process. For some unidentified reason, Gerald Ezra Sharkman is the one who has been specially selected to receive higher knowledge. He strives to piece this information together, to solve the riddle whose answer will illuminate the escape route from the sticky web of The Program. He also receives frequent, profound messages about an impending spiritual catastrophe.

"We must all begin to prepare now, today. There is no time to waste." He tells us with wide, frightened eyes. He transmits his fears with such passion that we are terrified, desperate to absorb his information and follow him before it is too late.

"This whole world is a disaster and the human species is headed toward extinction if we don't do something fast. We are destroying the planet with pollution. It is only a matter of time before it decides that it has had enough. The Earth will say, 'Next species', and wipe us out, in the same way it destroyed the dinosaurs. Following The Energy and learning how to use it is our only hope of survival. All the 'dead people' out there who don't eventually come to know what we know now, will be doomed. They had better smarten up fast. I have been getting messages that the end is very near. Next year at this time we won't be here anymore. By then, The Energy will have carried us out of this crazy thought system, and into everlasting life."

I believe that Gerald has special powers. I believe that he will live forever. This energy is something that only he can control and understand. It is our savior, our only source of hope in a necessarily dark and horrible future.

I enter the den one winter day and sit down quietly. Gerald is shaking his head vigorously and Bess is staring out the window at the falling snowflakes. She is reporting how his head shaking is affecting the snowfall. "Yes, The Energy is getting stronger. The snow is letting up a little."

Gerald replies gravely, after all, they are involved in a very important project, "That's good."

Keeping his eyes closed so that he can concentrate with the seriousness required by this task, he doubles his head shaking speed. I stare out of the window along with Bess, following her reports closely. I let myself be carried on this journey, rising inside as if on a magic carpet, propelled solely by the power of

Bess's confidence in her own beliefs. I feel everything that she is saying and its connection to his shaking. Half an hour later the snow lets up a little. She looks at him with respect in her eyes, smiling winningly,

"It's really disappearing now, thanks to The Energy. In fact, it's almost gone and I see a glow in the trees behind your back yard. You are glowing too! Gerald, you did it again!"

"It's going to get warmer now. The Energy broke the resistance in the weather," he answers.

"We sure are lucky to know you, Gerald."

"This is really exciting," he utters with wondrous, almost misty-eyed awe.

"Elizabeth," Gerald begins on another day, his eyes ablaze with pride, "Yesterday I was at Beatrice's and something incredible happened!"

"What?" I ask, eager to be in on any new discovery.

"Well I was shaking for about an hour on the deck when a few squirrels were drawn to The Energy. Soon more followed, and after awhile, there were about thirty of them sitting frozen, just staring up at me. The animals feel The Energy even more than the humans because they don't have the crazy thinking process to block them."

Beatrice sits on the love seat facing him, nodding exuberantly.

"Yes, Gerald was amazing, and as soon as he stopped shaking and went back into the house they all ran away. They were only interested in him!"

Yet another day in the den . . . "I have discovered something new," Gerald informs us, "The scientists are lying when they tell you that it harms your eyes to look at the sun. I looked directly into the sun yesterday for an hour and I am fine. The sun has a personality too, you know, and it plays games just like a human. It is no different from us. The molecules just take on a different form."

Soon we are all staring at the sun peeking through the trees as Gerald shakes his head. Bess describes what she sees,

"I just saw the sun run away. It must be afraid of The Energy."

"Yes," Gerald replies, "but it will come back. If I keep shaking, I can gain its trust and it will be our friend."

Awhile later Carl notices that the sun is getting bigger. Gerald explains why, "That is because it is coming closer to me. The Energy is winning over its fear. Right now I am actually having a conversation with it."

There are new and wonderful things like this happening every day; this makes Gerald's den the most exciting place to be, as long as you are willing to follow along with Gerald's logic . . .

Gerald lectures passionately one sunny Saturday afternoon as we sit grouped around him in the den.

"Gravity is bullshit, a lie we believe collectively. If we could release ourselves from this illusion, we would be able to fly around the room like they did in the movie, *Mary Poppins*. Remember when they floated up and had a tea party on the ceiling?"

An unanticipated surge of rage rises from deep inside my chest, reddening my cheeks. I tilt my face downwards to hide, but Gerald catches my reaction and makes an example of me.

"Elizabeth, do you have a problem with what I just said?" He glares, rising from his seat and approaching me threateningly.

"Yyyyyes," I stammer, cursing myself for always wearing my emotions on my sleeve, now forced to admit my lack of faith publicly.

"See everybody," he turns to face the rest of my comrades, "this proves my point. Elizabeth is defending the lie that we can't fly, and that lie is precisely what holds us all on the ground."

I recede into my chair in humiliation. His accusations make me feel personally responsible for keeping the entire human race weighted down on the Earth's surface . . . Another surge of rage passes through me, commanding me to jump up and argue, even attack him for what he has just claimed, but I hold myself back, suppressing my reaction, keeping my butt glued to my seat. Nonetheless, Gerald senses my continued opposition and turns, raising his voice, filling me with terror.

"You seem to still have a problem. What is it?"

"Nnnothing," my voice squeaks from the depths of my throat.

"You're lying," he bellows, "I can see it in your face . . . See what I mean people? Elizabeth is showing us something very important, how <u>not</u> to live. Gravity was created by our minds and our minds make it real. If we could release the true potential of our brains, we could do anything. We could fly; we will fly; I will find a way, you'll see, and when I do, it will be too late for Elizabeth. She'll miss out on the fun because she'd rather hold onto her stupid thoughts."

Bess, seated on the floor near his feet, looks up at him in gratitude, experiencing once again how fortunate she is to be part of it all. Feeling the sting from his public scolding, I try to examine it from his viewpoint. *What if Gerald is right and there are things I don't know about yet? I learned the Law of Gravity in eighth grade, but science is always developing and scientists frequently modify existing theories or define new laws for our physical universe. Isaac Newton had the last word until Albert Einstein came along. Perhaps there is more beyond Einstein, and maybe Gerald has the vision to see it.*

The following week Gerald reasserts that we will be able to fly soon. Again, that familiar rage swells up automatically from deep inside. However this time I attempt to correct myself. *There's that resistance again. Gerald must be right. This reaction occurs to stop progress. It's the same thing that has always happened when someone has a new idea. People are afraid of change and fight it. That's where my rage is coming from; I am afraid of change too. I must correct this in myself, get rid of the anger, so that I can have new experiences and enjoy the freedom they will bring. I must be flexible and open to new ideas. After all, a hundred years ago, no one would have believed that we could visit the moon or fly in an airplane! Maybe this is like that too. I've heard it said that whatever man can conceive, he can achieve. If all scientists possessed my negative attitude, they would never strive to achieve new heights of technology. I must force my mind to consider that someday, what Gerald predicts* <u>*could*</u> *happen.*

When Gerald mentions flying again later that week, the rage is still there, but I quickly push it back down, so deep now that it's almost completely out of view. Nevertheless, these rages have become regular companions in my life with Gerald. Although I usually manage to hide them from the others, they erupt almost daily as he makes his socially defiant claims of exclusive knowledge and extraordinary abilities. I desperately try to push away each reaction with all of my willpower, but the painful, conflict-ridden fury **will not go away**, no matter how hard I try. It twists my stomach while I attempt to distract myself with the conversation in Gerald's den or office. I feel like a traitor, unable to believe him, in fact often despising his claims and projections. He stresses almost daily that we must all be in agreement, on the same wavelength. As a team, focused on a group objective, we will cut through the resistance like a laser beam, and break out of our collectively oppressed states of being to realize the bliss of our true potential. Basking in the delirium of his visions, Gerald doesn't usually notice that I am having trouble being a team player, but sometimes, he senses my opposition and reprimands me.

"Elizabeth is making the intention, on purpose, to impede the mission and destroy the lives of the rest of us."

My other "friends" usually take the opportunity to gain a morsel Gerald's approval by jumping on board, adding their accusations to support his. In these moments I am cornered and come to sincerely believe that my "negative" thoughts are wrong, although try as I might, I remain powerless to evict them from my mind. I sit through these castigations, adrenalin pumping, hands shaking and mouth parching. Gerald criticizes me further for these physical signs of defensiveness, accusing me of receding because I am cowardly. Trapped, I focus only on surviving these sessions, retreating inside and numbing myself to my emotions, until the sessions end, and thankfully, I am released.

Having successfully seduced me and my mother, Gerald begins to break in the others. Lisa and Pauline don't seem to question his motives as he suggests they sit naked with him during their sessions. They are agreeable girls whose priority is to please others and to be perceived as nice. They have spent their lives in classrooms and libraries, believing like me, that attaining the praise of the authority or teacher, and the perfect grade, are all that is necessary to succeed in life. Also, like me, they believe his talk of breaking barriers, leading to personal growth. Soon he is sitting between them, kissing and fondling. He makes them feel special and needed with the attention he gives them and the invitation to be included in his experiments. They share in the excitement and momentum propelling them toward something wonderful. Nora gives in willingly as well. She and her husband live like brother and sister, rivals who spat constantly and share no intimacy. She enjoys viewing herself as a sexual and sensual being, ready to explore new and interesting territory. Beatrice, although married and old enough to be Gerald's mother, has a desire to worship and praise Gerald and would do anything for him. In her eyes, he is a wealthy woman's protege. Her husband unwittingly pays thousands for her "therapy", not realizing that while he conducts business at his Manhattan office, his wife is playing hostess to Gerald in their Westchester weekend home. He has no idea that her "therapist" stands on their deck at the back of her house shaking his entire body, stark naked. He also does not know that Gerald encourages Beatrice's hostility for the man whose riches support her lavish lifestyle. In The Group she speaks of her spouse with open contempt, emasculating him with references to his emotional insecurities and his trouble getting an erection . . . Bess has the personality of an insecure, little girl and Gerald is easily able to manipulate her into sexual encounters whenever he pleases. Caroline is the only one who turns him down. Besides choosing to remain faithful to her spouse, she doesn't understand what sex has to do with stress reduction therapy. Nonetheless, Gerald, unequipped to handle disobedience, endeavors to convince her otherwise. For more than a year, Caroline consistently declines his offers until finally he gives up, informing us behind her back that she is stupid and "giving up the opportunity of a lifetime".

Finally there is Mary, one of Gerald's students from the Demarest Adult School course he teaches twice a year. From the moment they meet, their mutual attraction is magnetic and engulfs them both completely. Mary attends The Group on Thursday nights, but only for a few short months. Then things change and Gerald begins to visit her house several times a week, always after her husband has left for work. Gerald no longer requires her to pay a fee in order to spend time in his presence, and instead brags about their marathon sexual sessions which often last up to six hours. From the way he describes their encounters, and the growth he attributes to each day of "discovery", he makes us feel that this liaison is necessary, even essential to his spiritual growth.

Gerald's children, Martin and Samantha, now high school freshman and sophomore respectively, know all about his relationship with Mary, but Gerald instructs them not to tell their mother. He has been explaining The Program and his wife's Female Game to them since they were old enough to speak,

"Your mother is too stupid to give up her destructive relationships with her parents and two sisters to go for something real. You kids will have to make a choice, to live like her and destroy your lives or to go for the good stuff and become big and truly alive."

One Thursday night, after several years of failed attempts, he finally convinces his wife to attend The Group in order to "break the lies in her head and start to understand the importance of what we are really doing in here". For an hour Doris sits in a rocking chair, saying nothing and shaking her legs restlessly, a stern look frozen on her face. Finally, well before the session is over, she sighs with apparent frustration and leaves the room; she never returns. The next day Gerald tells us that she "just doesn't get it". Soon he begins reporting that Doris hates The Group with a vengeance. In fact, she avoids the house whenever sessions are held, and passes a household law forbidding their children to take part in The Group's activities or have any contact whatsoever with the other members. Defiantly, each Thursday night Gerald insists that the kids join us after she leaves the house. At 9:25, when the headlights of her returning car shine down the driveway, he motions to them silently, but urgently. They jump from their seats immediately, sneaking out of the room and noiselessly closing the door behind them, throwing themselves on the couch in the adjoining family room. From the den, I can hear the remote click on the TV as the front door opens.

"Hi Mom, can we help you with the packages?" they greet her politely with feigned sincerity, "We were just watching a really good show. Do you want to hear about it?"

One day Gerald asks Martin to explain to the rest of us how he handles the conflict he experiences living with such contradictory parents.

"I was following my mother for a very long time. My father was trying to warn me that I was in danger, but I didn't listen. I thought I had all the answers. Then I realized that he was right and I quickly changed direction and followed him. I was so stupid; I almost destroyed my life, but I am OK now. My mother's life is going nowhere. My father is special and we must listen to him for the answers; I am sticking with him. My sister is smart, she always knew that my father had the right way and my mother didn't. Gerald is not only my father. He is father to us all."

According to Samantha, "My mother is stupid; she just never learns that Dad knows what's going on for real and she should give up her games and let him lead."

As the group members crave more time with Gerald he begins to invite us to visit each other's private sessions. On a typical Friday evening I take bus and subway to reach his office on 71st Street between Park and Lexington Avenues. I can still hear the squeaking and banging sound the heavy metal street door makes as I must throw my entire body against it to open it. In a moment I am in the narrow waiting area and sit expectantly. There are two offices opening off of this room, both sublet by practitioners who claim to be in the mental health field. Gerald's tiny office is on the left. It is only about fifty square feet and a love seat and two chairs fill it almost completely. I hear voices through the wall. Gerald is expounding excitedly on some new truth he has just discovered. I strain to listen to the dialogue; anything Gerald has to say, I want to know. I also want to know where everyone else is at, the gossip, so I can evaluate my current status in our family. Soon he opens the office door and yells out a friendly "Come on in."

Mumbling goodbye to Gerald, Laura rushes by, almost slamming against me, eyes down-turned. She is out on the street in a heartbeat and I am now permitted to enter the inner sanctum. Brimming with anticipation, I seat myself quickly on the couch, snuggling gratefully into the comfort zone of my now thrice weekly ritual of two-hour "stress reduction" sessions.

Gerald nods amicably, then immediately queries authoritatively, "What's doing?" I scramble to report a positive experience at work or expand on my growing awareness of one of his most recent theories. He nods his head continually as I chatter excitedly and then rewards me with the approval I hungrily seek, some short encouraging phrase like, "Oh boy, you're getting smart."

Lisa and Pauline arrive shortly thereafter. The discourse between Gerald and each of The Girls is similar to mine, although Pauline generally whines and sometimes eventually sobs hopelessly over her inability to put our leader's teachings into effect. Lisa doesn't usually have a lot to say, but appears serious and very apprehensive. When we three young girls have finally settled in, he proceeds with his agenda by inquiring suggestively, "How about if I take my clothes off?"

It is the same sweet voice he used that first day about six years ago when he asked me if I might like to try taking off my shirt. After he undresses, he sits in a chair, closes his eyes and begins to shake his head. His body shows no sign of sexual arousal. Gerald has told us many times that the wonderful feelings he obtains from the head shaking are "beyond sex". He no longer needs nor desires this backwards activity. "However," he tells us, "because I care about you, and I am the only man on the planet who can do this, I will lend you my body. You can experiment with your feelings. Do anything that you want. This will help you grow."

We focus on his spinning head and soon see clouds of light all around the room. Lisa's arm jolts with electricity and Pauline's head leans awkwardly to one side, pulled there by The Energy. This familiar exercise slows us down, preparing us to concentrate on the work we must each now begin to overcome our personal resistance . . . Painstakingly, one of the three girls removes an article of clothing from her body. There is no cue from anyone. It is entirely up to each of us to choose what she wants to do and when. Nevertheless, we all feel that we must push ourselves in this direction in order to take advantage of the "therapy". In fact, if you do not eventually strip and ultimately participate in the group activity by at least placing your naked body against the bodies of the others, you will be labeled as "holding back", which in our circle, where you only get praise when you "go for it", is a sin. I grit my teeth, close my eyes and slowly unbutton my shirt. The silence in the room is deafening while Gerald's chair squeaks relentlessly as he shakes his head back and forth. I want to know what the other two girls are doing, but I don't want to know . . . I strain to listen and hear more clothing rustle. I know that Pauline and Lisa, sitting next to me on the couch, are undertaking the same undressing as I have begun. The conflict increases as the minutes lag. It soon becomes overwhelming and since it is impossible to escape this room, my brain reinterprets my intolerable conflicted fear as electrical excitement. Within about half and hour there are three additional piles of clothes on the floor and three naked slim young women in their mid-twenties sitting terrified, silent on the couch while the naked man, eyes closed, continues his head shaking. The overhead light in the room seems brighter than ever as we are all painfully exposed. There is only one thing left to do now, approach Gerald, the prize. The air is charged with emotion — anticipation, competition and confusion. Each of us focuses on Gerald alone. We race against each other to get close to him. This agonizingly slow race takes nearly an hour to complete and every minute feels like ten. One of the three girls drops off the couch and onto the floor. With incredible concentration, she drags her body across the rug, limb by limb, one inch at a time. It takes fifteen minutes to cross the seemingly infinite span of three feet between the couch and Gerald's chair. The other two follow suit and rivalry develops quickly as we sense each other's actions. Yet, we, as individuals, have no personal desire for him. It's just the only role we can play. He has created a scene where, since we have committed ourselves to remain in the room, there is nowhere else to go, no alternate option for interaction. The first girl finally reaches his chair and remains there for a while, her head resting on his feet. Gerald continues shaking. The silence gets louder. The other two move along the carpet too, toward the oasis. Girl number two goes around the back. The first girl lifts herself up toward his chest. The chair creaks as she does this and she pulls back a little, afraid of breaking the silence and drawing attention to herself. There is no room for the third girl, the loser of the race, to be right next to Gerald, so she crouches on the floor behind the first girl. She must be satisfied with being next to the person who is next to Gerald. The second girl now becomes a little more bold and lifts herself up to reach Gerald's face. She finds his mouth with her lips. He continues to shake his head while the girl focuses on moving her head with the same rhythm as his so that their lips can remain together. After the session her mouth will be irritated, red and sore from the constant friction of rubbing flesh. This action gives the first girl more courage and she slides her head slowly down his chest and rests it on his thigh. Her hand creeps toward his pubic hair which she strokes softly, trying to convince herself that this is what she wants to be doing. Diligently forcing herself toward the ultimate, about ten minutes later she finally takes his still flaccid member into her mouth. Gerald continues shaking his head and soon his organ has become rock solid. Over the next several minutes, the girl does whatever she needs to in order to finish him off, while the third girl finds a way to maneuver herself into a position where she can assist the first girl. Sometimes their lips even touch as they apply themselves to their task. When Gerald finally climaxes he always says the same thing, "Whew, that was really big." He is referring to The Energy, released from the orgasm, which will propel him to a higher spiritual level. During the entire time he has not touched any one of the girls. According to him, the goal of the experience is to face uncomfortable feelings and learn from them, not to attain sexual pleasure. Our infinitely patient tutor, he explains,

"It was difficult for you girls to fight your resistance and move toward me and The Energy, but you did it. Knowing that you accomplished this is a tremendous reward and you will see the results of this growth in all areas of your life."

Soon, he turns scientific and asks us collectively, "So, what's going on, what did you feel?"

We each describe our reactions, thoughts etc. Then usually it comes out that one or two of the girls were "competing" or "playing a game". Once their crime is admitted, Gerald severely chastises them. In addition, one girl is deemed the courageous one who has grown the most that day. Which one of us is girl number one, two or three is unimportant. We are all drowning in the same cauldron, exchanging roles and actions randomly. Pauline often ends up crying, "I can't stop holding back. I am a failure."

He encourages the person he has selected as winner to advise her. Valuable suggestions such as, "Just go for it next time. Stop holding back."

Pauline replies tearfully, "But I don't know how to stop," and the helpful answer comes quickly,

"You just stop; you make a decision and do it."

If Gerald is in the mood, he berates her further. "If you don't start trying harder and cut the crap you will get left behind. You have to work harder and drop the games to get to our mission."

The competition we feel among ourselves for a prize that none of us wants, rises up like an angry demon and twists our guts until our life forces are asphyxiated almost entirely. What rage we suppress! We, unlike Mary, pay for every minute that we spend with Gerald, no matter how many orgasms we give him . . . Even outside of his sanctuary, in the Lexington Avenue diner where we three former college roommates share Swiss burgers, cheese omelettes, Gyros and coffee after our sessions, we are no longer comfortable together. As if obeying some invisible dictum, we never discuss what has just occurred or how much we paid him. The personal connections and sharing of our previous friendships are long gone. We monitor everything we say (and think) as if spies are all around. Although we all want to desperately, we never dare to even question Gerald's motives or actions. We know that any negative thoughts will be reported . . . and public humiliation, or worse, is something we must avoid at all cost.

These days Gerald's pants spend more time draped over the office chair than on his body. From 10:00 A.M. to 7:00 P.M. an almost hourly changing of the guard takes place as Beatrice visits first, replaced by Bess, then Jane, next Beatrice or Bess once again, and to wind up the day, a grand finale of me, Lisa and Pauline together. Sometimes, Gerald even adds Bess in with us — a group of five. With yet another female competitor, the emotional distress escalates. In response, I shut my eyes tightly; and I am almost positive that the other girls are doing the same. Bodies touch and hands probe with hesitation as our minds struggle to figure out what exactly we should do to win Gerald's approval. We know we must push at the envelope; it is in our own best interest — the whole point of these sessions, but the terror of failure is ever-present, and the overwhelming confusion. It is in this darkness that one day I feel a hand on my wrist. There is intent in the grasp and I shiver. Slowly it pushes down along someone's belly, centimeter by centimeter, finally dragging my hand toward the top of a feminine thigh. Revulsion bolts through my mind, freezing me in terror, but I am captive to momentum. When my fingers, shoved ever forward by Gerald's decisive grip, finally reach the private parts of my friend (I realize it is Pauline), forbidden feelings of outrage explode in my brain. Thoughts plead, *I don't want to be doing this. I hate this.* It takes all of my strength to stifle their expression, but somehow I manage, praying for this thousand-year moment to end. When twenty minutes later Gerald calls for a bathroom break, I say nothing to anyone. It will be several days before I can look directly at Pauline, I am so ashamed.

Break concluded, we immerse ourselves once more. Gerald suggests that Bess and I lie down on the couch naked, face, and focus on each other's eyes while masturbating ourselves. We protest weakly but he does not permit us to withdraw from this "lesson" so we reluctantly position ourselves as he has instructed. As I stare at Bess, trying to separate myself from this distasteful reality, I realize that she deplores this just as much as I do. Her body receives no sensation from her probing finger tips and after several tortured minutes, Gerald finally permits us to quit, criticizing us for holding back because neither of us could achieve any sexual pleasure.

We all build our days around visits to Gerald, fitting work and errands between our sacred obligation to this special therapy. Aside from Laura, who he seems to feel cannot be trusted to keep the nudity a secret, the scene is always the same. Dressed when we enter, he greets us cordially, chatting casually about truth, or sharing information about other Group member's progress or failure. Then he removes his clothing. The session is underway and it is time to work. Each female patient must now apply herself to the agonizing process of breaking her personal barriers, in order to permit herself the joyful freedom of experimenting with his body, which he donates generously and unconditionally, "because he cares about us in the right way". Sex with our husbands or boyfriends, if we have them, is no substitute for these sessions with Gerald, who is superior to every other man. He has eliminated all reactions and programming from his being. Therefore, each woman's experience of intimacy will be unfiltered and pure. Undistracted by another's insecurities, hidden agendas or thoughts, we can let ourselves go completely to feel The Energy. Although we begin by caressing him hesitantly, as our resistance breaks in levels we are able to proceed with more courage until we arrive at the ultimate where we give him oral sex. Sometimes, he will even invite one of us to have intercourse with him. This is a high honor and only reserved for a woman who is "really doing well". The rest of us feel jealous and terribly inferior to his chosen partner. In our minds, we scramble to figure out how we can attain this prestigious position the next time. None of us ever has an orgasm, but that is far less important than our opportunity to experience The Energy which Gerald releases when he climaxes.

Gerald has no problem sharing details about his intimate life with his wife either,

"This is how I have sex with Doris. I put my cock into her and lie there motionless, then I focus. The Energy comes out of my penis. This should give her an orgasm, but my wife is impatient and can't wait. She wants me to thrust like all of the other dumb jerk men. Those men just do that to perform for Mommy's approval. I refuse. Doris is really mad at me because she can't control me to get her way. If she ever decides to be smart, someday she will learn how to really have sex the right way."

One day I work up the courage to inquire about the double standard which seems to exist in our sessions,

"Gerald, when you, Lisa, Pauline and I are together, why do you always have an orgasm, but we never do?"

"Because you are not ready yet. You have to drop your baby games first and learn to be open to receive. Then The Energy will give you the orgasms just from being with me. I won't even need to touch you . . . "

One Friday evening, Lisa and Pauline are in Gerald's city office. All three are naked when suddenly, Gerald hears the outer street door opening. Doris was supposed to meet him in an hour but she is very early.

"Holy Shit," he mutters under his breath as he panics, hastily shoving his body back into his clothes. He motions for Lisa and Pauline to do the same. Unfortunately, they have not had sufficient practice in subversive clothing removal and redressing, and they do not move as quickly as he. Doris' footsteps echo up the short hall and into the tiny waiting-room. While politely waiting for Gerald to finish with his clients a sound enters her ears, the jingle of her husband's belt buckle. Instinctively, she bolts out of her seat and without knocking, grasps his doorknob and turns firmly, opening the door. Gerald has just made it back to his chair and although he has missed a couple of buttons, he looks pretty much in order. The Girls, however, have managed only to put back on their slacks and bras. Their shirts still remain crumpled on the floor. Upon viewing this scene, Doris' face reddens with the rage of a woman scorned. She yells out stridently, "What the hell is going on in here?"

Gerald puts on his instant innocent face mask and states confidently, "Nothing really, it's just that it was too hot in here so the girls decided to take off their shirts."

Doris commands Gerald to follow her to a private meeting in the waiting area as if he is an unruly schoolboy being dragged out of class by his ear.

"Did you have sex?" she asks directly.

"Oh no," he replies innocently, grasping at explanatory babble which ends up contradicting a previous statement of his, "We were just removing our clothes to explore how it feels to go against society's rules which were drilled into us with fear. This is only about breaking a barrier to free us from living small."

Doris leaves the office in an angry huff. When Gerald returns to The Girls he lets them know that this is their fault. Lisa and Pauline, terrified of his disdain, guiltily accept his blame and apologize profusely for having been too slow. For several weeks they beat themselves up mercilessly. Due to their personal inadequacies and an unwillingness to correct them, they believe they have come close to jeopardizing his marriage and ruining his life. Doris bans them from her house in Westwood, and like disgraced outcasts, they must sneak in for therapy sessions while she is at work.

The encounter with his wife does little to interrupt Gerald's schedule of creative experimentation. About a week later, he suggests that Nora and I remove our clothing and sit naked during an afternoon group session in his den.

"Society has programmed us to be ashamed of our bodies, but they are very natural. Just sit through the embarrassment until it lifts and you will feel comfortable in your own skin," he directs.

Dropping my head in shame, I stare at the floor and pray for my mind to stop sending me thoughts of panic as I imagine the others, Beatrice, Carl and Gerald, ogling me. Nora, on the other hand, seems comfortable with the exhibitionism and continues her stream of intellectual chatter as if nothing is amiss. Suddenly I hear the doorknob turn and Gerald's daughter enters unannounced. Samantha appears mildly surprised at the scene before her but hides her reaction with a slight smirk. Gerald laughs at this unexpected intrusion while she quickly finds a seat. Then conversation resumes with no explanation offered to the teenager. I can't understand how Samantha can accept it all so nonchalantly . . .

One day, as I arrive at Gerald's office in the city, he tells me that my mother has decided to leave The Group. He gives no explanation other than to declare her a "stupid fool who doesn't respect him", and that her life will most certainly go down the tubes without his energy. I can't believe it. How could she leave our mission? Where else is there to go? The stream of my life and my allegiance lies only in The Group, under Gerald's direction. She is now on the other side of the fence, a traitor. Over the next several months I hardly speak to her, and it never even occurs to me to ask her why she left or how she is doing without The Group.

After about two years, Grace suddenly returns. On the phone with her a week later, I finally probe her for information.

"After Gerald moved to New Jersey and stopped using our apartment for the group meetings, he didn't treat me well. He never appreciated, nor thanked me for helping him when he was in need. He just used me selfishly."

"Then, why did you come back?"

"Because I want his Energy. It is unique and special. There is nowhere else to get it except from him. I need it to discover myself and to grow."

"Don't you care about how he treats you anymore?"

"No, I am willing to put up with his imperfections to get The Energy."

Now that she has returned, I see my mother twice a week in Gerald's den. She just blends in with the rest of his soldiers for the truth. We are estranged from each other and there is no special significance to our relationship anymore, no personal allegiance. The sole focus of both of our lives is on our membership and participation in The Group. About twice a year I visit her apartment, usually for Christmas and Mother's Day. These meetings are awkward and the conversation always leads to Gerald, the only subject we have in common, our only link to each other.

Unexpectedly, after more than four years of intensive involvement, Gerald tells us that he has broken up with Mary.

"She refuses to believe in The Energy. I can't have a relationship with someone who wants to die."

The immense importance of this event hits each woman in Gerald's circle like a tidal wave. Now there is an opening for one of us to participate as his partner in a relationship! Each of us silently hopes and prays that she will be selected. I am sure I will be the one. I was his first. I am the smartest and best student. I am more passionate than the rest. From the day Gerald first kissed me on the cheek in Dr.

Rogers' office, I have experienced an unrequited love for him. It is as if, in one pivotal moment, a specter took residence in my body and never departed. The yearning for Gerald has become so familiar that I never doubt its continual demand that I must, at all costs, find a way to one day make him my own. I have never questioned the validity or intelligence of this intention, the feeling is too overpowering, and it feels so right. I know I would experience total completion, ecstasy, if only I could fulfill my longing, and today the opportunity has finally arrived to get one step closer to my goal.

However, rather than waiting for him to choose, Bess decides to take the step and volunteer herself; Gerald agrees. Feeling betrayed, I complain to him. He derides me and praises Bess for her courage.

"You missed the boat. You should have taken a shot but you were too distracted with your Female Game of seduction. You wanted to make me chase you and that would never happen in a million years."

Bess in her new role gets special treatment just like Mary did. She is instructed to arrive half an hour early on Saturday mornings, at 8:00 A.M., so that they can experiment with sex. Engaging ever so quietly on the den couch, they hide from the ignorant Doris who sleeps soundly in the master bedroom, literally right over their heads. Bess also stays after the rest of us leave at 2:00 P.M. for a repeat performance. Sometimes, when Doris is visiting her sister on Long Island, Gerald even invites her back on Sunday.

One Saturday afternoon, Laura begins to gripe. It isn't that she wants him for her boyfriend, but she guesses that Bess isn't paying for all of the extra personal time she gets.

"It isn't fair. Bess gets special treatment and the rest of us must pay for every single second that we spend with you. You are always watching the clock and counting the money. Why do you need so much anyway? You always tell us that you're going to a place beyond where money doesn't even exist!" Her voice gets louder and mocks him, "You just love Bess. Bess, Bess, Bess. She's your girlfriend. She's not so wonderful!"

"Shhhh, quiet," Gerald hisses, "Do you want Doris to hear you?"

But Laura, forgetting with whom she is dealing, loses control and releases her uncensored feelings, "You're so greedy; you don't care if I starve just so that you can have all of my money! And how come you are always the one telling us what to do? Nobody ever corrects you! Are you perfect? You sit here feeling superior while we are constantly criticized."

"Oh believe me, you have it easy," Gerald spits out, "You only have to interact with a human being, but I get disciplined by The Energy and it's a hundred times worse than anything you have ever gone through; you wouldn't be able to last two minutes in the pain I feel when it corrects me."

"Yeah, well I don't believe you; I think you're making it up."

"Sister, you better respect me and cut the shit! Last week my thoughts were leading me the wrong way when all of a sudden this terrible stench came out of my body. It was so bad; it made me want to vomit. Then, The Energy grabbed me and slammed my body up against the wall. It let me know I'd better clean up my act, or else!! Beatrice was there and saw the whole thing."

Beatrice nods obsequiously, but Laura doesn't seem to want to buy it. Gerald, fed up with her insubordination, leaps from his seat. He lunges, grabs her collar, shoves her toward the door and bellows,

"That's it; I don't need you here. You've got to get out now; you can't stay here any longer."

I feel the same way she does about the money, his frequent reprimands and Bess' privileges, but as the dispute unfolds I tighten, averting fear-filled eyes in the fervent hope that he won't turn on me as well. I could never support her, lest he force me to share her punishment. Beatrice and Pauline glare judgmentally, criticizing Laura for daring to raise her voice against our mentor.

"What if Doris is in the kitchen listening? Do you want to get Gerald in trouble and screw everything up? You know she will never understand his reasons for what he does. How could you be so stupid?"

Reacting to his rough handling, Laura instantly changes from confrontational to pitiful.

"Please don't make me leave," she pleads as he slams the door behind her.

She drives home in a fog of terror, knowing that she can never survive without The Energy and Gerald's guidance. That night she calls him and apologizes. He accepts graciously and permits her to "try again". The next day she returns. Sitting humbly in the corner, she is relieved just to be accepted back into the kingdom.

Of course there are consequences to being chosen as Gerald's woman . . .

It is a Tuesday afternoon. The phone rings in Gerald's den, interrupting his shaking. Holding the receiver in silence for a few moments, he makes a strange face and looks annoyed. He calls his daughter, Samantha, to his side and whispers something in her ear, after which she exits immediately. About an hour later Samantha returns, mission completed, followed by Bess. Bess' shirt is bloody and an ugly gash scars her forehead. There is dried blood on her face as well. She sits down miserably while Gerald explains to the rest of us gravely,

"Bess just fucked up big time. She was sitting at a traffic light up on Route 59 in Nanuet, N.Y. when a car crashed into her from behind. Last night we were alone and she was playing her female games on me. She couldn't control me so she decided to get into this car accident to try to make me feel sorry for her. Well, I won't be manipulated! I've told you over and over, you can't make me react, not even if you decide to stab yourself right in front of me."

With that he starts shaking his head, tuning us all out. Several other patients enter and leave during the next several hours while Bess sits in a corner, motionless and speechless, her face still smeared with dried blood. Many of the others don't even notice that there is anything wrong. Those few who experience a natural impulse to help her quickly stifle it, seating themselves slowly and averting their eyes. The unspoken message in the room is sovereign and must command everyone's actions, an invisible rule that no one, no matter how they feel, has the courage to break, *Do not reach out to Bess, she defied Gerald and must pay for her sins.* No one comforts her or even inquires how she feels. No one asks her if she'd like to borrow a clean shirt, or if she needs to lie down and rest, or drink, or eat.

Lisa and Pauline's schedule has evolved to include spending lunch hours with Gerald. Every Monday, Wednesday and Friday they grab a taxi at noon, bringing sandwiches to share with him. Including round trip travel, they desert their offices for nearly an hour and a half. When I find out about this arrangement, I am enraged. If their bosses realize they are taking so much extra time, they could miss out on a promotion or even lose their jobs! They are already seeing Gerald two hours after work on those same three days, as well as Thursday night and all day Saturday. This behavior is obsessive and costing them too much. They can't save for their futures and they never have any money for themselves now either. Nonetheless, Gerald seems very happy with the arrangement and the egotistical part of me is personally hurt, realizing that Lisa and Pauline have replaced me as his new model students. When Gerald senses my disapproval, he reprimands me for concerning myself with their affairs,

"You people are all competing with each other instead of focusing on your own growth. The Girls are willing to make the sacrifice to invest in their future. Why won't you do the same?"

Gerald begins to see us in groups of three to ten people during the hours that used to be devoted to private sessions. Whether you have the rare good fortune to be alone with him, or you share him with several other companions, the charge is the same, now $40 per hour per person. He reminds us all frequently, reassuringly,

"The more time you spend with me, the more progress you will make. Do not worry about the money. The Energy will bring it back to you."

Finally Lisa, egged on by Gerald, breaks the barrier of separation forever. She spends her entire vacation week at his office — arriving at 10:00 A.M. when he starts, and leaving at 7:30 P.M. when he finishes. At noon she purchases lunch for both from a local deli, and they share it in his tiny office so that she won't miss a single moment. Gerald reports on this new arrangement proudly,

"Lisa is my new wife; she spent the whole day with me; she is really committed to her life!"

That week she spends more than forty hours (and more than $1600) with him. Soon, despite the unaffordable costs, others feel obligated to follow suit. We try to remind ourselves that we are breaking our ties to society and The Program by paying him so much, convincing ourselves that this release, a catharsis, feels good.

Pauline, like a competitive sibling, follows right behind her roommate and spends her next vacation week with Gerald. As a result, because she has no resources outside of her present $25,000 per year job as a legal secretary, she immediately forces herself into debt. When her salary runs out, she takes cash advances on credit cards.

Beatrice has no job to keep her busy. She spends three full days a week, every week, with him. The budget of $600 per week given to her by her husband doesn't go very far to cover all of these hours. Exploiting any available resource, she begins to secretly sell off the antiques she has collected from thirty years of world travel with her spouse to pay the balance. Gerald proudly reports that she has sold more than $30,000 worth to invest in her future freedom.

Laura, the nurse, gives all of her salary to Gerald that is not spent on her studio apartment and food bill. Clearly in conflict, she frequently protests,

"Why don't I just sign over my paycheck to you?"

Gerald simply ignores her, changing the subject, and Laura keeps paying, like an obese person with a food addiction who desperately wants to lose weight but can't say "no" to the relentless impulses to cram food down her throat. The walls of professional privacy have been completely dismantled and his practice, both in the New York Office, Monday, Wednesday, and Friday, and in his New Jersey home, Tuesday, Thursday and Saturday, has evolved into an open house.

With so many people in the room the private sex occurs with much less frequency. One day Laura, who normally sees Gerald from 4:00 to 5:00 P.M. on Fridays, remains to sit in on my session with Lisa and Pauline, which for the past few years has consistently been the scene of intense erotic activity. This day, for the first time, we all remain clothed. The following week Laura is there again. This arrangement becomes permanent and the former encounters between me, The Girls and Gerald are gone forever. Strangely, Gerald seems totally content to separate himself from us so suddenly, as if he has grown out of a former hobby and replaced it with a new one. However, I feel dumped. The intense intimacy, as one-sided as it was physically, filled me emotionally. After all of our shared experiences and the exciting discoveries born from them, I have come to believe that I am special to Gerald. Whereas I undergo profound separation anxiety from our former activities, I am appalled to realize that Gerald has simply moved on without even looking back. Harsh reality slaps me in the face. From his perspective, no personal bond exists between us and he has simply used us as lab rats for his personal research. Rage rises, almost as intensely as when I experienced his response to Joe's death. I battle these feelings privately, but they take several months to subside.

The money pours into Gerald's bank account in truckloads and I am shocked to realize that no one is doing the basic arithmetic to calculate his salary, now over a quarter of a million dollars a year. He has gone from being barely able to support the maintenance on his *V.W. Beetle*, to a healthy stock portfolio. Because he has eliminated private sessions but charges the same per head for groups of up to ten people, what used to be a salary of $40 per hour has now escalated into a potential $400 per hour. The subject of his financial circumstances is strictly forbidden territory. Like a dirty family secret that no one admits to, there is an unspoken command that we are not permitted to even think about it, let alone mention it aloud. Occasionally Laura, whose frustration drives her to break the vow of silence, complains vocally, usually in front of several others. However, Gerald cuts off these emotional displays immediately, rising threateningly from his seat and throwing her physically onto the floor or even out of the room, sending her home for the day. Fear of Gerald's retaliation creates a heavy weight on my chest which presses firmly inward, threatening to squeeze the breath out of my lungs should I even consider embarking on such discussions. Several people, including Laura, Bess, my mother and Pauline, have difficulty buying groceries even with up to $50,000-a-year salaries. Nonetheless, Gerald ignores our increasingly severe problems and continues to insist that money is meaningless.

"What do you mean?" Bess asks one day, "We need it for rent and food."

"No, people only believe this lie because they buy into an illusion created by the universal mind," Gerald explains, "It is possible to become hidden from the system and live for free, but first you must break your attachments to money, release yourself from its importance. A few nights ago, Marty and I had some fun. While Doris was out, we burned cash in the fireplace. I began with a fifty-dollar-bill, lighting one corner and sitting through my reactions, watching the flames engulf it. The first time it was hard, but we kept going and it became a lot easier. After about two hours of burning all kinds of bills, one by one, Marty and I were having a ball, rolling around on the floor, laughing our guts out. Because we released ourselves from another lie in The Program, the next day I discovered something brand new." Gerald points to his kitchen screen door. "See this door? I got it for free, a gift from the store," he states proudly.

"How?" we respond in unison, intensely curious.

He laughs, "I just walked out of the front door of *Pergament's* with it, right past the registers. In fact the stupid manager was in such a fog that he opened the door for me and smiled as I left."

Bess looks distressed. "I really don't understand."

Gerald continues, shaking his fist, gaining passion as he progresses,

"Just think about the system. It is greedy, selfish and governed by stupidity. It does nothing except rip everyone off. People are trained like good children to give their money away to big business and the federal bureaucracy, but they end up just getting screwed because the people managing the finances waste most of what they collect. It is time we stop cowering in the corner and take back what is rightfully ours. Money shouldn't exist anyway. It is all part of the lying thoughts that everyone believes. Someone has to write some new rules and have the courage to make a stand and live by them. I have the truth and even if thirty million

Frenchmen think I'm wrong, I am willing to stand up against the whole world, against the entire crazy thought system that everyone is following."

As he reaches his climax, we find ourselves rising unified, prepared to follow, an organized regiment of troops who have just been summoned to battle. It is not his specific ideas that convince us, but the strength of his passion and commitment to his beliefs which make us all feel that whatever he is saying, he surely must be right. Gerald instinctively knows that he has captured our allegiance to his new direction and he quickly switches into the mentor mode to explain the ropes to us.

"People get caught because they are still playing in The Program. Their training has taught them that they are doing something wrong; so they feel they must hide the items in order to escape detection. Then they look around furtively to make sure they are not being observed and this body language invites the suspicions of the store's employees. The perfect invitation to get arrested! You must learn to suspend your thoughts, take your mind out of the loop, go beyond to the real truth, that everything has really always belonged to us; we were just too afraid to claim it. You must be convinced of this truth to be confident, and if you exit the store with this evolved perspective, you will no longer be part of the game everyone is playing and therefore, no one will pay any attention to you. You will be invisible."

Soon, like it or not, we all try to follow suit. Martin, now a high school senior, is the superstar. His store of choice is also *Pergament's* in Spring Valley, N.Y. There he obtains a microwave oven, dishes, paint, power tools, anything he wants. Because I am hesitant about this new activity, one Saturday Gerald sends me to train with his son. When we enter the store, I immediately sense that Martin has put himself into a deeply calm state. I ask him if he is at all nervous and he answers me impatiently, hissing under his breath as if I were an annoying, stupid third-grader,

"Why should I be? I am doing nothing wrong. Didn't you listen to what my father told us? It is our right to walk out with whatever we want without paying for it. You must train yourself to eliminate the thoughts from your head that you are being watched and the physical reactions associated with the fear of being caught; they are all lies anyway."

Martin has learned well from his father. He selects whatever items please him, of course making sure that there are no magnetic inventory tags attached, and we head toward the exit with a shopping cart full of unpaid merchandise worth more than $300. I follow right on Marty's heels, focusing inward, desperately to try to calm the fluttering in my chest and my shaking knees, praying no one will notice, and that if they do, they will not realize that I am part of it. To my great relief and awe, no one stops us.

With this new experiment to attain another level of personal growth underway, we now enter Gerald's den for our daily sessions eager to report what we have acquired by "shopping for free". Gerald beams with pride when Mitchell walks out of *Pier One Imports* in Paramus with a five foot in diameter, "papasan" chair. Pauline brags that she draped a sweater over her arm at *Annie Sez*, convinced herself that she had taken it from her closet in the morning, and strolled right past the register, throwing a friendly smile to the salesgirl en route to the exit. Laura exits a local deli, around the corner from her nursing job at Columbia Presbyterian Hospital, without paying for her coffee. The most popular and frequent maneuver is to walk out of restaurants without paying, particularly diners where the management relies on the customer to bring up the check. Even the faint of heart among us muster the courage to grab the check and sufficient cash in one hand, head toward the register, take a deep breath and continue through the exit, acting as if we believe that someone else in our party is planning to take care of the bill. We also develop an almost fool-proof back-up plan, should this ploy fail. One day Lisa, Pauline and I walk out of a coffee shop in Tenafly, but the waitress chases us into the parking lot. Because we are three well-dressed young women she doesn't dare let herself think that we intended not to pay. That objective would be too incongruous to our appearance and demeanor. I am holding the check, so I turn to her with trained calm and feigned sincerity,

"I'm really sorry; I got distracted and forgot."

Falsely humble, I expose the check, folded around a twenty-dollar-bill, and follow her inside to pay. Later that week Lisa points out to Gerald that in some establishments missing checks are deducted from the waitresses' salaries, but he ignores the statement and instead reminds us that the managements of large corporations do little to eliminate waste and that this leads to unjustly inflated prices and consumer rip-off. In light of this larger mess, like a drop of water removed from the ocean, the loss of income from the items we claim for ourselves could not possibly have any effect on the well-being of the company.

Although it is fun to get stuff for free, there are two greater attractions for most of us — what little money we save gives us a momentary sense of relief from the onerous burden of paying for Gerald, and more important, each success story wins a coveted slice of his heartfelt approval.

Martin and Gerald make weekly visits to the Westwood, *Grand Union Supermarket*. They place open brown bags in a cart and stroll the aisles, nonchalantly filling them. Once satisfied, they simply walk past the check out. No one ever stops them. Even after my private tutoring with Martin I am hesitant to try anything on my own, so Gerald recommends the Closter *K-Mart*. The registers are positioned far away from the exit door; it is easy to walk out. I screw up my courage and try some small things, a hammer, a flashlight, a picture frame. I have one priority only, not to get caught, and thank God, I never do. Mitchell has more bravado than I, and one day he tries to take a vacuum cleaner from *K-mart*. However, on this day a manager spots and detains him. The store calls the police and presses charges. A few weeks later he is required to appear in the Closter courtroom where he is fined. Gerald is very annoyed. He accuses Mitchell of being an asshole and ignoring The Energy which would have protected him . . . Another day, while shopping with her father, Samantha approaches the *K-Mart* checkout with an item, planning to pay for it. She doesn't feel comfortable about taking things; not for moral reasons, she is just too afraid of getting caught. Gerald picks up her intention, pulls her into an empty aisle and scolds her. She is commanded to walk out with the items; The Energy wants us to do it this way; she must not be defiant. Samantha has no choice but to obey . . . Several weeks later my mother gets caught by the store manager of *Sloan's Supermarket* on 97th and Broadway. She has a can of tuna wrapped in a newspaper. The store management, viewing her as a harmless and piteous old woman, lets her go, provided that she stays out of the store in the future . . . Wealthy Beatrice is fond of hiding food items under the supermarket circulars at the bottom of her cart. One day she too gets caught. A court date is set. Her husband, an upstanding citizen of their Westchester community, is mortified. However, Beatrice explains to her lawyer that she is currently writing a novel which portrays the life of a thief. The shoplifting was merely an experiment to help her relate to her main character and therefore improve her narrative skills. On the day that the court lets her off with just a slap on the wrist, Gerald spends several hours bragging about Beatrice's creativity. She is credited with knowing how to use The Energy properly to escape the system. Then one day Martin is finally arrested for nabbing groceries in the *Grand Union*. He is seventeen. The police handcuff him and release him to his father. Gerald brings Martin home in tears, all the while excoriating him for ignoring the signals sent by The Energy that today was not a good day to be in that store. Gerald hires a lawyer, but his son never makes it to court. The store management has other priorities and drops the charges.

Thanksgiving Morning
9:00 A.M. to 1:00 P.M.
1987 to the present

Today is a national holiday and a treasured day off from work, but we all get up early. Lisa and Pauline rise at 6:00 A.M. because they must travel to Gerald's in N.J., all the way from Queens, N.Y. My alarm jolts me out of a deep sleep at 8:45. I pull my clothes on and grab a coffee. At 9:05 I drive up Westwood's main drag, making a left onto his street. His white house is the first on the left. All of the others are already there, their cars selfishly crowding the tiny, residential block. I see Laura's white *Toyota*, Beatrice's green *Jaguar*, *Acura Integras* (the official Group car of choice) belonging to Nora, Lisa, Martin, Samantha and Mitchell, Bess's light blue *Honda Civic*, and Carl's blue *Ford Escort* wagon. My stomach turns sickeningly in fear and anticipation. As I walk down the driveway I wish desperately that I could be somewhere else, not only because of the unaffordable amount of money I am about to spend, but also because of the conflict that will almost certainly lie within. I push these feelings down very deep, below my conscious mind, so that I quickly forget I ever felt them, and struggle to come up with some positive event that I can attribute to the power of The Energy, something I can recount to Gerald when I enter the room and he throws me his typical, "What's going on?"

I force a bright cheery smile onto my face just as I ascend the stairs of his deck, turn left and open the wooden door which leads into his den. Standing on the tiled floor in the entry, I take off my coat and place it on the floor. There is a full house today and the coat rack to my right already has more garments than it can accommodate. I pause to quickly scan the room. A wave of tension passes over me; I hate being here, but I push past these feelings too. To my left is a blue and green plaid couch on which Pauline, Bess and Carl are perched. A large picture window above them illuminates the room. Gerald is two feet away, his back to me, in an overstuffed armchair with matching fabric. A love seat across from him, occupied by Nora and Beatrice, completes the set. Laura sits in an oak rocker to their right, her eyes squeezed shut, and Samantha occupies a white swivel chair, next to her father, just to the right of where I stand. Her unreadable visage always makes me nervous, and I avoid looking at her most of all. Martin is nowhere to be seen, probably in his basement office doing a graphic arts project on his computer. Lisa and Mitchell sit on narrow green velveteen folding chairs behind the love seat. My mother, now in her late sixties, occupies one of these uncomfortable seats as well.

As usual, later than the rest, I have missed all of the good seats. There is nothing left to sit on besides a fourth awful folding chair. It is too painful to occupy one of them for four hours, so I slip as unassumingly as possible between Gerald's chair and Samantha's knees, and plop down on the carpet beneath the fish tank, right next to Jane, the teacher, whose earthy personality generally directs her to sit on the floor. I am merely one of twelve eager students who feel they must obtain a healthy dose of Energy before they head for the family holiday dinner war zone.

Beatrice and Nora, pasty complexioned, appear to be in a sort of trance. Carl looks nervous and twiddles his thumbs rapidly while Mitchell rocks back and forth on his tiny folding chair. Samantha, by contrast, looks serene and tranquil — like royalty observing her subjects. Her thick wavy black hair, cut in a shoulder length shag, contrasts with her bloodless complexion. Completely clothed in black, her favorite color, she wears glasses and long silver star-shaped earrings. With her coloring she could easily pass for one of Dracula's wives except that she is not pretty enough. Her weak chin and puffy features are far from easy on the eye. In reality, she resembles her father in female form. Of Gerald's two offspring, Martin, who resembles his mother, got all the looks. Bess, sitting right next to Pauline on the couch, looks terribly worried, while Pauline is sitting so close to Gerald that their knees almost touch. As I scan the room, trying to avoid being noticed, I observe that conversation is already in progress with Gerald confronting Pauline energetically,

"Why don't you want to grow?"

Pauline is visibly upset. Her skin is yellow-gray and her dry hands clench the fabric of the couch. "I don't know how."

"Yes you do. You're just holding back."

"I can't do it. I don't know what to do."

"Why don't you just let The Energy lead you? It's your only friend."

Pauline's voice trembles, "I really don't know, I just try and try but I never get it."

Annoyed, Gerald raises his voice. "You know that you're wasting my time; you have all the answers inside of you but you're too lazy to make an effort."

Pauline's face is paling by the minute. "No, I don't know what to do. Can't you help me?"

Gerald switches gears for the moment and explains like a supportive teacher, "I can't help you if you're not willing to take the first step; you have to want to help yourself. I can only assist you when you begin on your own. You have to go for it," he adds vocal force, "Just drop your selfish manipulation, get on your bicycle, and start pedaling."

Pauline whimpers, "I can't. I don't have any answers. I can't find them inside of me like you say."

Gerald irritated once more, becomes louder, "You're lying, I know that you know what to do but instead, you prefer to play games with me, games I have no time for. I have an important job to do and you are holding me back on purpose."

Pauline continues to insist, "I really can't do it; I need help; I'm just stupid and I can't get it."

Now Gerald rises up menacingly with eyes glaring, conceiving fear in all of our hearts, "You stupid waste! Why the hell should I spend my time trying to help you when you don't care about yourself? You don't belong here. I'm giving you one more chance, but you better switch your attitude right now or you're out. The Energy doesn't have time for your crap."

Tears begin to roll down Pauline's face as she pleads with him, "Please don't throw me out; I'll try harder. I know I'm making mistakes but I can't help it. I'm weak, please help me to get through this. I don't know what I'm doing anymore. Please don't throw me out."

"Do you actually think I am stupid enough to fall for your fake tears? I don't know why I waste my time with you people at all when there is all this wonderful stuff to experience and none of you want it. You'd rather stay in your misery like a bunch of babies then grow up and take a stand against the bullshit. Why is it that I am always alone in the end, the only one who sees the truth? Why do you people even come here if you don't want what I have? Isn't there anyone who understands what a sacrifice you have to make to get this? Doesn't anyone have the courage to go all the way? None of you want to work. You just want to be taken care of, babies sucking your thumbs and waiting for a free ride."

Pauline is now sobbing outright with her head down and her entire, scrawny body shaking. She rocks back and forth, her hands wringing each other, and her throat is so tight that she can't even speak. This fit seems to anger Gerald even more and he soon reaches full-blown rage, thundering at the top of his lungs,

"You fool! Drop it now! You are holding us all back. I have no more time to waste with you. We must move ahead _now_ if we are ever to get out of this lousy world. If you don't want to grow that's your problem. I know you think you can stop me from moving ahead with this phony drama but I have news for you sister, it won't work. You must really think I'm stupid. If you want to throw away your life that's your problem. There are others here who want the good stuff, who know how important what we are doing here is, who appreciate me and don't hold back. I can't make everyone else pay because of you. When you finally decide you want to drop it, it will be too late anyway because I will be too far ahead to see you. Like always, I have no support. I'm just going to have to go for myself because that's all that's really important."

Having had his fill of assassinating Pauline's character, he abruptly severs his connection to her and begins to shake his head vigorously. The rest of the people in the room display no evidence of any sympathy for Pauline, except Bess. The two women now work closely in the same law office and Bess feels emotionally obligated to her fellow co-worker. She leans toward Pauline on the couch and attempts to reassure her. Sweet and patient, she takes the stance of a person possessing intimate understanding of the rebelliousness Pauline is experiencing.

"You know Pauline, if you just tried a little harder you could do it. Yesterday I was at work and I felt myself holding back so I just focused on the wall for five minutes and I thought, *What am I complaining about? Why am I such a baby? I know Gerald. I am part of this wonderful mission, truly part of the chosen people. I must really be strong underneath to have stayed with him for all these years and worked so hard.* Then I felt so much better and right after that Arthur (her lawyer boss) came by the desk and told me he got a new client. In that moment, I put it all together — when I let go of my self pity, The Energy brought in more business."

Gerald interrupts his shaking, abandons his previous tantrum and transforms into a gentle mentor.

"There, that's what I mean, does everybody understand? Bess was all screwed up and then she chose to remember what is important; she made a decision to let it go and good things came immediately. The Energy rewarded her for deciding to drop the games. Now, why can't all of you just do that more often? It would make my job so much easier. Don't you realize how much it holds me back from discovering new things, if I have to constantly stop and change your dirty diapers? Just tie a string around your finger so that the next time you will remember what Bess just told you."

This scene has become our daily diet. Six days a week, eight to ten hours a day, people come and go. Most spend at least four hours at a time. The faces change throughout the day but Gerald's stance remains the same. He has incredible stamina, often yelling at one of us for more than two hours at a time. His voice is so loud and resounding that the window panes rattle, threatening to crack. The object of his rage, different almost every day, recedes to the extreme, their face turning ashen. The rest of us, secretly grateful not to be on the hot seat, sit quietly, with pious and knowing looks on our faces, trying to give the impression that we, unlike the person who is being scolded, do try, and know how to "get it". If there is an opening in the conversation, we interject the evidence that we are fiercely working on ourselves to grow. In reality, we are really just praying that he won't shift his focus to us, that we won't be included in his terrifying arraignment. To strengthen the positive impression we are trying to make we add our supportive comments to his, our attempt at purchasing a day's worth of insurance.

Pauline apologizes, "I'm sorry, I just don't appreciate what we have here enough. I'm so ungrateful; I'll try harder to drop my games."

Gerald responds sympathetically, "See, that's all it takes; just admit that you are small and then let The Energy take over. Maybe next time I won't have to waste so much of my time breaking your resistence. You know this is for your own good. Your mind is so thick with lies that the only way I can wake you up is to ram the truth about your mistakes down your throat. This sends a message through to your brain so that it will make the necessary changes and allow you to grow beyond your baby Program world."

Gerald directs his eyes to hers and she returns his gaze. Her sobbing fades and eventually dies away. After about five minutes, as the focusing progresses, she slips into a staring trance, her body jolting from The Energy. She reports that she sees green light around his head and the rest of us understand that all is well; the conflict is over for today. Gerald continues to focus on her and slowly his head moves again, gaining speed. Exhausted from adrenalin rushes triggered by the continual fear of attack, we focus on his spinning head, as one would on a hypnotist's swinging pendulum. Soon, we too feel The Energy. As the shaking continues, the tension releases from our bodies and we relax, close our eyes and nod off. Martin comes upstairs from the basement, entering through the kitchen door at the end of the den near where his father is seated. He lies down on his back on the floor next to Samantha's chair and falls under almost instantly. Gerald himself, after half an hour of continuous head shaking, begins to let go. His head rolls back in his armchair and he slips into a state of deep sleep. I find solace in this familiar, peaceful state of relaxing nothingness — no thoughts, no conflict, just relief from stress.

I am intimate with everything in this den — the diagonal, knotty pine paneling . . . the white Berber carpeting . . . the tiny bathroom to the left of the entrance with its inspirational poster entitled "Footprints in the Sand" posted on the back of its door . . . Gerald's oak roll-top desk in the corner opposite, overstuffed with personal paperwork and our checks to him which peek out from a cubbyhole and the matching square coffee table where we rest our feet from his couch . . . the sound of the wind chimes ringing on the deck . . . This place feels like home to me. There is total silence as fourteen people and Gerald's two cats, B.J. and Tyler, succumb to a drugged sleep.

The doorbell rings and his black Labrador Retriever, Ben, in another part of the house barks, but no one hears a thing. Our bodies must weigh a thousand pounds; we couldn't move our limbs if we wanted to. After an additional hour of sleep Gerald comes to. It is 12:55 P.M., exactly five minutes before the hour he has intended to finish. Gently and sweetly he rouses us,

"OK everybody, it's time to get going."

We all groan as we drag ourselves out of the oppressive sleep which has engulfed us. Feet begin to find shoes and one by one, we rise slowly from our seats. Gerald, watching over his flock, asks how everybody is doing, and Pauline replies first,

"I feel much better. I think I understand more what you mean."

Gerald replies lovingly, like a proud father, "Now you're getting smarter!" and then coaches the rest of us, "You know we are all in this together and we need each other; we have to be on the same side, not work at cross purposes. This mission is too critical to waste time on nonsense."

Pauline looks at him gratefully, her face shining. She thanks him and follows with a hug which he receives without emotion. Then she writes him a check, but as she hands it to him she cautions, "Don't cash this until Monday. I can't give you everything today; I'll have to wait for my paycheck next Wednesday."

He nods in acknowledgment and continues his lecture, "We all went up a level today and learned a lot. Now everybody, make sure you don't throw it away as soon as you go out the door. At your Thanksgiving dinners today, just observe your families, but don't get involved. Learn from them; use them to grow, to break your connections to the garbage and games they are drowning in. If you can get strong then maybe you can lead them out too, if they want something better for themselves than the worthless life they have now. Just remember that The Energy is always with you and working for you, if you can just let go of your need to control and give in to it. It knows what to do for you; it will take care of you. All you have to do is stop resisting and enjoy the ride!"

Beatrice kisses him on the cheek as she heads for the door and he smiles sweetly. Bess follows suit and then asks, "What are you doing for Thanksgiving?"

"Doris has some stupid crap planned with her disgusting sister. We're driving out to Long Island so that me, Samantha and Martin can spend the day watching her sister and brother-in-law act like babies. Her house is filthy and her cooking sucks. Well, this is the price we have to pay right now. Holidays stink. They are total nonsense. We all have to put up with it until we get enough knowledge to leave this world, even if none of the crazy people out there want anything better for themselves."

"I know. I'm going to my brother's. His kids are nuts, his wife's controlling him with the Female Program, and he doesn't have a clue. Every time I try to tell him that he could have so much more if he came here, he ignores me and changes the subject. I don't know why he is so stupid when the answer is right under his nose."

"Yeah, I know what you mean. Parents in The Program are so crazy that it's amazing our mothers didn't put us in the oven instead of the Thanksgiving turkey! Hah. Hah."

"Right you are, Gerald! Well, take it easy and I'll see you tomorrow, first thing in the morning when you start. I have the whole day off from work. How late are you going tomorrow?"

"From 9:00 until 5:00. I'll need to work extra hard to break the holiday con that will sink into all of you today."

"OK, I can stay the whole time; See you at 9:00 . . . I'll bring some bagels."

Bess leaves, smiling in anticipation of their next meeting. Tomorrow's bill will be $320. This price tag of half a week's salary will buy her the opportunity to watch Gerald shake his head while she alternates between sitting inertly on the couch in a state of non-thought staring at him, and sleeping upright, wrapped in one of his spare blankets.

Laura shares her plans also as she leaves. "I'm going to my brother's in Harrington Park for dinner. They just had a new baby."

"Well, just observe and don't let yourself get sucked in. Watch them put your niece on a pedestal and worship her. Observe that they have no lives for themselves. If you can sneak to the side with the baby, hold her and get some of The Energy into her. It will build up and might even help her deal with her crazy parents when she gets older."

"OK, I'll see you tomorrow. I'll be here from 10:00 to 2:00." (Bill for tomorrow, $160.) Laura pulls a stack of twenties out of her pocket and peels off one for herself. The rest she gives to him. (Bill for today, $160).

The rest of us file out, handing him checks or cash, all of which he receives without expression and immediately pockets. Samantha and Martin, the princess and the prince, remain seated. They silently observe The Group members' exodus and the transfer of cash, the growing fortune they will one day inherit. Today, this holiday morning, from 9:00 A.M. to 1:00 P.M., he has scolded Pauline, eaten bagels and fruit brought to him by Lisa, Nora and Laura at the spontaneous lunch break he took somewhere within his two-hour tirade, and finally head-shaken himself into a deep two-hour slumber. He has earned $1760.

Fall to Winter — 1987

"Lisa, Pauline and Carl have just gotten married." Gerald smiles mysteriously at me one Friday evening as I enter his office in the city.

"What do you mean?" I inquire, not comprehending.

"They have just started a business."

I notice that their faces are glowing with anticipation. "What are they going to do?"

Lisa answers, "It is called *New Life Design*. We are going to sell custom Formica furniture, window treatments and wooden cabinets."

I accept this without question. Gerald always makes it seem like anything is possible . . . with The Energy. Soon, everyone in The Group seems to be starting a business. Our collective passion persists. Our idealism prevails convincing us, *Whatever you conceive of, try hard and you will arrive. The Energy is the wind in your sails.* Beatrice begins writing a novel about a girl afflicted with an eating disorder. Lisa starts a murder mystery. Nora and my mother throw themselves into a children's book, *Dashiki,* about a little colored girl. Beatrice and my mother commence another joint project, a custom roller-skating bag which they have designed and plan to sell to stores in Manhattan. Bess and Pauline establish a resume writing and editing service. Nora's vocation is a private school referral service. Mitchell draws from his business experience at his father's printing shop. He advises us on the ins and outs, such as designing effective business cards and selecting the proper paper stock for business stationery. Soon our wallets are filled with each other's business cards. We hand out as many as we can, to waitresses, shop owners, pedestrians . . . Visions of our futures overflowing with guaranteed wealth, the fruit of our dreams, whirl in our brains and lift us upwards on a cloud of ecstatic anticipation.

A week later I enter Gerald's office amidst an animated conversation. I scan the room to see Carl, Lisa, Pauline and Beatrice.

"You just got here in time. We are about to do something really big," they tell me. A wave of uncertainty passes through me as I probe Gerald's face inquisitively, but Carl explains,

"Well, the three of us are going to turn *New Life Design* into a corporation and we need some start-up capital. I have a wealthy aunt in Australia who really likes me. I'm going to call and see if she can help us out."

I tighten immediately as extreme discomfort rises in my chest. I do not understand why, but I cannot share their excitement, quite the opposite. I try to hide what I am truly feeling with a counterfeit, encouraging smile. However, as if he could read my mind, Gerald senses my true response and grills me immediately, raising his voice threateningly,

"What is wrong with you? You must be jealous of their new venture. Why must you always demand center stage? You are a dream crusher. I know that you want to fail in your life and you want the others to fail along with you, but that is not what we are here for. I suggest you change your attitude quickly or else you are out of here. I don't want any bad intentions screwing up this phone call."

As I recede from the attack, I muster the strength to promise aloud that I will change my attitude right now, although I know I am lying because try as I might, I am not able to crush this presence which inhabits my chest and insists that there is something terribly wrong with this picture. Nonetheless, Gerald does trigger my self-doubt with his reference to jealousy and my mind begins to repeat his logic over and over in a willful attempt to drown out my feelings of uneasiness. Meanwhile, Carl picks up the phone and using his calling card soon reaches his aunt in Australia. My discomfort storms as he chats with her superficially and then slowly moves onto the subject of their exciting new enterprise. On the surface everything seems normal, so why do I feel it is all so wrong? His aunt is taken with the idea. Although she has not seen her nephew for more than fifteen years, she was always fond of him. Finally, he gives her the figure. They will need $20,000. He does not identify it as a loan but that is understood, isn't it? Of course he will be good for it . . . !Miraculously she agrees, and as he hangs up the phone a sort of cheer arises from the occupants of Gerald's tiny office. My own smile covers a set of gritting teeth.

Over the next several months Carl feeds some of that money into the new corporation. The rest he uses to pay Gerald because he, like the others, has begun to spend entire days in Gerald's office. With additional funds from Lisa, they purchase a $22,000 computer, expensive stationary and booths at several trade shows. They have invested all of this to give birth to a business where they have no clients, no product knowledge and no business experience. Soon their bank account runs dry and Carl calls his aunt again. This time she refuses him . . .

It is 6:00 A.M. and I am startled out of a deep sleep. Staring at the ceiling, Mitchell's light snores floating into my ears, an idea comes to me with powerful certainty; a product's title resounds in my mind — *Chemistry in a Flash*. Desire, curiosity and commitment flood me, and in this decisive moment I am determined to follow this idea wherever it will lead me . . . Currently, I am tutoring about ten students a week in high school chemistry. To each I dictate the same vocabulary list, the same equations. Why not make flash cards for high school chemistry to make my job easier and to help them learn more efficiently? I figure that there must be some already on the market, so I ask at *Barnes & Noble*, but they have never heard of flash cards for high school courses. They add that other customers have asked for them too. I try several additional bookstores and receive the same response. Why hasn't a publisher created this product already? There is such an obvious need! People have always used flash cards and every year a fresh group of high school students take a chemistry course. In this huge country we live in, the United States, I have no direct competition. What tremendous potential! I will have to write them myself and somehow, I will get my product to the market. I grab my typewriter and my textbook and put together several sample cards. Mitchell suggests that I create a prototype, something to show a potential publisher, and I hire a college student to draw cartoons for the package. I am in love with the idea and I truly believe it will help millions of students. In the next few months I invest many hours to complete samples of three science titles, *Chemistry, Biology and Physics in a Flash.* Mitchell teaches me how to paste up typesetting on acetate overlays. Finally, I make color xeroxes of each box cover and spray mount them to empty business card boxes. I set them on my kitchen table and just look at them, entranced. Now I must manufacture the cards, but a typesetting quote from a large, Manhattan printer is more than $6000, way out of my budget. I hit a brick wall and my lovingly designed prototypes are soon retired to a shelf where they commence gathering dust. But they beckon me each time I pass by,

"Elizabeth, you have to find a way to publish us."

"I know I must publish you," I tell them, "but I don't know how. I must wait for the answer . . ."

When Mitchell and I first moved into the apartment, I cashed some government bonds worth about $10,000. I thought that this money would cover me temporarily until I figured out what to do with my career. I promised myself that I would find a way to make a reasonable salary before that sum ran out. Three years later tutoring is still my main source of income. At $40 per hour I feel like I am making big bucks. Nevertheless, the $10,000 runs out. I cry and rage inside of myself. *What happened? I have been working and trying so hard. How could I have spent it all? What went wrong?* I point my finger at the world. It isn't fair; it owes me a return for all of my effort and hope. After this tantrum has exhausted itself, my scientific side emerges to calculate expenses. It takes about fifteen minutes to arrive at the awful conclusion that the wear and tear on my car from driving to all of those students' homes, and my gas and insurance expenses are exactly equal to the amount I have earned in my years as a tutor! Stupid fool that I am, I realize that the seduction of the hourly rate distracted me from examining the big picture. I have been living a lie, and waking up feels like being kicked in the stomach. Now I must make a change, but I have no idea how . . .

One bright November day I find myself peering into the window of a storefront near Gerald's house which posts a "For Rent" sign. As if following the counsel of some unseen advisor, I contact the realtor, surprising even myself as I inform them that I want to open a photography studio there. This concept has sprung out of nowhere and I don't know why, but I feel compelled to carry it through. I don't analyze, seek advice from others, or weigh the pros and cons; I simply begin, and to say that I don't know what the hell I am doing is an understatement! Photography has always been a favorite hobby and I have held a few part-time jobs over the past three years in the field . . . yet, I have no business sales experience nor any potential clients. My only saving grace is that I don't require a loan; the start-up capital will come from my father's inheritance. In fact I've never even heard of a business loan, nor do I understand financial planning, sales projections, cash flow, accounting, marketing or advertising. Most important, I haven't figured out that making money requires sales skills and the art of negotiation. This requires confidence and personally, I have none. I am afraid to ask anyone for anything, especially money; the potential threat of rejection terrifies me. I am also gullible and believe that all people are like me, that they tell the truth and have forthright, cooperative intentions. However, thanks to Mitchell, I do know how to create business cards, letterheads and price lists. I also find it easy to shop, purchasing equipment, furniture and props. In fact, I do these things very well.

Once rented for $1000 per month, I apply myself to creating a business environment in my new store. The picturesque location, at the Demarest Duck Pond, is ideal for a family and children's portrait studio, and there is nothing I won't do for my new baby. I plan every square inch of that five hundred-square-foot space, selecting a rich burgundy carpet and matching Formica counter for the sales area. I find a local, wholesale picture framer and obtain samples. There is so much to figure out . . . I make endless lists of essential items to complete my collection of necessary photography equipment and the studio's decor. Setting up the place takes two solid months and I work night and day. I eat, drink and sleep with that studio in my mind, often waking in the middle of the night to jot down an idea which has just hit me. I hire Martin, now a college freshman, to paint the walls and install a tile floor in the future shooting room. Not very reliable, he completes half of the job and then disappears on a school ski trip, forcing me to finish the rest alone before my grand opening deadline. On the day he leaves I work until 1:00 A.M. wielding a huge roller high in the air to paint the eleven foot prewar tin ceiling. The following night I sit up even later, cutting odd shaped pieces of "peel-and-stick" tile with an Exacto knife to finish my studio floor. Mitchell is annoyed because his personal chef and maid is no longer home to serve him. Feeling neglected, he accuses me in nasty tones of being "obsessed". He is correct, I am driven; I want to succeed more than anything and despite my lack of experience, I will not stop until I arrive . . .

January 1988 to December 1990

Expressions Photography Studio opens February first. I don't know what to expect. I pace in circles the entire day, straightening this or moving that. I hope some customers will come in and start the ball rolling, but they don't. How do you get them to come in anyway? I have no idea. The second day I decide that I need sample portraits for the window and begin photographing my retail neighbors' children for free. The butcher on the right lends me his three-year-old, red-headed son, Vito Junior. The beauty salon on the left donates their French poodle for an hour. My first paying customer finally walks through the door about two months later. A grandmother and customer of Vito Senior, she brings in her five-year-old granddaughter and I make a $45 sale. Every month the funds run out of my checkbook like a waterfall: rent, heat, garbage disposal, electricity, telephone, film, office supplies, equipment, lab costs. I work ten to twelve hour days, and when I am not at the studio, I think of nothing else. As if I am walking a tightrope and any mistake could destroy my precious enterprise, I agonize over every decision: film speeds, formatting my price list, framing styles, positioning portraits on my walls. I attend professional seminars and read books by successful photographers. I buy props and equipment to imitate their shooting styles. I draw diagrams of lighting angles and measure lighting ratios. I get the technical stuff

down pretty well but I still can't figure out one thing, how to get the customers to walk through the door and how to get them to buy. All alone with my thoughts each day, I struggle with helpless feelings about my lack of cash flow. A hundred times that year my head commands me to quit. *It's not going to work; you have wasted your time; you are a failure.* Temper tantrums rage through my body as I drive home from work, my mind screaming mercilessly to give up and get a real job. More than anything, I detest writing those rent checks. I can't see how I will ever overcome this downward momentum of spending without earning.

I am all alone in a beautifully planned and decorated studio with no customers, no experience and no confidence.

One sunny spring day a woman walks through my door. Her name is Melissa Goldsmith and she has lived in town most of her life. She seems to like me immediately, although I can't imagine why. With my file of so far, nonexistent, "paid" receipts still painfully empty, I don't think much of myself these days. As if she instinctively knows that I am in trouble, perhaps even better than I do, she unselfishly offers her help with no request for compensation. For the next several weeks she hauls my portfolio around to local businesses and promotes me. Soon she escorts more than twenty local shop owners, their families and their dogs into my studio for free sittings. We hang those free portraits on the walls of their stores along with business cards and special coupons for their customers. In October she gives me a free booth at the "Demarest Oktoberfest", a local crafts fair which she happens to coordinate. I book a few jobs at the event and finally my phone starts ringing. I find the flow or the flow finds me, I'm not sure which. The first year I lose $25,000, but I truly believe that next year will be better.

By working diligently the second year I manage to break even, and in my third year I actually make a profit. However, the walls of the retail space which seemed so ample almost three years ago are now closing in on me. I begin to search for larger quarters and fall in love with a loft, over double the size, in the neighboring town of Closter. The final three months of 1990 and the entire year's profits are spent fixing up the interior. On January 1, 1991, I move the business.

The new suite is perfect. Gazing at the fruits of my dedicated labor, I realize how much I have grown in the past three years. Although I have struggled with my disappointment when customers didn't buy, I have figured out ways to deter them from taking advantage of me. I no longer obsess over an ideally formatted price list or letterhead. I have slowly come to realize that business is about relating with and reaching people, not setting up the perfect environment. I have survived the first three rocky years and have begun to earn a reputation as a family portrait photographer with a unique style. Business is finally flowing, albeit slowly, and if it continues, this coming year I will finally be able to take a salary for the first time since I opened the studio . . .

Although all of my time is devoted to growing my business, Gerald seems to feel I have a little to spare for a special project of his own invention . . . And one Friday night as our session ends at his Manhattan office he pulls me to the side. Grinning with paternal pride, he informs me crudely,

"Marty's cock is getting so big that he doesn't know what to do with it. I think you're the perfect person to teach him. Of course Mitchell needn't know about this. He's not grown up enough to understand why this is important."

"Really? Are you sure?" I query.

After hundreds of hours with Gerald, I have become numb to his bluntness and crude choice of words. Outrageous, socially unacceptable assignments are the norm in our circle. I tremble with trepidation and confusion which are soon mixed with anticipation. After all, I must be very special indeed to have been chosen from among all the girls for this important assignment — to initiate his handsome, precious and enlightened son into the world of adult intimacy. After a heart-to-heart with his father that evening, Marty pays me a visit at my studio the following afternoon. Upon entering for his lesson, the first words out his mouth are,

"I feel I have to make a commitment to you."

However, later that day Gerald corrects him. "That is not for you to do; just have the experience and learn."

Like a stab in the back I get the message. I am not worth a commitment. I am just to be used for his son's growth. When Martin has learned all that he requires, he will leave, and a few weeks later, that is exactly what happens. I push aside my resentment, trying to convince myself that I must have learned something valuable as well from this special experience.

February to December 1991

It is a late Tuesday afternoon. I am slumped on the couch in Gerald's den. Dizzy, nauseous and exhausted from overwork, I feel miserable. I have to deliver proofs to a bride and groom that evening at 7:00 P.M., and I am afraid that I will not be able to make it through the meeting. Samantha, seated in a chair opposite me, has become a regular in her father's groups since she graduated last June from SUNY New Paltz with a B.A. in communications. I am thirty-one and she is twenty-three. She has been working several part-time jobs for almost nine months and is currently a cocktail waitress at *Medieval Times*, an entertainment restaurant in Lyndhurst. In addition, a few times a week, she fills in as substitute teacher for the Westwood grade school. The rest of the time she hangs out at the house. Her father begins to get annoyed. He can see that her college degree did not earn her a ticket into a well-paying job, and that she is not motivated enough to create a meaningful and productive stream for herself which will lead to a healthy career. A radio station has just offered her a full-time job with a starting salary of $6 per hour. However, Samantha and Gerald both feel that this paltry amount would hardly compensate her for her value, so she has turned them down.

Gerald notices that I look pale and sick. When I mention my evening appointment he gently suggests that Samantha might be able to help me out. Surprised at this unanticipated suggestion, I appreciate his thoughtfulness and agree. So that evening she accompanies me to my office. Confident in herself, Samantha insists on handling the appointment alone. I am hesitant, but my stomach is rolling and my head is banging; I don't feel strong enough to contradict her. After the couple leaves, she asks me if there might be a little work for her. The possibility of bringing another person into the business has never occurred to me, but here she is and I don't mind trying something new. I spend the next few days pouring three years of acquired knowledge from my head into hers. She listens and absorbs. I tell her that while she is training in sales I will give her a 5% commission, and when she has learned enough, I will raise it to 10%. Unexpectedly, she glares at me and I recede automatically from her piercing gaze.

"I will do the sales myself now. Five percent is not going to do anything for me."

I really don't feel she is ready to deliver what it has taken me three years to learn, but I lack the emotional resources to go up against that willful rage I have just perceived in her eyes, so I agree to allow her to do it her way, convincing myself that it will probably work out OK.

Over the next few months Samantha spends more and more time at the office, finally working herself up to over twenty hours per week. By now, she is handling all of the sales. Naturally I am concerned with her methods of dealing with the customers, and if she is selling effectively in order to maximize the company's profits. However, she does not take constructive criticism or suggestions well. Any time I approach she rises defensively and accuses me of putting her down.

"Do you think I am stupid? Don't interfere. I am perfectly capable of learning on my own."

In addition, she reports to her father that I disapprove of her, and during my sessions he frequently chastises me for my lack of respect for his daughter. I can't fight her, and I certainly can't fight him, so I learn to deny my better judgment and let her have free reign. Soon Gerald is bragging to The Group that his daughter has saved my business from failure because I am a poor saleswoman.

"Samantha is gifted with the powerful confident personality that Elizabeth is too weak to develop. Samantha has the drive to take the business to the stars. In fact she could run five businesses at once if she wanted to!"

At the office, Samantha makes suggestions which she insists will help us grow. Only minimally experienced in business, I believe her promises of a brighter future. She hires a new photographer so that we can manage more jobs and begins to make reasonably sized sales. After the customers leave, she usually explains how she has overcome their objections and resistance and convinced them to buy much more than they had originally intended. I have never been comfortable with selling and have always had difficulty asking for money at the end of the sale. Although, before she arrived I did find the means to force myself anyway. Therefore I am grateful that she has relieved me of this distasteful task. Within four months Samantha demands a salary on top of the sales commissions. She justifies this with a reference to the extra time she has been spending at the office, because I need so much help. I hesitate; I can't afford it. After three years of start-up costs, I still don't have enough cash flow to pay myself a salary. She scowls at me disapprovingly,

"Don't you want to grow? You have to sacrifice. I must have a salary in order to stay here, and you don't have the character of a business person. Your business will fail without me."

That night she tells her father that I don't want to pay her a salary because I don't value her and the next morning he attacks me,

"You are turning down the opportunity of a lifetime. When it comes to business, your personality sucks. Without Samantha, *Expressions Photography* will go right down the drain. She has more experience dealing with people than you do. Just climb on her back and she will take you with her."

This idea offends me. I don't want to climb on her back; I want to evolve myself. Every time he praises her my stomach twists. I do not see the evidence that

Samantha is so great. However, in addition to Gerald and his daughter, the rest of The Group encourages me to let her "save the business". The peer pressure is too much. I question my instincts. I convince myself that I <u>must</u> be missing something. I <u>must</u> still need to learn. She <u>must</u> have advanced knowledge, ingested from spending so many hours with Gerald since she was a toddler, that I have yet to obtain. There are so many unanswered questions, and I know that I am not being given the opportunity to discover Samantha's natural place in my business. All of a sudden, against my will and common sense, she is grabbing the steering wheel from my hands. However, she and her father seem so sure and confident, and I can't overcome their unified wall of intention. I agree to give her the salary I can't afford now, reasoning that if I compensate her from my personal resources, it will come back later when Samantha has time to put some of her new ideas into place — Gerald's "Law of Reciprocity". Our mentor has carefully taught us to make the investment and be patient. The fruit will come if you follow directions. About a month later Samantha informs me that she has quit her waitress job. She will now devote herself full time to the studio. However, she requires another raise in salary. With the additional time she spends, she will do even more good things for the business. I repress my hesitation once more and give in . . .

One day in the summer, Samantha notices my flash card prototypes on a high shelf in the office. "What's that?" she asks.

I tell her about my project, my aspirations and the unaffordable $6000 cost for typesetting. Within the next fifteen minutes she is on the phone with her father telling him that she will get them published. True to her promise, she quickly secures an appointment at *Prentice Hall* in Englewood Cliffs. Gerald brags to The Group that I am too intimidated by the "big people" so Samantha will carve the path to success. The following week, clothed in business attire, we drive to our meeting. Sitting in the passenger seat, I clutch my precious prototypes close to my chest. *Prentice Hall*, a division of *Simon and Schuster*, one of the world's largest publishers, looks like a great big daddy to me. *I have a wonderful idea. Surely they will want to find a way to get it to the market*, I tell myself with conviction. Our meeting goes well. Euphoric and hopeful, we infect Wynn Happauch, an assistant editor in the mail order division, with our excitement. He schedules a follow-up meeting with some other editors to discuss more specifics. We leave high on a cloud.

"This is really going to happen," Samantha says confidently, "and we will split it 50-50."

Split it evenly? This doesn't sound fair. It was my passion, brainstorm and years of experience as teacher and tutor that conceived of and developed this idea. How is she entitled to half of my profits just for setting up a meeting? Very upset, I call Gerald to complain. Instead of defending his daughter as I fear, he responds gently, calming my reaction,

"Nothing has happened yet. Why don't you just wait and see when the time comes?"

I accept his answer as logical. The next week we attend our next meeting. The other editors show some preliminary interest and set off to get quotes on production costs. Apparently, the printing costs turn out to be too high and a week later we receive a gracious letter of refusal . . .

When Samantha took those three-year-old prototypes off the shelf, and I dusted them off, my passion reignited. Despite our first failure, my mind begins to fantasize in dramatic proportions. I envision the product on the shelves of all 30,000 retail bookstores in the United States. I calculate the potential profits which would reach into the millions! Samantha and Gerald immediately jump on the bandwagon. Another assignment for The Energy! The three of us spend much of my session time planning our next move. There is so much potential: retail stores, mail-order, translation to computer disks, international sales . . . We see ourselves taking on the entire planet. One day I comment to Samantha,

"This is the perfect vehicle to get your father's information out into the public. We can write things about The Energy in the card sets, and with millions of boxes of flash cards out there, a lot of people will start understanding our mission and begin to think like us!"

From my experience with the *Prentice Hall* meetings, I have become aware that I am easily intimidated and lack the aggressive personality necessary to make headway into the towering monster which is the publishing industry. In contrast, Samantha appears fearless. I watch her in awe as she picks up the telephone, over and over, calling anyone she desires — manager, chief editor, president of the company — she has the courage to apply herself to any strategy, no matter how outrageous. I have come to feel that I really do need her. After the *Prentice Hall* turndown, we decide to try to publish the cards ourselves. We have no idea what it will cost but she and I come to a verbal agreement that since this is my brainchild, I will pay all of the costs: production, travel, advertising, and so forth, (from my inheritance) and she will donate her time to make connections and ultimately, sales. We will split the profits between us. Within the next weeks she schedules appointments at several major book chains. Our first stop is *Barnes & Noble*, of course. That is my dream, to see my product on their shelves. Meanwhile, Mitchell suggests that I make a sample run of the product, say one hundred copies of each title, and try to sell them to local stores. Anything to get these cards in front of the public. He refers me to a printer and we work out the details. Technology has advanced in three years and the $6000 typesetting charge is no longer necessary. I will be able to output the flash card's text from my computer. I purchase science study guides and get to work, writing my first three titles.

Finally, after many late nights, I am ready to print. The Group is elated with the project. Our excitement is infectious and since this seems like it is really going to happen, the rest jump on board. Gerald is involved as advisor at every stage, every decision. Best of all, he is pleased with me. Through his interest in the flash cards, I can obtain his attention whenever I need it. I register the business name *Flash Enterprises* as a sole-proprietorship and just like the photography business, *Expressions Photography*, I own 100%; Samantha remains my employee. The first print run costs me $11 per box for three hundred boxes — $3300. Samantha runs into her former high school teacher and asks her what we should retail them for. The woman's opinion is $15.95. I feel the price is too high, it should be close to $10, but Samantha is adamant. The Energy has spoken through this woman.

Our first, glossy, sales flyers go to print. "New for 1991, *Flash Enterprises* presents, *In a Flash Study Cards*." With a $15.95 retail we are wholesaling them for $8 each. I am losing $3 per box, but I don't care. I am in business. Things will turn around. I must invest my time and money now. Later there will be enormous profit. Samantha, the go-getter, drives to several local *B. Dalton* and *WaldenBooks* stores. Walking in without an appointment, she speaks to the managers and convinces them to purchase an introductory package. I force myself to follow suit, my profound fear of rejection choking me relentlessly. Surprisingly, most of the stores say yes, and soon we have placed those three hundred pieces on their shelves; it is time to make more. With all of these sales, I have developed immense confidence in our future, so I decide to make five hundred of each title this time, to cut my per unit cost. I have no idea how we will sell them all, but Gerald reassures us, "Just go for it and it will work out."

Those fifteen hundred pieces cost me $11,000. At $7.33 each, I can actually make a profit of $0.66 per box! However, soon after that, some of the stores object to the price and we are forced to lower it to $12.95. Now, at a wholesale of $6.50, I am losing $0.83 each time we sell one. On this print run I will lose close to $1200.

We just have to keep pushing to get bigger, I tell myself to soothe my disappointment. *After we build up our account base I will be able to make ten thousand at a time. The cost will come down per unit and then we will make a profit.*

During the next few months I decide to produce a corporate video, aimed at enticing buyers to purchase more flash cards, and hire the *Expressions* wedding videographer — "Dave the Video-Man", to complete the project. Dave, in his early thirties, is recently separated from his wife, so I decide to introduce him to Lisa. They take an immediate liking to each other, begin to date regularly, and soon she is bringing him to The Group. Gerald, feeling he has met a kindred soul who can appreciate his personal gifts, tries to convince Dave to start his own group down where he lives in Southern New Jersey, to teach people about The Energy.

Dave doesn't feel comfortable at all, and after attending one or two more meetings he starts making excuses not to show up. A disappointed Gerald criticizes Lisa for failing to convince her boyfriend otherwise, and pressures her,

"If Dave doesn't join soon, you will have to stop seeing him."

Lisa is torn. She really likes him, but her fear of Gerald's disapproval wins. Finally, she feels she must give Dave the ultimatum to either join or she won't see him anymore. Dave really likes her, but he knows he will never be a part of Gerald's entourage. If these are the only two choices, he will have to give her up. Lisa begs him to come to one last group meeting because for this evening, Gerald has come up with a strategy to push Dave over the edge. That night, half an hour into The Group, Martin enters with a very attractive woman, his "date". Unexpectedly, after a few preliminary remarks to the woman about our group, Gerald turns on the stereo. Thus cued, Marty's companion rises from her seat and, revolving languidly around the coffee table, commences to slowly remove her clothing. The Group men, Gerald, Marty, Mitchell, and Carl, who have apparently been in on this plot, take turns dancing with the voluptuous female. They remove their shirts and gyrate seductively, gluttonously relishing this sensual pleasure. Dave in contrast, considering his girlfriend's feelings, invites Lisa to join him in a dance. We women stand on the side in shock, not knowing what to make of this. In the presence of this woman our men are behaving in an extraordinary manner. Although I can't consciously label it, betrayal engulfs me as I suddenly become aware that we are never respected as women; to the men we are androgynous, neither valued nor complimented for our feminine attributes. The next day, having picked up our distress the previous evening, Gerald makes fun of us, accusing us of being stupid fools for our jealous reactions to the stripper. Then he calls Dave to see how he liked The Group. Dave tells him that he enjoyed himself very much but he still doesn't want to join, and the following week Lisa breaks up with him.

With our completed corporate video, I have high hopes for *Flash Enterprises* and *Expressions Photography* too. However, Samantha, now my almost constant companion, throws me a curve . . . One day, a few weeks after the stripper show, I walk into the office to find her sitting at my desk looking angry. I inquire if something is wrong and she glares at me, righteous indignation written all over her face,

"I have been here for several months now. I have helped you make improvements because I care about you and the business, but you still don't appreciate me. All you do is criticize me."

Samantha terrifies me. I have never met anyone like her in my life. When these moods strike her, she is so angry, cutting, nasty and cruel that I experience an uncontrollable drive to run out of the room, as far away for her as I can get. Her accusations trigger me to recede until my face is pale, my mouth parched and my hands sweaty. I feel as if I will pass out from the flood of fear and anguish which rises up inside me. During these confrontations, nothing I say will change her mind or stop her attack, no matter how incorrect her assertions are. When I try to escape she orders me to return, parroting what her father teaches in The Group, *Sit through the war until it breaks and then you will be stronger.* Nevertheless, with the acidity of my reactions coursing through every vessel in my body, escalating in intensity as she utters each new allegation, I feel as if I am being commanded to force my hand to remain in a flame until the pain passes; the sensations are unbearable and I quickly learn to numb myself in order to survive. I know that if I don't obey her, she will tell her father and his vengeance will be even worse than hers.

Although eight years her senior and the owner of this business, today, as usual, I shrink from her in cowardice.

"I'm leaving," she threatens, "You can fail on your own."

After hearing from her mouth, and Gerald's, over the past several months how skilled Samantha is, and what a failure I am, their opinions through sheer repetition are sinking into my mind, and unconsciously I am beginning to accept them as true. They have pointed out that I am afraid to ask for money from our photography customers and afraid to ask buyers to make appointments for the flash cards. They are right. If I am unable to do these things, my businesses won't succeed. My personality is inadequate and I do need Samantha to fill in these gaps. Therefore, when she threatens to leave, I feel myself sinking to the floor. I believe that I have committed the worst crime in the world. Although I can't figure out exactly what it is that I have done, in her ranting Samantha has offered no specific details, I know that if I don't win her back I will be doomed.

During that afternoon's stress-reduction session I face Gerald with a pale terrified countenance. He immediately reinforces his daughter's position.

"Samantha is the best thing that ever happened to you, and you are too stupid to see it. If you let her go, you will lose everything."

The next few days are awful. I drown in a state of constant fear and impeding ruin. Samantha is present at the office, but makes it clear that her days are numbered. I feel that at any moment the rug will be pulled out from under me, and not only will I lose my only chance at success, but I will incur Gerald's eternal wrath for screwing up with his daughter. I want desperately to find a resolution, and yet I still don't understand exactly what the problem is. From both all I hear is, "You really screwed up this time. You're gonna pay. I feel sorry for you without Samantha in your business."

I feel like a helpless rabbit in the middle of an open field being attacked by a swarm of crows. I endure the horror of nowhere to run for cover and no weapons to ward off the enemy. A couple of evenings later Samantha calls me into a meeting. This is it; my worst fears are about to come true; my life is over. But observing the pathetic heap of a woman shaking in her seat, she gazes intensely and surprises me, delivering these unexpected and magical words,

"Elizabeth, I was definitely prepared to leave, but I have decided to stay . . . , with one condition; I must have a 20% commission from now on."

I almost cry out. The doubled commission, from 10% to 20%, doesn't even seem important in this moment. I simply drown in incredible relief as she presses a button and releases me instantaneously from the unbearable terror which has haunted me mercilessly for the past few days. However, in this moment I also make a vow to myself. I do not know how, but I will find a way to overcome the control Samantha has over me. She must be stopped. One day she will attack me and I will have the strength to stand up to her. In fact, the next time she strikes, this promise to myself will be my anchor. I will refuse to retreat; I will fight the war until I figure out my enemy's strategy and learn how to disarm her. Despite the pitiful, weak fool I have just made of myself, I will do better next time; I must. I believe in my ability to overcome, no matter what the odds. I tell no one about this oath; it is my private secret.

Over the next several months I can't afford to take a salary while Samantha earns hers plus commissions. In addition, after our last confrontation, I have no more say in my business. Samantha is in charge, and I am advised in my sessions with Gerald that if I will just let her lead, she will only do good things. This simply requires patience on my part. When feelings of injustice rise in me, which they do quite often, I learn to oppress them, repeating in my mind the mantra of Gerald's logic, *It will be all right if I can just wait and let Samantha lead. The Energy is running the business now. After all, Gerald is the source of The Energy. Samantha is Gerald's daughter, and has inherited her father's gifts. The Energy flows through her to the customers. This attracts them to the business and commands them to spend large sums.* How could I think otherwise . . . ? Gerald has explained it all several times,

"If you had been my daughter, you would have been just like her, but you were not so fortunate. Therefore, the best thing you can do is let her take charge."

By the end of that year I have actually earned $9000, my first salary ever, but Samantha has taken home $25,000 . . .

Samantha, heartened by the pecuniary gains at *Expressions Photography*, reaches out for other opportunities to expand her capitalistic success. One evening in spring, while listening to the New York City radio station, CD 101.9., she is taken by that week's featured band, New Age artist, David Arkenstone. She purchases a copy of his latest cassette and immediately his music becomes The Group's theme. All day long our leader shakes his head in rhythm to David's music, and each time the tape is played, Gerald claims he can hear the music improving as he inserts his Energy into it. Samantha and Bess, encouraged by this evidence that The Energy can make a band sound better, decide to go into the concert promotion business. Gerald is very proud of them.

"The audience will feel The Energy while they are being distracted by the music. Because we know that their minds would resist us, we will get The Energy into them through the back door, for their own good."

The two women reserve the *John Harms Theater* in Englewood. Soon, contracts are faxed to Mr. Arkenstone and for the next several months, all group energies are swallowed up by this new endeavor. We set about promoting the concert, handing out more than 10,000 flyers at local pizza parlors, dry cleaners and record stores. Samantha purchases several hundred dollars worth of advertising on CD 101.9 radio. The theater holds approximately two thousand people. The tickets will average $25 so Samantha and Bess figure they will make about $25,000 after expenses.

The band flies out three days before the concert date and Samantha puts them up at an expensive Tenafly hotel. On Thursday night Gerald advises his daughter to bring the band leader and his flautist to The Group. An unprepared David enters the room and stands frozen, staring incomprehensibly at the twelve or so sober faces basking in The Energy. Within less than thirty seconds his face turns ghost white and he mutters in distress,

"I have to get out of here."

Making an abrupt about-face, without explanation, he flees the den and flies down the dark Westwood street toward the main road. There, in the middle of nowhere he waves at passing cars, hoping to find a taxi. Within the next minute Gerald sends Samantha and Bess after him and David agrees to let them drive him back to his hotel. After they leave, Gerald explains why he reacted so strangely,

"You see, a celebrity expects to be treated like a god wherever he goes. We know that he isn't superior to us, so we just acted like he was a normal person when he visited instead of bowing down to him. His ego couldn't take it so he ran."

We all believe his explanation. We know that the crazy people are very insecure and don't understand how to live as equals, the way we are learning to.

The next evening the concert takes place. Seated in the back of the theater, Gerald shakes his head during the entire show. Martin makes a video which we all watch the following day. On the film, we all observe The Energy glowing around David's head. Gerald explains that it is in him now, even though he tried to run away the other night. Aside from the regular group members and some of their family, only ten additional people purchase tickets and the two "concert promoters" lose a combined $40,000 on the concert. However, this doesn't seem to bother Samantha in the least. Instead, she immediately throws herself back into the soup and begins planning two additional concerts at the same theater.

Down the hall from my new Closter studio the sign on Suite 1 reads "Education Dynamics", a company which sells encyclopedias and other study aids door to door. One Friday night I return to my office at about 8:30 P.M. after a city session with Gerald. The building is locked and dark, but I notice a shaft of light spilling out from under their door. Perhaps they will be interested in my flash cards? Bursting with anticipation, I race down the hallway to my office, grab my samples, and return to knock.

"Come in," a man yells from an inner office.

Peter is tall — 6'2", dark hair, suntan, lots of gold jewelry, quite handsome and sexy too. From the first moment our eyes connect and light up in unison — as if we have instantly recognized each other as friends. I begin describing all of the wonderful attributes of my product to him and we talk for over an hour about our respective businesses. I leave feeling sort of shaky, excited and alive. The next day we pass in the hall. The mutual attraction is there again, just as strong as the night before. He is fifty-one years old and has been separated from his wife of twenty years for five months. They have two children, now in their early twenties. The feeling between us is compelling, as if we can't get enough of each other. We make a lunch date for the following week and I feel as if I am walking on a cloud.

Gerald and The Group know everything about me, so they soon find out about Peter. At first they find my new liaison amusing. Peter invites me to an off-Broadway play in the city and Gerald encourages me to take advantage of the opportunity "to at least get a free meal". Peter has told me that his company is worth a few million. Realizing that there may be potential to benefit from his coffers in some way, Gerald advises me sagely,

"You never know what you can get out of him, so go for it."

Mitchell however, does not appreciate the concept of me dating another man while I am sharing his bed every night. He senses that I am doing what any woman in an unhappy relationship would do; I am comparing both men. This is true. For the first time in many years I am experiencing how wonderful it feels to be treated like a woman. This man has something to offer, a successful business, friends, good looks, life experience . . . Even more important, as I get to know Peter, I come to truly respect him for overcoming a painful childhood spent in foster homes, and establishing a fruitful business with nothing but his own wits and chutzpah. I see a man dedicated to his children and his employees, who enjoys his life and spreads his enthusiasm to those around him. He is genuine and sincere, even about his shortcomings. I like who this man is . . .

In contrast, it is finally becoming clear to me that Mitchell has absolutely nothing to offer, and never will. In the seven years that I have lived with him, he has yet to manage to tap into the stream of income that he always promises is "just around the corner". I am beginning to realize that "the corner" doesn't exist. In addition, he has an immature and self-focused personality. Over the course of our many fights it has become painfully obvious that he has never seen nor appreciated who I am as a person. To him I have simply represented a set of female genitalia, and a checkbook with a pen. I crave the emotions that my short relationship with Peter has unleashed. I relish feeling like a woman — an adult who can experience give and take, a relationship of growth, and yes, passion. I begin to realize that by allowing myself to fall into this trap with Mitchell, I have committed a devastating crime against myself. I have imprisoned myself with a fool (which makes me a bigger one), thus denying myself a healthy fulfilling relationship. In fact, since I have become friends with Peter I find it increasingly difficult to relate with Mitchell in the way I used to. More and more, I can barely tolerate his presence at all. When I come home at night I avoid him, and when we retire to bed I bury myself in my red goose-down sleeping bag, left over from my teen-age camping and hiking days, to insure that he won't be able to make contact with my body in any way at all. After several years of trying everything in my power to make us work, I have finally lost the motivation to continue. I am beginning to wake up, to realize that our relationship has always been one-sided and that Mitchell will never change because he has no desire to. I have pursued the objective to improve our life together all alone, while Mitchell has been satisfied with the status quo. Something powerful is happening and through no conscious intent, I feel myself being propelled away from Mitchell.

One Saturday evening once again, I fight with Mitchell over money. After seven years I am still paying almost of all of the bills while he works part-time, at his convenience, when he doesn't feel too emotionally taxed, occasionally donating a few spare pennies to take me out for a hamburger. As usual he refuses to validate my position, but instead draws upon a seemingly endless vat of excuses which he throws in my face relentlessly and without compassion. Frustrated, still trying to convince him to change, I stare into his glaring eyes and unexpectedly, I am propelled beyond them, into the carefully concealed lair where his soul abides. Suddenly a powerful and horrifying vision emerges. I see myself trapped in a cage in the basement. I am hungry but Mitchell is feeding me infrequently, only when he feels like it. He laughs at my obvious distress over being unable to escape. Sometimes, when the fancy strikes him, he enters the cage to play with my body as if I am no more than a Barbie Doll. All at once that New Year's Eve with him at Lisa's apartment seven years ago comes back to me and I experience once again that unholy feeling of entrapment. It is the same sensation I had growing up with my mother. I finally make the connection. This set-up is familiar, reminiscent of my childhood, and that is why I have been willing to endure his injustice for so long. What I am seeing is the real Mitchell and I know now for sure that I will never change him; I will never be happy; I must leave him.

The following Monday, I complain to Gerald about Mitchell, as I have several times before. Gerald always responds the same way,

"You are right, but Mitchell is trying and you need to have more patience. Besides, you are not ready to leave him; you still have things to learn. I know it is frustrating to pay most of the bills but look at it positively; you are <u>paying for your education</u>. Don't forget, it takes two to create a problem. If you do not resolve your personality defects which contribute to the difficulties in the relationship you will take them with you to your next relationship. Stay with your uncomfortable reactions to him until they break. Then we will see what you should do next."

What he says seems logical; I want to follow Gerald's instructions, but I can't. The repellant is becoming too strong. The following week Gerald takes a vacation. On that first evening I return home and find that I simply can't stand spending one more night under the same roof with Mitchell. It is as if I am about to be shot out of a cannon; I am barely able to tolerate the pressure in my chest as I quickly pack a bag and throw it into my car. Against Gerald's orders I run away from Mitchell for a week. I jump from hotel to hotel and even sleep in my photography studio one night. Although Gerald does not know I have defied him, Samantha does. She becomes enraged and makes my life miserable at the office. She lets me know that when her father returns, it will be ten times worse. This is true. On Gerald's first day back my knees are shaking as I walk into his den. He doesn't say anything for awhile, but I know what is coming. Finally he looks my way and delivers his pent up venom,

"You just couldn't wait for the right moment, could you? I knew you would ruin everything while I was on vacation so I wouldn't be here to straighten it out. I told everyone not to do anything except lay low while I was gone, but you just wouldn't listen, would you?"

He rises, still raving, and grabs me by the collar, shoving me against the wall with such force that two framed posters fall to the floor.

"Damn," he sputters, "Look what you made me do. The glass is broken on these pictures and I'll expect you to pay for it."

I can't take Gerald's opposition, and I move back in with Mitchell. Besides, I have nowhere to go . . .

Nonetheless, it is not long before those same horrible feelings emerge again, commanding me to leave Mitchell. Still Gerald informs me I am not ready. However, he has a suggestion that might make things easier. Samantha has been looking into renting a house that several of us could share. If she, Pauline, Carl, Lisa, Mitchell and I could split the rent, we would reduce our expenses and have a really nice place to live too.

"This way," Gerald adds encouragingly, "you and Mitchell will have others around you and will be less focused on each other."

I don't want to do this. I see enough of Samantha at the office, and if I live with her our existences will be totally merged. She is not the person to whom I want to make that kind of a commitment. Besides, I would feel like I am back at my college dorm. I am almost thirty-one; I want a more adult lifestyle.

I pick up a grey striped kitten on the back poach of a house overrun by strays. She is so tiny, pocket-sized, that she fits into the palm of my hand. I feed her with a baby bottle and keep her on clean towels because she is too young to use the litter. Sleeping in a cardboard box, she throws her paw over the stuffed mouse I have given her for company. She sighs to the sound of the ticking clock positioned under her towel to replace mother cat's heartbeat and comfort her. I make her first baby portraits and hang them fondly on my bedroom wall. At home, in my office, in my car, she is my constant companion. While I am driving, she sits on the driver's seat between my legs. I want to name this baby kitten after something that is close to my heart, so I chose "Flash" after my flash card project. Of course she attends my sessions with Gerald too. Another experiment, he holds her upright, his hand around her belly. Her back legs hang straight down while he shakes his head vigorously. The Energy field from his body knocks her out, and her now limp body, in a deep state of relaxation, begins to vibrate rapidly as electricity runs through her nervous system and triggers her muscles to

Baby "Flash" could fit in the palm of your hand.

twitch. It is a bizarre sight, but he doesn't seem to be hurting her, I believe. Gerald laughs as he touches her jolting paws.

"See everybody," he enlightens us, "The Energy calms her down, knocks out her programmed cat behavior, and transforms her into a calm being with the wisdom and intelligence of the 'other place'. Maybe we should let the animals lead us. They are less crazy than the humans because they do not have thoughts on top of their instinctual reactions. Humans have both, and this makes it more difficult to reach our true natures."

Gerald also works on Samantha's orange and grey cat, B.J. He holds her in his lap, seated like a small person. When she struggles to break free, he forces her to stay until she gives up, having learned that an attempt at escape is hopeless. Now she sits, for hours at a time, in a completely motionless state, as if mesmerized. Looking as wise as the Sphinx of Egypt, Gerald praises her as the example of

perfection which we should all strive for. He refers to her as "our leader, the all-knowing being, if only we could learn to communicate with her." The rest worship her too. I try to follow suit, but I have a hard time convincing myself that this cat is more intelligent and wonderful than I am . . . Gerald also works on Martin's black Labrador mutt, Ben.

"Ben is a lunatic. His dog program makes him run too fast and ignore his well-being. No wonder dogs only live until twelve years old. They are too self-destructive."

Gerald spends hours lying on the floor clutching the dog in a wrestler's hold, restricting Ben's motion each time he tries to free himself. At mealtime he teaches the dog not to bolt his food down by holding his head and restricting his jaw motion so that he is forced to chew more slowly. The more Gerald is able to control and change the behavior of his animals, the more he lifts them up as spiritual examples for the rest of The Group,

"My animals are more alive than we are. We must follow them. They have knowledge of the place we need to get to. I have forced them to drop their crazy programs and they are no longer part of this crazy world."

It is late November and I have reached the end. Hiding in my office, avoiding Mitchell at home, and submerging the conflict I experience in his presence has become intolerable. I have given up trying to convince him that he should be fair to me, and it has become impossible to find a comfortable place to relate. In fact, I can rarely force myself to hold a superficial conversation. I have grown out of him. It is strange, but Mitchell, my intimate companion for the past eight years, is completely insensitive to these drastic changes in my psyche. I complain to Gerald once again, and this time my will so powerful that he is unable to change my mind. Apparently, I am not Mitchell's in the spiritual place as Gerald tried to convince us when he put us together, and now I am going to leave no matter what. Gerald realizes that he can't hold me back any longer, he has lost this round, so he quickly reverses his stance and supports me, as confidently as if he had never promoted any other position.

"It's OK, you can leave him if you want to. It will be good for you to move on to new experiences."

I am neither angry nor bitter. I am way beyond these emotions by now. Instead, I regret sadly the loss of eight precious years of my life. I suffer over my newfound awareness of the low self-esteem which permitted a man like him to take advantage of me for so long . . . In secret I begin my apartment search. The last weeks with him are so strange, a sensation that a spaceship is on its way to pick me up. Unbelievably, he suspects nothing! This painful revelation, that he lives in a state of total disconnection from any of my personal feelings or struggles, pushes away any final shreds of doubt. At the office I ask Samantha if she would like to accompany me to see a few apartments I have been considering. She suggests that while we are at it, she would like to look at some of the houses that she's been thinking of renting with the others. We spend the day exploring local rental apartments and homes and then the realtor suggests a beautiful house in Closter with a very reasonable rent. Immediately upon entering the front door, a powerful sensation overcomes me, as if I am being sucked into a tornado. Before I even have a chance to think, I discover that I have made a commitment and the two of us are signing a lease. What I never wanted to happen is happening nonetheless; Samantha and I have merged our lives — out of the frying pan and into the fire. Regardless, the relief over finally leaving Mitchell and the prospect of starting fresh in this wonderful big house with a fireplace at the end of a dirt road, just like I dreamed of ever since I was a little girl, conquers any sense of doubt — for the moment. A week later, Mitchell comes home from an appointment to make the unexpected discovery that all of my things have been removed. I had no other choice but to sneak out while he was away, because Mitchell, as he always has before, would have employed brute force to stop me.

New Year's Eve 1991 to December 1992

Several Group members spend the last remaining hours of 1991, and the first few of 1992, at our new house with Samantha and me, assisting us in unpacking and setting up. Carl, Pauline and Lisa paint my bedroom, white walls and blue trim. They hang white lace curtains to complement my floral bedspread. Nora and Marty help Samantha decorate her room: black mini-blinds, black sheets, and various medieval props — swords, wizards, dragons . . . Our tastes certainly contrast!

Samantha and I are now an item. Because we are involved in two businesses and I share a house with her, I have finally managed to climb past all of the others on the ladder of The Group's hierarchy. In fact, I rest only one rung below Gerald's children. If I work hard enough, I believe that I will earn equality with them, and then one blessed day in the future, with Gerald. As for now, Samantha and Elizabeth are the team that is really going places. Suddenly we seem to have the answers and experience for the others to learn from. In The Group, with everyone involved in some entrepreneurial project, business is generally the subject of choice. We all take booths at mall trade shows together where we offer all of our services on one table. In fact, we promote each other's enterprises wherever we go, often handing a receptive stranger over half a pound of paper as we proudly recite all of the amazing things that The Group members do — books, printing business, Formica furniture, photography, stress-reduction exercises, etc. We travel in a cloud of euphoria, drowning in the hopes and visions we generate.

All of this activity makes Gerald's den or city office the only place to be, the official headquarters for expert guidance, whenever you can get there. My flash cards get plenty of attention and as the project progresses, I become addicted to my visits to Gerald where I share the latest developments and seek his advice for our next steps. Because the photography studio operates by appointment only, Samantha soon arranges for it to be closed three afternoons a week so that we can "go into the city", to her father's office. We spend hours in that cramped room, brainstorming about our two businesses and advising the others about theirs. Samantha is not paying for this exciting time but I am, at a rate of $40 per hour. Because we live and work together, we operate somewhat like a married couple and drive in one car, often hers. If we arrive at 2:00 P.M., Samantha insists of course, on remaining until 7:30 P.M. when her father finishes his day. This obligates me to pay for more than five hours of his time. I can't drive my own car in order to cut my session short, because if I oppose any of the individual decisions which compose Samantha's overall strategy for success, I will be considered a traitor and accused of wanting to fail. As upset as I am about this arrangement, I try to convince myself that the "Law of Reciprocity" will work in my favor. I just need more patience. All of the ingredients have not yet been put into the cake. I talk to myself to pacify my anxiety, *I know that you are spending a lot on Gerald and on the flash cards, but it will be well worth it when your product is in every chain across the country. You will be making so much that even if you had to pay Gerald $100,000 per year, compared to your total salary, it would seem like nothing.*

Meanwhile my checks to him every two weeks have begun to exceed a distressing $2000. Since the time I complained to my mother about giving him half of my teaching salary I have always resented paying him. I never wanted to drain my small inheritance, now down to about $75,000. My schedule is as follows: Monday, Wednesday, Friday — 8:30 to 9:30 A.M. in his New Jersey den and approximately 3:00 to 7:30 P.M. at his Manhattan office; Tuesday, Thursday — 2:00 to 7:30 P.M. and Saturday — 1:00 to 5:00 P.M. back in the den. With these frequent visits my troubled feelings are rapidly turning to alarm and anger. I resent every check, wishing it was the last, but I push back my hostility and recite the explanation he has trained, *This is an investment in your future. The money will come back.* I dutifully submerge my conflict each time it rises up because I have learned a justification and a mental comeback for any complaint. Yet my life feels like a speeding train moving too fast for me to jump off, even though I clearly see the brick wall way up ahead. These days the others are also increasing their hours, and often his tiny city office holds so many people that there isn't even enough room to sit on the floor. We leave the door open and a person or two sits on the hallway carpeting. Sometimes as many as ten people cram themselves into that five by ten foot space, each paying $40 per hour, except of course for Samantha and Martin who are often there all day and always for free. Everyone envies his kids. They don't have to drain their bank accounts and live like paupers, struggling over food bills because it all goes to Gerald. To make it worse, he always cites them as the best examples of the success of The Energy. They have inherited the approval from him that the rest of us are all paying thousands of dollars to try to win, and for us the coveted prize of his respect is always just a little beyond our reach . . .

Yet, Gerald claims that he treats everyone the same.

"I don't have any favorites; everyone is equal in my eyes," Gerald states proudly one afternoon, spotlighting his unprejudiced nature.

This feels wrong to me and I challenge him.

"What about your children, you must feel something special with them because they are a part of you."

"No, I feel the same about everyone. The fact that they share some of my chromosomes is only relevant in the physical world. It has no effect on our true spiritual relationships with each other."

"How can that be? And if it is, then why don't you have sex with Samantha or Martin too, to break a social barrier, like you do with us? Why would it make a difference?"

I think back to the time my mother touched my breast in the middle of the night, how she used Gerald's reasoning to justify this action as having no significance, just "flesh against flesh".

Gerald looks at the floor. For a moment, trapped in a contradiction within his own logic, he doesn't know where to find a loophole. Finally, grasping at straws, he mumbles,

"I have decided to let them have their own experiences."

What kind of an answer is that? It doesn't make any sense . . .

Aside from my distress over my finances, since the move into the new house my physical symptoms have worsened. Severe allergies constantly trigger me to itch and sneeze. My nasal membranes are so swollen that most of the time I must breathe through my mouth. Many of the business contacts I speak with ask me why I am always sick. I develop a post nasal drip and all day long mucus flows into my lungs, collecting there. Each night I spend up to two hours coughing the phlegm out before I can finally rest, often sleeping sitting up, an eerie echo of my mother's nocturnal problems when I was a teenager. I develop asthma and my lungs are perpetually irritated. Mild physical exertion causes them to tighten, forcing me to gasp for breath. During the night I shake my head like Gerald does to try to calm my constricted chest. Sometimes it helps . . . In addition, I have never overcome my perpetual fatigue and most of each day I find myself fervently praying for the time when I will be able to return to my bed. Attacks of anxiety and indecisiveness plague me as well. I cope as best as I can and it does not occur to me to go to a doctor. Actually, this is not an option; Samantha is ever-present in my home and office and aware of my every move. Gerald would excoriate me fiercely if I ever sought help outside of his jurisdiction; it would prove my disrespect for The Energy and his wisdom. Feeling hopeless, I try to convince myself that The Energy will take care of it; I must have patience and keep pushing past my resistance.

My relationship with my new roommate is a constant source of anxiety as well. One Friday night, about 8:00 P.M., I am reading in bed when I hear footsteps on the stairs. Samantha appears presently, making her way toward her bedroom across from mine. She looks fairly placid as she waves a greeting to me. Just after her friendly gesture something strange and unexplainable happens. All in an instant I sense an intense build-up of electricity in the air. I look at her and, as if a hostile ghost has just invaded her body and seized control, her face contorts and immediately transforms from her previously peaceful countenance into a twisted expression of rage. Without warning she begins to yell at me about a pipe in the basement which is dripping water onto the furnace. Standing in the narrow hallway outside my room she grills me, making no sense whatsoever,

"Why didn't you know it was doing that and get it fixed? The house could blow up!"

In moments she is screaming out of control and I don't even understand what she is referring to. I try to reason with her but she will not be silenced. Turning up the volume, her face turns beet red and her veins pop out of her forehead; it looks as if she might explode. All of a sudden, after about ten minutes of relentless interrogation and accusation, she stops short and runs into the third bedroom, her office, across the hall. Dropping onto the couch, she buries her face in her hands and begins crying. Although my feelings are hurt by her unreasonable attack, I am also concerned. I leave my room to go and sit near her, settling on the carpet near her feet. She seems to be ashamed that she is crying and wishes I wasn't there to witness this vulnerability. I sit quietly waiting for an opening to soothe her, to connect with her. I do not put my arms around her or stroke her head because she sends an unspoken message which I hear all too clearly, *Don't you dare touch me or else!*

I am intimidated by this silent dictum and do not have the courage to defy it in order to give her the comfort that I believe she genuinely needs. In a little while she lifts her face and sobs,

"Everyone only sees the outside of my personality. They do not realize how horrible I feel inside when this anger happens."

I listen sympathetically, knowing that the storm has passed and she will soon find relief. I do not understand what has just happened, but I do know one thing, Samantha, with all of her bravado, self-confidence and intimidation, is a tormented person . . .

I see Peter on and off. Relating with him I experience my inner self, free and safe. Samantha, on the other hand, does not approve and reports to her father that I spend all day at the office dreaming of the man down the hall and don't get my work done. She tells Gerald that we are losing sales because of this, and he believes her, warning me several times that I had better drop the games with Peter and return to what is important, or else . . .

I begin to feel that I must hide my connection to him. In fact, a silent message that I am committing some grave sin weighs on my mind continually. There is a wall of resistance between me and Peter, as if I must run a gauntlet of invisible entities to reach him, enemies which lacerate, flog and choke me while I attempt to pass. They send the message that there will be terrible consequences to pay if

I don't give up immediately and rededicate my life to The Group. But in spite of my growing conflict I won't give it up; I can't; Peter is just about the only thing in my life that feels good. Samantha continues to press the issue, claiming that I am obsessed with him, and soon The Group chimes in, humiliating me as a pathetic stupid fool for chasing one of the "crazy people".

"He seems like a nice man," Gerald observes, having met him one day at our office, "but if he doesn't come here to learn, you are not safe. One day he will hurt you."

I beg Peter several times to visit our group but he always refuses me and Gerald finally lays down the law.

"Your business is suffering and you have to get rid of Peter for your own good."

I am torn in half. I don't want anything to happen to my business, I depend on my salary, but I really like Peter. Still, because I fear the consequences of Gerald's disapproval more than anything, I decide to end it with Peter and later that evening I call him from my office, dialing his car phone to deliver the news. When he hears my voice he responds with pleasure, showing how he truly feels about me. I, in contrast, cut myself off and inform him coldly,

"Peter, I can't see you anymore."

Taken off his guard and clearly distressed, he questions, "Why?" and I feel his pain, as if I have just kicked him in the stomach. Samantha sits a few feet away, observing my conflict indifferently, insuring that I won't back down. I feel awful. I can't answer Peter's question. How could I ever explain about Gerald's commands and our dedication to The Energy? I babble and hesitate, praying that some miracle will occur in the next minute to save me from doing this awful thing, but instead his anguish builds and he blurts out,

"I swear to God on my children's graves, if you don't tell me why you can't see me anymore I will never speak to you again."

I am trapped. I keep insisting that I can't tell him why, still hoping that magically he will figure out the truth and find a way to save our relationship. Instead he hangs up on me. Agony is written all over my face, as if I have just lost my best friend, and that is how I feel inside. Samantha's cold shark's eyes continue to focus on me for a moment, and then she rises, disappearing to pursue some other important task, her mission accomplished. Deep guilt is born in my soul, twisted from the sin I have just committed, and I return home broken, shutting myself in my room. The next day I resolve that I will correct the mistake. I must win back Peter no matter what it takes. Although we work in the same building, just a few doors from each other, unbelievably, for the next six months our paths never cross. When I do finally run into him he tells me to keep my distance; he doesn't trust me. Although crushed, I don't blame him. Nevertheless, I sense that he is softening. Our mutual attraction is still there, the recognition of two kindred souls for each other. In another month or so I manage to regain his precious trust, some of it anyway. Grateful, I promise myself that I will never repeat such a mistake and that someday I will explain to him what really happened. Then I will be able to truly apologize . . .

With Peter basically out of the way, Samantha rededicates herself to new and innovative flash card promotion schemes. For her next move she decides we should win the endorsements of some influential people. Her first choice goes right to the top, the wife of the President of the United States, Barbara Bush. After all, Barbara is into education; she will surely want to help! So one day in her father's den, Samantha, with a hint of merriment, like a student planning to pull a prank, suggests that I pick up the phone and call Barbara. Taken aback, I try to throw some common sense into the equation,

"Why would she want to endorse our product just so we can profit from her name?"

But my partner glares at me for hesitating. This is more evidence that I want to fail. Soon the rest get on my back too. I don't want to admit that I am a coward and the word "no" is not an optional response to Samantha's suggestions, so nervously, I call information for the number. After being transferred a few times, I finally reach a secretary's secretary's secretary who tells me that they don't make appointments for this type of thing and besides, Barbara would not be able to put her name on any product. I sigh with relief, but only for a moment before Samantha concludes that I just wasn't confident enough. To prove me wrong, she calls the number and requests to speak to Barbara Bush herself. I think it is really rude to try to disturb people for our insignificant (to anyone but us) project. Regardless, Gerald beams with pride at his daughter's courage.

"They are not any better than us," he explains, "We just turn them into parents and then fear and worship them. Politicians are really our employees and it is our legal right to meet with them and give them our ideas whenever we want."

I know that in a general sense he is correct, although I still don't feel comfortable with the idea. Samantha's call yields no better results than mine, still, a few days later she brings it up again, pushing the phone in my hands with a grin. My face turns waxen. This is the last thing in the world I want to do. I get through to a secretary who remembers our previous call and seems annoyed. I don't know how I manage to accomplish our objective, but by babbling and forcing her to stay on the telephone I get an appointment. She probably says "yes" just to get rid of me. Barbara's personal secretary will be willing to meet with us, although I am told flat out that they won't be able to help us with an endorsement.

The next week Samantha and I are off to Washington, D.C. to bring The Energy into the White House. Based on our verbal business agreement I finance the trip, paying the tab for hotel and train. We do indeed meet with Barbara's secretary. Seated in cushioned chairs, we chatter about the future of the country and how the flash cards will help American students compete better with the

Japanese. Although Gerald has assured us that The Energy will attract Barbara, that she won't be able to stop herself from coming in to meet us, this does not occur. Later Gerald explains that it doesn't matter because the secretary will transmit The Energy to Barbara when she sees her, and the effect will be the same. I am beginning to understand that The Energy spreads in the same way a virus does.

After the meeting we feel glorious from breaking another barrier of fear. We have made our presence known to the "higher ups". We tour the White House and then head home on the train victorious.

"Yes," we tell The Group, "the meeting was a big success. The Energy was so thick that it looked like fog in the room. Now Barbara will carry our special force right to President Bush!"

We are beside ourselves with excitement, and the following week when an important piece of tax legislation passes the Senate, Gerald informs us that our visit with the flash cards had something to do with it . . .

After the Barbara Bush trip Samantha schedules many more. We travel to the Connecticut, *WaldenBooks* headquarters; to the Massachusetts, *Lauriat's* offices; to *Encore Books* in Pennsylvania, and to *Barnes & Noble* in Manhattan. At each meeting the buyers shake our hands heartily, supply us with the proper forms in order to list our titles in their database, and promise that they'll consider it seriously . . . but we receive zero orders. I have invested so much of my creativity and common sense to design a viable product and I don't understand why the buyers don't see what I do. What are we doing wrong? Nevertheless, I purchase a cellular telephone and obtain an 800 number so that I will always be reachable. I even sleep with it. Samantha and I make so many calls that my bill is more than $1000 for the first two months.

One week we meet with the *Barnes & Noble* buyer for the third time. Consulting his computer, he confirms that our product, thanks to Samantha's face to face meetings with store managers, is on the shelves of eight New Jersey stores. He tells us to come back in a month. If there are sales, he will try a small order. We leave his office giddy with anticipation, and while approaching the elevators, we formulate our strategy. Over the next two weeks we proceed to send several members of The Group to those eight stores with the cash to buy our product and clear their shelves. A month later we report to the buyer for our follow-up meeting. He looks pleased with the unbeknownst to him, bogus sales and promises an order, but it never arrives. My high hopes are smashed on the pavement and I complain to Gerald about the lack of sales. He seems to understand the problem fully and explains how I am responsible for these circumstances,

"Elizabeth, you are not succeeding because you send a nonverbal message into the spiritual airwaves that you want to fail. The buyers in other states, even if they have never met you, pick this up, follow your instructions without even realizing it, and pass over your product."

Then he adds gently, "Let's see if we can reverse the negative energy coming from you with the positive energy coming from me."

With that, he volunteers to call the buyer himself. I sit there biting my nails while I watch him demand (not at all politely) that the secretary put the buyer on the phone right away because he has "something very important to tell him". Gerald extols the virtues of our flash cards and throws in a little about The Energy while he is at it. I believe that Gerald can do anything, but he doesn't get the sale either. Nonetheless, he tells me that it doesn't matter. The buyer felt The Energy and that will lead to bigger things later on . . .

Meanwhile, Samantha schedules meetings with the Canadian book chains, *Cole's* and *W. H. Smith.* In February we make an expensive and exhausting, week-long trip to Toronto. I am beginning to notice that the buyers typically have the same reaction to us. I can see it in their faces even though they try to cover it up to be polite . . .*Who the hell are these two and how did they get an appointment?* We have no sales history to show them, no marketing data, no demographics, no significant connections and no evidence of any financial support. We haven't a clue about how to structure a publishing deal let alone how the business even works. We are just two young girls excitedly chattering about a product which we have fantasized will make us millions, and our behavior broadcasts our naivete. To anyone other than ourselves and The Group members, we look like ignorant and at times rude and presumptuous fools. Although I am trying so hard to satisfy Gerald and Samantha's program, somewhere deep inside of myself I know this. Samantha usually tells the buyers that the product is flying off the shelves in New Jersey. In reality, our only significant retail sale was to a physics teacher who bought eight boxes for his class from one of the *Brentano's* stores we managed to push our way into. I feel ashamed of our presentation and the lack of significant valid data to back up our claims, but Samantha is relentless. She has her father's wisdom in her mind. *You can convince anyone to buy anything if you just make yourself excited enough about the product to get them excited.* The buyer from *Cole's* asks us to describe our discount schedule and we look at each other confused. After a pregnant pause, we cannot concoct any other reply than,

"What is a discount schedule, and what do you want ours to read . . . ?"

At the end of our trip, before boarding the plane, Samantha telephones her father, a twice daily ritual on every trip we take. She tells him about our wonderful success, how the buyers felt The Energy, and the orders for flash cards they have promised. She asks him, as always, to shake his head over the phone, to put The Energy inside of us, to protect us on the trip home. After she speaks with him I am obligated to take a turn as well; to refuse would be total betrayal. I dread these conversations. Gerald is always so warm and friendly to his daughter, but with me he is cold and stern. It is clear that he favors Samantha, even though I do everything in my power to please him. I must endure the head shaking as well, although I feel awkward and stupid about the ritual. I hear his body shaking at the other end of the line and the receiver banging against his cheek. Finally, after a few minutes he stops and I must respond as he expects. A part of me feels like a phony, that I am being submissive only to satisfy him. I despise the subservient person I have become.

"Yes, Gerald, I feel waves of lightness; my whole body is alive. Thank you so much. I feel much better now."

However, today Gerald is in the middle of a rage when we call. After shaking, he switches gears and complains,

"Everyone here is holding me back. They don't appreciate me. I don't want to wait for them to wake up any more. I'm seriously thinking of dropping the whole Group and just going ahead on my own. I can always open a hardware store to support myself."

A wave of fear passes through me. How could I survive without Gerald? My needy vulnerable self speaks with total commitment,

"Gerald, whatever you do and wherever you go, I'll always find a way to be there with you, no matter what. I love you."

In the spring Martin asks me to sign a petition from a local Westwood group working to get Ross Perot elected. I have no idea who this man is, but soon after, I see him on TV. He talks straight, telling citizens that they have a right to the true facts about how our taxes are spent. Truth? A national political hopeful is advertising Truth? Gerald is thrilled. Finally, a man who thinks like him — expose the hidden secrets of the elected officials who control and exploit the rest of us. Empower the people and give them the right to demand what's best from our legislators, our "employees". Gerald is all for this, disassembling the current failing unjust system and finding a better way. Isn't that what we are working for in The Group? Exposing and demolishing the current Program to enable higher spiritual forces to mold a better life out of the wreckage. Gerald has always told us,

"I could never be on public TV because my message is too powerful. The politicians want to stay in control. If they ever knew about The Energy they would sense the threat I represent and do the same thing to me that they did to Jesus Christ. I must build up our forces behind the scenes and find a way to sneak in through the back door."

Now Ross Perot has appeared almost magically and he seems to be in line with Gerald . . . One day Gerald has a revelation,

"It just came to me why Ross Perot is here. He didn't decide to do this; he is a man like any other. He is being used by The Energy, merely a vehicle to transmit our message. Perot is my back door!"

A few months later Perot drops out of the election. About ten of us sit around the following Saturday morning calling him stupid, coward and jerk. Then Gerald has another revelation,

"Perot has changed the minds of the people, he has done the groundwork for us by waking them up. Thanks to him they will now be receptive to our information. We do not need him to win the election. The Energy has already used him to open the doors for us. Now his work is done and it is time to step in and replace him. We will run for President!"

On that morning, the ticket of Lesser/Stavos (Carl and Mitchell) is created and we set about getting ourselves elected to the White House. Delirious ambition passes among us like a tornado as we brainstorm. Pauline, currently dating Carl, will be the First Lady. Mitchell, still intent on getting me back, points out that I "really blew it". I could have lived in the White House too if I hadn't left him six months ago. Martin supplies us with the Perot headquarters' fax numbers in all fifty states and Samantha, Mitchell and I immediately rush over to his father's shop, *Printing Today* in Bergenfield, now our official campaign headquarters, to fax press releases all over the country. Samantha, the BA in communications, is media crazy anyway. Contacting them and rubbing shoulders with celebrities and politicians is her favorite pastime. After all, Gerald believes that the higher up we go and the larger audience we reach, the more The Energy will spread. She adds several major newspapers, TV and radio stations to our fax list. Our announcement reads, *Perot has withdrawn, but hope is not lost. We know what he was trying to achieve and we can do it. The ticket of Lesser/Stavos is officially entering the race in his place. We will carry on Perot's mission!*

We fax all afternoon and by Monday we receive a few responses. UPI contacts Mitchell and interviews him on the phone. He chatters about truth, people's rights and how we are going to make it all take place. Wheels are turning and the train is moving. We are really gonna make it this time; everyone can feel it! Now we must spread Carl and Mitchell's names around so that the people become aware of our presence. We all chip in (except Gerald) to pay for buttons and bumper stickers which respectively, we wear proudly and place on our cars. The graphic design on these beautiful promotional articles uplifts us into a dizzying euphoria; we are bound to win . . . !

Mitchell hands out buttons to all of his father's printing customers and walks up and down the main street of Bergenfield shaking people's hands and introducing himself.

"Hello, I'm Mr. Mitchell Stavos. I'm going to be the next President."

And the people respond, "Oh that's wonderful, president of what?"

"Of the United States of America, of course!" he replies with a grin.

They look at him strangely, not knowing what to make of this glowing, confident young man with such a beautiful red and blue campaign button pinned to his chest.

In order to be elected we must get on the ballot, so Samantha calls Trenton to do the official investigating. One evening I return home to find her sitting on the floor of her bedroom office surrounded by xeroxes.

"What's going on?" I ask.

"I called up to find out about getting Carl and Mitchell on the ballot. In New York State we need 20,000 signatures and in New Jersey, 5,000. We have a month to get them."

"Oh, Samantha," I respond sympathetically, "that's so many, we can't possibly do it."

My business partner glares at me as if she would like to pick up a knife and stab me.

"What's the matter with you?" she hisses, "Don't you believe in The Energy?"

I shut my mouth. Even though her stubborn insistence stirs doubt in my mind, underneath I know that I am right. Over the next several weeks I watch everyone, except Gerald, scurrying about collecting signatures. Meanwhile, Carl notices a black limo with heavily tinted glass following him near his house. With the secret service watching us now, we must really be making an impression. After all of those faxes, maybe they are!

Every minute of free time we work at collecting signatures in malls, grocery stores and office buildings. One Sunday, feeling depressed and alone, I take my clipboard to the *WillowBrook Mall*, about 45 minutes from home. Embarrassed, I force myself to approach people, and after two hours I have actually obtained twenty-three signatures. People have responded in interesting ways . . .

"Anyone is better than what we've got now. I'll sign." or, "I would even vote for Batman if he ran!"

Finally, a man asks me what our platform is. Unprepared, I stammer in confusion, "What's a platform?"

"You know, what they stand for. How do they stand on abortion?"

I babble something about changing the system and walk away feeling profoundly stupid. In this moment, I realize how ridiculous it all is. We don't know what the hell we are doing, yet we exuberantly expend our time and energy to promote absolutely nothing. On my way toward the mall's exit I end up handing a Philippine woman with a baby stroller one of my photography brochures instead. This business is the only legitimate enterprise in my life, in fact, the only venture undertaken by any Group member which has ever been profitable (aside from Gerald's sessions). A week or so later the deadline for signatures passes and Perot returns to the election ballot soon thereafter. Still, our leader assures us that our efforts to carry on Perot's mission have resulted in his change of heart . . .

Although he can no longer offer her a bedroom in the White House, Carl has not given up on unifying with Pauline and one day I enter Gerald's city office to discover the two "lovers" sitting on the floor, locked in an intense embrace.

"We are going to have a wedding soon; I have decided that this will be a good experience for all of us," Gerald informs me.

I scrutinize their blissful faces and wonder how this is possible. They are always fighting and I have never seen any evidence of genuine love between them. However, as always when we are embarking on a new project, I figure that Gerald knows more than me. Wedding plans take center stage for the next several weeks; Pauline, genuinely excited, calls Virginia to inform her family; Beatrice offers her Westchester home for the reception; rings are inspected at local jewelry stores. The following month Pauline leaves Lisa in Queens and moves into Carl's New Jersey basement apartment.

The move forces Lisa to make a change too and she decides to buy a house, something she has been wanting to do for several years. On the first day out with the realtor she finds a lovely three-bedroom colonial in Bergenfield. The price is right and the next day she puts down a deposit. Although she is giving Gerald almost all of her salary in order to compete with the other girls, her father's stock investments afford her a decent down payment. However, the mortgage amounts to much more than her Queens co-op apartment expenses. Wrestling with this new financial obligation, she begins to have serious trouble making ends meet. Finally, she does her math and realizes she has to make some changes; the only place to cut back on is Gerald. When she explains this to him, he does not take it well and berates her, declaring her "unfaithful to the mission". The fact that she is going broke is evidence that she isn't trying hard enough or following his instructions, otherwise, it wouldn't be happening. Lisa knows her calculator isn't lying, but to Gerald, calculators have no validity either. The hurt she feels from the injustice of his demand that she solve this impossible equation is almost unbearable. However, for the moment she suppresses her feelings, knowing they will surely resurface later. At the same time Gerald offers to drive her home, three times a week, from his Manhattan office. Each day, after they cross the George Washington Bridge and head North on the Palisades Parkway, he suggests, ever so gently, that Lisa might enjoy giving him oral sex while he drives. After all, he really misses being with her since Laura started attending our sessions, forcing us to keep our clothes on. Gerald has been so generous to honor her with these rides that Lisa feels she can't refuse . . . Besides, she soon notices that since she has been accommodating him regularly, she is no longer selected to be publicly criticized during Group meetings.

About two months after the wedding plans begin, Samantha escorts "the bride to be" to the Paramus Park Mall to select a gown for the big day. Unable to make a decision, the girls consult our father. Surprising them both, Gerald suddenly acts like he has neither time nor concern for this topic. In a single decisive moment the dream marriage evaporates in a puff of smoke as Gerald informs a crushed Pauline,

"We put ourselves into the project so we could experience the feelings and reactions which would result. You didn't think we were really going to go through with it, did you?"

The most Samantha and I ever gain from our faithful and frequent journeys to chain book buyers is an order for five hundred pieces from a couple of Upstate New York *WaldenBooks* district managers, and a $3000 order from the *World of Science* chain in Rochester. Neither of these sales result in a reorder and much of the *WaldenBooks* merchandise is returned over the next couple of years due to their numerous store closings. I keep trying to figure out why we can't make more sales. What is it? The price, the packaging or the market? Why isn't this dream that tastes so real to all of us being fulfilled? Yet my want to succeed is so great that I refuse to give up, and each time one idea fails, another replaces it without delay. We hit educators' trade shows, first in Boston and then St. Louis. We stand in the aisles forcing expensive color flyers into the hands of the visiting teachers. Handing out flyers anywhere and everywhere is Samantha's specialty. She believes that a little bit of The Energy rubs off on each flyer, and that will bring the customers. We receive many interested smiles or "Oh that's a wonderful idea!", but after it is all over only one teacher calls our 800 line and we make a $45 sale. (The phone call costs me $10.) Brainstorming once again, we decide that we need to shoot higher. From a list of wholesalers, I randomly call Brooklyn's *Golden-Lee Distributors* to set up a meeting. One of the vice-presidents, Lee Spellman, picks up the phone. *Workman Publishing* has just come out with *Brain Quest* and sales are skyrocketing into the millions. When he hears that we have flash cards for children he becomes genuinely excited and relating to the current *Brain Quest* success, asks me if I could handle sales of a few million units over the next year. From this one question a rocket of feeling shoots through me, and for the next three days I drown in a whirlpool of ecstatic, hopeful greed. My emotions create so much internal heat that my face looks like I have a sunburn . . . I believe that this man, Mr. Spellman, represents the doorway through which our future success lies, and I conclude that if I am going to be so big, I must develop a larger product line. Therefore, I decide to expand from my three science titles to fifteen titles covering most basic courses offered in high schools. I name the series *Exambusters Study Cards*, geared for standardized test preparation (SAT, GED, MCAT, etc.)

When we finally meet, Mr. Spellman is more than positive. It's a definite winner for *Caldor's*, his largest account, but we have to make one minor change first. The package needs more color and he suggests a yellow star on the front. We leave exuberant, promising we'll be back in six months, yellow star in hand, for our *Caldor's* order.

The next several months are filled with activity. In between seeing Gerald twenty hours per week and photographing portraits and Bar-Mitzvahs, I am writing flash cards in *WordPerfect*. I put in hundreds of hours of computer time, often typing until 2:00 or 3:00 A.M. to write several of the science and math titles. Other group members volunteer for many of the remaining subjects: Carl writes English Vocabulary, Pauline — American History, Beatrice — World History, Lisa — French, and Martin — both Algebra 2/Trig. and Physics. Samantha is unable to write a title of her own, she was never a good enough student. I hire independent teachers for the remaining subjects. New packaging is also under construction. The project's costs begin to mount rapidly, but I am like a wealthy woman redecorating her house; price is the last consideration. "I want this and I want that; just give me what I want." Everything <u>feels</u> so right; I <u>know</u> it will all work out. Martin has just graduated from college with a computer graphics major. According to Gerald, he is the best artist in the county and the perfect, no, the only person to co-ordinate the package design project. It turns out that Martin isn't as experienced as he claims, yet he bills me by the hour for the time he is taking to learn his computer programs, as well as the work he is supposedly doing. His invoices begin reaching into the multi-thousands, and I feel like I am being raped. However, I can't confront him, he always has an air-tight alibi. Any mild complaints I do manage are met with vicious reproach as he criticizes me for making false and unfair accusations. I certainly can't take him off the project, that would be total treason against what has become the entire Group's mission. His sister, Samantha, is having an all-expense-paid adventure into the publishing world, but where are all of those sales she promised so sincerely as her end of the bargain? They are "just around the corner" and according to her father they would have happened sooner, if I hadn't been holding back the operation, because I "wanted to fail". In addition, I still pay Gerald more than $600 per week. Almost every day I find myself writing a check to another Sharkman: Gerald, Samantha, Martin, Samantha, Gerald, Martin, Gerald, Samantha . . . *Why must I give all of my money to the Sharkmans?* I cry inside my head. It feels as if Gerald and his two children have each placed an IV in one of my veins and are simultaneously, slowly, draining all of my blood. I hate this, but I honestly for the life of me haven't a clue how to extricate myself. *Help me please, someone, help . . .*

Faithful to our promise to Mr. Spellman, six months later we return to Golden-Lee, our briefcases filled with samples of the new box, complete with yellow star per his instruction. *Caldor's* here we come . . . However, we don't receive the reception we had anticipated. Mr. Spellman is friendly but hesitant, and instead of handing us our purchase order in accordance with our verbal agreement, he begins to make excuses — *It's not really buying season right now . . . They have too much stock in their book department . . . I think you need to gather some testimonials from students and teachers that I can present to the buyer . . . Leave a few samples and I'll pass them around . . .* I exit the meeting feeling deceived. Although his behavior was so convincing, I fear that he was always just stringing us along and never intended to buy our product. Now I am out another $2000 for the new package design he requested . . . When will we ever get a break?

My partner, in contrast, is so optimistic that I feel guilty and childish about my miserable mood,

"Oh well, we just have to keep trying. We'll hit it next time."

In fact, these days, Samantha is in her element. We have distributed thousands of flash card flyers to an eagerly waiting public and she has just completed her first book, Volume I of *The Dark Powers Trilogy*, a science fiction fantasy novel based on characters she created playing *Dungeons and Dragons* in college. The story is juvenile and poorly written but she invests more than $3000 to hire a local artist to create a painting for the book's cover. The cover art work is superior to many others on the *Barnes & Noble* science-fiction shelf and Samantha sees a bright future for her creation. With her project, my flash cards and several books the other group members are working on, she envisions a prosperous and influential publishing company about to be born. Therefore, she reasons, to protect us from potential lawsuits, we must incorporate. In fact, while we are at it, we had better incorporate *Expressions Photography* as well. She sets an appointment with Alan Brown, the Sharkman family lawyer, to arrange things. I hesitate. Although my ego feels a rush from the fantasy of becoming a corporate officer, I know nothing of corporate law and I am not as sure as she that this is truly necessary. However, Samantha pushes on with her father cheering behind her. "You have to step out and make a commitment." The corporate paper signing day arrives, and before our scheduled meeting with the lawyer, I sit on Gerald's couch shaking. I don't know why, but I hesitate about going through with it. Gerald, disgusted with my weak personality, rises up to chastise me as Lisa, Beatrice and Samantha look on. Glaring down, he accuses me of "wanting to fail like always". I am no match for him and less than an hour later I obediently report to the lawyer's office with Samantha at my side . . . I select the name *Flash Blasters* for our new corporation because, with our innovative products and ideas stemming from Gerald's Group, we are going to "blast through the conventional lies and teach the world a new way to live".

Receding from my internal conflict, my brain is sluggish, as if I have been drugged. I can't think clearly; I feel pressure in my chest and must allow Samantha to answer the lawyer's questions for me. Mr. Brown asks,

"Who will be the vice-president?"

Samantha replies, "I will."

"Who will be president?"

"Elizabeth will."

"How will the shares be divided?"

"I will get ten and Elizabeth will get ten. The rest are reserved for the investors we will be looking for."

My brainwashed thoughts remind me of how generous Samantha is to let me be the president instead of her . . . With the commitment finalized, my former hesitation is soon replaced by a lift of excitement from the anticipation of our new venture. After the meeting her eyes sparkle as she explains,

"Now we are really partners in both businesses. You don't have to pay me a salary anymore. We will split the hours and the profit in half. We will build up the photography business really big and then sell it. When we do, you can get back your original start-up capital investment of $66,000 from the sale."

Because she has promised me my fair share sometime in the future, I can't find any way to argue with her logic.

January to December 1993

One winter day, we receive a call from the Bergen County, Ross Perot organization. Although he has lost the election, his support group has not given up, and *United We Stand America — UWSA,* is forming local chapters in each of the fifty states. Samantha decides to attend. The grassroots citizen's group will work first at reaching local government officials, and then state and federal politicians. A new mission set in a larger playing field has been identified for our group.

The local *UWSA* chapter is led by a dedicated young woman named Hilary. In the past year, she has spent hundreds of hours and much of her own money to support Perot's candidacy. At that first organizational meeting, Samantha makes a silent wish that she will be in charge of the county — she wants Hilary's position. Our photography studio soon becomes a meeting place for the *UWSA* group. With several strong egos present, there is discord among the members as they struggle to invent a new system where there had been none before. Not everyone agrees with Hilary. Without drawing attention to herself, Samantha encourages the conflict behind Hilary's back. A couple of months later, things came to a head at one of these "core group" meetings. Suddenly, almost everyone seems dissatisfied with Hilary although I do not understand why. They have no better way; they simply oppose her. Finally a vote is taken and she is voted out almost unanimously. She leaves in tears. After that evening, she changes her phone number and no one ever hears from her again.

Immediately, Samantha throws herself in as "Interim Coordinator". She organizes a monthly county meeting at the Hackensack *Riverside Square Mall.* With Samantha in charge, Gerald encourages all the members of The Group to become involved. Nora, Pauline, Carl, Martin, myself and even occasionally Gerald, attend meetings. We form an active telephone tree. Samantha puts Martin in charge of data-basing the names of the few hundred county members. She sets up committees and makes sure that each of the ninety meeting attendees join one. We are instructed by the Texas *UWSA* headquarters to conduct an official election for county officers, but no one runs against Samantha, so she wins the official title of County Coordinator by default. Bergen County is divided into seven regions and each region contains ten towns. Directly under Samantha, I volunteer as regional coordinator for our area. Nora, Pauline, Carl and Martin serve directly below me as town coordinators. Beatrice, my mother and Bess, New York residents, join the *UWSA* New York State chapter.

One Saturday, Lisa brings her visiting parents from Oregon to The Group. For a few hours they sit at the back of the den looking uncomfortable. At dinner that evening her mother, with some measure of distress, speaks out,

"I don't like what's going on in there even though I don't understand it."

Her father quickly rushes to his daughter's defense,

"Come on, Lisa is too smart. I know she wouldn't do anything stupid."

Lisa stops dead, her fork in mid-air and ponders, *Would I?*

In the past ten years with Gerald, she has spent more than $100,000. *What have I gained from the investment?* she asks herself for the very first time.

The following Monday Lisa makes a life-changing decision. Instead of participating in The Group, she forces herself to observe. Always unhappy about the outrageous costs and the constant fighting, she begins to question what is really going on in this small, intensely involved, group of adults. She decides to acknowledge the contradictions which she had previously dismissed. There was the day that Gerald criticized her for taking her cat to the vet. He told her that the cat didn't need shots, he only needed The Energy to protect him from disease. As fate would have it, a few moments later Martin had entered the den from the adjoining kitchen and asked where the cat carrier was so that he could take the Sharkman's cat, B.J., to the vet . . . Then there is the health insurance he forbids us to purchase while his entire family is covered by *Blue Cross* . . . Over the next several weeks, she becomes aware that she is terrified of Gerald and figures out that he has set this up on purpose to control her. She asks herself provocative questions, such as, *What if The Energy doesn't really exist? Is there another explanation for the phenomena in this room — the auras we all see, the bodies jolting?* Once asked, she sets her mind to figuring out the answers . . . She observes him towering over me, Bess or Laura when we disagree with him, glaring at us and often physically throwing us from the room. The failure of the Lesser/Stavos election ticket, the lack of revenue from her *New Life Design* business, the misery she feels competing with Pauline and Bess to spend the most hours with Gerald or to be the one he will choose to have sex with today . . . She begins to realize that her life is not turning out to be the wonderful paradise Gerald promised. Our group activities have generated acute excitement and distraction but none of them — Samantha and Bess's concerts, the books currently in progress, my flash cards — have ever borne any fruit. When one enterprise fails, Gerald either blames the participants for holding back and wanting to fail, or finds some explanation of the personal and group growth which that activity has fostered just by the fact that we attempted it. As Lisa forces herself to step back from the emotions, fantasies and diversions of the moment, to look at the big picture, she begins to see a group of fifteen hopeful immature naive fools creating fantasies in their heads and then spending thousands of dollars to try to make those lies come true, and they never do . . . Lisa realizes that she does not want to be a part of this circus anymore and she begins the process of emotional withdrawal. Strangely, no one even notices that she has changed her intention. Of everyone I should be sensitive to her, because of our inseparable college days, but that was years ago and since then The Group has come to supersede our friendship. These days, I hardly even notice her. Besides, I am knee deep in my own conflict.

Determined to find her way out of the maze, it takes her eight months to disconnect the ten years of wiring binding her to this incestuous circle which has steadily evolved to represent her only legitimate family, in fact, her whole life. Despite the fact that she is working fifteen or more hours of overtime per week, on top of her full-time schedule, she is slipping financially. Paying Gerald and her mortgage takes her entire paycheck and overtime is all there is left to buy food and other essentials. When she finally works up the courage to complain, Samantha and Gerald supply her with their solution. Pauline will move in with her for income and personal growth. However, Lisa can never agree to this. It has taken her too many years to get away from Pauline, a person with whom she was never happy, and this self-serving insensitive suggestion pushes her over the edge. A week later she announces that she is leaving. She has finally completed the necessary emotional work to separate herself; she realizes that if she had fled any sooner, she wouldn't have been able to find a reason to get up in the morning. Completely out of touch with Lisa's needs and feelings, I can't comprehend her decision. She is one of us, a member of the team; how can she just walk out? We are in this for life; there is nowhere else to go in this world. Like an unexpected death, I experience shock. Gerald is determined to change her mind and instructs all of us, her comrades, to visit her house, to wake her up to what she is walking away from. For the next two weeks, we all take different evenings. Lisa allows us into her home because she feels that if she really believes in her newly found principles, she ought to stand up for them. We lecture passionately about her commitment to *New Life Design* and its potential profit. We speak of the French flash cards she had just written and the millions of copies which will soon sell worldwide.

At my assigned meeting, I sit stunned as Lisa patiently explains why she is truly leaving. As if she is speaking a foreign language, the sounds coming from her lips make no sense to my brain. It is like watching a TV show with no volume and I scream back at her, trying to bridge the impossible gap between us with fervent reminders of The Energy, helpless to create a light powerful enough to find her in this thick fog, to lead her back where she belongs . . . Finally, she shares her hope and desire that we will still be friends, but I counter,

"No, that will be impossible if you leave The Group."

She looks genuinely disappointed and perplexed; I don't know why I have declared this, but I know it must be so.

Pauline and Bess, visiting together an evening later, remind her intimately and intensely,

"You know there are no people out there that you can trust. We are your only friends. Without us you will have no one. You will be alone forever."

We all speak of her years of investment to master the exclusive sensitivity to The Energy which only we, the few chosen ones, possess . . . but then she floors us,

"I don't believe in The Energy anymore."

What? How could this be? She has become possessed by the dead world; she is beyond reach. We don't understand how this has happened, but we realize that we must let her go and we tell her so. We only know one thing for sure, her fate is sealed and her future doomed . . .

A week goes by and Gerald, unable to accept defeat, asks her to visit his office one more time. Lisa agrees; she feels strong. After all, she has survived the week of enraged tirades, the threats of a destroyed future and her friends' passionately delivered speeches about the necessity of The Energy. She will find the strength to handle Gerald. When Lisa arrives at his office, she observes that he has cleared everyone else out. This is not normal for a noon meeting when there are generally about five people. He greets her with a friendly relaxed smile and asks how she is. She tells him she is fine and sits down. With benign behavior, he attempts to coax her into admitting that she has missed us and made a mistake. She lets him know politely that her decision is firm. Frustrated, he becomes more passionate, extolling the virtues of The Energy and the personal investment she has made to be a part of our closely knit team of privileged warriors. How could she be so stupid to throw that away? Still, she maintains her position. Finally his face changes to demonic rage. He shrieks at her,

"If you don't come back, your life will be worthless. You will fail at everything you attempt. You will lose your job. Without The Energy, you will die impoverished, friendless and soon."

Lisa is outraged. The veil has been lifted from her eyes and reality rushes in all too explicitly. Gerald is banking on the fact that she still believes these outrageous fabrications; therefore, his declarations would terrify her into returning to the fold. Until today, she has lived in a world where fear prevails over logic, where free choice, critical thinking and objective reasoning is consistently short-circuited by Gerald's strategic phobia indoctrination. She loathes him for this cruel manipulation — exploitation of the fears he has methodically implanted and fertilized in her mind, his invisible weapons against her. Nonetheless, on the surface Lisa maintains her composure. She permits him to play out his routine and when the hour is complete, calmly hands him a final $40 check, shakes his hand

and states that she still cares about everyone, but she isn't coming back. She exits the office where she has spent thousands of dollars for "therapy" and hundreds of hours competing with her "friends" for the honor of pleasing him sexually. She reflects wistfully upon the years of precious time she has wasted ingesting Gerald's fanatical warnings of certain doom destined for those who continue to screw up and refuse to follow The Energy, lies she has finally erased from her mind after ten years of blind submission. She closes the door softly behind her and emerges, a free woman, into the spring sunlight of 71st Street between Park and Lexington Avenues.

A few weeks after Lisa's exit, Samantha and I drive up to the *WaldenBooks* headquarters for the third time. We meet with yet another buyer who promises, once again, to place that opening order we seek so desperately, and once again, we believe her. The scene following our "successful meetings" has always been the same. The two of us return to Gerald's den, jumping up and down exuberantly, reporting all of the wonderful things the buyer said about the product and the huge orders they have promised to place, which inevitably never come. On this day, as usual, we rush home quickly to replay our favorite scene. However, when we enter, we discover Gerald, Martin, Beatrice and Pauline drowning in a cloud of gloom. Gerald tells us why and I detect fear in his eyes.

"About an hour ago I went upstairs for a moment when I heard a cry and a thud. Ben fell, his back legs collapsing under him."

We notice that Gerald's black Labrador is lying on the floor, breathing heavily and in obvious distress. Samantha and I immediately shift from our previous elation to soberness and Gerald instructs us to gather around him and lay our hands on him. We touch him gently while Gerald holds Ben's head in his lap and starts his head shaking to help the dog. The thought that he is dying runs through our terrified minds, but Gerald senses our thoughts and commands us to eliminate all negativity, to force ourselves into a positive place <u>immediately</u>. The gentle caress of our voices and hands over the next fifteen minutes does nothing to encourage Ben to stand up and walk again. Aware that we are failing, now Gerald changes to a stern tone, commanding Ben to stop "playing bullshit games" and come back to life. Ben just groans. As other Group members visit later that day, they are told that Ben can't walk because he is holding back The Energy in his body. We must all focus our energy on him so that we can help release his blockage. After all, Ben is the most intelligent dog on the planet because he has been saturated with Gerald's energy for the last twelve years. He is a special part of our mission.

Returning to my office later that afternoon, my mind returns to its concerns over our next business move. However, the ring of my phone interrupts my pondering. A man is cold-calling from a brokerage firm in Paramus.

"No, I don't have any money to invest," I tell him, "I am putting it all into my publishing business."

The man begins to ask me questions about this enterprise. Normally I would blow him off, not wanting to waste time in idle chatter with a stranger. However, today for some reason I decide to answer him, describing the flash cards I am having such a hard time getting to the retail shelf. He asks me if I would mind if a friend of his calls me, a man who has just retired from *Western Publishing* (publishers of "Little Golden Books" among others) and might have some advice for us. I don't mind . . .

A week later his friend, Bob Doscher, calls me from Pennsylvania. I describe our product and he likes what he hears. We agree to meet in Miami Beach the following month at the June 1993 *American Book Association* trade show (now called *Book Expo America*, the largest industry show in the world) at which I have just taken a booth for $1600 . . .

At the show, Bob is encouraging but tells us that we need professional reps to make sales for us.

"What's a rep?" I ask.

"A guy that sells your stuff to the stores," he replies.

"You mean these angels exist!?"

That afternoon, he introduces us to the top group in the Ohio territory, Terry Wybel Associates. They agree to take us on but only if we drop our retail price from $12.95 to $9.95. Samantha is enraged. She refuses to give in, declaring indignantly that the rep simply doesn't understand the value of our product. I however, agree with Terry, and I want desperately to hire them. Samantha, throws in my face that she is now my legal partner, and blocks me with no negotiation.

During the five-day trade show Samantha debuts her preferred method of product marketing, a sure-fire strategy to claw ourselves into significance. She promises much greater results than Terry Wybel Assoc. ever could deliver. This consists of approaching celebrities (visiting authors signing their recently published books) and handing them a "gift", a box of our flash cards. By exposing our products to those who occupy a lofty position in the hierarchy of our society, she feels that the word will spread and big things will happen naturally. First on the list is Oprah Winfrey, a guest at the trade show. Samantha takes a Polaroid picture with her and then slips her a box of *Spanish in a Flash*. Oprah thanks her politely. Later that day she accosts the body guard of Great Britain's former prime minister, Margaret Thatcher, as Mrs. Thatcher's entourage escorts her into an author signing. The guard, slightly miffed, nevertheless receives a box of *Physics in a Flash*. That night on the phone, Gerald praises her highly for this courageous action on behalf of The Energy. After Samantha, I take my turn with him.

"Gerald," I ask timidly, "I don't understand; isn't it rude to push the product on these people? They don't seem to want it."

Ever-patient, he explains, "No, we must do this. The people are dead and if we don't force The Energy, which will make them alive, down their throats like medicine, they will never know its benefits."

I am not comfortable with his explanation, but as usual, I remind myself that he has access to higher information which I am not yet ready to understand. I feel stupid and obnoxious but compelled to follow Samantha's lead. The following day I stand in line to receive an autographed copy of actor Leslie Nielsen's newly published book. Once in front of him, I present him with a box of *French in a Flash*. He looks at me strangely but accepts it with a smile.

All told, the Miami trade show costs me over $4000, but we only write about $300 in sales. About two months later, as we continue our current rate of almost zero sales, Samantha finally agrees to lower our retail price to $9.95 and give the sales reps a try. Within a few months we retain six more teams which cover bookstores in all fifty states. It's full steam ahead at *Flash Blasters Inc.* With all of these reps, the big time is surely not too far down the road!

Nevertheless, with the new $9.95 price I am losing even more than before. I restructure the package and find a new printer, but the best deal I can work out is $4.50 per box, providing I print one thousand at a time of each title. I would have to put out $67,500, which I barely have. With about $70,000 now remaining of my inheritance I would bankrupt myself. Besides, how are we going to sell 15,000 pieces when the last two years' sales combined were 1,800 pieces? However, Samantha, the eternal optimist, has confidence in our future sales and regarding my conflict, she knows the answer as well. Spend someone else's money; find an investor!! I don't want to. There are too many unknowns and I would never be able to live with myself if I lost another person's capital. In contrast, Samantha is convinced.

"That's how all businesses do it," she exclaims with total confidence . . . and she knows who she'll call first, someone she introduced herself to in our Miami Beach hotel elevator. A man in a wheelchair who confided in her that he was semi-retired with a few million bucks to blow on some appealing entrepreneurial venture. Between the lobby and the fourth floor, Samantha had succeeded in capturing his interest in our future plans for the company — laced with a dollop of nonsense too, such as, "We have orders coming from all the major book chains." Samantha has developed the expert talent of enticing an innocent bystander with important sounding projections which have, in reality, no facts to back them up. We schedule a meeting with her future investor at a restaurant in Central New Jersey. Although I feel more than a little uncomfortable about our new scheme, nevertheless, I follow my partner as I always have. I know of no other alternative, and my overwhelming compulsion to bring my product to the market supercedes any shred of common sense which might still remain in my brain. The night before our big meeting, we sit up late together in Samantha's bedroom fantasizing about our glorious future with the product once we have obtained Mr. Investor's capitol to really go "big time". She asks me what I want to do when I make my first million and the energy of this vision lifts me, even though in some remote corner of my mind I can't truly believe it . . . The next day we present our business plan to Samantha's contact. It includes sales projections of 500,000 units for the 1994-95 season. We paint the picture of a huge publishing company, even describing the decor and color scheme of each office in our main headquarters. We will flood the retail market and public awareness with advertising, local contests, buttons, tee shirts and joint ventures with McDonald's and children's charities. The necessary start-up investment is $850,000. When he hears this, poor Mr. Investor almost falls out of his wheelchair! Trying to be polite, he asks if we might be able to take less. Samantha replies, after several moments of serious pondering, that we would be willing to downsize our plans temporarily and accept $250,000 if we had to. He promises he will earnestly consider our proposal, words which leave us more than a little hopeful. My partner, satisfied that we have accomplished what we set out to do, signals for the check. When the waitress returns our change, we realize that she has apparently miscalculated, leaving us $20 more than we deserve.

"What a gift!" Samantha exclaims with confidence once we are safely inside her car. "This is proof that money will soon come from the investor too!"

It would never occur to us to return the money to the establishment. After all, Gerald has taught us about things like this. "Just take the gift; you deserve it. Their mistake is their problem and not your responsibility to correct, so don't waste your time mothering other people. They are grown up and can take care of themselves."

An hour later, once again, we report the meeting's big success to Gerald. Yet, a week later, Mr. Investor excuses himself from the deal, explaining sincerely, "Although it seems very promising, my daughter just asked me for $30,000 to purchase a restaurant franchise. Unfortunately, I really must focus my available funds in her direction."

The wheelchair-investor failure propels me into a deep depression. However, Samantha throws herself in with renewed energy. She has become the queen of "fake it 'til you make it" and she injects so much energy and enthusiasm into her act that uneducated parties actually believe her extraordinary sales projections, that is until they see the facts on paper. I keep trying to tell people the truth. I don't want to misrepresent the sales history of our company. She scolds me, coaching me on how to climb the ladder of success,

"People want to feel excited. We create that with <u>big</u> plans and <u>big</u> projections. You are too serious and passive. We will never get an investor at this rate."

Our next victim is one of our photography customers, Lynn Brignola. With two young children, she has a natural interest in education and agrees to meet with us at her husband's office. (He's in the construction business.) By now the investor's price tag has been reduced to $500,000, for which they will own one third of the company. Samantha and I will own the other two-thirds because it was our idea and we have done all the leg work — handing out flyers at the trade shows and traveling to Toronto, etc. During the next few weeks, we actually get through two meetings with the Brignolas, but for the third meeting, they ask us to bring our sales orders. The thick manila folder filled with orders generated from our reps in the fifty states inspires confidence in our hearts; today, they will surely bite. Sitting in their waiting room, I am jittery with anticipation. I don't want to screw it up. As always, I call Gerald on my cell phone for reinforcement. He tells me to stay still and focus, and I hear the phone banging against his ear as he shakes his head. A wave of calm passes over me. He pauses and asks if I feel better. I tell him that I do. He replies softly with what sounds to me like paternal pride,

"OK, now go and be a success."

Soon after, we are ushered into the Brignola offices. After some introductory chit-chat, they open our file; the first order is for five pieces from a mom-and-pop store in Ohio — $25. Other orders total $35 and $50. All told, we are able to present them with about $1000 worth of business. Nevertheless, our sales projections for the next quarter are $625,000. The Brignolas appease us; they will "think about it", but a week later we follow up with Lynn to obtain our rejection.

During the year, there are many others: Neil, president of *Sulzberger and Graham*, a publisher of study guides for medical and law students; Ronald, a former New York City publishing executive; Irwin, president of *Bookazine*, distributors to *Barnes & Noble*; Ted, the multimillionaire, cosmetics mogul from Long Island; Hal, Ted's friend, a loan shark who makes his second home in Atlantic City; Angelo, owner of a large magazine publishing company and former Yonkers, New York mayor; Bob, a Yonkers real estate entrepreneur; Jonathan, president of *Queue Publishing*, an educational software company; Lee, president of *Golden-Lee Book Distributors*; Chris & Chris, professional investors in just about anything which appears profitable . . . Wasted hours of business plan preparation, meetings, expensive lunches and hundreds of dollars worth of free samples . . . All dead ends; each prospect another miserable ride on the hopefulness — disappointment loop.

Impossibly dedicated to creating the future success of the flash cards purely from my own will, I am beginning to feel like a gerbil on a wheel. While Samantha spends every Sunday with her father, I usually collapse on the couch for most of the afternoon, exhausted from the week's stress and the breathing problem which keeps me up most nights. These past few months, my asthma is starting to scare me and one Sunday, safe from Samantha's scrutiny, I finally decide to defy Gerald's orders, break the ever-present invisible wall of resistence, and visit a doctor. I share this with no one; if he finds out, there will be hell to pay.

I have no idea what my problem is and I tell the doctor that I have a cold; I am always blowing my nose. He corrects me. I have allergies and the asthma is from a constant post nasal drip which fills my lungs. He gives me a yellow inhaler, rescue medicine to arrest muscular spasms during an asthma attack. The medicine relieves me in an emergency but does nothing to stop the post nasal drip.

As the months pass, my symptoms worsen. My period, which has never been regular, stops completely. Brain fog surrounds me like a cloud, and I pass through each day as if walking in a dream. I have more and more trouble eating. Every time my stomach tightens with hunger, my thoughts deny that I need nourishment. *Food is not your priority. Just keep working. You must make the flash cards succeed. They are the key to your future.*

Instead, I drink another cup of coffee; I'm up to eight cups a day. Gerald claims that we really shouldn't have to eat or sleep anyway.

"The molecules in our bodies originally came from stars. We are made of stars, and stars are made of energy. Well, energy doesn't need to eat and sleep in order to survive, and neither should we. If we weren't so hooked to our crazy training, our bodies would adjust to making their own food just like the sun does. I hardly sleep at all anymore, maybe just an hour or so at night. I can go without food for many, many hours without any problems. Once you break The Program, everything changes."

I eat one meal a day, usually late at night; I never seem to be able to find the time during the day. Working and attending Gerald's groups are much more of a pressing priority. Between the cost of Gerald's therapy and the never-ceasing expenses to get the flash cards off the ground, my inheritance is quickly dwindling. If I do not maintain my businesses, I will have nothing to pay for food and rent. I know that I could not trust my mother to take me in if I were really in trouble, and that is the last place I would want to be anyway . . . The other people in my life, The Group, would perceive me as a failure if I fell apart physically, emotionally or financially. After all, we all know that The Energy brings only good things to the people who faithfully follow it. Deep down I shudder to think of falling so low that I would ever need to ask them for help. Ironically, at the same time, I anchor myself emotionally to the sense of family brought about by our constant group activities. In my other mind I am convinced that these people really do care about me and depend on my presence and participation. After all, look at how much time and energy I have given them! I believe that somewhere, somehow, these feelings would surface should I ever really be in trouble . . . Nevertheless, terrifying fear-riddled visions of myself penniless and on the street plague me. I cannot alter the negative direction my life has taken, no matter how hard I try, and I do try . . . These days, my energy and ability to swim against the current are waning and my physical well-being and emotions are rapidly and consistently failing. Over the past ten years my feelings about the future of my life have changed drastically. What started in 1984 as confusion, when I dropped my ambition to enter medical school, is now passing through stages of anxiety and fear, and rapidly approaching a state of genuine helplessness and terror. Life every day, every hour, is becoming purely a matter of survival.

UWSA is all we talk about in The Group, and in June, Samantha suggests that I join the "Say No to *NAFTA*" committee. A couple of times a month I drive down to the Edison, N.J. *UWSA* headquarters to meet with the other members of this statewide team. Our goal is to educate all of our N.J. politicians. Once enlightened, we hope they will vote against it. I decide to organize a group meeting with my local Representative, Marge Roukema, and on Friday evening, July 16, 1993, about fifty people attend. For over an hour, *UWSA* members passionately enlighten her about the potential evils of *NAFTA*. At the end of the meeting, as pictures are snapped with Marge and the meeting's coordinators, Gerald approaches her. Gently placing his hand on her back, he whispers in her ear softly,

"Don't forget that we depend on you to bring the truth to the rest of the government."

While he speaks, he shakes his hand ever so slightly to make sure that The Energy goes into her body . . .

The following day dawns, Saturday, July 17, a day of victory for Gerald's group. Governor Jim Florio is coming up for re-election this November. *UWSA* members appear to be a viable source of future votes and Samantha has been able to convince Florio's office to agree to a meeting with the Bergen County *UWSA* officers. In fact, the big event is scheduled to take place in Gerald's dining room and adjoining living room at 1:00 P.M. today! Hours before, we all powwow, in awe of what is about to happen. Gerald delivers his pep talk,

"People, this is what we have been working for all of these years, to be able to capture the ear of a politician who has influence over large groups of people, to be able to get him to experience, and maybe even understand, The Energy."

Between 12:00 and 12:30, the rest of the *UWSA* members begin to arrive and I greet them in front of Gerald's house. When most are safely inside, a white *Mercedes* appears at the end of the block. I recognize the driver, Judy Carlone, the Bergenfield town coordinator. I have spoken with her on the phone several times because, as regional coordinator, I am her superior in the *UWSA* hierarchy and she answers to me. She passes the house and parks. Locking her car, she strides toward me with a confident grin and greets me with a kiss on the cheek. I immediately wonder why she is acting so friendly, I barely know her, and then I figure it out . . . *She's Italian, that must be why!*

Secret service arrives right after Judy and at 12:45, Florio's black limo finally appears. Gerald's tiny living room is crowded with about twenty eager members seated on folding chairs. They face the dining room where Samantha, Martin, Gerald and I sit, right next to the Governor. Mitchell is positioned on Gerald's stairs at the back of the living room with a video camera, anxious to record this momentous event on film. Florio's primary agenda is to encourage us to vote for him. Therefore, his speech recounts all of the positive things he has done for our state. He remains standing and speaks passionately, gripping the back of one of Gerald's dining room chairs. Ten minutes into the meeting, Gerald, seated directly in front of him, begins to shake his head slowly. Florio doesn't know what to make of this and he is clearly more than a little uncomfortable. He pretends to ignore Gerald, who is now picking up speed, and continues his speech. The secret service men observe this weird display suspiciously. In contrast, we Group members are so used to Gerald's habits that it all feels perfectly normal to us. In a little while, Bess raises her hand. When Florio calls on her, she suggests gently, yet subtly condescending,

"Governor, you appear tense. We are all equals here. Why don't you sit down on the same level as the rest of us?"

Gerald speaks up immediately to support her.

"You see, Governor, the way society is set up, it enforces a program which demands politicians to stand above us like teachers and superiors. Citizens view themselves as children who must look up to you. Wouldn't it be better if we all cooperated instead?"

Florio appears terribly flustered and I pity him. I sense that he is not equipped to deal with this unique type of a challenge to his personal habits and innermost intentions. So, under the pressure, he decides to yield and seats himself hesitantly. The meeting lasts about half an hour in total. At the end, we present the Governor with a box of items we have collected from our various Group entrepreneurial enterprises. They include: copies of Samantha's and Gerald's books, a box of *Physics in a Flash*, Bess' music demo tape, brochures advertising Martin's graphic design business and Mitchell's printing shop. Perhaps we can turn Governor Florio into a customer! In front of Gerald's house I shoot a couple of rolls before the Governor finally drives away in his limo. After the meeting, Gerald reviews the day's events with us and Bess receives The Group's accolades for having had the courage to tell Florio the truth. I envy her for that and for another, much more ancient issue, the fact that she managed to fill the role of Gerald's mistress where I failed. Amidst the conflict-ridden relationship I have had with him, an old familiar voice, dating back to our first meetings in Dr. Rogers' office, still emerges frequently, often when I am alone driving my car. It insists that Gerald should really be mine; I mustn't settle for less than the best. It is only a matter of time until I find the means to make it so; I haven't tried hard enough. Good things are worth waiting for . . . Sometimes I argue, trying to contradict this voice's insistence with logic of my own, that I despise Gerald and how he treats me, but its will is stubborn and won't release me from its so far impossible demands. Other times I brainstorm, trying to cook up the means to satisfy this unrequited longing. There is still a large part of me that is totally fascinated with our leader, a part which believes that I, above all others, deserve to win the most advanced man on the planet for my own.

Shaking myself out of my introspection, I catch the tail-end of Gerald's speech as he proclaims,

"Now Florio will win the election in November because he has listened to us and The Energy is inside of him."

About ten days later, gubernatorial candidate Christie Whitman makes her own journey to Gerald's home to meet with the same group of *UWSA* members. The

Governor Florio and me after the meeting.

meeting is fast and uneventful. Whitman stands off in a corner, speaks and departs. There is no interaction with any of the audience and Gerald does not shake his head. In November, Florio loses the election to Christie Whitman.

In the months to come, the *NAFTA* committee meets with Rep. Robert Torricelli in his Hackensack office. Our two New Jersey senators, Bill Bradley and Frank Lautenberg, receive our small but dedicated group in their respective Newark offices. At the conclusion of the latter visit, I make an offer to Lautenberg's secretary to organize a statewide members' meeting featuring him as guest speaker. A week later, his office accepts. For the next couple of months I throw myself into the task of organizing this meeting. After drawing so few participants to hear Marge Roukema, I am determined to increase the attendance, so I double my efforts, sending flyers and press releases through every channel open to me in the *UWSA* organization. I mail invitations to the offices of every state representative in New Jersey, the press, and TV and radio stations countywide. The meeting is structured as a question and answer session with the Senator, and a mediator is required to select the questions and control the behavior of the audience. The only obvious choice, in my opinion, is Gerald. However, during the next couple of weeks there is terrible unrest among the non-Group *UWSA* members. Apparently, they <u>absolutely</u> do not want him as mediator and I genuinely don't understand why. They appear hostile and angry but like many people, are at the same time too polite to communicate what they truly feel and why. Samantha attempts to make peace, and they eventually reveal that because of his head shaking at the Florio meeting, they fear a repeat performance in front of Senator Lautenberg. Gerald takes their reaction as a high compliment,

"This just proves how advanced we are; all of those people are too small to handle the intensity of The Energy. They are afraid of its power."

Samantha assures the members that her father will comply, and they finally give in. On November 4, 1993 about three hundred *UWSA* members from all over the state fill the Ridgefield Community Center to capacity. Gerald behaves himself; he does not shake his head at the meeting.

My name is Judith Carlone. A native of Hoboken, N.J., I was raised in a middle-class Italian-American neighborhood. I am forty-four years old, married with no children, spiritual by nature, and appreciative and loving of all animals. My indoctrination into Catholicism was the foundation and the springboard that facilitated my spiritual growth. I discovered at a very young age that we have little control over navigating our lives, and that it is our personal relationship with God which lights the way to our salvation, not the repetitive rituals of religion. I can still remember the first time I felt the Holy Spirit. It happened in church one day after Sunday School. I sat quietly in the back row. To me this was the best seat in the house, especially after mass. The view was spectacular. I watched the many rows of bright red flickering candles, eagerly delivering the prayers that brought them to life. The sun penetrated its rays through huge stained glass windows, illuminating the altar with vibrant color, while faint clouds of frankincense hovered in the air. I love the church; its silent atmosphere always helped me to get in touch with myself. Enchanted by this visual feast, I asked God to help me remember the new prayers I had just learned in catechism class. The nuns were tough and demanded that we know all that was required of us, inside and out. The fear they instilled in me created performance anxiety, and I needed help. As I looked up at the giant crucifix suspended above the altar, I suddenly felt an internal lift. Something invisible had entered my body and was pulling me upward, filling me with a sensation of love and ecstasy. In that moment I knew God truly existed. He showed himself to me. He let me know He was with me, and that with Him, I could do anything. The feeling was fragile and left quickly. He added something to me that day, something special. I'll always be thankful for that experience, and the memory of it, for the rest of my life.

I am involved in the Real Estate and Insurance business and run a small agency in town. I never had any interest in politics and never voted in any of the elections. Politics always seemed to be a corrupt system. The intentions of the candidates were clearly evident, and the games they played to get elected had little effect in seducing my vote. However, all of that changed in 1992 after seeing Ross Perot on TV. He spoke the truth and sparked my interest. He uncovered the buried love I had for my country and gave me hope that the United States could heal its immorality and become a better place to live. I was so impressed that someone had the courage to speak the truth and uncover the lies that were going on in our system, that I registered to vote and joined the local chapter of his grassroots movement, United We Stand America. This is where I first met a woman named Elizabeth Burchard.

The week following the Lautenberg meeting, Ross Perot debates Vice President Al Gore on The Larry King Show. Judy Carlone invites about ten of us to her house to watch the show on her big screen TV. I arrive earlier than the rest and she suggests that I sit at her kitchen table while she prepares the munchies she will serve later. All of a sudden she seats herself across from me. Probing with considerable surety, Judy commences to make some very direct statements about my personality and behavior.

I have always been perceptive about people. Even though I don't know Elizabeth very well, for some reason, I can't hold back sharing my feelings with her. I feel driven to break the ice, and ask her permission to be frank.

"Would you mind if I tell you something personal? I know what your problem is; you are a little girl and not a woman; you are looking for a parent, someone to take care of you; you perform to get approval from others; you look to the outside for validation because you don't know who you are; you don't have an identity."

I don't know why, but I feel strangely separate from any normal social response such as, *My private feelings are none of your business.* or, *You don't really know me. What right do you have to judge?* I do not defend myself, explain or make excuses. Instead, I allow my mind to absorb Judy's observations without analyzing, interfering, modifying or interpreting; I leave it alone. Pausing for a moment, she catches herself, apologizing,

"You know, I am getting very personal and I have only just met you. I am sorry. I hope I am not offending you."

Without thought I respond automatically, "No. If you are telling me the truth and this is something that will help me, then I want to hear it. It is OK. Please continue."

Judy is direct. I am fascinated by this ability above all else. Intuitively, because honesty seems to be her priority, not fashioning statements to avoid people disliking her, I trust her and value her opinions. For the remainder of my visit I am constantly aware of her presence. In fact, to me she is the only person in the room. However, soon after I leave her house that evening, her comments slip from my mind . . .

Later in November our *UWSA* chapter stages a Walk-a-Thon to raise money. Samantha, Nora, Pauline, Judy, and I organize the event, scheduled to take place at a local park. On the big day about thirty members show up ready to walk for the cause, but I can only think of one thing, where is Judy? Finally she arrives. It's strange, I know so little about her, and yet just the sight of her makes me feel warm and safe. So, at the conclusion of the event I linger behind and hesitating like a school girl waiting for the perfect moment to approach an idolized teacher, I finally work my way over to her and sit down. I want something from her but I don't know what and I don't know why. I ask if she would like to go for lunch and she agrees. We jump into her car and head for *Kenny Rogers Roasters* in Englewood. At the table, over our platters filled with chicken, mashed potatoes and string beans, we happen to look simultaneously, and unexpectedly our gazes lock with intensity. It is as if she possesses some special knowledge that I must at all costs gain. I feel compelled to get to know her much, much better. A little while later, when she drops me off at my car, I don't want to break the connection between us.

I notice from the very beginning that there is something special about Elizabeth. She seems sweet and gentle and has a higher intelligence that attracts me. She is passionate about everything that she does and yet, sometimes I watch her wandering aimlessly. She looks lost, lonely and full of emptiness and somehow I understand her. At times I experience an empathy so profound that tears fill my eyes and my heart swells with sorrow for her. I can see how full of conflict she is, and the convincing act she has created to cover it up. I struggle for answers and wonder why I have these deep feelings. At organizational gatherings I find myself constantly distracted by her. I watch her every move and the way she talks and gestures. I admire her. She is smart and it shows. Her business partner, Samantha, does not appear as well educated or refined as Elizabeth. Samantha's vocabulary is limited and she uses a lot of slang to express herself when addressing the organization. The contrast is noticeable. I see who Elizabeth is. As if we are internally connected, I know what she feels and how she thinks. I am in awe of what is happening — of the strong magnetic field that seems to be pulling us together. Our involvement in politics becomes the foundation for our friendship. With few answers and little to go on, I am compelled to move forward . . .

We often have our core group meetings at Elizabeth's photography studio. The core group consists of twelve to fifteen regulars and several significant others. As I get to know some of the members, I notice that quite a few have a personal connection to Elizabeth, Samantha and each other. Their perception of politics and the world is different from the rest of the members, and all of their opinions are identical. On the surface they look normal, but when I face them one-on-one they all seem to stare glassy-eyed with an empty penetrating focus which reminds me of the characters in the movie, *Children of the Damned*. I know something is wrong but can't put my finger on it, until one day when Elizabeth mentions that she and Samantha both attend a support group for stress reduction. It is held at the home of Samantha's father, Gerald Sharkman. When I ask them to explain what it is all about, they tell me that I have to come and experience it myself to understand. They avoid giving me a straight answer and I sense that they are hiding something as spooky as their glassy-eyed stares. One evening, I notice a table against the wall which displays various business cards. Curiously, I glance at them and discover that they bear the names of several core group members. Later, I find out that these people also attend Samantha's father's stress group. A surge of heat flushes my face as I react to this information. I worry about what I might be getting into, and what Elizabeth is already a part of. Why are all of these people so weird? Why are they all together in this political group, and why do they all go to these stress sessions? Something inside of me feels as irritating as sandpaper. I sense an unholy hidden agenda.

About ten days after the walk-a-thon, twenty of the county's core members gather in Samantha's and my Closter den to watch the fast-track vote for *NAFTA* on TV. We have gained enough publicity from our Lautenberg meeting that Channel 7 decides to visit the house and film our active citizens group's reactions to what will take place on the TV tonight. Despite the application of our best efforts, *NAFTA* passes anyway. The following week it reaches Samantha's ears that various members who had visited our den that night were suspicious that we were devil worshipers. In fact, they sense something creepy and are even afraid of us. Samantha laughs it off, blaming the Halloween decorations and trinkets she still has lying around the house from last month's holiday as the cause of their bad feelings.

Once a month we have county meetings in a large public facility to accommodate the hundred or so supporters of our cause. All of the members gather to hear the latest news, and the town coordinators get their instructions. At one particular meeting I notice a man in the back of the room shaking his head back and forth continuously. Initially I react in fear. When this passes, I conclude that he has some sort of medical condition so I avoid looking at him altogether. Later I find out that this man is Samantha's father, Gerald Sharkman, the leader of the so often mentioned, "Stress Reduction Group". This guy is weird. What is he doing when he is shaking his head? I begin to ask questions. However, the only information I gain is that his strange behavior has something to do with energy. I wonder, *Is there really stress reduction going on or is this some kind of evil cult?* The more I participate in *UWSA*, the more I try to figure out this other group. Samantha appoints each of her zombie friends to various positions; they are now her administration. Their controlling attitude and strange behavior become the thorn in the side of the Bergen County chapter of *UWSA*. As the months pass, we try to get organized, but the core group begins to divide. Samantha and her people want to run the organization with as little documentation as possible. Their ideas are not realistic and the other members feel we need structure. Some of them have previous experience managing other organizations. They know you cannot effectively run a political movement without chronicling the meetings' minutes and other events and plans. So, our encounters get longer and longer, and because of the constant dissension we endure hours of brainstorming, writing endless pages of bylaws and agreeing to disagree. We struggle to stay awake, watching immature adults gain satisfaction from listening to themselves talk, scoring points with each other and showcasing their inspired proposals. It is exhausting and fruitless! Relating with Samantha's group becomes almost impossible.

Everyone not connected with Samantha and her friends senses their group's need for control and their willful intention to insert their hidden agenda into the organization. In fact, we all feel an evil energy exuding from them. Elizabeth, however, is different. She follows, but I sense she doesn't truly believe. I feel comfortable in her presence. So what is she doing with these dark people?

From observing Elizabeth's interactions with her "friends", it doesn't take me long to conclude that many of the people in her circle have in some way abused her, each with his own specific method of control. Samantha and some of the others are bossy and parental. They belittle her frequently. I also begin to realize that Elizabeth is doing about 80% of the work in her photography and publishing businesses, and yet I discover, splitting the profits in half with Samantha. What is wrong with this picture? An alarm goes off in my head. This woman is working seven days a week, sometimes more than twelve hours a day. She never takes a vacation and never has a boyfriend that will stay. She is chronically fatigued, acutely allergic and dangerously asthmatic. Underweight from poor eating habits and enduring incredible stress, I wonder where she ever gets the fuel to accomplish everything she has to each day. She endures periods of depression almost weekly where she puts herself down so fiercely that she almost cannot function. Yet at other times, she is more alive and loving than almost anyone I have ever met. I know she is not like the rest of them and it seems obvious to me that she does not belong there. In fact, I fear that there may be grave consequences for her if she does not get out soon and reclaim herself.

I decide to pay closer attention to Elizabeth's behavior, and I begin to connect the dots. At thirty-three, she is emotionally and socially undeveloped. Elizabeth tells me that she has been "on the psychological couch" since the age of eight. She was raised to believe that she must consult an outside professional before making any personal decisions. Her mother was unable to deliver any love or affection to her; she was nasty and never gave her validity. Her inability to mother Elizabeth left her a lonely child, starving for any human contact she could obtain to fill her needs. I sense quickly how incomplete she is, and that she is in serious trouble. Sometimes, when we are together, she recedes, becomes childlike and stares at me like a little girl, desperate to be picked up and held, to be protected. As the weeks roll by I feel her clinging to me emotionally, tighter and tighter, and I become aware of my own compelling desire to take care of her. Something incredibly powerful is pulling me to fill her needs, to support her, to be the family she never had, and to create a safe place for her. So I do, and soon discover that I have become her anchor, the doorway to her truth and the only opening she will ever have to escape.

January to August 1994

One winter evening my mother slips on the ice in Gerald's driveway. He hasn't put enough salt down and in addition, the path is poorly lit. When she enters the room, she tells Gerald that she has just fallen and suggests that he add more salt right away so others don't fall as well. He shoots her an annoyed look and I read his thoughts, *Don't blame me because you can't pay attention to where you put your feet . . . Thanks for criticizing me about how I keep my house . . . I might get around to it later if I remember and I am not too busy.* To her he responds impatiently,

"Go past it. You didn't really hurt yourself."

About ten minutes later Grace's face turns pale. Sounding scared and small, she calls out to him weakly, "Gerald I don't feel very well."

Immediately her eyes roll back in their sockets, out of sight. Bolting across the room, he lands on the floor at her feet. He grabs her arms and yells,

"Grace, don't leave us. Come back. Don't give in to the game."

A single awful phrase flashes through my mind. *She's dying.* My face turns ashen and I cry out spontaneously, "No!"

In that moment all of our differences fly out the window and I realize how much I truly love her. I am stricken with anxiety, grief, horror . . . the rest of the people in the room simply stare vacantly, like mannequins in a department store window. Tears roll down my face, but mercifully, in about a minute she comes back. The rest of The Group, including myself, praise Gerald for "saving her life".

The following morning he informs me that he did not approve of my emotional outburst during the episode, nor do the others in The Group. My heart twists from the blow, yet my mind doubts, and attempts to go along with his thinking, *What did I do wrong? Did I let my weaker side take over instead of focusing on The Energy and trusting in Gerald's abilities to save her?* After delivering his message, Gerald changes the subject.

The following week my mother complains of pain.

"I'm afraid I've broken something in the arm I fell on," she tells Gerald, seeking his advice.

Insistently and forcefully he responds,

"You're inventing a story, Grace. You didn't hurt yourself. Just leave it alone and stop using it as a distraction."

However, the pain persists and three months later she finally has an x-ray done. The results show that she has indeed broken her wrist. Furthermore, because she went so long without a splint to set it properly, it has healed crooked and her wrist is now permanently deformed. The next day she informs Gerald that he was wrong about her injury.

"I did break my wrist that night and you told me not to see a doctor. Now my bone has set permanently in the wrong position."

"I was just giving you my opinion," he counters immediately, "You didn't have to listen to me. Your life is your responsibility. There will be no finger-pointing in this room. Just remember, every time you point a finger at me, there are **three** which point back to you!"

It seems unthinkable that I have reached the point where, even in such an extreme circumstance, I do not rise up to retaliate on behalf of my mother. My oppression has grown so overwhelming that I find myself trapped in a deep dark cave, incapable of experiencing any feelings whatsoever. My personality on the surface is usually exuberant, nervous and giddy, a failed attempt to rev up my body's adrenalin in order to generate some kind of emotional experience. I would not dare to even consider confronting Gerald. His years of constructing our thinking and instilling fear into our hearts have created a protective shield around him, a thick wall of thorns which would rip me to shreds should I ever follow through on a personal challenge. Deep down I suffer the blow from Gerald's injustice to my mother, a person who innocently followed his arbitrary instruction, advice which resulted in permanent damage to the one and only body that God gave her, but my feelings are securely chained, incapable of expressing themselves. Although I do not comprehend all of this consciously, the truth lives somewhere inside of me. Gerald's bullying has rendered me an emotional rag doll.

The following month, I attend a Long Island, educational trade show on behalf of *Flash Blasters Inc.* After I have finished my business, I think of calling Judy G., my mother's old friend. I have not seen her in more than ten years, not since she and her two daughters, Brigette and Jeannie, quit coming to The Group at our apartment in the mid-eighties. While I was growing up, they had practically been members of the family and I miss them. Judy answers the phone and several minutes later I am standing on her doorstep in Valley Stream. We are so happy to see each other; it is as if no time has passed since our last meeting. In the past several years, Brigette, now twenty-five, has been married, and separated. She has two children, Craig, age four, and Lacey, age three. Jeannie's daughter Crystal, an infant when I last saw her, is now in junior high school. Judy wants us all to get together. We schedule a date for a Saturday the following month. I offer to make portraits of Brigette and her children at my studio so we decide to meet in New Jersey. I plan the day. Judy and her family will come to Gerald's house in the morning. After that, we will go for lunch and finally to my studio. Judy finds this plan unusual. She really wants to visit with me and my mother, not go to a therapy session with Gerald. However, I have taken control and she is too polite to oppose me.

At noon on the scheduled day, her family of six arrives. With ten of the regular group members already crowded into Gerald's den, many of us move onto the floor to open up seating for the guests. Gerald is excited. Perhaps they will want to return to him. He fills them in on some of the important "new information" we are working on today.

"You know, ladies, just this morning we were all brainstorming and came up with something incredible. You see a lot of hostility and fighting in this world. Right? Well, WE just figured out why . . . not that any of the crazy people in The Program will want to admit this is true . . . Let's start from here . . . Everybody's gonna die someday and they know it. Right? Well no matter who or where people are, everybody, I mean EVERYBODY is always aware of this, consciously or unconsciously, and they are terrified. After all, what's the point of living if it all ends up six feet under? This means that in the end, our lives are really pointless. So, all the people are really very angry and they can't do anything to change their impeding demise, so they fill their lives with anything that will divert them from the terrible truth. Starting a fight is a terrific distraction. Every interaction between two people, I don't care who or where they are, is really used for this; the people start a fight to avoid feeling that they are dying every second. Now, if you want to change this, you have to start by reversing your intention . . . you have to know that there's a better way, we are discovering it here in this room . . . you have to admit your hostility . . ."

My mother cuts in, "Gerald, I really have trouble with this one. I don't always feel hostile."

"Oh you better believe that you do!!! You're just insensitive to what's going on inside of you; but then again, what else is new!?" He sneers with authoritative sarcasm.

"Well, all right," she capitulates without hesitation, "on Monday at the office I'm certainly going to examine all of my conversations and look for that hostility. Actually, I know what you mean. People are all so phony and polite, but their friendliness is only social. If you don't give them what they want, you know, compliment them on their looks, praise their cooking, they'll turn on you in two seconds. All relationships are sort of . . . conditional."

Brigette unexpectedly bursts into tears,

"I am so sorry I ever left. I feel like I have finally come home," she sobs, apparently profoundly moved by what she is experiencing.

The rest of her family members, however, do not share her feelings. Quite the opposite. Jeannie and her daughter, Crystal, find Gerald to be nonsensical and have to stifle their impulses to laugh at him outright. The three-year-old, Lacey, screams relentlessly in an agonizing temper tantrum, as if the den's atmosphere is completely intolerable to her young psyche. Craig, squirming perpetually, finally walks up to Gerald and informs him,

"I don't like you."

The rest are uncomfortable and can't wait to leave.

After that day, Brigette rejoins The Group. She makes the hour and a half journey from Jericho, Long Island, twice a week. She often brings her two children, who continue to despise the sessions with Gerald. As if no time has passed since her previous visits with him fifteen years ago, she automatically seems to catch onto everything Gerald is professing. He is thrilled and gives her special treatment. She soon becomes Gerald's model, the example that the rest of us, his perpetually inadequate students, must follow. Bess, Pauline, Beatrice, Nora and the others seem to be willing to accept that Brigette is superior to them, that they are ungrateful under-performers in Gerald's squadron, barely worthy to even sit in his presence. I don't understand how they can not only tolerate but promote such a demeaning opinion of themselves. Sensing that I am not going along with his assessment, Gerald willfully endeavors to convince me that I too, am less than Brigette. I refuse to swallow this and he becomes enraged, attempting to verbally beat me into submission. Lately, our relationship seems to be frequently estranged.

The following month *The Celestine Prophecy* hits the bestseller list and Gerald picks up a copy. Soon it becomes our bible and during daily sessions we take turns reading aloud. All of us own a well-underlined copy and promote it to anyone with whom we make contact — customers, co-workers, shop-owners . . . Encouraged by the success of this spiritual book, Gerald decides to republish his own book, *Biofeedback Without Machines* and with it, an audio tape entitled *Minus Stress*. Martin revises the previous plain brown cover, replacing it with a modern shiny black and white one. He also helps his sister edit the copy, but neither have much skill at grammar or spelling. The book hits the shelves filled with mistakes; even the subtitle is misspelled on the first page! Nora, the librarian, distressed by the Sharkmans' lack of respect for the potential reader, informs Gerald that his book would probably sell better if it was more professionally presented. He is far from receptive to her constructive criticism and instantly, his eyes light up in fury.

"It doesn't matter if it's perfect or not. The crazy people are in such a fog that they don't know the difference anyway. They will still get my message; that is all that is important. Besides, I don't need to prove myself to any of those assholes. They are supposed to listen to me; I am the authority."

Publishing seems to have replaced shoplifting as The Group's favored activity, and Samantha makes her official author's debut with her *Dark Chronicles*,

Volume One, by arranging a book signing at a small science fiction bookstore in Fairlawn. Samantha is not shy. She shoves a flyer at each person who enters the store that Saturday. By the end of the day she has sold twenty-four books. Heartened by her success, she seeks any and every opportunity she can to get herself in front of the public with her precious volume in hand. She approaches several other stores in the area and establishes a signing circuit. A few months later, she attends the LUNACON Science Fiction Convention and volunteers to participate on an author's panel. As fortune would have it, she attracts the interest of the *Barnes & Noble* science-fiction buyer who happens to be in the audience and is impressed by her excellent cover artwork. He invites her to meet with him a few weeks later and purchases five hundred copies. Now, with her book for sale in all two hundred of their superstores nationwide, she has the perfect platform to do as many author signings as she wants. At this point, Gerald jumps on board and they each give free lectures every few weeks, rotating between several local *Barnes & Noble* superstores in New Jersey — Paramus, West Paterson, Ledgewood, Hoboken, Edgewater, and New York — Yonkers and Nanuet. Samantha also obtains her first radio interview. She devotes herself to actively seeking as much publicity as she can for herself, her book and her father's book. Unlike the other Group members who for the novelty attend the debut signings of Gerald and Samantha, I arrange to be present at virtually all of their lectures. Among all of his followers, I believe that I am still the most committed and involved devotee of Gerald E. Sharkman's strategy for living.

At his signings, Gerald promotes his expertise in stress reduction. A blurb in the monthly *Barnes & Noble* newsletter reads "Gerald E. Sharkman, author of *Biofeedback Without Machines*, presents his first of four workshops in his *Evening of Life* series. This evening he will introduce you to his unique methods of stress management." He begins to draw peripheral followers, people who come to hear him speak each time he appears at their local store; people who are clearly interested in what he has to say; people who swear by his book, which is filled with his "revolutionary methods that achieve real results".

Along with the book signings, our commitment to *UWSA* continues, and in March, we hold our second official election. Naturally, Samantha joins the race in order to claim a second term. The same group of people who opposed Gerald as mediator at the Senator Lautenberg meeting five months ago grooms another young member, Mark North, to run against her. A month before the election, Mark and his supporters launch a full scale campaign. There are telephone parties, postcard mailings and information meetings. Samantha, the confident incumbent, does nothing to promote herself, and none of us see why she should. The day of the election dawns and eight members of Gerald's group enter the meeting hall to join eighty or so other members of *UWSA*. This election is a mere formality. Of course Samantha will emerge victorious. How could it be any other way?

Samantha speaks first. She recites an impressive list of valuable contributions during her six-month term. It all seems so unnecessary, until Mark takes his turn. From the moment he commences his five-minute speech, I unexpectedly perceive a sudden shift in the *UWSA* group's energy, as if they have all just woken up simultaneously. I sense a direct line of focus from the entire audience to their candidate. They are alive and supportive. Inside I am confused. I don't understand what is going on, but I certainly feel how real it is, an irrevocable changing of the guard, out with the old and in with the new. The foreboding increases in intensity as the ballots are cast and counted, and twenty minutes later the new county coordinator is announced — Mark North. Samantha has only received nine votes out of a total of ninety, and these may all be attributed to the members of Gerald's group. I am astounded; I was so sure we would prevail! During the next five minutes, Nora, Carl, Pauline, and Martin, who had planned to run again for their respective town coordinators positions, huddle. They all reach the conclusion that the other members are fools and not worth their time. They withdraw their candidacy immediately. I hesitate, but from peer pressure, finally withdraw mine as well. I don't believe that Mark North's supporters are worthy of ridicule. I am simply puzzled by the day's events. In the next moment I notice that Samantha looks pale and dizzy, a reaction to her disappointment. Aware that I have never earned her trust and therefore can't help her, I run outside the meeting hall and into the gravel parking lot. There, I call Gerald, our leader, on my cell phone.

"Gerald, Samantha just lost the election, what should we do?"

He appears shocked too, temporarily at a loss for words. In fact I realize that this man, who I thought <u>always</u> had all the answers, apparently has none in this moment. Uncomfortable in the void, I stammer to fill in for him,

"There must be a really good reason for this. There is something better coming, a greater mission."

This logic sounds good to him; it fits in with his philosophy, so he agrees. Then I chase Samantha down and shove the phone into her hand.

"Here, Samantha, talk to your father," I command her.

I feel empathy for her; I know she needs emotional support and Gerald is the only one she will accept it from.

Samantha and the rest of them become nasty and irate over the election's outcome. Their excuse is that her opponent gained his support by unscrupulously influencing potential voters with campaign flyers and phone calls. Because no official election guidelines or protocol exist, Samantha doesn't have a leg to stand on. However, losing the battle fuels her and she becomes hard-willed and hostile. She demands obedience, respect and another election. The rage her group exhibits does not subside, evidence that their primary goal has been to maintain control of the *UWSA* Bergen County chapter, not to work toward the common mission of government reform shared by most of the other members. Why do they fight so hard for control? Why is it so imperative? Everyone feels their wrath. They send letters and faxes to all the higher-ups — State and District Coordinators, and even Ross Perot himself. They harass other members by telephone, complaining of how they have been mistreated. They organize a petition to get Mark North impeached. They won't give up. There is a power driving these people, some stubborn evil force that seems to have a life of its own. The new administration finally has to ban them from holding any positions of authority, and attending any more core meetings. Nonetheless, they insist on crashing these meetings. The members are fed up and exhausted and wish they would just go away. Soon Samantha's group attempts to use me as a diplomat to smooth things over. I find myself playing both sides of the fence because I have devoted so much time to this movement, and I know that the breakup could sever my relationship with Elizabeth. I don't want that, so I write a few letters on their behalf, but it is useless. The members want these people out.

Our meetings in Gerald's den focus on complaining about Mark North's abuse of Samantha and our strategies to convince him and his entourage of their unjust way of handling the election. One evening Mark meets secretly with his new cabinet in his home. Somehow Martin finds out and decides to take this opportunity to assert his rights. He drives there and shamelessly rings the doorbell. The people inside deny him entrance, but Martin insists.

"I have a right to attend the meeting; I am a card-carrying member of *UWSA*."

Mark will not let him in, warning that this is private property and he'll call the police if necessary.

This is too much for Gerald. He decides to double his efforts to overthrow Mark's regime. Toward this goal, seven of us form a team to confront them. Samantha calls Mark and requests a joint meeting on neutral territory to "talk things over". Mark agrees and selects his office. Judy Carlone, because of her friendship with me, seems to be the only person who might agree to act as a bridge to the other group. Gerald suggests that I invite her to his den during an afternoon session to discuss the problem with all of us. I invite a few other *UWSA* members as well, but only Judy shows up.

I shiver at the thought of visiting Samantha's father's house. This is the dreaded place where they hold their stress reduction sessions. Elizabeth assures me that several of the other *UWSA* members will be there, so I accept reluctantly. However, when I arrive, there is no one else from the movement present, just the members of Samantha's father's group. I walk into his den. Sitting on the couch are several group-goers including Samantha and Elizabeth. Samantha's father, Gerald, observes from a rocking chair in the back. I quickly position myself in a folding chair next to the nearest possible exit. Instantly, I feel an energy field as everyone focuses on me with expressionless faces, their eyes staring, piercing me. I feel their intention to penetrate me and insert something into my being. I freeze in terror from the evil sensation which seems to be trying to consume me as I silently pray to God. I jingle my keys nervously, trying not to let them see how petrified I really am. I want to jump out of a window but I force myself to calm down and sit through my uncomfortable feelings. I must take this opportunity to find out what is really going on in here.

They ask me questions about the election and present their point of view. They also tell me a little about the energy force that comes out of Gerald. I have always been sensitive to energy fields, so why is this one so terribly frightening? I answer their questions as best as I can and wait for an internal message to leave. When I feel there is nothing left to say, I rise and flee the den with relief. Walking toward my car, I feel terribly betrayed by Elizabeth. I conclude that because I have consistently refused all of their invitations to Gerald's sessions, she has set me up and tricked me to finally get me into his den. No one has ever manipulated me like this in my entire life and I feel violated beyond description.

When Judy enters and scans the room, I sense that something is wrong. I do not know what she is feeling, but she appears to be severely agitated. Gerald observes, silent for the moment as we vent our frustration on Judy, sounding like school children complaining to the principal about extra homework.

"It's not fair how Samantha lost the election. Can you convince them to listen to our side?" we implore her.

Finally, she agrees to fax Mark a letter stating that she has heard our concerns and that we have the right to have our side considered. Then Gerald speaks, telling her that it will be well worth it to help us. It will accomplish positive things, even for her. Warm and encouraging, he crosses the room to shake her hand and pat her on the back, just like he did to Rep. Marge Roukema and the other politicians.

That evening our team, Samantha, Mitchell, Nora, Pauline, Carl, Martin and me, gather in our Closter den to brainstorm. Forming a circle, we create an exhaustive list of contributions: meetings organized with governors and senators, dedicated xeroxing, faxing and mailing, the walk-a-thon, the Christmas fundraiser, etc. We certainly impress ourselves with how much we have accomplished! This resume will serve as our ammunition against the West group. Our intention is to remind them that we are indispensable and then convince them that they gathered votes for Mark unfairly, that they violated *UWSA* election rules and that we must have a new vote in fairness to Samantha. The next afternoon, we gather in Coach Gerald's den for a pep talk and then we are off to certain victory!

In Mark's office we form a ring of seats. Each of the fifteen or so participants is given the floor for a few minutes. Mark's team makes their position very clear. The election was conducted fairly and there is no negotiation. During their turns, Pauline and Nora are polite, asserting sweetly that the new administration just isn't seeing things our way. They claim that Samantha was a great leader and that they simply aren't being fair. In contrast, Carl and Martin decide to employ the tactics that Gerald uses to get his way with members of The Group. After all, he has assured us that we will win; we just have to show them how powerful and right we are. They begin to yell, accuse and curse. As they rise up like angry bulls, some of the women in the West group become offended at their choice of four-letter words. Mark warns them, politely at first, that they must cut out the obscenities. At this, Carl boils,

"How dare you correct my language or my delivery?"

Defiantly, he continues to yell as before. Mark stands up, walks over to him and escorts him to the door. The rest of us sit bewildered. This isn't working out the way we had planned. We are helpless, at a loss to turn the situation in our favor, a total contradiction to Gerald's fervent promises of triumph this afternoon.

Meanwhile, I am more aware of Judy standing in the back of the room than anything else. Somehow I sense that she is my ally. I don't know why; this makes no sense based on what Gerald has taught us about outsiders. Nevertheless, I want to feel her presence, and when a little while later she slips out quietly, I run to the door and peer through a tiny pane of glass near the top, plaintively watching her take out her car key. She turns and looks directly into my eyes with no expression. Wistfully, I watch her car pull away into the dark street. Something is disturbing her. She has cut herself off from me and I have no idea why.

The next day I am glad that I am not scheduled to see Gerald in the morning; I know there will be hell to pay. I am right. When I arrive in the afternoon, Pauline and Nora are sitting on the sofa sobbing. Gerald has been raging all day because we have failed to win back the county leadership for his daughter. I inconspicuously make my way to my seat and hold myself stock still, hardly breathing. I don't want to receive what he has just dished out to my tearful teammates. However, I am not meant to escape. A few minutes later he focuses his punitive intention on me.

"Why did you fail last night? Why are you a failure?"

I really have no answer. We did our best, but the people refused to give in. In a barely audible voice I squeak,

"I didn't fail." Then, a little louder, "I am not a failure."

I don't want to submit to the agony of feeling worthless, in fact despicable, again. I don't want to join the tearful Pauline, in this moment in agony on the couch across from me, feeling like a child who had just been brutally beaten for a bad grade in school. I make a decision. With my willpower, I will oppose Gerald's opinions. Even though he is pushing me down, I will not allow him to win. Fortunately, most of his wrath is exhausted from the previous seven hours he has just spent verbally beating the others and he doesn't have much left for me. With my weak but determined opposition I manage to get him off my back. He gives up and starts shaking his head, dropping us all in disgust and reaching toward new growth for himself.

After that fateful meeting at Mark North's office, I don't hear from Judy at all. Although I have been in touch with her regarding *UWSA* on at least a semiweekly basis for the past several months, I hesitate to call her; I fear her rebuff. A couple of weeks later we are scheduled to attend a lecture given by the Mayor of Jersey City, and when the evening arrives I hope to meet her there. A few minutes after we have taken our seats, she enters the room. I can tell that she notices me as I gaze at her poignantly, like a puppy dog in a pet shop window pleading with a passerby to take him home. However, she stubbornly ignores me, seating herself far away, on the other side of the room. I am hurt and confused and do not understand what is wrong. At intermission I try again, approaching her with a big smile, but she snubs me. I leave the meeting sad and empty. Helpless to change her mind, I try to get on with my life.

I refuse to speak to Elizabeth; it's about three weeks now. I tell everyone in the political movement how she set me up to be trapped alone in a room with the members of Samantha's father's group. Each time I relate the story, it helps me to heal from the terrifying experience. Finally, I decide to call her and inform her of how I feel. I blast her and she does not defend, but simply listens, allowing me to express myself. I begin to realize that her higher self, the person I am attracted to, and her behavior are in direct opposition. I try to let some of my hostility go. Despite what she has done, I know that underneath I have great affection for her. In fact, most of the *UWSA* members do like Elizabeth. They find her a decent soul; it is only her involvement with Samantha that keeps them from feeling comfortable in her presence.

When the telephone rings at the studio and I hear Judy's voice, I am overjoyed; hope fills me once again. However, she is raging from hurt and informs me in no uncertain terms that she never wanted to be in Gerald's den with our Group, especially not by herself. She doesn't like what she feels in there. In fact, she declares adamantly,

"God doesn't like it either."

I take this strange statement in stride. To me it seems irritating, even religiously zealous, and I have no idea what she means. Yet I decide to suspend judgment. My intuition tells me that someday I will understand. Judy goes on to state that I manipulated, even tricked her into attending that meeting, and she feels betrayed. I do not grasp the true meaning of the word "betray". It is not a working concept in my system of thinking. Besides, members of Gerald's group make a regular habit of inviting others to experience our unique philosophies. We believe that the more people we can involve, the stronger The Energy will get, and we know that it does good for everyone, even if the new people don't realize it until later. Judy has been approached several times by Nora, Pauline, myself and Samantha. She always refuses and I can never understand her rigidity, why she won't at least try it before making a decision. Nevertheless, I know I would never intentionally do her harm. On the phone today, instead of fighting, I just listen and let her blow steam. After about twenty minutes, she slows down and asks almost sadly,

"I thought you liked me?"

I respond immediately to reassure her.

"I do. Don't you remember the kinship we felt in *Kenny Rogers Roasters Restaurant* last November? I still feel a connection to you. It never changed."

She absorbs my affection as truth and I know our relationship will resume.

Life is very busy between the *UWSA* incidents and my business obligations. It is early April before I realize that I have postponed doing my income taxes for almost too long. Finally, one Sunday afternoon, I spread all the paperwork on the coffee table and throw myself in, adding columns of numbers. I avoid the two-inch-thick stack of Gerald's checks until the last possible moment; I dread knowing the sum. The pain in my stomach goes up another notch with each click of the calculator's buttons, and when the green digits finally display the total, more than $42,000 for 1993, my eyes fill with tears of frustration and resentment. I hate him; I hate The Group. Nonetheless, I try to remind myself that there is nothing I can do. Next year, I reason, the flash cards will flourish and this fee will feel like nothing. Despite this logic, intended to calm me down and accept the situation, my rage takes more than twenty-four hours to subside . . .

Later that month, our long-awaited breakthrough finally arrives when *Cliff's Notes*, one of the nation's largest educational study aids publishers, opens a new division called *Centennial Press* with the intention of distributing about five small publishers. I submit samples of *Exambusters Study Cards* and they are accepted. The company is an ideal distributor because they already market a similar type of product. I am sure that they can accomplish much for us. However, now I am under the gun to finance the printing of more product, and we have failed to find a willing investor. The only opening that presents itself comes from a local lawyer who is willing to lend us $30,000 at 12% interest for six months. Desperate to meet the inventory requirements for *Cliff's Notes*, I devote most of my remaining inheritance to finance the remainder of the printing costs.

The May monthly meeting under Mark North's administration takes place and for the first time, Gerald's group members enter the room without being in charge of anything. It is strange, and I begin to wonder why we are really here at all. A little while later, I notice Judy across the room. I haven't spoken to her since our last phone call and I am not sure if she has really dropped her hurt. I fear that perhaps she has changed her mind again and will give me the cold shoulder. Timidly, I look directly at her. She catches my eye and throws me a big warm smile. What a relief! Gazing at her in that moment, I suddenly experience an intense sensation of bright white light and seltzer. I remember back to the first time I met Joe in high school French class; the feeling of sameness of soul and instinctive trust is identical. I can hardly wait to talk to her at the break . . . Mark North puts forth our agenda and soon new committees are formed. Our next mission is to fight *GATT/WTO* — supposed to be worse than *NAFTA*. Samantha and another man volunteer to organize the *GATT* committee. Now she is back in the swing of things. Judy forms a group too, "The Property Tax Committee", and twenty people sign up, including me.

Continuing to donate my time to *UWSA*, I start a Tax Payers Committee and Elizabeth signs up. I know she has no interest; she doesn't own any property to be taxed, so why would she? Instead, I feel that this is her way of staying in touch with me to continue our friendship. I call her a few days after the county meeting, inviting her to co-chair with me, and she agrees.

Judy and I embark on committee responsibilities. The necessity of planning meetings supplies me with a reason to telephone her, and also to visit her new real estate office in the neighboring town of Dumont. She is quickly becoming a regular part of my life and I feel compelled to spend more and more time with her. Our first meeting takes place at the Bergenfield Library. We enjoy a large attendance and make big plans. Are there any other kind? After the meeting I follow her to her car. She gets into her driver's seat, closes the door and rolls down the window. I stand outside just looking at her as if mesmerized. I don't know what I am doing here; I have nothing to say, but I don't want to separate. Finally she asks me if I have something I want to tell her.

Not very sure of myself, I reply,

"No, I just want to talk to you, about anything."

Why do I feel this way? It seems so strange. However, I don't try to figure it out. This is just the way it is, the way it must be. She invites me into the car and we drive to a local diner. Sipping coffee, I begin to openly reveal several personal details about myself and my past. I really trust her . . .

The following day, I decide to buy her a plant as a gift for her new office. Unsure of what to write on the card, I let my heart lead me. *Congratulations on your new office . . . You are a miracle.* I know nothing of miracles outside of Gerald's jurisdiction. Why did I write that?

Elizabeth and I soon become inseparable. We go to movies, out to dinner and wander through the aisles of *Barnes and Noble.* She spends a lot of time at my house watching the big screen TV and chatting with my husband. She also continues to try to get me into her group; the more I resist the harder she tries. She tells me that she has been getting some flack about her friendship with me from her mother, also a member, Samantha, Gerald and the rest. It seems that none of the groupies have any relationships with outsiders. For some reason this is not permitted. But why? Why do they all think the same? Each time I go out with Elizabeth she talks incessantly about The Group. She sings the praises of Gerald's abilities, giving him the credit for everything in existence. It is obvious that she worships him in every way and I often wonder if they have sex.

Frequently I invite Judy to visit a Thursday night group. She always refuses me, but I can't let it go. I feel that I <u>must</u> convince her to come and share the experience. In fact, a need rages within me and my asking leads to begging. One night I feel unusually desperate and drop to my knees at her feet. She looks down into my pleading eyes and asks abruptly,

"Do you want me to sit there and look at Gerald with cow eyes like all of those other women?"

"Oh no," I reply without even thinking, "I don't want you to ever be like those other women, or even like me, but there is something there that is good. You will understand if you come. I want you to have that for yourself. It will help you in your life."

"All right, I will think about it. Maybe sometime I will."

Satisfied at having gained ground for the moment, I know I will persist until she gives in.

A few days after Independence Day, the *GATT* committees of both N.Y. and N.J. stage a walk over the George Washington Bridge. The night before, I spray-paint several signs on our lawn. "*GATT* = Liberty Lost", "*GATT* = No U.S. jobs", "*GATT* is Economic Treason and Unconstitutional". The next day, about one hundred N.J. and N.Y. members walk across the bridge waving those signs to

passing cars. Despite our obvious visibility, we don't get any publicity. The media is losing interest in *U W S A* . O u r organization hasn't accomplished what it set out to, and our original strategy of developing the huge mass of constituents outside the perimeter of Republican and Democrat, whose influence could turn future elections one way or the other, the swing vote, isn't coming to pass. Instead, *UWSA* is choking itself with ego

Protesting GATT on the George Washington Bridge

battles, hidden agendas and a rigid hierarchy. In fact, we are turning into a political party just like any other. *UWSA* is losing members as well. The seed planted by Ross Perot, which was going to grow into a mighty oak as it collected more and more citizens nationwide, seems to be experiencing stunted growth. The excitement spurred from our hopes and dreams is dying as we are all slowly coming to terms with the fact that our efforts are bearing little fruit. Besides, with Samantha no longer in charge, the members of Gerald's Group are rapidly losing interest. The *GATT* walk over the bridge is our last hurrah. The eighteen months that we were active, even obsessed members, have been filled with activity and exhilaration and now that time has clearly come to an end. We all know it. The Group withdraws from *UWSA* and stops attending their meetings.

For the past year, since Ben's fall the previous summer, he has been one of Gerald's primary focuses. In spite of Gerald's claims, Ben never does walk again. He begins to sleep more and our group sessions usually include him lying on a mattress at one end of the den or often even in Gerald's arms. As he sleeps his body jolts, often quickly and violently. Gerald claims that he is now "in the other place, in total ecstasy, and we must try to follow him there." Ben must be picked up and carried outside to evacuate and Gerald proudly states that he doesn't care if the dog pees or craps right on his hands, he loves him that much. Even though Ben requires a "walking" every couple of hours, Gerald and Martin never complain about how oppressive and restrictive it is to be tied to their house every day, all day, to care for the dog. In fact, Gerald states with confidence,

"Ben is going to live forever and I don't mind caring for him for that long. It is worth it."

I try to comprehend their side, to justify the love and dedication, evidence of a supreme selflessness which could only exist in a highly spiritual person. I cannot. Instead, this inordinate, even ridiculous attention to the dog enrages me. However, I keep my mouth shut. Everyone else seems to go along with the significance of the dog and what Gerald claims we will learn from him. Ben soon develops an insatiable thirst. However, Gerald limits his water to avoid more frequent trips outside. This blatant cruelty cuts into my heart. I want to see the dog's suffering alleviated so I timidly ask Gerald if he might consult a vet to help Ben, but Gerald will have none of that.

"Vets don't know what's going on. We'll solve the problem ourselves with The Energy."

There is no swaying Gerald's opinion. I wouldn't even dare to try. Then Ben begins to lose his hair. The inert helpless animal with large bare patches on his body looks terribly decayed, as if he is already dead. Nevertheless, Gerald insists that he will reverse the process and restore Ben to the strong beautiful creature he was twelve years ago when Dr. Rogers found him during a mountain vacation in the N.Y. Catskills. He holds him on his lap for hours, rubbing his body and insisting that he detects new hair growth.

Saturday, August 27, 1994
and the weeks that follow

I enter the den one Saturday afternoon. An oppressive gloom hangs in the air and I quickly ascertain that Ben is not doing well. In fact, Gerald is holding him with poignant sadness written across his face. The other ten or so faces reflect his mood. I feel exceedingly uncomfortable. Not just for the inevitable loss of a living creature whom we have known and loved, but an impending, unknown transformation which is much, much worse. I don't know what to do with this feeling, or with myself, so I sit in silent observation. Soon Gerald announces that he is too involved and that perhaps someone less emotionally connected should hold the dog. He places him painstakingly on Beatrice's lap. The minutes drag by in agonizing anticipation, of what, we have no idea. All of us feel helpless and yet responsible, as if there is something that we should be doing, which we are not doing, to stop the process taking place. Finally it is 5:00 P.M. and time to leave. Gerald and Martin debate about taking the dog to the Oradell Animal Hospital nearby. Each of the others assures Gerald that things will turn around for Ben. Bess tries to bolster his confidence, telling him that he mustn't give up.

"You have the right stuff to help him. Just believe in yourself," she reassures with a supportive smile, reaching out to gently rub Gerald's back.

I gaze at Gerald helplessly on my way out, asking him if I can do anything, but he waves me out the door. In my mind I want to believe that Gerald will foster some miracle this night, after we have left, but in my heart I know that Ben is dying. I sense an indomitable spiritual process taking place which none of us can influence, and simultaneously I sense Gerald's willful insistence that he, and we as a group, <u>must</u> alter this process to satisfy his heart's desire. Gerald stands at the door watching us slowly depart and he looks terrified, like a lost little boy.

That night I accompany Samantha to a book signing. When we return home, Samantha calls her father and discovers that he and Marty have decided to leave Ben at the animal hospital overnight. The sense of transition, which commenced this afternoon, is ever present and even stronger. I believe that an important milestone is about to be passed and I want to experience every moment of it, so when Samantha retires about midnight, I remain awake, sitting in my recliner in the dark, just staring at the wall. At about 2:00 A.M. I experience a definite lift, a release. Soon after, I fall asleep. Our phone rings at 8:00 A.M. It is Gerald. He tells Samantha that Ben is gone. It happened somewhere between 2:00 and 2:30 A.M., exactly the time I felt that strange sense of freedom. Samantha cries for the loss of her pet and also because today is her brother's twenty-fourth birthday, and Ben was his best friend. Later that afternoon, Ben comes home in a white cardboard box and is buried in the backyard by father and son. Gerald tells us that the local health codes forbid this, but he wants Ben to be within reach always. Martin carves a headstone out of wood. It reads, "Ben — a true friend". A carved paw print lies below this eulogy. At his grave side, the men talk to their dog, telling him how much they miss him. When they have said all that they can, Gerald stands over the grave. Shaking his head furiously, he raises his arms high in the air in a desperate plea to make it not so.

Monday dawns and I dread going to Gerald. I don't know what to expect but I know it won't be pleasant. I am correct. For the entire week, in the Jewish tradition, he sits Shiva in his den for the dog. Gerald cries without stopping. Tears stream down his face in an endless river. His features are red and blotchy, the picture of perfect misery. Martin howls and bawls frequently. Gerald's wife, Doris, hearing this drama through the closed door, is embarrassed beyond description at what she feels is a ridiculous and pointless spectacle taking place in her own home. Gerald ridicules his wife for her insensitivity. All of The Group members attend regular sessions. We sit rigidly, sober and forlorn, competing with each other to see who can mirror Gerald's agony the most effectively. I try to keep my face blank and pray that Gerald will not notice that I am much less distraught than the rest. Although I try to force myself to feel the agony he is feeling, I just can't manage.

On Tuesday afternoon, the second day of mourning, I arrive in the early afternoon. Spotting Beatrice and Pauline on the love seat, I immediately read the identical expression on both faces, *I deserve to be punished because I was very, very bad.* Instinctively, I know there is trouble and wish I could sink deep into the couch, out of sight. However, I am unable to transform into the invisible woman and soon Gerald swings his attention to me, his reprimand accompanied by an intense glare.

"Tell me what part you played in Ben's death. How did you help to kill him?"

I stare in disbelief, although I am not surprised. Since Saturday afternoon, I have been fearing that he would force me into some inescapable trap like this. I reply truthfully, attempting to keep my voice steady and unemotional so as not to trigger him even more,

"I didn't kill him. I didn't want him to die. I offered my help the other day, but there was nothing I could do."

My voice doesn't deliver any confidence; I am too afraid of Gerald, but I try. It is obvious that all the others in the room, Laura, Nora, Beatrice and Bess, have swallowed his accusation that we collectively killed the dog, and that from this sin there is no redemption. Gerald rages upon receiving my blasphemous response and I recede. I grope desperately in my mental storehouse for some kind of double-talk which will satisfy him, so that he will leave me alone before my rapidly constricting veins completely cut off the blood supply to my brain and I pass out from sheer terror. Therefore, for the sake of my survival, I do the one thing I abhor more than anything, I lie. I mumble something about bad intentions that I see in myself and haven't been able to correct — that I will try harder — that I am sorry and feel terrible about my mistakes. Eventually I manage to appease him. Then Laura, seated next to me, demands our leader's attention and Gerald moves on. She has just received an inspirational message, profound wisdom which if sufficiently explored might prevent this dreadful event from ever recurring. The rest of my comrades, with Gerald at the helm, brainstorm about her ideas for the next hour, but I stay out of it. Late in the afternoon Gerald telephones the vet to ask why Ben couldn't have been saved. The vet really doesn't know how to answer him because obviously Gerald refuses to acknowledge that it was simply the dog's time to go — that his physical body had given out. He asks the vet if there wasn't something that we could have done, or something that we could still do even now, informing her with conviction, "I just want him back. I'm willing to do whatever it takes to make that happen."

After that, Gerald refers to the death as a "mistake" and a "tragedy". Ben's merciful passage from the pain of his decaying body and the ugly conflict, ever-present in his owner's den, becomes in Gerald's eyes the worst thing that has ever happened to him.

"We will pay for this mistake the rest of our lives," he assures us.

At Thursday night group, we are all terribly sober. Gerald tells us we must now strive to understand our mistake so that we can learn from it. Beatrice concedes that when she had the animal on her lap that fateful afternoon, (she was the last of us to hold him), she felt her negativity go into him. Because of this, she believes that she, more than the rest of us, is responsible for his death.

Gerald praises her for this humble admission and then declares that we must all try to move on now. As he begins shaking his head slowly and solemnly, his arms float up into the air as they often do. All of a sudden, he is overcome with emotion. His voice choking back tears, Gerald reports with genuine awe that he can feel the weight of Ben's body in his hands. He calls Martin over to him and Marty kneels on the floor at his feet. Slowly, Gerald lowers his arms as if they are supporting some great weight and hands the unseen body of Ben to his son. Martin begins to cry uncontrollably, sobbing that he feels the dog too. Next Gerald invites us one by one to experience this miracle. When it is my turn, I concentrate hard. I nod to him with serious intensity, telling him I feel it a little. Satisfied, he moves on to the next person. I had hoped to feel something as powerful as Gerald and Martin; I wanted it to be real, but honestly, although I feel terribly guilty for my sacrilegious thoughts, I am not sure that there was really anything there to feel at all.

About an hour later Samantha interrupts our silent sobriety and the steady rhythm of her father's head shaking. "Dad. Dad. Look out the window!"

She stares at the big picture window over the couch which overlooks their backyard.

"I see Ben. I see him floating. He is with us!"

Gerald looks toward the window, tears running freely once again down his cheeks as he too beholds Samantha's vision. In the next moment, Bess and Pauline begin to see the faint outline of Ben's body too, suspended in the black night over the yard. All the other women envy Samantha. She has earned tremendous accolades from her father for this discovery, praise that they themselves sorely need. If only they had seen Ben first . . .

The next couple of weeks are awful. Misery is rampant among us and there is no hope in sight. Gerald is depressed and unreachable; he hardly speaks and spends most of the day somberly shaking his head and ignoring us. Without his enthusiasm to lead us through another day, to encourage us along the next leg of our journey toward the ultimate truth, we collapse like deflated balloons. The oppressive stagnation is intolerable. Although I do everything I can to fight it, I feel as if I am being dragged down into a bottomless pit from which I will never be able to escape. There is emptiness everywhere, no fun, excitement or light. I cannot imagine that Hell could possibly be any worse than this.

It is Wednesday, lunchtime, about ten days after Ben's passage. Samantha receives a call at the office from her father. There is little conversation. She hangs up the phone quickly, her face paling noticeably, and without explanation rushes out mumbling, "I've got to go."

Her behavior is more than strange, but I have learned not to ask questions when no information is being volunteered. The Sharkmans reserve their secrets exclusively for those worthy of their sacred possession. After that day, Gerald seems happier. In fact, the following evening, when I enter the room for the 7:30 group, he is laughing and winking at Martin. Very much his old self, he lectures,

"We are now going to a new level, beyond the physical. We will explore the spiritual realm. Everything is really spiritual. The physical world is just an illusion, a lie."

There is a strange pungent smell in the room, as if too much air-spray has been used, but I ignore it and sit quietly observing, not understanding the reason Gerald's mood has changed so drastically. I know something is up, but it all seems to be a big mystery which they choose not to share with me, and I don't dare ask about it. In fact, all of the other members of The Group are silently and desperately competing to see who can be the first to solve the puzzle whose solution only the three Sharkmans possess. Finally, one Thursday night a few weeks later, while sitting on Gerald's couch, I look up at him, and suddenly, I don't know how or from where, the answer comes to me. Smiling in collusion, thrilled to be "in the know", I catch his eye. It is all so clear — the reason Samantha turned ghostly pale before scurrying off to carry out her father's command. Gerald, spurred by a momentous inspiration, had called his daughter from his Manhattan office and ordered her to meet Martin at the family house in Westwood. There, they were both instructed to dig up the dog's carcass, to bring Ben home, into Gerald's den.

The next morning, I report for my 8:30 A.M., before-work session and I am nervous. Gerald questions me and I inform him verbally what I had only shown him in my eyes the preceding night.

"Now it's time to take a look at it," he tells me.

I really don't want to. To postpone the inevitable, I slip into the bathroom. While I am inside, he removes Ben from his hiding place behind the couch. Now I know what that apple-scented can of air-spray on the coffee table is for! Finally, I can't find an excuse to remain in the bathroom no longer. I suck in my breath and bravely walk out to face the music. Before my eyes I behold poor Ben's body lying on a slab of wood on the floor. The first emotion that passes through me is poignant sadness for all living beings which must die. I tell Gerald what I have felt. He coaches me gently,

"You have to get over that. The emotion is a lie. There are much more joyful feelings when you get past those reactions."

Immediately after, I am nauseous, revolted. After being dead for about a month, the carcass is putrid. It has also been bleeding. Evidence of this is obvious in the matted fur and red stains on the wooden board. Gerald counsels, as he instructs me to touch Ben,

"Our disgust forms a barrier we must break in order to arrive at new discoveries."

I am obligated to comply and so I ignore my feelings as usual, but after sixteen years, I am used to this. It takes me about ten minutes to screw in my courage but I finally sit down Indian-style on the floor next to Ben and gingerly place my fingertips on his back. I recoil and then try again. With a sigh of determination, I close my eyes and push myself through the barrier of life and death until I am able to put my whole hand on his back and keep it there. Gerald is very proud. However, for once in my life his pride doesn't feel like the reward it usually does. A few days later, for some unexplained reason, he decides to bury the body again. He and Martin do this. . .

About a week later, Gerald and his wife visit her older sister on Long Island. Gerald thinks obsessively of his best friend Ben while taking a solitary walk on the beach. Suddenly, he is drawn to a palm-sized white stone with a small hole in the middle, lying in the sand. He picks it up and on Monday he gives us the news,

"Ben has come back to us. His soul is in this rock. I have a job to do now. I must transfer the soul from the rock back into the body. Then Ben will walk and live again."

The white rock, "the Ben Rock", becomes Gerald's constant companion. Only in a blessed moment might he let one of us touch it. At these times we are terribly honored, gently holding it for a few precious minutes until he reclaims it and "brings it home" to the safety of his pocket. God forbid that we would drop it or hurt it in any other way. All day long he keeps it close to him. He even places it in his mouth, sucking on it for hours while shaking his head. This rock is truly sacred and we feel its specialness as much as he does. We are in awe of the "Ben Rock". We revere and fear it.

Gerald's body puts out so much heat from the head shaking that soon the rock is physically affected. The hole becomes larger. It looks like a belly button. Some additional colors, brown, black, grey, appear on the rock's surface as well. He declares that The Energy is transforming the rock and making it ready to transfer the soul to the body of Ben. The following week, as Gerald and I are sitting by the grave focusing and "experiencing", he picks up a white rock from the ground which looks like a small potato.

"Here," he says, "a gift."

I slip it in my pocket proudly, thinking to myself, *It's just like it always was; whenever he starts something new, I am always the first because I am the person most like him.* During the next few days he gives rock "gifts" to the rest of The Group, and in the weeks that follow, we even begin to exchange rocks with non-Group family members, explaining,

"The rocks will help you calm down when you are stressed out and speeding."

Every day we sit with Gerald holding rocks, feeling their energy, watching them change and grow.

One Saturday soon after, I arrive at Gerald's around 2:00 P.M. as usual. As I make the left at the end of his driveway and approach the deck, I look to my right to see The Group standing solemnly about thirty feet away, by Ben's backyard grave. *Oh God*, I think, *Now what?* I really don't want to find out. Regardless, I walk over to The Group. Laura, Beatrice, Pauline, Bess . . . each is sober and serious with eyes down-turned, while Martin is just removing the white box with Ben's body in it from the grave. Gerald is in the house getting something, but soon I spot him running across the yard toward us. My heart leaps expectantly as it always has at the sight of my revered mentor, but as he comes closer, for some unknown reason, I find myself looking directly into his eyes. They seem to approach my face rapidly, like blinding headlights from an oncoming car on an otherwise completely dark and deserted road. In that moment, I see something I have never seen before. There is blatant unmistakable and consummate insanity in those eyes. I realize that he has gone over the edge and I am profoundly scared.

Gerald is glowing with enthusiasm, "This is the biggest thing that we have ever done and no one except us will ever understand. Marty and I will have to hide this from Doris. You are all present at this birth, the beginning of Ben's new life!"

Laura states in wonder, "This is really great. We are doing something truly important together."

Pauline, also enthusiastic, adds, "Yes. We are finally cooperating instead of fighting!"

Soon we are inside with the carcass. It, along with the white rock, is to become a holy sacred item, an object of worship, the total focus of our existence for the unforeseeable future.

When that afternoon session is finally over, I walk toward Gerald's driveway and my car. It is here, on the concrete path I have crossed thousands of times, that in one exquisite and awesome moment a realization rips though me with extraordinary force. *My God! Look at what we have become; we will do anything for Gerald; he could even convince us to murder if he wanted to . . .* This awareness shocks me firmly into reality. I come to a full stop, a brick wall, as my oppressed inner voice finally triumphs over my rigid orthodox thinking and finds the freedom to declare undeniably, and with commitment, *I hate the Black Dog Religion. I hate what is going on in The Group!* Our unique, rocky, crazy, exhilarating, challenging journey has culminated in this — the exaltation of a black dog's carcass. Although I never would have believed that this day could possibly arrive, it has, and this is where I must get off. Something deeply buried inside of me has just woken up and is taking the reins. My inborn morals, personal standards for my conduct, are forcing me to change direction, leading me away from this ridiculous drama. Gerald has crossed a new barrier, and for the first time, his most faithful disciple cannot, and will not follow him. This day he has declared that he has the power to resurrect a dead dog. He and the dog, as a team, will lead us to our ultimate salvation.

"I, Gerald, am the Alpha and the Omega. I will know the beginning and I will lead you to the end." He has pronounced himself to be the true Messiah. "Everyone in the universe will eventually have to come my way or they will perish. 'Dog' is 'God' spelled backwards and <u>Ben is God</u>. He has traveled to the other side and now he will come back to lead us all there."

How did I ever stray this far from myself? Where have I been all of these years? On this day, I hear my inner voice commanding me. It proclaims clearly and distinctly, *You must stop the game, now.* It is the authority and there is no negotiation; I have no choice but to follow its directive. As if someone has just turned on a light, in these moments of revelation, I discover the role I have always been playing with Gerald — my perpetual performance to gain his recognition. However, from the instant that voice speaks, I cross into a new realm. I will never again throw him another flirtatious look or flatter him for his superhuman powers.

I will never again report my accomplishments to him for brownie points. My unhooking of a very long addiction is about to begin . . .

Fall 1994

My sessions take a one hundred eighty degree turn. I enter the room as unassumingly as possible, hoping no one will notice me and encourage me to relate. Inside, my needs crush my chest. A desire to participate screams relentlessly, but I endure instead of satisfying the demand, for an hour or two, however long I am scheduled to be there. Urges pass through me to look around, talk, comment and act out the role of enthusiastic follower which I have played for so many years. However, I am unable to interact no matter how much I want to. As if I am been strapped to my seat with my mouth taped shut, I am restrained by an invisible power much stronger than my own willpower could ever overcome; therefore, I have no option but to sit through my assigned time in his den in silence. I discipline myself to focus on the doorknob or a knot in his diagonal wooden paneling, anything I can use to fix my eyes on. Day in and day out I work on breaking my connection to this group of people who have become my family, and my whole life, to our common belief system, to the fear I carry with me always — of displeasing Gerald and being punished for it. This assignment compels me, but strangely, I do not question why, or where it will lead.

As if I have just signed up for a correspondence course, the lessons arrive regularly, automatically, through no effort of my own. My job is not to seek them, but simply to absorb them. I come to understand and abhor the person I have become and the life that I have lived. As the days turn to weeks, and I invest my time in observing rather than participating, I am horrified to feel how powerful my attachments to this group and their thinking really are. Like Gulliver tied down on the beach by the Lilliputians, thousands of tiny little threads hold me captive. Each strand represents a thought, memory or action. Taken alone, each thread seems innocuous, easily broken. However, because they all comprise a single intention, in entirety they form a trap which seems virtually impossible to escape. A mass of emotional responses and intellectual evaluations which has been brilliantly fostered, so slowly and carefully, right before my eyes while I was looking the other way. The group activities Gerald encouraged have created the sense of belonging, of family, the glue which binds us to The Group, to him, and to his ideology. Every day, while we thought we were attending relaxation therapy sessions, and were distracted by intellectual concepts and gossip, he had secretly hooked another tiny imperceptible thread into our being. A master craftsman of control, he has wielded concealed weapons of willpower and seduction to construct his masterpiece, an army of perfect soldiers who exist solely to serve him, in any way he desires, for the rest of his days. We are simply marionettes at the ends of the hundreds of strings which he has painstakingly embedded into us, one at a time. Whenever the whim passes through him to pull on those strings, we dance — his dance . . .

Along with focusing on Ben's body to see it changing and growing, we now spend most of our time focusing with each other. The days of bonding through group activities (*UWSA*, concerts, business projects), personal discussions (problems at the office, or with spouses and family), even discussing the books on our reading list, have ended abruptly, and during our sessions we do nothing but work at Gerald's new mission. Our mentor severs all interactions and becomes completely unreachable — a machine programmed for one function only, resurrecting the dog. Nothing will deter him from the task at hand. Each time I enter the den, the air is thick with the unspoken message that the details of my life no longer hold any significance to him at all, none of ours do. After years of shared experiences, he has cut himself off emotionally and no longer views any of us as individuals; our only relevance is the energy we can supply to further the cause. Stray chatting is now against the rules as he commands us daily,

"Come on everybody, it's time to get to work on Ben. There's nothing else important aside from this, so cut the distractions, people, and let's get going."

Gerald commonly selects the person he feels is most open to his Energy with whom to focus. Once he has made his pick, the others in the room select a focusing partner. Samantha commonly chooses Bess or Pauline. It is clear that they both feel honored to have the opportunity to focus with a person as advanced as Samantha. They look up at her with the same cow eyes that they turn upwards toward her father, appearing to experience an emotional rush from the absorption of Samantha's superior knowledge. Personally, I hate to focus with her. Her eyes are cold and empty, like marbles. I sense something ugly in her. Looking at her, I feel creepy. No matter where we are, I routinely find ways to avoid her penetrating gaze. Nora and my mother choose each other. Because they are writing a children's book together, this focusing is good practice for them to form a more cohesive partnership and ensure their success at obtaining a publisher for their book.

Bess flatters Gerald for his faithfulness to the cause,

"I have never met anyone who has as much determination as you. It's amazing, and that's why you get the incredible results that you do!"

Gerald bows his head in humble recognition of this sincere and justified compliment . . .

It is a fall Saturday afternoon, another bright and breezy day when I wish I could be outside enjoying the weather, not about to be trapped in the dimly lit den, focusing on Ben. As I approach the door, about to enter for my afternoon session, I realize that over the last few months, this house has been transformed into a church dedicated to the dog. A flag with a black Labrador's image sways in the breeze on Gerald's deck. There are several statues of black Labradors in varying sizes strewn across the coffee table and sideboard. Mugs with painted black dogs keep the statues company. An afghan, a gift from Samantha which sports several Labrador images, is pinned to the wall. There are posters, T-shirts, light switch plates and throw pillows, almost all offerings to Gerald from various Group members. As I enter, Bess, Pauline and Beatrice are seated on the couch and intensely absorbed in a conversation about the development of Ben's carcass. Gerald turns to me with excitement,

"I have big news. Ben is creating worms. They are brand-new life forms, born from The Energy I have put into him."

I look down quickly and observe small white specks all over Ben's legs.

"Oh, I see," I reply, not knowing what to make of it. Not really wanting to believe him, and yet too afraid not to.

Gerald continues, "Earlier today I saw one growing out of my arm too!"

Pauline giggles, "I certainly don't want to ask how that happened!"

Next Gerald picks up a robin's egg which had been nestled next to Ben's leg. "I've been holding this egg for two days now. I can feel the life inside of it already. It is communicating with Ben and he is telling it to hatch!"

The dog's body is covered with many items, donations from The Group members: a dollar bill, a business card, a piece of jewelry, a feather. These items are placed there to absorb The Energy, after which they will be taken home as charms to end family conflict, or on the job to help get a raise. I listen to Gerald recount with childlike glee how he and Martin manage to keep the carcass hidden from Doris. On Monday, Wednesday and Friday, when Gerald goes to his office in the city, Martin, while driving around to keep appointments with his graphic design customers, carries his best friend in the trunk of his white Acura Integra under a blanket. At night they hide Ben in the garage, only removing him after Doris leaves for work in the morning.

Sitting in the rocking chair, I stare at a doorknob, not wanting to look at anyone in the room. I suddenly experience a strange sensation. It feels as if a golf ball which has been circling a hole for a very long time has finally fallen into it. I realize that all of the years of perpetual personal attacks, accusations and degradations have finally broken my friends in. They have been tamed like wild horses and I sense that they have handed their wills over completely to Gerald. They are now docile and agreeable, willing to follow him wherever he goes, never to question or oppose him again. An unholy peace hovers in the den and Gerald appears relaxed, as if his mission is finally accomplished and he can rest, confident that his devotees are following right on his tail. However, I, unable as always to submit to Gerald with blind trust and commitment, discover that I am on the other side of a fence looking at them in horror.

My God, I think, *That was supposed to be me too. Gerald meant to have me join them, a zombie, a puppet following an eternal master!*

In one phenomenal moment, I realize that although I have traveled the same path as the others, for some incomprehensible reason, I have been saved from this dreadful fate. I do not know how to thank God by name, but nonetheless, my heart extends out its gratitude. It is an eerie sensation. I can see them all and they can see me, but, as if separated by a pane of glass, I cannot connect with them any more. I am all alone on my side. However, I am not upset. In these moments I actually feel myself being propelled upwards as I watch the rest receding slowly and purposefully, as if floating away on an iceberg. Over the past several weeks, since the day I renounced the "Black Dog Religion", I have had the sensation that I am a passenger on a train which is carrying me somewhere unknown. In other words, I am coming to realize that I am in some type of transition. I don't know where I am going or why, but instinctively, I trust the process. In addition, I know that I have no choice in this matter. Whatever has been happening will continue, with or without my approval. I don't even want to try to figure out what the future will hold. I just take it one day at a time . . .

I have always displayed such enthusiasm for the mission, relentlessly demanding Gerald's attention and monopolizing most conversations. Now I am separate. Strange, but the others don't seem to even notice the drastic change in my behavior. I begin to realize that they don't miss my participation either. I have always believed I was relevant, necessary and important. After all of the experiences we have shared together, and the enormous piece of myself that I have invested in The Group and into my relationships with each individual, I can't believe that my detachment doesn't affect them. Yet, as I slowly withdraw the spirit and the energy which is me, I realize that it doesn't make any difference to them at all.

I have felt Elizabeth's pain since the moment I met her, and I have come to believe that our connection has been divinely fostered so that I can help free her from the sticky spider web she is trapped in . . . These days we struggle for hours — on the phone, driving in my car, or over cappuccino at a local café. Our attraction to each other is powerful. In fact, there is nothing that can pull us apart, not the others in our lives, not even our own minds, which sometimes wrestle with our increasingly intense relationship. Through our conversations I discover that Elizabeth has been thoroughly brainwashed to believe that Gerald has all the answers, that she will die if she leaves him. However, her heart speaks differently, which results in her almost unbearable conflict. It is her soul that bonds with me, not her mind, for that is owned by Gerald, Samantha and her mother. I can only give her information in small doses, so that she can break the bars of her jail one at a time. I have never seen a more eager and passionate student. She grasps my perspective willingly, even though it is in direct opposition to what she has believed for two decades, and then returns to The Group to verify it. Now an observer, she soon begins to feel like an impostor. She confronts her addiction directly and works on instinct, completely in unknown territory. I support her behind the scenes, twenty-four hours a day.

Without the political group's activities to supply us with a reason to meet, Judy and I continue our relationship on the telephone and in diners — conversations which often last for more than four hours, not infrequently until 3:00 A.M. We are so comfortable with each other, as if we have been together all of our lives. One evening we take a ride to Hoboken, N.J., the neighborhood where she grew up. Judy's childhood was such a contrast to mine; her father drove a truck; she never went to college. We seem to come from two different worlds and yet, there exists an uncanny familiarity of soul. She genuinely likes me and I feel it, not for my personality or my mind, but for who I am, for my spirit. In her presence, I feel as if I have come home; my struggles cease and I am safe and peaceful. Judy genuinely respects me too and she points out the reasons why. My character is kind, generous and fair. I am a good business woman, intelligent and perceptive, a success. My response to her is always the same,

"Huh? What do you mean? Really?"

I live in a fog of self-denigration, having forgotten that I have any intrinsic value whatsoever. All of my thoughts have been focused on the part I play in Gerald's world. I believe I am nothing, a person with no merit, a person no one likes. I feel like the walking dead, cut off from myself completely, no emotions, only conflict. I cannot cry, laugh, play, feel excitement, love or hope.

One night while out for a drive in Judy's car, she pulls over. Focusing her attention on me she playfully teases and jokes with me as if I was her little sister. Seriously stiff, as usual, I withdraw and pull away. Then, unexpectedly I let go and begin to giggle. She looks at me with a warm smile.

"I have never heard you laugh like that; it is a wonderful sound. It is good to see you happy."

Elizabeth admires me to the point of fascination. In fact, it seems as if I am the first person in her life who ever paid any attention to her. She absorbs every inch of me like a sponge, and brings it all back to The Group and to Gerald.

Judy Carlone is a wonderful person. She is passionate and direct, never afraid to speak her mind. I respect her honesty. The energy I draw from our relationship leaves me feeling exhilarated, even delirious, and I can't help mentioning her to The Group several times a week. Although at first I am tolerated, (Gerald is convinced that The Energy is drawing Judy into our friendship) they soon become irritated and begin to warn me that I am being childish. I am obsessed and she is nothing but a mommy to me. One day Bess lectures me with heartfelt sincerity.

"Elizabeth, I know what it means to be seduced into thinking that one of the 'crazy people' has something going for them. This is a weakness I've come up against many times, but you know that unless she comes to The Group, the relationship is really not good for you. It is just a distraction. You really should concentrate on getting her into The Group on a regular basis."

Gerald chimes in, warning me, "Judy is a powerful person. You better watch out or she will start to control you and take you off track. Your connection to her could ruin your business . . ."

"Ben's body was really glowing all morning," Gerald relates one Tuesday afternoon, "Beatrice threw her arms around him and hugged him. Then she said, 'I love you Ben, you are the best', and kissed him."

Gerald seems prouder of Ben than he ever was of Samantha or Martin. In fact, he admits that he loves the decaying remains of his former canine companion more than his own children, principally because of Ben's divine status and the profound effect it will have on our future spiritual survival. As we sit, Gerald holding the dog, I concentrate on focusing into his eyes as I am always required to do when we are alone. In a moment of weakness, betraying my commitment to withdraw, I find myself seduced to share his personal aspirations as I used to. I return to my old self, the faithful Group member, wanting desperately to satisfy Gerald's heart's desire, to resurrect Ben, no matter how. My solution is both creative and bizarre. In a cloud of fantasy, I convince myself that I feel my ears growing longer, changing into a dog's ears. This is just the type of thing which will capture Gerald's attention. I alert him, and he is instantly excited, following my every word with awe. Together we focus on completing the transformation and soon a snout and tail appear. I experience an uncontrollable desire to bark and pant, and within about fifteen minutes I have become Ben for real. Gerald can see his soul hovering, surrounding me like a ghost. Happy to be relieved of the conflict which has been building between us for a few years now, even if only for these brief moments, I inform him with delight,

"Gerald, I can actually feel Ben's personality in the air; in fact, I just heard him tell a joke!"

When our time is up I rise and head toward the door uplifted, smiling and patting Gerald on the back in intimate comradeship. A moment before I reach the exit, he rewards me for my participation, handing me a small piece of matted fur from Ben's decomposing belly. I slip this precious talisman into my wallet, evidence of my connection to Gerald, but really to myself, the only life I have known . . .

These past few months of self-imposed separation have been more than difficult. Abandoning my resolve, albeit temporarily, I have found a way to obtain a rare injection of Gerald's approval, the substance of my addiction. I feel uplifted and content for the rest of the day . . .

When he is not applying himself to Ben's rebirth, Gerald is making his rounds, book signings arranged by Samantha who serves as his manager. His first Manhattan lecture takes place at the *Barnes & Noble* near East 86th Street. My mother, Bess, Pauline, Laura and Beatrice attend, seating themselves in the front row like the ardent fans of a revered rock singer. I arrive, a little later than the rest, and when I scan the crowd I spot them immediately. An aura of worship seeps from their pores and I want no part of them. Grabbing a chair in the back unobtrusively, I pray that they won't notice me or pick up my true feelings, revulsion so powerful that I fear that even if I freeze my face in a neutral expression it will be perceived. I do not want to be punished tomorrow for tonight's traitorous attitude.

Gerald talks for a while and then tells the audience he has a surprise for them. Laughing, he warns,

"I am a weirdo but do not be afraid."

With that, he seats himself on a stool and begins to shake his head with slow determination. *Oh God*, I think, *Why is he embarrassing himself like this in public.* I look around wondering how the audience, and a few managers standing in the back, are receiving his bizarre behavior. I grit my teeth and pray for him to finish. Faster and faster he goes until the whole stool is shaking. His activity creates a loud, repetitive clatter as the metal stool bumps against an adjacent bookcase and he draws a small curious crowd. When he stops, he asks the audience if they feel The Energy. A few people say that they do, but several others walk away shaking their heads in disgust. Gerald selects a woman in the second row with whom to focus. She seems to slip into a trance-like state under his intense gaze and claims that she feels calmer. After the signing Gerald hands out business cards and invites several people to his N.J. group next Thursday night "if they want to learn more". A few purchase an autographed copy of his book.

All of the local *Barnes & Noble* managers know Gerald and Samantha well. What they don't know is that the image of the sleeping dog on Gerald's business card is of Ben's carcass, hidden even now behind the den couch while his master is on the road. They have no idea Gerald believes that the heated white rock he offers gingerly for them to hold for a moment contains Ben's soul. They don't notice that he is sucking on something small while he is lecturing, and that something is a toenail from Ben's carcass. They have no idea that their customers might get hurt, should they take Gerald's offer and attend a Thursday night group.

The following month he holds a book signing at the *Barnes & Noble* in Nanuet, N.Y. During the first several minutes he informs the audience that their life and everything that happens to them is their responsibility. If only they would accept this and stop blaming other people and the world for their misfortunes, they could be the architects of their own lives and eventually have anything that they want. A woman raises her hand to disagree.

"How can absolutely everything be within your control?" she asks, "There are things that happen every day that no one has any power over. What about the people who were just killed in the Oklahoma City bombing? They didn't ask to die."

"Yes, even they were responsible," Gerald replies, "Those victims sent out a message to the spiritual universe that it's OK to kill me."

Several members of the audience groan and within the next few minutes, some walk away. Later during his hour-long lecture he states with surety,

"I know that you don't want to believe it, but you are God; if only you had the self-confidence to accept it."

An instantaneous rage passes across the face of a sixty-something Italian man wearing a cross who has been standing at the back of the crowd for several minutes. He exits abruptly, delivering a clear message that he is severely offended. Gerald decides to make an example of him.

"See, my point is proven. That man's reaction is evidence that he can't handle the fact that he is God. He is too small-minded and doesn't have the courage to experience how big he could really be; so instead, he runs away like a baby."

Winter 1994 to Spring 1995

One afternoon I arrive at Gerald's to find a buzz of activity. Small black rocks are scattered everywhere and his tables are covered with black and grey velvet pouches. Beatrice looks up excitedly.

"A new enterprise has been born. Gerald is moving ahead and will soon be all over the globe."

I turn to see him sitting in his armchair shaking his head with the "Ben Rock" in one hand and about fifty small black "baby" rocks strewn all over his body.

"Ben just gave birth to all of these," he pauses for a moment and jokes, "Take one."

Gerald hands me a rock resting on his thigh. "Meet the *Ezra Touchstone*, the *Pet Rock* of the Nineties! Ezra is my middle name, you know."

The rocks are soon individually packed by an assembly line of Group members, each into its own velvet bag. Martin produces a tag on his laser printer which states — *The stone contained within will foster a connection between your spiritual self and the universal energy field. Hold it and you can feel the vibrations of the cosmos moving through your body.* Gerald explains, exhilarated,

"All I have to do is shake and put The Energy into these rocks. Any person who buys one will be connected to us through the rock. The rocks will form a network, like telephone lines, and those people will receive new information as we discover it. This is how we will build our army to fight for the truth. Samantha is already on the phone making deals with major department store chains to carry them. These rocks will connect all the people on this globe someday!"

Ben's initials, printed on the bag's tag, have been declared as The Group's official new slogan — "Be Everywhere Now". The rock retails for $10 and thanks to Samantha's sales efforts, over the next month about five local New-Age gift shops agree to stock a few. Gerald claims that each rock possesses a special and unique character, and because a rock doesn't have a mind, it is more alive than people are. We must now model our lives after the simplicity of these rocks.

Gerald's obsession with rocks increases and he constructs a four-foot-high wall of loose rocks around his entire yard, to connect Ben's now empty grave to his house, completing an "electrical circuit" so that the energy from the dog's presence can flow around the property. The Group members collect rocks wherever they can and bring them to him daily, as offerings. We sit holding rocks in our laps, hands and even in our mouths as we focus with each other during group sessions. Gerald shakes and holds a thirty-pound rock on top of his head, claiming he is changing its shape. As we spend our days focusing with those rocks, we begin to see the same aura around them that we have seen around each other's heads, evidence, our leader claims, that they are becoming alive and developing individual personalities. Ben's body is covered with rocks and Gerald

Ben's grave covered with rocks. The rock wall extends behind.

reports that during the night, Ben moves and throws them from his body. Each of The Group members buys several of the *Ezra Touchstones* from Gerald at $10 each.

Beatrice purchases a dozen — Christmas gifts to her entire family. She returns with glowing reports of how peaceful and serene her children and grandchildren became once they held their stones, how grateful they were for the wonderful gift.

My mother distributes them at her office. She offers one to a bus driver, and when a bum on 86th and Broadway begs her for a quarter, she places a rock in his hand instead, telling him that it is the key to a new life for him. Our French cousin Michelle, recently diagnosed with cancer, receives an airmail package containing a precious black stone as a gift. My mother proudly reads Michelle's thank-you letter in The Group as everyone nods their heads in agreement. If she uses the rock properly, her cancer will be cured.

Pauline sends one to her own mother in Roanoke, Virginia, who is about to have an operation. When she receives a telephone call a week later — the operation was a success — she gives the rock the credit.

Nora makes good use of the rocks as well. After years of empty relating, it seems that her husband has found someone more compatible and one day Nora accidentally discovers them sharing an intimate lunch at a local restaurant. Her first response is jealous hurt, but Gerald advises her to "sit on her reaction" until she can go beyond it. He also suggests she offer a rock to the woman to connect her to "something greater". Nora obeys, reporting how her spouse's paramour was profoundly affected by The Energy and as a result, they have become fast friends.

In fact, every day there is another joyous report to Gerald about the amazing responses from outsiders to the rocks, how family members, co-workers and even total strangers come instantly alive, how these people all want to know more about our mission. In the past I would have embraced any new project. In fact, I probably would have been the first horse out of the gate. However now, while the rest dash about dispersing rocks like raindrops, I hesitate. Finally, with all of the peer pressure, and the praise everyone is earning for telling rock success stories, I decide to purchase three rocks. The following week I visit Peter at his new office in Hackensack. (He moved from our building to larger quarters last year.) He greets me warmly; we haven't seen each other for several months. After a few minutes I hand him his gift, the rock in a bag. Recalling my fellow soldiers' sweeping victories, I wait expectantly for a miraculous response. Instead, he glances at it briefly, comments that it seems "very interesting" and shoves it into his top desk drawer. Then he looks back at me and grins boyishly.

"I want to hear all about you and what you've been up to."

I leave his office giddy. He couldn't have cared less about the rock! Relating with _me_ was the only important thing! After that day I don't give out any more rocks. I am quite sure that they aren't going to cure cancer either . . .

There is conflict at our office, much of it over Judy, and one afternoon while I'm on the phone with her, Samantha bursts into the room, pierces me with her gaze and motions for me to hang up . . . immediately. When I have obeyed, she vents her frustration in no uncertain terms.

"I really don't think it's a good idea to have her calling here in the middle of the work day. She is interfering with the business."

The tone of her voice indicates that there will be hell to pay if I don't listen, so later, I ask Judy to page me instead of calling. Regardless, the following week when Samantha hears my pager go off, she instinctively knows who it is and turns from her desk to reprimand me,

"I told you not to talk to her during the work day. We are losing sales because of your friendship with her. Tell her not to do it anymore."

Quickly I silence the beeping sound. A half hour later, while Samantha telephones Gerald, her daily ritual to report in to headquarters, I slip out to the diner across the street and call my friend.

Each day Judy has made a habit of contacting me to make sure I am OK, but today I tell her not to page me anymore either, that I will call her every afternoon instead. That evening Samantha returns home from sitting with her father at about 10:00 P.M. to find me on the phone with Judy. Disapproval written across her face, she motions for me to hang up immediately.

"You are obsessed with Judy," she accuses, "Our business is suffering more and more from your relationship with her. That is why you have no money. You should stay away from her and spend more time with my father. Why must you continue when my father warned you repeatedly that it is dangerous? You have no respect for any one of us anymore. All you care about is Judy. Besides, I don't want her calling the house in the evening. I could be on *America-On-Line*, and the call-waiting gets triggered and bumps me off."

I wait patiently while she drains her stockpile of complaints and accusations, robotically nodding my head in silence. Like a henpecked husband, I have learned that this is the only way I can handle Samantha's unreasonable tantrums. Judy wants me to put her in her place, to tell her that she is not allowed treat me this way. After all, I am a thirty-five-year-old adult. Asserting myself to Samantha seems simple to Judy and she can't understand why I won't just do it. I try to explain that I am too fragile, but I can't make her feel what it is like to be inside my body, how Samantha's anger causes me to recede into impotent terror. These days, I am more aware than ever of my weaknesses and how very much I want to conquer them . . .

As the months roll by, Elizabeth and I cultivate a powerful bond. According to Samantha, she has never seen anything like it. She labels our friendship as an "unhealthy obsession" which, she warns Elizabeth, will surely bring about her total downfall if she does not wrench herself away from it. Soon, everyone directly connected to Elizabeth makes it clear that they despise me — her mother, Mitchell Stavos, Samantha and especially, the head honcho himself, Gerald. Policed by all of them, twenty-four hours a day, her only safe zone is in her car. My close connection to Elizabeth now triggers all of their malevolence to surface. The people who are gaining the most from her try desperately to prevent it from continuing. While we are working toward her freedom, they are instilling doubt in her about my intentions, reinforcing her insecurities and making false accusations about the nature of our relationship. This is evidence to me that I have become Gerald's competition. His ego is now threatened because his most passionate follower has met someone whom she admires more than him. This creates a battle for control that makes me the object of hatred and jealousy, and Elizabeth the pawn.

When I was growing up, Hoboken's population consisted of mostly blue collar Europeans. Women did not work outside of the home. Their responsibility was to raise the children, usually four or five, while their husbands worked many long hours to support the family. Life was not easy. Who would want to give up so much of their time and energy for a paycheck that barely covered the expenses? I lived in a cold water flat with my three siblings. Our only source of heat was generated from a kitchen stove which had to warm five, large, box rooms. At a young age I understood my parents' sacrifice to raise us, how most of the time they struggled to gather whatever emotional resources they could to deal with their own areas of weakness. The rest of the time was spent fighting and taking their frustration out on the children and each other.

I never really knew my father, I mean, who he was inside. He had a violent temper which he directed at my mother and siblings. I was the only one who figured out how to stay out of his way and avoid the beatings. The evidence of his rages covered the doors and walls of our apartment. There were dents in the sides of the refrigerator and cracks in the wooden door to the pantry. I spent my entire childhood in a state of fear and oppression, knowing that I lived with an enemy who could destroy me at any moment if I wasn't on guard duty all of the time. While still a toddler, I learned to keep myself in an emotional straitjacket when he was around. Any outburst of laughing or sibling fighting could drive him over the edge into an uncontrollable tantrum directed at any of us. To me, he appeared like a giant monster towering over us with his abusive verbal attacks, glaring eyes and fists flying often out of control. We were basically good kids and nothing we could have ever done, warranted this degree of reprimand. I despised his behavior and his lack of remorse for the damage he did to us. At the age of six I remember a terrible fight between my parents. Observing them, I panicked that his rage might drive him to hurt my mother. Not knowing how to stop him before he went too far, I picked up the telephone to call the police, taking the chance that my father would turn on me for challenging him. Thank God he didn't. Instead, he simply removed the phone from my hand and everything suddenly ended.

My father was one way in the house and another in public. It was never spoken out loud, but my parents instilled in us the silent, indisputable message that we were forbidden to reveal what took place in our private home, even though we knew the things that went on there were not right. Our house was not unique. At night you could hear cries coming from other nearby apartments; violence and abuse were a disease which had invaded our entire neighborhood.

Despite his temper, I respected my father's craving for knowledge and excellent discernment skills. He could pick up a bad intention like a rat smells cheese. These qualities I inherited from him.

It's funny how persecution holds no prejudice. It doesn't care who you are, what you are or where you come from. Gerald's kingdom was a familiar scene to me, a deja vu. Much of Gerald's personality was the same as my father's — the unfounded rages, the intention to oppress, the need to control at any cost, the glaring, the intimidation tactics and the disregard for the well-being of those in his camp. You never forget these spiritual crimes once committed. If I had not been a spectator of my father, I would probably never have been able to understand Gerald's motivations and the depth of Elizabeth's suffering so profoundly. This, to me, is evidence of God's intervention.

Judy begins to question me about my business, asking me how Samantha and I came to be partners, who paid the start-up costs, and how we distribute the profit. Some internal instinct tells me to water down the truth, to avoid the questions and change the subject.

"Oh, Samantha and I contribute equally," I answer, thinking that she brings Gerald's energy which attracts customers and success, and that this is more than equivalent to my contributions of financing, time and talent. However, I realize that I can never make a person who is not a member of our Group understand, so I try to push Judy off the subject, but she is persistent and brings it up again, pinning me down to give more specific details.

"Did you pay for the start-up costs during those first three years when you ran the photography business alone?" she asks.

"Yes, of course," I respond.

"Did Samantha pay anything to become a 50% partner?"

"No."

Again my mind tells me that The Energy is more valuable than my money. Otherwise, there would be no business no matter how much I invested, but I can't explain this to her. She has not taken the journey I have and would not understand.

"Does Samantha have any talent as a photographer?" she continues.

"Not really."

"Who spends more hours at the job? Did you ever think about it?"

I think for a moment of all the late nights I have spent while Samantha keeps regularly scheduled hours and is always out the door when her time is up, like an employee, not a business partner.

"I think I do . . . Oh no. You don't understand why Samantha is here. You don't realize what she contributes, that she has to be here."

My unspoken thoughts are filled with Gerald's voice, a speech he gave me just last week, *If it weren't for Samantha your business would have failed a long time ago. Samantha has the drive and passion to push through the resistance and get the money out of the customers. No matter what kinds of games the customers play, she will not fall for them, but you are a wimp and would give away the store if Samantha left it up to you. She is not lazy like you either, because she spends so much time with me and I force her to focus on The Energy. Last Sunday, I shook my head for eleven hours, from 12:00 noon to 11:00 P.M., and Samantha and Martin were here with me. Of course they wanted to run but I forced them to stay so that they can learn to be more powerful. You are not my daughter; you are not so lucky to have all that time with me. You can't help being inferior to her. You must let her lead the business to success which you will both share.*

"Honey," Judy says ever so gently, ending my thoughts, "I think you're being exploited."

Judy repeats what she has just said and patiently asks me to verify again, "Who started the business and paid for the start-up costs?"

"I did."

"Who takes the pictures?"

"I do."

"What does Samantha do?"

"She does the sales; I am not good at that; I am afraid of the customers; she is not."

"Who did the sales in the first three years, before she came into the business?"

"I did."

"Then why can't you do them now? Where did you lose the ability that you had? Didn't you make a good profit your third year in business all by yourself?"

I am in a corner. Her clear and simple logic shows me that there is something missing in mine; my thoughts have somehow become twisted. I can't help but admit that she is right. I begin to question why I am so sure that I can't do the sales when I was able to do them before. How have I come to deny, so absolutely, my own achievements and abilities?

Exploited, exploited, exploited, what is that? I turn the word over and over in my head. Of course I know the dictionary definition. I scored in the 98th percentile on my high school SAT exam! Yet, I do not seem to be able to apply this word to my own life. It is not in my working vocabulary. Everything Judy has just said makes sense. I can acknowledge it all to be the truth when I separate from my emotions and habits and just evaluate the situation objectively, but looking at my life from this foreign perspective is excruciatingly uncomfortable. My mind is filled with excuses, rationalizations and unjustified affection for my leader, Gerald, the perpetrator of the crimes against me. This affection is based on familiarity, social obligation, my emotional needs and projections, and it forms a knotted tangle of thoughts and habits which bind me with my "family", quicksand which restricts my movements almost completely.

As shaky as a six-year-old struggling through his very first addition problem, I repeat back to Judy mechanically, almost without comprehension,

"I am being exploited because — I paid the start-up costs for the business; I worked without a salary for three years to get it on its feet; I spend more hours now than Samantha does; I have the photographic talent and she doesn't . . . "

It feels so strange; there is no arguing with the facts, but at the same time, it all feels wrong. There are other factors, The Energy and the irrevocable dictum that Samantha _must_ be there. This way of thinking is familiar to me, my only reality. It must be true because I have repeated Gerald's logical conclusions about his daughter a hundred times in my mind over the last four years. I have heard them repeated another hundred times by The Group members. On the few occasions when I questioned these "facts", I was publicly humiliated, beaten down until I learned not to question, but instead to repeat Gerald's logic to myself whenever doubts rose in my mind, until those doubts were pushed deep down once again. _Samantha brings The Energy. She must be in the business._ However, those explanations never could quite kill my doubts, which often torment me still, especially when I am exhausted from overwork. Over the past eight years, since I have invested so much into this photography business and then again, into the flash cards, since I have taken Samantha as a partner and paid her half the profits, since Gerald's demands for attendance have increased, I have been running out of money at such a rapid pace that it terrifies me. The only solution I know to stave off this powerful downward momentum is to work harder and faster, and to struggle to find ways to work smarter. Nevertheless, no matter what I do, I can never relieve myself or turn things around. My financial state continues to worsen and my physical body is at the point of giving out from sheer exhaustion, drained from fighting this impossible battle. Due to the rapid decline of my personal well-being, doubts arise from my mind with even greater frequency, and I must apply all that much more effort to push them away.

It is in this gentle but persistent and intelligent manner that Judy begins to expose Gerald's lies. Her assertion that I am being exploited is just the reinforcement I need to support what I have always truly felt, but haven't had the strength to stand up for. Although her logic _feels_ so unfamiliar and sounds so wrong, instinctively, I know it is right, and I trust Judy because she treats me with love and respect. Still, based on Gerald's accusations that Judy has ulterior motives, I cross-examine her in my mind, but always end up concluding that she has nothing to gain from my agreeing with her. She seems to genuinely want to help. Brainwashing is accomplished by a repetition of thoughts until they become part of you, and by eliminating conflicting stimulus. Judy's input marks the birth of that crucial conflicting stimulus, and once I determine that what she says is correct, I begin the exhausting work of repetition of new thoughts, developed from my interactions with her, to oppose my existing ones. Slowly, I allow her to lead me like a blindfolded horse out of a burning barn while Gerald claims continually that I am becoming her follower and that she is playing the role of a mother. However, this is far from true. In fact, initially, I oppose most of her "opinions" because they are in direct opposition to what I believe in my mind. I frequently defend Gerald to her, telling her that she is wrong about him and doesn't understand our group, that Gerald is a good man who knows more than we know, who is on an important mission. I never give in easily or automatically as he professes, as if I am just simply throwing out his belief system and absorbing hers without a mind of my own. In reality, two powerful forces run neck and neck inside of me, both desperately struggling for control. One is my insatiable thirst for the information which will solve the agonizing conflict in my soul. The other is the pronouncement from my brainwashed mind that everything Judy says is wrong. I have come to firmly believe that any thoughts which haven't been approved of by Gerald are wrong; I am terrified to think otherwise. Therefore, I fight against my current way of thinking, accepted by The Group, with gut instinct and faith alone. It is painful and scary, but I truly have no choice. I sense that my survival is reaching a critical point. I refuse to let myself become impoverished and I must not let my body fail. I will make whatever changes are necessary to solve my problems; there is no negotiation. I must survive . . .

I accept Judy's help and she becomes the life preserver that is thrown to the drowning man thrashing in the sea, the strong arms that pull you struggling and shivering up the rope and over the deck to safety. In making the choice to examine my own thinking and remold it, I begin to gently tease apart the wires of the time bomb which is about to blow up and destroy me. The job is slow, requiring patience and constant attention in order to avoid disaster, and nervous breakdown always seems just about an inch away. I know that Judy sees the entire ugly picture, while I only see the tip of the iceberg. As impatient, lost and frustrated as I know she sometimes feels, Judy can only feed me one spoonful of reality at a time. She must wait for me to swallow and digest before feeding me the next one.

Elizabeth never gives up trying to get me into that group. Most of the time I can tolerate her persistence, but at other times it becomes unbearable, so I finally give in and agree to go. This time I am not upset. I know I have to put myself into the war-zone so that I can get more information to help her. This Thursday night when I enter the "devil's den" I come to see the truth at a much deeper level . . . The air seems thick, as if I've just walked into an opium den, and my senses lose their sharpness as a wave of sluggishness hits me. It feels as if my abilities to reason, analyze and challenge are being completely drained from me; I feel heavy and empty. Gerald sits in a big armchair with a cane across his lap. He quickly explains that he needs it to walk because a special energy has filled his foot, swelling it painfully. This is a necessary part of his body's spiritual transformation. The group members look like the living dead, pale zombies who seem to only vitalize themselves momentarily in order to spit out some venomous, judgmental or intellectual comment before dropping back into oblivion. I notice that all of the groupies are women with the exception of two weak-willed men. They appear to share common characteristics of low self-esteem, an inability to assert themselves and personal isolation. His devotees gather around him, seated on sofas, folding chairs and some even at his feet on the floor. They all stare at him as he shakes his head back and forth — slowly at first, then faster and faster for about one or two minutes. This is supposed to release the energy from his body, energy he believes can heal and protect — everything that God can do for us, only he has convinced himself and his followers that he is the Almighty. He is sure that in the near future he will discover the key to life and death, and achieve immortality. I observe an outrageous ego which will accept no challenge, and a status quo of hero-worship as his followers perpetually reinforce his position as omnipotent leader. In fact, they believe that only he is the key to their ultimate wisdom, happiness and everlasting life. Like a vampire, he feeds off of the energy of his devotees and requires their adoration to survive; without them he would be completely deflated. I am distressed and offended by the twisted lies that are being promoted and defended in this room. I think of a treasured picture of Gerald that Elizabeth carries in her wallet. This revolts me. The allegiance she and the rest have to Gerald is incredible. My experience attending this session confirms what I and a few of the others in *UWSA* had suspected, that this is a cult, and Gerald has definitely set the whole thing up simply to benefit himself.

In addition, what is this head shaking all about? Groping for answers, it finally dawns on me. I remember a day, after a particularly hard workout in my Karate class, when I slipped into a state of deep calm, created by the release of endorphin in my brain. I realize that Gerald, instead of using drugs or alcohol, is keeping himself high all day long by shaking and triggering his brain to release the chemicals which will separate him from reality!

I sit there for two long hours, focusing on the leaves of his Ficus tree and praying for protection. When we are finally released, I do not even pause to speak with Elizabeth, but with gut-wrenching stomach sickness, rush home to my bathroom where I vomit, a reaction to the profound evil I have just experienced in that room . . .

The information I gather from my own personal observations and additional facts from Elizabeth helps me to discern Gerald's unique con. The psychological elements of Gerald's past are the seeds for his current choices and behaviors. Elizabeth has told me about Gerald's abusive mother. It is clear that he never resolved his hatred for her, so he created his own personal dictatorship where he continually punishes his followers for his mother's crimes. He hates any kind of nurturing or feminine behavior and demands the women to eliminate all natural expressions of love and affection by convincing them that this is "mothering" and part of the destructive "Female Game" whose sole purpose is to manipulate men. I would describe him as a malevolent genius who constructed his own kingdom where all of his obedient subjects never question him and offer the total allegiance he demands at the expense of their own personal well-being. He controls their minds and behavior by restricting their natural curiosity and instinct to form their own opinions, by not permitting them to discover anything on their own, especially their personal feelings. He must conclude everything first, and if he doesn't agree with what they say then it isn't so. Anyone who tries to contribute any new information, not approved by him, is cut off with a display of raging put downs, glaring hostile eyes and strong arm threats. Emotional domination is used to direct all of their thoughts and actions back to The Group's doctrine and to block all possible exits. The consequence is that all ability to make a moral choice, or distinguish right from wrong, is repressed or even removed from their beings.

In his meeting, I observe this myself. He even tests his approach on me, but gives up quickly, sensing that I am on the edge of throwing it back into his face. I am not afraid and would never allow him to make me recede. Unfortunately, he has found weak, vulnerable, empty women to victimize with few personal resources to defend themselves, and he is having a field day with them. His followers are isolated planets with no sign of life, circling him, while he falsely accuses them of interpersonal transgressions, so that they are constantly in a state of guilt and unworthiness in his awesome presence. In essence, he has taken their souls and inserted his will. He has unified their minds with his by robbing them of their individuality and spirit. He has convinced his followers that the more time they put in with him, the closer they will approach their goal of immortality. In addition, their financial investment will be returned to them some other way. Clearly, this is Gerald's reinterpretation of the spiritual "Law of Reciprocity" for his own benefit.

When I discover that Elizabeth sees him more than twenty hours a week, I hit the roof. The injustice and exploitation throw me into a rage and I confront her,

"What? Are you crazy? You've been in there for more than fifteen years. You have no other life. What's he offering you for all of your time, devotion and money? You know, a relationship should be a two-way street. Unless there is give and take, an even exchange, then one person is being taken advantage of. In addition, no man in his right mind would ever stay with you as long as he has to compete with Gerald. Do you want to wake up in twenty years and realize that you have wasted your whole life in his den?"

I hope the truth will find its way to Elizabeth. She looks bewildered, hesitantly agreeing that she wouldn't want that to happen, and I know there is hope for her.

Elizabeth finally admits that Gerald has had sex with most of the women, who now range from thirty-two to seventy-two. He has directed them against their wills to kiss and fondle each other and to pleasure him (while they pay for the honor!) but he never reciprocates. I can't believe that this is going on a couple of minutes away from my home. With all that I have discovered, I am beside myself with outrage and I have to hold myself back from going right up to that son-of-a-bitch and poking both of his eyes out! I know I can't fight Elizabeth's battle for her; I must find patience and reinforce my trust in God, whose hand I see in both of our lives . . .

A little bit at a time, Judy encourages me to acknowledge the accomplishments I have made in my life. Her respect is refreshing salve on a burning wound . . . She reminds me that the people I choose to be a part of my life should lift me, not bring me down. What a revelation that an alternative even exists to the interminable condemnations and humiliations which have been my steady diet in The Group! I feel like a child just learning to walk, discovering that there is a whole world outside of the four walls of the tiny crib. I watch Judy as she strokes the face of her little niece, telling me how sweet she is. I look at her in amazement, dumbfounded. This concept is new and strange to me. Sweet? What is that? A person can take joy in the beauty and innocence of another? In the place where I come from everyone is inadequate, even despicable, to be judged and hopefully corrected by Gerald's Energy. Failure as a person is perpetual and unavoidable.

I grasp each new concept Judy presents me, turning it over and over in my mind, commanding it to stay, even though it feels like a strange foreign object. Absorption is slow, but my eyes are opening, as if I have just remembered a movie I saw so long ago. Like Rip Van Winkle waking up after his twenty-year sleep of nothingness, I can't believe all that I have missed. It is so incredible to feel alive, too magnificent to ever allow anyone to cut me off from myself again. The more of myself I reclaim, the more I understand what is going on in my circle. The Group can only exist when each individual severs the connection to her own self-worth, leaving Gerald's approval as the only possible source of personal satisfaction or value. Like selling our souls to Satan, we have transferred ownership of our lives to Gerald, and I can't figure out what valuable commodity we receive in return for the donation of our most precious possession. As I pass my sessions in observation, the mechanics of control and oppression for the personal gain of Gerald and his children slowly expose themselves. I gather new information each day and compare notes with Judy each evening . . .

As I look at the world around me with new eyes I realize how cut off I have been from others. I begin to notice the people I ignored before, having heartlessly judged them with Gerald's prejudices, as dead robots with no feelings. Now, I look into their eyes and see sweetness and struggle, fear and hope, a sameness of soul. I realize that their lives are like mine, with tragedy and joy and the dream of a better tomorrow. They have personal victories and failures which they experience just as profoundly as I do. Although I haven't known it for many years, I begin to see that I am a part of this mass of spirit and humanity, not above and separate as Gerald has taught us. I realize that other people have something to offer me, an aliveness and intelligence which I can share. These people could be friends. How extraordinary this seems!

One evening I view a football game on Judy's TV. I notice a light blue glow around the white helmets of one of the teams. Interpreting this phenomenon from Gerald's viewpoint, my mind drifts to The Energy we saw around David Arkenstone's head on Marty's video of the concert. Suddenly I wake up to my own faulty conclusion. Bolting out of the recliner, I rush into the kitchen, jumping up and down like a little kid, barely able to contain the exhilaration of my discovery.

"Jude," I declare, feeling like a baby bird who has just pecked his way out of his shell, "Before I would have believed that the glow around the helmets was from The Energy. Its presence would have meant that the team is going to win. I just realized that the glow is only from the TV tube. There is a physical explanation for what I saw. It's all about electrons and magnetic fields. It has nothing to do with Gerald and spiritual forces!"

Relieved from the burden of yet another one of his lies, I throw my arms around her, "Thank you for being my friend."

May to August 1995

I am driving home from work when something suddenly darts in front of my car and falls in the middle of the road. I pull over and jump out. Holding up my hand to stop the traffic, I dash out to discover that it is a baby squirrel. Hesitantly, I pick him up. His head is bloody, but when I clean him up, he seems to be OK. "Rocky" becomes my constant companion. He is only a few weeks old and must be fed with a baby bottle. He comes to the office with me every day where he sits on my shoulder and plays with my hair while I am on the computer. Gerald is delighted with this new creature for his experiments. He holds him during each session and shakes his head until Rocky becomes knocked out from The Energy and hangs limp in his hand, his body jolting from electrical surges, just as my kitten, Flash, did four years ago. One day Rocky has a seizure. The vet tells me that he probably fell out of a tree on his head, and there is nothing we can do. He is not sure if the squirrel will survive.

Soon Rocky is eating peanuts, apples and almonds. I am afraid to let him back into the wild. I fear that with no parent to train him, he won't know how to find food. A month later the seizures worsen. My heart breaks every time they come, wracking his tiny body with painfully overpowering spasms.

Saturday, July 3, noon
I enter the den with Rocky. In the silent room there are about eight people sitting around focusing on the carcass, but although I expected her to be here, my mother is not among them. I seat myself on the floor Indian-style and open his pet case as I usually do. In an instant, Rocky bolts from the carrier and escapes to hide behind the couch in an adjacent room. There he has a massive seizure. Samantha reacts immediately. She races to the squirrel, grabs him roughly as if he were a piece of garbage she is about to throw out, tosses him back into the carrier, shuts the lid and glares, freezing me with her gaze.

"You have disturbed my father's group while he was doing something important, just because you wanted attention."

"No, that's not true." I whimper impotently.

I can't understand what is happening, but in the next instant, Gerald jumps out of his seat, rushes toward me with no explanation, and grabbing me by my hair, literally picking me up into the air. Nora reacts to this violence and sucks in her breath audibly, but the rest simply sit motionless, as if in a trance, staring blankly. With burning eyes, he commands,

"Get out of here now."

The shock dazes me and I feel little pain. I cannot comprehend what I have done to deserve this. This tornado of persecution has manifested out of nowhere in the space of only two minutes. Gerald grabs Rocky's case and shoves it into my hand. He drags me toward the exit and throws me out onto the deck, firmly slamming the door behind us. My eyes fill with tears as I drive the few blocks home. Once safe inside the house, Rocky has another seizure. I sit next to his thrashing body, watching helplessly, praying he will get better, until finally a couple of hours later he calms down. We both fall asleep from exhaustion, my outstretched hand touching his tiny paw. Late in the afternoon Judy calls. The day before I had promised I would drop by her house today for a barbecue, and I never showed up. Naturally, she is more than a little concerned. I make a lame excuse that I am tired and don't feel up to it. She is upset and disappointed. She senses that I am hiding something and probes for more information. I resist and change the subject. How can I explain the real truth? I must deter her inevitable reaction. I know her fiery Italian temper will explode like the Fourth of July fireworks. She will want to grab her husband, drive to Gerald's house and put her fist through his face. Although I love her for her dedication, I know that she can't go into combat for me. It will be many weeks before I tell her the truth . . .

These days I am losing weight rapidly; I look pale and exhausted. No one in The Group seems to notice or care, including my mother. Gerald and Samantha observe from their spiritual thrones, dispassionately contemplating my downfall. When the mood strikes them, they excoriate me for my poor health. I must be disobeying The Energy to look so terrible. Funny, every other person in that room, including them, looks just like me — denied, deprived, empty and lifeless.

Gerald reminds us sometimes that we don't need to eat anyway. "The Energy will fill our stomachs. Eating is nonsense. The brain is miraculous and can take care of the body without food, if we would just let it do its thing". Picking up a rock, he jokingly mimics taking a bite.

"If we didn't have the barriers of The Program, we would be able to nourish ourselves with these rocks!"

Pauline, even more haggard than I, enthusiastically agrees,

"Yes. I know. My stomach feels full and I haven't eaten for eighteen hours!"

Daily at my office, I drive myself relentlessly to perform, to fix the mistakes in my life. Sometimes I think of breaking for food, but a voice in my head commands, "Don't eat. You'll be OK without food. Just keep working. You'll make it. Get the more important stuff done first."

Inside my mind an intention controls me. Denying food consistently, there seems to be a drive to deliberately starve myself to death. One day a photography customer notices that I look peaked, much worse than the last time she saw me about a year ago. Unconsciously, she senses that there is something terribly wrong and invites me to lunch. The next day I mention her gesture to Gerald.

"Oh she is just mothering you and feeling sorry for you," he responds.

Meanwhile, Judy struggles to get food into me. She cooks sumptuous Italian meals. Grinning with delight, she even puts the fork-full of food into my mouth herself and watches while I chew and swallow. Gently, she encourages me to finish what is on my plate and praises me when I do. Each day she asks if I have eaten and what I have eaten. She reminds me to make sure that I eat, "Your body can't run without fuel."

Judy is also concerned that I don't get enough exercise.

"We don't need it," I answer automatically, based on Gerald's assertions.

"Of course you do," she replies, "Your heart will grow weak without it. That is one of the reasons that you are always so tired. You spend too much time sitting in Gerald's den. You know that swollen foot he had at the group meeting I attended last month? That was gout, due to inactivity, because he spends all day in his armchair."

Suddenly, I feel like a fool. Of course she is right! That swelling was not The Energy at all. I am ashamed of myself. A pre-med major with a college education and I believe his ridiculous explanation. I had learned about gout in high school science. How could I have forgotten?

Later that week Judy escorts me to the *Jack La Lanne* health club in Englewood Cliffs. I haven't been to a gym since I was on the swim team in college, nearly twenty years ago. On the way in I observe several people on exercise bicycles.

"They look like ridiculous assholes," I spit out judgmentally.

"That is what Gerald taught you. It's not really true. Exercise is good for you," Judy explains patiently.

She puts me on a treadmill and as I begin to jog my lungs clamp up with asthma, my symptom doubling me over. At thirty-five, I feel as weak and helpless as a doddering nonagenarian! I remember my dedication to physical fitness eighteen years ago — swimming, jogging, weight-lifting.

My God. What have I done to myself? I cry in my mind as a powerful wave of self-realization passes through me. I have neglected myself so much that my body feels almost useless. How can I ever repair the damage?

One bright summer afternoon, Caroline brings her 91-year-old mother to The Group. Gerald shakes his head and spends at least an hour focusing with her. The elderly woman experiences profound calm in his presence, and although she has been afraid of cats her entire life, she allows B.J., the Sharkman's orange and gray cat, to sit on her lap for most of the two-hour session. Gerald is thrilled. Thanks to his energy, a miracle has taken place in front of our eyes. This woman has broken her barrier of fear toward cats.

Caroline's mother has cancer. After today's success, Gerald is sure that a cure is in sight, provided of course, that Caroline brings her back for regular sessions. Caroline chooses not to do this although she doesn't explain why, and a disappointed Gerald accuses her of not caring about her mother. In his presence, he insists, her mother's life can be saved. During the weeks that follow, Gerald spends hours lecturing Caroline. He insists that we have the answers to cure disease and she is avoiding her responsibility to share this exclusive knowledge with others. Several times Gerald even accuses Caroline of wishing her mother dead. The evidence lies in her refusal to bring her mother back for more help.

Brigette, on the other hand, brings her two children, now four and five years old, to The Group every week. They protest every time; they hate "going to New Jersey", but their mother doesn't care about their feelings. Eventually, powerless to change the circumstances, they give up their complaints. I feel sorry for them. They sit together in a big white chair, two beautiful little dolls with jet black hair and creamy white skin, gazing into space, waiting impotently for their two hours to be through. Gerald frequently asks them if they want to "sit on his lap and go for a ride". Once he tries to force Lacey, but she screams and pounds her fists on him until he lets her go. Instinctively, they want no part of him. Their mother knows all about the dead dog, but Gerald never shows it to the kids, explaining that they are "too young to handle Ben's power", but he gives them each a rock as a gift, reminding them that it is precious and they should carry it in their pockets always; it will help them with their schoolwork and solve conflicts with their friends. With Craig, he talks "man to man", telling him that he has special knowledge because he comes to The Group. He should remember that he is superior to his little friends who are not so fortunate. He should be their leader. Gerald makes an example of Lacey as The Female Program in training,

"Look at her. Even though she is only four, she knows how to seduce and control men. She is already a little witch."

Lacey glares at him. Silently I cheer and pray for her to be strong. *Keep pushing him away until you grow up and can tell your mother that you will never come back.*

One day in the car, on the way to Gerald's, the kids inform their mother, "Gerald doesn't care about us, he only cares about his rocks."

Brigette laughs as she recounts this to Gerald and The Group. "My children are still too young to understand that you are able to care about them more than anyone else in their lives, but you do it without false emotion and fake behavior."

As summer passes and fall approaches, Judy volunteers to help me select clothing for the cooler months. In fact she would like to teach me how to dress in a more feminine and tasteful style, to help me mature from the unconfident woman I am now, a person who unconsciously leans toward her mother's bargain store clothing tastes. She escorts me to the *WillowBrook Mall* (the scene of my pathetic signature-collection efforts for the "Lesser-Stavos for President" campaign three short years ago!) We spend several wonderful hours exploring stores, examining skirts, shoes and jewelry. In one of the shops, Judy encourages me to try on a cocktail dress, just for fun. As I emerge from the dressing-room hesitantly, uncomfortable in this unfamiliar role, she compliments me,

"You know, Liz, you are really quite pretty; with a little make-up and a stylish haircut, any man would find you sexy."

Her response confuses me. I don't understand how she sees these things. I would never even consider applying such adjectives to myself. Aware of my bewilderment, she inquires,

"Didn't your mother ever teach you how to be feminine?"

"No. What does that mean? Isn't femininity a specific type of behavior that women put on when they intend to trap a man so that they can manipulate him?"

"No, Liz, Gerald taught you that because he doesn't like women."

Grabbing me by the shoulders, she forces me to face my image in the dressing-room mirror.

"Look at that face. Look at the womanly beauty coming out of it. That is not there to control men. That is there to enjoy. God gave you that!"

Glancing at my reflection, I see something I never have before. There is a glow of confidence in my face, a sparkle in my eyes.

"Wow. That's really me; I am really not ugly like I thought."

"Yes, that inner radiance is what attracted me to you in the first place," Judy's voice encourages me to appreciate my own value.

"Well, if this is true, then why don't the people in The Group feel the same?"

She shakes her head in puzzlement. "I don't know Lizzy; I think they are blind and crazy."

The following week, I decide to give in to Elizabeth's relentless insistence that I attend another one of Gerald's meetings. I walk into the den an hour into the meeting, and position myself on a folding chair at the back of the crowded room. I notice a foul smell that is quite revolting. There isn't another place to sit, so I try to tolerate it. However, when someone gets up to leave, I quickly jump into the vacant seat. Unfortunately, I can't escape this pungent odor. I struggle to try to identify it, but the only conclusion I can come to is that one of the women sitting near me has poor hygiene.

Apparently, The Group has just finished viewing a video movie portraying Jesus Christ as a modern day citizen. I notice that as Gerald asks various members what they have learned, he reprimands them when their interpretations are not correct, that is, when they are not the same as his. While he puts them down, others rally to support him, hoping to score points. He particularly attacks Elizabeth's mother, Grace, and I feel sorry for her. It seems unusually cruel, especially for a woman in her mid-seventies. Later that evening, Gerald turns to focus on me.

"You are quite new to our group. What do you think is going on here?"

Feeling put on the spot, I try to respond as neutrally as possible.

"Well, I really don't know much about your group, but I do know that I am very happy to have a friendship with Elizabeth."

I look over at her with a swollen heart and address the room, suddenly wanting to release my true feelings.

"I am very proud that I know her. She is smart and alive and has brought so much joy to my life. She is a diamond."

I notice Elizabeth looking away in shame and I realize that what I have just said is totally unacceptable to The Group. Grace intervenes to take the focus of positive feelings away from her daughter by interrogating me. Her cold nasty voice expresses her intention to set me up as a fool.

"How is your relationship with your husband?"

I try to tell the truth, "We have our ups and downs, but he is a good man and we love each other very much."

I know this isn't the answer they want to hear, since they believe that all married couples are role-playing and don't experience any real feelings for each other. I realize that my honest and forthright answer will confirm in their minds that I am a bimbo, certain to pull Elizabeth the wrong way.

The following morning in the den an annoyed Gerald demands, "Why did Judy lie last night? You don't really expect me to believe the lies she fed us about her relationship with her husband! All married people are in a game with each other, like two children playing house. They are only together because they are co-dependent. Underneath, they really hate each other. It is not possible to live together in harmony unless you have The Energy. You had better watch your step with this woman. Her life is a wreck and she can easily screw up yours too."

Gerald's insistence creates doubts in my mind, and they are still present that weekend when Judy invites me to her back yard for a barbecue. Soon after arriving, I make my way over to her husband, Michael, seated at their picnic table with a sleeveless shirt on. Approaching him to say hello, I notice his tatoo.

"Wow, that's Judy's name on your arm," I remark.

"Yep, that's my Jude." His voice caresses her name as he looks into my eyes intensely.

In that moment I understand the commitment he made to his wife when they took their vows of marriage, twenty-two years ago. Michael has given his heart to a person he genuinely loves. In addition, true to his nature, although he knows very little about me, because he senses that she enjoys my company, he has never stood in the way of our friendship, even though these days Judy dedicates most of her time to me!

However Gerald, in his ever present attempt to separate me from Judy, warns again the following day, "You could be in real danger. One day her husband might wake up and realize that you are taking away his mommy. He might lose control, take a gun and shoot you. You should stop spending so much time with her."

Although I feel guilty about betraying the privacy of my meetings with Gerald, I can't stop myself from spilling it out to Michael on the phone that evening, but he simply laughs.

"That's ridiculous. I would never hurt you. I

Judy, Michael and me at her kitchen table
on my thirty-fourth birthday.

understand that you need Judy. She needs you too and I would never try to take you away from her. The only one I might want to shoot is Gerald!"

Despite all of our monumental efforts, Samantha and I have never been able to find a willing investor for the flash cards. Finally, we decide to apply for an SBA (Small Business Association) loan from Bergen County and are referred to the Paramus branch of SCORE — Service Corps of Retired Executives, to complete our application. Our mentor, Tom Perrone, a former *IBM* executive, is kindhearted and perceptive. He takes an immediate interest in the product. However, he explains that we must learn some basic accounting principles.

That night I toss restlessly and the next day I realize why. I have been repeating the same grievous mistake in my attitude toward this venture. I have never made the effort to learn how to properly run this type of business. Instead, I have tried to convince potential investors to hand us their money to cover up my mistakes, ignorance and lack of business skills. I am horrified that it has taken me this long to realize something so obvious. Finally awake, I am grateful that no one ever invested in our doomed venture. I realize that I would have surely lost their money; I would have never been able to live with myself. The following week I resolutely begin my tutelage under the direction of Tom Perrone.

Samantha, on the other hand, appears to have no interest and elects not to attend any more meetings. Over the next few months we cover the basics of managing a corporation's finances, rudiments I should have grasped a long time ago. I learn how to create a cash flow statement, make projections and calculate profit and loss. Most important, Tom and I discover my biggest problem. I am simply paying too much to make the product. We figure out how to cut production costs for future print runs. With Tom's encouragement I come to realize that I am responsible for the numbers of the company, figures which may be analyzed in a logical and simple way. I should never make a decision to spend without looking at the facts, the big financial picture. Gerald's philosophy about running a business, *Just try it because, you never know. No matter what you do, it'll work out somehow if you believe in The Energy*, is rapidly flying out of the window.

Finally, the plan is complete and we apply to the *United Jersey Bank* for a $30,000 loan. The Bank's regional and local managers visit the photography studio to hear my verbal presentation. With an overhead projector and Tom coaching me from the side, I do an impressive job. Samantha has so little to contribute that our guests don't even realize that she is my partner. I notice her sitting on the side, pale and very angry. As Tom leaves he hugs me; I have come a long way and he is proud.

After our guests have parted, Samantha motions me over, evaluating my performance with cold calculation. "You did very well today, but I pick up that underneath, you still want to fail."

I deny it, genuinely confused. All the time and preparation I invested in this meeting should be evidence enough that I am trying very hard to succeed, despite the mistakes we have made. However, Samantha persists with more energy. For the next half an hour she interrogates me as she always has, willful and relentless. She corners me, glowering, accusing, twisting all of my responses against me. Weakening from her repetitive insistence, I finally believe that I sense this failure sensation she refers to somewhere deep down. I tell her that I think I understand what she is talking about. Satisfied, she dismisses me. I didn't want to fail earlier today, so how did this intention come to be inside of me? It is as if, by sheer force of her will, and despite my genuine protests, she has rammed this negative and ugly feeling down my throat on purpose, to prove her point . . . The following week our loan application is approved, but Samantha, my legal partner, declines. In the weeks that follow, I sell the last of my stocks to pay expenses. However, still short on funds, I look to my only remaining asset, a zero-coupon bond worth $5000, bought for me fifteen years ago to start the retirement fund I have never been able to add to. Despite the 10% penalty for early withdrawal from my IRA, it is all I have left; I see no option but to cash it in. As I stare piteously at my *Fidelity Brokerage* statement which contained assets of more than $100,000 a few short years ago, tears and frustration explode. *That IRA bond was supposed to be there to take care of me,* I cry helplessly to no one listening, *How much longer will this go on?* I beg whoever it is that is pulling the strings to please release me from this torment.

I cut back expenses everywhere I can, denying myself anything other than essential groceries and clothing, never taking a vacation or eating in restaurants. Worrying about money is constant. Any small amount that I earn goes to Gerald or to the money-pit, *Flash Blasters Inc.*, a ravenous insatiable beast. After selling off the remains of my inherited portfolio, despite my better judgment, I have nowhere else to turn but credit cards. I do not know how I will repay them, but I pray for a miracle, a better tomorrow if I could only find the right combination to make my business succeed. My credit card debt, with interest accruing at more than 14%, seems to mount exponentially, quickly surpassing the $30,000 mark. Desperate for solutions, I wonder if I should stop buying coffee in the *Dunkin' Donuts* down the street to save a few pennies. Perhaps I could put that $10 a week toward my bills? While photographing weddings and Bar-Mitzvahs I survey the dance-floor for an eligible man. Opportunistic thoughts flash across my brain, *Perhaps I can attract someone wealthy, someone who will want to support me?*

The downward avalanche toward financial ruin continues. More and more frequently I experience the horrifying vision of myself broke and on the street, worrying where my next meal will come from. Each day this image looms closer, threatening to rip the veil between prophesy and reality and engulf me. The bars of my jail close in tighter and tighter until there is barely room to breathe. It takes all of my energy just to coach myself to make it through another hour, another day. As if a thick emotional wall of resistance and pressure impedes my passage, I feel as if I can barely walk. The powerlessness to solve my problems of financial debt weighs upon me constantly. Each morning I wake up exhausted. During the night, I know that Samantha can hear my relentless hacking cough from her bedroom across the hall, but she never asks if I am OK. Sometimes, afraid that I am getting too loud, I tiptoe downstairs to sit in my recliner in the den, out of her earshot. I feel guilty that the noise may be disturbing her sleep. These days my lungs struggle with almost continual asthma and I cannot mount a flight of stairs without pausing to catch my breath . . .

I push myself through photography assignments, feeling like a slave, fervently trying to push the truth out of my mind, that all of the money which I can barely find the energy to earn, will go to Gerald. No matter how much sleep I get at night, during the day I constantly want to lie down and rest, to relieve myself of the interminable struggle to keep my body in motion. When occasionally I do, I am unconscious in less than three minutes. I undergo a desperation I could have never imagined was possible. There is something seriously wrong with my entire life — my body, my mind, my spirit, my soul. I do not know how much longer I can go on without relief . . .

I think back to the riding camp I attended when I was eight in Upstate New York's Adirondack Mountains. That summer temperatures soared. About twenty horses walked a circuit with children on their backs, eight hours a day in the brutal sunlight. There was no break as each group of campers was cycled through the horse-riding activity. One day I noticed that the horse in front of me was sweating profusely. A little while later he collapsed. He just couldn't take another step.

Now I feel like that horse, worked almost to death. I barely have another thimbleful of resource or energy inside of me and I lean on Judy heavily for emotional support, yet I know she can't carry me.

I struggle to pay Gerald. What other choice do I have? I keep hoping that things will turn around but they never do. Finally, ashamed to admit that I need it, I ask him for help . . .

"Gerald, I'm having problems with money; I don't know what to do . . . "

My eyes turn toward him pathetically; I believe that he must have the solution; I just need to show him that I am willing to yield to his direction; he is the source.

But Gerald looks down at me, sending me the unspoken message that I am annoying and stupid and tackling my predicament isn't worth the breath in his body. However, as if doing me a big favor, he offers his solution . . . That morning one of his new recruits, a rabbi who first met him at a book signing in the Nanuet, N.Y. *Barnes & Noble*, has offered to help him grow his flock.

"The rabbi agreed to approach people at my next book signing. He will sell my rocks and encourage them to join The Group. Why don't you try the same thing and I will pay you a commission?"

This is his solution to my oppressive debt!? Where is his common sense? The man who claims to have all the answers, wisdom beyond my own capabilities, can't even do basic mathematics! I calculate quickly in my head. Even at a 20% commission, in order to pay off my credit card debt I would have to refer one hundred people who would each see him once a week for two years. He currently has twenty paying clients. How could this ever happen?

With no solutions in sight, my shameful circumstances force me to cut back my time with him to a bare minimum — five hours a week plus the Thursday night meeting, $900 a month. Beatrice, Bess and Pauline still spend their twenty hours per week at Gerald's side, and I feel left out, like a naughty child who must stay indoors during recess, pressing his nose against the classroom window, watching all of his little friends play. Although my withdrawal is so significant to me, the fact that I am hardly ever there anymore goes unnoticed by the rest. They just keep moving right along, business as usual.

I live inside a bubble, a detached state of catalepsy, my sole reality existing completely inside me, and there a nightmare rages. Rapidly, the most awful truth of all is sinking in; hurt erupts like a geyser, as all of the evidence points to one inescapable truth which I must now face and somehow accept, an incomprehensible truth . . . *My God, Gerald really doesn't care if I'm in his life or not. I am not special or necessary at all. He has no desire to spend time with me and I can only be next to him if I can afford the admission price at the door. Otherwise, he doesn't give me a second thought. If today was the last time he ever saw me, I would be forgotten in a matter of minutes. I do not matter to him, and I never did.* I see clearly now, for the first time, that if I lose everything and go over the edge, Gerald will simply say,

"Oh well, Elizabeth didn't use The Energy properly. She was too defiant and wanted to do it her way."

Now, when I need a friend, the man I have dedicated my life to for almost two decades is not there for me . . . I imagine myself floundering in the icy water at the base of a large ocean liner. I look up to see Gerald, my mother and the rest standing on the deck looking down at me. Gerald is telling me that the position I am in now is my fault, that when the vessel lurched moments ago and I lost my footing on the slippery deck to slide over the edge, that somehow I was responsible for these circumstances. The others nod in agreement as they emotionlessly watch me struggle to stay afloat. I beg them to throw me the life preserver resting only inches away from their hands. However, they ignore my plea and sing their chorus of "I told you so. You didn't listen to us when we gave you advice because we cared about you. Now you must live with the consequences."

When they have had their fill of inflating their self-importance and reinforcing their self-righteousness they walk away, moving on to other interesting activities on board the ship which will bring them pleasure and stimulation. Instantly, they erase me from their minds, leaving me to drown in the sea.

For the first time I understand betrayal and the terrible consequences of trusting someone blindly. I finally realize that despite The Group's repeated assertions, "We are all here to help each other; you just have to ask; you have the greatest possible source of power in the universe right in this room," I truly am, and for that matter always have been, on my own. No wonder from the first moment I met Gerald, I have experienced such enduring subconscious conflict.

So far, our *Cliff's Notes* sales have been present but disappointing, and after completing my daily commitments to *Expressions Photography*, I continue my efforts to promote *Exambusters Study Cards* in new and innovative ways, perpetually searching for that big opening where the product will finally take off and insure my financial security. However, instead of ever making a profit, I have only succeeded in increasing my already huge loan to the corporation. To make matters worse, after three years of dedicated service with no pay, Samantha begins to insist on drawing a salary. With the company operating at a loss, this salary only adds to my increasing credit card debt. Nevertheless, something inside of me refuses to give up that business, my baby, because I still believe in it. I continue to keep the business alive on more than fifteen credit cards, rotating balances between them when I can't make the minimum payments.

One Sunday, feeling I can no longer tolerate this constant failure and despair, I force myself for the first time to sit down and analyze my situation on paper. Gerald, with his spiritual philosophies about running a business, would not have supported this action, and thanks to his advice I haven't kept records of profit and loss or analyzed my cash flow. For the past four years I have been spending money thoughtlessly, basing my decisions on what "feels right" to me or to Samantha. How easy it has been to indulge our desires and how impossible to earn! Samantha has been just as careless as I, using The Energy to justify any expenditure. On the few occasions when I opposed one of her suggestions she promptly reported to her father who yelled at me until gave in. As long as I was able write a check this situation has perpetuated. However, now the well has run dry.

I dig up my tax documents from 1991 to 1995 and form a pile of the checks written for *Flash Blasters Inc.,* next selecting categories such as travel, development and printing. I organize the checks accordingly, calculate the totals and list them in a table, by year and by category. Four hours pass. A hundred times I want to run from the table, to throw everything in the garbage and go back to Gerald's convenient way of thinking. *Everything will work out OK if you just do what feels right.* However, there is a drill sergeant inside my head tying me to the chair; he holds his gun to my head and I must finish no matter what. Shame mounts and rage pours through my veins as the unavoidable horror of my massive mistake slowly reveals itself. I have spent more than $165,000, and after five years I have succeeded only in creating an additional $40,000 in debt on credit cards! All of this money has been squandered to the ignorance and self-importance of Samantha and myself, two women who believed that what we conceived of so passionately in our minds was destined to become reality because we, the faithful followers of The Energy, wanted it so much. Toxicity floods my system, but there is nowhere to run. I cannot blame Samantha and Gerald completely for this. Yes, they certainly encouraged me, but I have been a victim of my own ego as well. I have embraced my fantasies without seeking a reality check, and like an addicted gambler, I have depleted my funds to pacify my needs. **I despise myself!** In this moment, drained of any remaining willfulness or creative solutions, I experience humility for the first time. I understand now how I was fooled. I remember the sensation I experienced during all of those decisive instants before I wrote another multi-thousand-dollar check to pay for some attractive, but ultimately fruitless, advertising campaign. A special uplifting feeling of false mental empowerment would flood my senses, filling me with a temporary assurance that I was going the right way. However, the figures I have calculated today are clear. I have been lying to myself and those lies, collectively, have forced me to the brink of self-destruction. I vow that it is time to take matters into my own hands. I must turn my life around, correct the mistake and end this ridiculous drama. I must stop listening to Gerald and Samantha once and for all . . .

My first thought is to declare bankruptcy in order to wipe out my credit card debt, money which has financed print runs of flash cards, merchandise still selling at a loss of fifty cents a box. Can you imagine the degree of stupid thinking which drives a person to such decisions? I always knew full well that I was losing on every sale — the more sales, the more money lost — and yet in my ridiculous rejection of common sense, I believed that somehow it would work out anyway. Now I leave this logic behind. I grab myself by the scruff of the neck and scream, "Face the facts." No matter how distasteful, I will force them down my throat.

The following week I visit a *Jacoby and Meyers* law firm for a free consultation. The lawyer examines my liabilities,

"You don't have to worry anymore; we'll take care of you. It's easy to declare bankruptcy. People do it every day. It is a legal way to get a fresh start. Just sign this paper, pay $1000 (I take credit cards if that's necessary), and in three weeks you will be debt-free," he smiles like a reassuring father.

A wave of excitement and relief surges. What a joy to wipe away those years of mistakes in one sweep of the pen! I feel seduced to give in. Yet, despite his optimistic encouragement and my feelings of hopelessness, I hesitate. Of course I desire a solution to my problems more than anything, but my conscience and sense of dignity won't allow me to proceed. Having accepted my mistakes, I would prefer to repair them myself, not seek the wave of a magic wand. I also sense that there are consequences to this course of action upon which he has not touched. Although it is difficult, I walk out of his office, telling him I will call next week. I want a second opinion.

In late August, on the one-year anniversary of Ben's death, Rocky, whose seizures plague him daily, mercifully passes away in his animal carrier. Although I know it is for the best, as I hold his limp body in my hands, grief grips me for the loss of my tiny wild friend, a faithful companion who trusted me enough to sit motionless on my leg for hours at a time, sighing contentedly. I bury him in the woods behind our house, surrounding the grave with his favorite nuts — peanuts and almonds which I purchased only last week especially for him. In the days following, Gerald, who always claimed he would cure and tame the squirrel, informs The Group that I killed Rocky because I wanted to draw our attention away from Ben's first birthday. During the Thursday night meeting he instructs my friends to interrogate me so they can discover for themselves why I committed this ghastly crime against the innocent animal which Gerald had been trying to help. So, for the next hour they take turns accusing me of murder and my attempts to defend myself fall on their deaf ears. Then, for no apparent reason, Bess breaks the momentum,

"Elizabeth, I realize it must have been very painful to lose Rocky . . ."

With this statement the wall of abuse suddenly dissolves and I am released. Gerald immediately moves on to another topic, never to mention Rocky again.

Knowing how bad I feel about the squirrel, Judy invites me to sleep at her house that night. I gratefully accept but shudder at the thought of calling my housemate, Samantha, to tell her I won't be home. Mustering sufficient false courage, my fingers tremble as I pick up the receiver, inform her quickly and hang up, not allowing her the opportunity to protest.

In the morning I lie in the guest bed, enjoying the cozy country decor. Judy and Michael's voices drift up the stairway from the living room. They chat casually about nothing special: mowing the lawn, flavored coffee or visiting the mall. It is the most beautiful music I have ever heard and I drink it in. These people will not hurt me. They will never demand, force or lie. I am safe.

"Rocky"

Then things get much worse . . . The owners of the building where I rent my photography studio retired to Las Vegas in 1992. As absentee landlords, they are less interested than they could be in the condition of the public areas. The back staircase leaks in rainy weather; the hall carpet is worn. Samantha has been calling them long distance for quite some time, complaining and leaving angry messages. Finally, she photographs various trouble spots with her Polaroid. Unbeknownst to me, these photos soon arrive in Las Vegas, accompanied by a not-too-gentle letter. In less than a week, Samantha receives her reply, a certified letter notifying us that after December 31, 1995, our lease will not be renewed because we "seem so unhappy".

I have set up a studio twice in the last seven years and our current premises serve our needs perfectly. I fear that another suitable retail space would be impossible to come by. We could lose our business. In addition, there are significant moving costs involved, costs I have no way of affording. It is clear the landlords were so highly offended by Samantha's approach that no apology from me will turn the situation around.

Samantha's reaction is the opposite of mine, "This is great. A change and a new opportunity. We will take a step up."

I try to promote some common sense, "Samantha, it is very expensive to move. There are walls to knock down and build, carpeting to install, painting, signs to make. You have no idea how the costs mount."

But she only glares at my words. "No, it is a good thing that this happened. You just don't trust me. I will find a way."

The next day she appears with a grin on her face. "Elizabeth, I have a great idea. With our combined rent for the house and this studio we could pay for a mortgage, so let's buy a house! The business could be downstairs and our bedrooms upstairs."

"But where will we get the down payment? I have no money to put down."

"We will work it out," she replies optimistically.

I know we won't; there is no way, but what can I say? She whirls in an exuberant dance for the next two months, contacting just about every real estate broker in the area. She is so enthusiastic that most of them take her seriously and not one bothers to pre-qualify us for a mortgage. Samantha drags me on these escapades. She struts through the premises like a rich man's wife, declaring with self-importance,

"Isn't this room lovely? I'll take this bedroom. You can have that bathroom. We'll put the studio in here. Is the room long enough? No? Well, we'll knock a wall down if necessary."

I shuffle disconsolately in her wake. I can't believe this is happening. How will I ever survive without the income from my business? However, there is no stopping her, so I just "yes" her. Her iron will always prevails and our fights never resolve anything anyway . . .

Later that week, *Cliff's Notes* notifies us that they have finally sold out most of our inventory, those 10,000 pieces in expensive packaging which lost money on every sale. They have established some new accounts, albeit slowly, and things seem to be headed in a positive direction at last. If our business is to continue I must replenish their stock, but this time repackaged at a much lower cost. I open up the *Business to Business* yellow pages and begin my search for a new manufacturer. After several days of intensive research, I manage to redesign the package for less than half the former per unit price. Of course the packaging is not as pretty as before, but there will be profit from our sales. Within a few months I complete the print run and *Cliff's Notes* receives three thousand pieces of the new *Exambusters Study Cards*. The entire project adds about $6000 to my debt but with *Cliff's Notes* supporting us, I know this is the turning point.

Although Samantha has not participated at all, out of courtesy, I take her to meet our new printer. When I introduce them, he mentions that he didn't know I had a partner. Samantha does not take this well. In a split second, I am aware of the intense ugly reaction she is suffering, even as she carefully hides it from this stranger. I sense impending doom and recoil deep inside myself, praying that the inevitable will not come. After the meeting, we drive back to the studio in pregnant silence. When we arrive, my partner immediately closes and locks the door to our suite. My jaw tightens; I anticipate her reprimand. Finally protected by privacy, her face reddens, twisting into a vicious rage as she releases her venom.

"I didn't exist to him! We are supposed to be partners, fifty-fifty, but you are pushing me out!" she states indignantly.

I don't know what to say. I try to explain that I have no bad intentions, that all I care about is putting the company in the black. I am willing to do the necessary work, as long as I get results. However, the engine fueling her crazed rage is boiling and nothing I can say will halt the furnace of her temper. She accuses me of wanting to fail, defying The Energy, being impossibly self-destructive, scheming to hurt her, not valuing her contributions to the company — the same unfounded criticisms I have heard hundreds of times before. Winding herself up until she loses control, Samantha lunges toward me and grabs me by the throat, pushing me onto the counter top. She shakes my head, screaming like a banshee and threatening to kill me.

"You have contributed nothing to the company. I am the source of its success, the one who really cares. Without me it would have failed before it even started."

During these moments everything slows down. In my mind, I silently and purposefully interview myself. *Elizabeth, what do you want to do?* I answer back, *Well, we are both about the same weight and height, but right now she is hysterical. I do remember learning a little Judo when I was twelve. Although that was long ago, I have not lost the ability to focus my fist. I know that if I want to, I can punch her lights out. She's not really harming me right now, just scaring me and hurting my feelings. I really don't want to be violent, so I will do nothing.*

Internally I become limp; I yield, neither defending nor fighting back. I focus past her wrath, into a place of calm and safety, and wait. A little while later, for no apparent reason, her tantrum ends. She releases me from her grip and walks away without further comment.

Finally liberated, my delayed reaction bursts forth and I strike back in frustration and hurt, screaming, "What's the matter with you? We never get along. We're always fighting. I have good intentions for this company, I work hard and you attack me like an animal for something I had nothing to do with."

Pain wells up higher, choking me. I can't tolerate another minute in her presence and I run out of the office, seeking the safety of our home. Inside I vow once again that this injustice must end; I do not deserve to be treated like this. My surging adrenalin creates the sensation of possessing the power of ten men, and in this moment I could pick her up and throw her off the planet, all the way to the moon. Pacing my den in frustration, I take deep breaths to prevent myself from hyperventilating . . .

The next day I am afraid to face Gerald; I am sure that he knows all about the fight and will blame me. However, he surprises me,

"Samantha is a real witch," he states with a glint of pride in his eyes. Then he adds reassuringly, "It's OK now."

Yet, I stay away from her. Not being able to face going to work, I return home. Sometime that afternoon the phone rings. It is Samantha. She sounds sweet.

"I don't think all of this fighting is good so I have scheduled a meeting with a business advisor. His name is Louis Gavin and he will meet with us tomorrow at 3:00 P.M."

She doesn't say she was wrong; there is no apology, but I realize that this is her attempt to remedy things. Relieved that the fight is over, I relax.

"That sounds like a good idea, Samantha, OK."

Actually, when Samantha and I aren't fighting, I often feel friendly toward her. There have been many times that we have enjoyed relating. We share bonds born from common experiences — the discoveries and activities in The Group, our struggles in both businesses, our experiences in *United We Stand America*. Samantha has even made me a character in her fantasy trilogy — Eliza, the buxom barmaid! We have spent many hours relaxing on her bed, playfully throwing around plot ideas for her books or watching TV, like college roommates, in between all of the rest of everything.

The following afternoon a new character enters the stage of our lives. Louis Gavin, a "professional business consultant", is a strange bird. Neither lawyer nor accountant, he explains that he simply freelances, giving advice, writing contracts and assisting business people with negotiations to obtain financing. He claims to be fifty-eight, but his weathered face looks at least fifteen years older. He is skinny, average height and at the moment, single. His body language delivers a failed attempt at seductiveness; in his jaded leather jacket and black polyester pants, he moves like a swinger on the make. He smokes thin brown cigarettes and drives a beat up *Honda Civic*. During our first meeting he tells us that he has been married and divorced six times and had lived all over the world, including Paris. He is now looking for wife number seven. When Samantha asks him why, since he has already failed several times, he pauses to ponder his motivations before answering. Finally he delivers his conclusion,

"I don't like to be alone, and it would be nice to have someone to do my laundry."

He also tells us that he has been indicted for insider trading and has recently served a short jail term after paying a one-million-dollar fine. It is clear that he has only just recently begun rebuilding his life and is hungry for cash. How has this unconventional creature entered our lives? Samantha had called four listings in the *Yellow Pages* and he was the only one to answer his telephone!

In between all of my confusion, I finally find the courage to tell Judy about Ben. As I recount the grotesque details, she listens without comment. In fact, she seems to accept it all. Judy is the first outsider to find out. When I explain Gerald's interpretation about the "worms" Ben is creating, she corrects me, pointing out that they are maggots feeding on his rotting flesh. I could kick myself! I have seen as many horror films as the next person. This is basic, "Biology — 101" information. How did I come to throw away all the science I learned?

The next day I inform Gerald that Judy knows about the dog, but he does not take it well.

"Why did you go and do a stupid thing like that? She might want to hurt him." Then he becomes pensive. "No, she can't hurt me or Ben because The Energy protects us, but she can hurt you."

"Why would she want to?" I ponder.

When Elizabeth tells me about Ben and Gerald's plans to bring the dog back from the dead, it confirms what I have known all along; his goal is to compete with God, to transform himself into the one and only true Messiah, endowed with powers possessed solely by Jesus Christ himself, miracles, healing and, the most revered, resurrection. I realize that there are truly two spiritual intentions which can pass through a human being — one which sustains a person's well-being, and another which exploits and destroys. The entire picture comes into focus — the oppression that Elizabeth is under, Gerald's self-serving lies, the absolute denial of truth and love, and the reason I have such a drive to help free her from the control of this malevolent man. Elizabeth's explanation also confirms the source of that awful smell permeating his den the last time I went to The Group. According to her, the carcass was laid out on a board on the floor, hidden under a towel, only two feet away from me! It seems that Gerald hides Ben from anyone who is not an inner circle member. I conclude that he must know that what he is doing is wrong. If he truly had faith in his mission, he would have no reason to conceal it! It is now clear to me that this man is not only devious and manipulative, but also deranged and potentially dangerous to himself and those who have put their trust in him. With what I have just learned, I am more afraid than ever for Elizabeth . . .

Samantha continues her massive real estate effort in search of the perfect house, and one day she schedules a visit to a potential property in Cresskill, only five minutes from us. It faces a Dumpster in back of a Chinese take-out restaurant and the scent of rotting food wafts across the street, reaching my nostrils as we enter the front door. After the tour, a seventy-year-old house with sagging ceilings, cheap paneling and tiny rooms connected by poor architectural design, I excuse myself to return to our office for an appointment. However, Samantha remains with the realtor, excited and vibrant. They soon return to the real estate office where Samantha starts to "talk turkey". She compiles a detailed list of requests to the current owners which will compose our bid. Finally, the realtor asks her the magic question.

"How much can you put down?"

Samantha replies, "Wait a minute, I'll ask my partner."

She telephones, "I really love this house. Anyway, it's time we made a commitment. I want to put in a bid. How much can we put down?"

"Put down! I have nothing to put down. I've been telling you that!"

"What's wrong with you? Don't you want to move up and get bigger? You always try to stop me when I'm trying to create progress for us."

"But Samantha, I'm telling you. I can't. I have nothing. You know that."

"You always betray me. You are a lousy partner. I can't trust you. You are no good."

"What do you want me to do, Samantha? I have no solutions for you."

"Why don't you put it on a credit card!?" she finally hisses in frustration.

Somewhere deep inside of me I am glad that she has said this, for in this moment she has exposed who she truly is. For months she has acted empathetic toward my agonizing dilemma over the mounting credit card debt and my thwarted attempts to get out from under. Now I have proof that she is a liar and a hypocrite, that underneath her concerned behavior, she doesn't give a damn what happens to me as long as she gets her way. She has no remorse over encouraging me to bury myself all that much deeper, just so she can satisfy her personal desires. I see my enemy before me in full splendor. Although I keep this secret from the rest of The Group, I hold the knowledge close to my chest like a precious jewel . . .

At our first meeting, Louis Gavin has agreed, for a fee of $500, to put together a partnership agreement for *Expressions Photography Inc.* Over the next several weeks, we meet with him a few more times at our studio. As he comes to know us, he learns of our search for a new office and he can't understand why we would want to leave such lovely and ample premises. We describe the landlords' reactions to Samantha's letter a few months ago which Louis finds ludicrous. He offers to negotiate a new lease for us, for an additional $500. This option never occurred to me, to let them cool down and then try to make amends. I just assumed that their decision was final and we would have to leave. After several phone calls, faxes and letters to Las Vegas, not only does he get our lease back but we gain a $250-a-month rent reduction, locked it in for two years, as well! I don't know what he said to them; he refuses to tell us; trade secrets I guess. Whatever it was, it worked, and Samantha's hunt for the ideal house ends as abruptly as it started.

It is the morning of September 15. This afternoon, we will sign the partnership agreement for *Expressions Photography*. It occurs to me that perhaps Louis could also help us find a way to finance the flash cards. We are still looking for an investor, a loan or something, anything, so I make the suggestion to Samantha. Samantha's favorite activity is scheduling and attending meetings, and she especially enjoys preparing agendas and proposals. However, today her reaction is abnormal and strange. She shoots me an ugly look, stating unequivocally,

"That is a bad idea. I don't want to do it. Furthermore, I don't want you talking to him behind my back. He shouldn't get more involved than he already is."

"Why? I don't understand. Give me a good reason," I protest.

She offers no coherent explanation, but instead her expression injects fear into my heart of dreadful consequences, should I defy her decision. Then she changes the subject. This is the girl who dragged us all over creation to meet with everyone conceivable about the flash cards. Now we have a viable person in our lives who has just helped us out of a major bind, and she doesn't want to even talk to him. Why? Later that day Louis arrives and we sign and notarize the agreement. It mainly contains details regarding the disposition of partners' shares upon breakup or death. According to the agreement, we each own half of the business, currently valued at $80,000. After we have finished, Samantha, true to her daily habit, rushes out. She can't wait to go and sit with her father and the carcass. As she exits, she glances back at me to make it clear that I had better stay in line.

However I can't. I must save *Exambusters Study Cards*; I must find a way to repair my finances. This is an emergency and the imbedded instructions to keep my mouth shut, planted by Samantha and her father, can no longer paralyze me. I drag Louis into the other room to show him product samples. This is the first he has heard of our other enterprise. For the next hour I passionately, almost hysterically, recount my entire eight-year journey of hope, frustration and defeat. I describe how the idea came to me from my teaching and tutoring careers, the endless meetings with book chain buyers and investors, the potential I see and my frustration at failure after failure. *Help me; help me; please*, my expression pleads. Louis is riveted to every detail of my saga. His eyes widen as he relives the entire roller-coaster experience with me. He is impressed with my persistence and ambition. Most important, he genuinely understands why I believe in the flash cards, and after that day he comes to believe in them too. A connection has been forged between us. Where it will lead, I do not know . . .

Louis begins to ask the questions which Samantha's lawyer should have, but never did, on the day he made us legal partners. He wants to know how Samantha has paid for her half of the *Expressions* shares to match my start-up investment of $66,000, my time and my talent. The justification that Samantha's contribution of $0.00 was offset by The Energy she brings into the business will only work in her father's den, and she knows this. Therefore, whenever he challenges her, she answers a different question, referring to her highly developed sales talents. Louis also appreciates the portraits which grace our walls. He asks if we are both photographers. Samantha proudly says yes, but when he inquires which ones she has created, she can only point to some unimpressive head shots on one small wall of our waiting area. The creative and lively images of children, pets and families are all mine.

Louis telephones me regularly, calls which don't include Samantha. He continually challenges the details of our partnerships, exclaiming with loud fervor,

"You can't gift shares of a corporation. They must be bought or given in exchange for something tangible, such as labor, accounts or contacts . . . something."

What he says sounds logical, and yet, as if my mind were an empty blackboard with one single definitive phrase scrawled authoritatively across it, I respond in monotone programmed determination,

"Samantha **must** be my partner. I can't explain it to make you understand, but she just has to be."

However, Louis is a relentless drill. He possesses a drive to convince me, to split my head open with the facts he knows to be true. Propelled by an engine whose origin I cannot comprehend, he confronts the brick wall of my thinking process again and again. He will not stop blasting me. Over and over he repeats with force,

"You can't just give away shares of a corporation. How did she earn them?"

In my head, even as I drive to work or sit at home alone at night, his strident, demanding voice rants. Nevertheless, the *Expressions Photography* agreement has already been signed. What can I possibly do? Hire a lawyer and take her to court? I could never afford that and I am too afraid of her father. The dots just aren't connecting.

October 1995

Early in the month, we all hear that Caroline's 91-year-old mother is going down. Her cancer has taken over her body and she is in intensive care at a nearby hospital.

"Well," Gerald lectures Caroline, "I warned you. Your mother felt The Energy, but you didn't bring her back. Now, if you don't do something fast, she is going to die. There is still time to save her but you must yield and let me take over."

The next evening, he visits the hospital. For over an hour he shakes his head at the bedside. Although her mother is half unconscious, he is convinced that when he places his hand on her head, she recognizes him from their last meeting. What's more, she knows Gerald is there to save her and she is glad. He makes several more trips to the hospital within the next two weeks, shaking his head with the intention of turning her disease around. The mother's condition stabilizes for a few days and then continues its descent. Meanwhile, back at the den, Caroline schedules extra therapy sessions to help her get through. The entire Group focuses on offering their advice.

"Caroline," Bess donates her insight, "you must have a secret desire that you are not facing, to see your mother die. This is the reason that Gerald is having trouble saving her."

The rest chime in, encouraging her to face her destructive intentions, her hidden hatred toward her mother. She must confess it if her mother is to ever have a chance. Caroline, appearing dazed and confused, protests continuously. She can't understand how to locate these unpardonable thoughts inside of her mind.

Within a few weeks her mother passes away. Due to the funeral, Caroline misses a few of her regular weekly sessions, but finally returns to Gerald's den one Saturday morning, to try to strengthen herself with his stress reduction therapy. A group of eight or so is present, and they barely give her time to seat herself before they all proceed to shoot incisive "truths" at her. She could have saved her mother by helping Gerald, but instead, she preferred to harbor her lifelong feelings of resentment toward her mother which even now, after the tragedy, she refuses to admit to. Caroline is as helpless as a rabbit being attacked in an open field by a flock of crows. Overwhelmed with grief from the loss of her mother, she has no emotional resources to stand up to this onslaught from the people who have claimed for years to be her only caring friends. Finally Bess concludes,

"Caroline, I hate to say it, but I have just realized that it is because of you that your mother died. By hiding your real hostility toward her, you interfered with Gerald's selfless attempt to cure her."

Once this core truth has been revealed, the entire group rises up to side with Bess. Tears of disbelief and injustice rise in Caroline's eyes. She wonders how she will ever make it through the remaining half-hour of her session. Finally it is over, but even as she is leaving, Samantha adds the coup de grace,

"Why won't you just admit that you killed her? You have betrayed us, your true friends. We have spent weeks trying to help you see the truth, and you just spit on us by ignoring us. You especially owe my father an apology."

Caroline barely makes it out the door and into her car, parked in front of Gerald's house. That evening Gerald receives a telephone call from Caroline. She has invested more than a decade of her life, but after today, she won't be able to return. She excuses herself politely by explaining that she just doesn't feel there is anything more for her to learn in The Group.

During the following week Nora, Bess and Pauline each telephone Caroline on separate evenings to convince her to come back.

"You don't realize how bad your life will become without The Energy."

And after several days, Gerald calls himself, wearing the parental sarcastic tone which always got him his way in the past,

"Well Caroline, are you through with your little vacation? Are you ready to come back?"

Caroline is shaky, sad and confused, but she knows one thing for sure, she wants no part of us. Hesitantly, but with inner resolve, she replies,

"No Gerald, I don't think I'll be able to."

Gerald's face instantaneously turns three shades brighter and he roars, "You have used The Energy for fifteen years now, without it, you will never survive, Caroline. Your health will decline quickly and you will be dead soon."

The next day he fills us in. "Caroline is just another stupid fool who has walked away from The Energy. It was nice knowing her, but now it's time to move on. We have more important things to do. Next."

With that, he begins shaking his head and eliminates her from his mind forever.

━━━━━━━━━━━━━━━━━━━━━━━━━━━━━━━━━━━━━

It is Thursday night and Ben is resting in his favorite spot, on Gerald's lap, on his wooden board-bed. The dog expired more than a year ago and his carcass has passed through several stages — bleeding, flesh rotting and additional hair growth. Now the skull is partially exposed near the snout and the bone inside the eye sockets is clearly visible. Dry, leathery skin clings to the ribs and small patches of hair remain here and there. One of the legs has broken off, but those bone fragments are painstakingly positioned in their former location, awaiting the day when Ben will need them to walk again. Gerald compliments us on our patience and persistence regarding Ben's resurrection.

"Each of you has become conditioned from many hours of focusing. You know, if I showed this to an inexperienced person they would freak out from the enormous power of what is happening here. People can't just walk in and look at Ben, they have to be prepared; they need to train with The Energy first. This is not a stupid baby game; this is real; it is really going to happen!"

Gerald picks up a light bulb and begins to shake vigorously. We all focus on the bulb.

"Just give me a little time and I will make it light," he insists.

Soon Bess sees something amazing and declares in her typically soft, subservient voice, "The light bulb is getting longer!"

Within minutes several other people declare that they see the light bulb changing shape, glowing slightly and becoming soft and pliable. Gerald continues shaking. Wanting to participate, I concentrate as well. I see the light bulb get a little longer, and then, suddenly, for the first time, the concept of the power of suggestion becomes very clear to me. Finally, after so many years, I know the truth. Nothing is happening, not now, not ever, to the light bulb, to the rocks, or to Ben! As a group, we have made a profession out of focusing our mental energy to convince ourselves that we are seeing what we desire to see, what our minds have only imagined . . .

It is 8:30 A.M. the next day. Focusing with Gerald as I usually do during these morning sessions, I slip into a familiar state of foggy relaxed oblivion. Unexpectedly, Gerald breaks the silence and his words stun me.

"Doris left. She moved out in August. Don't tell anyone. No one else knows except Samantha and Martin. I was taking a nap in the morning one Monday. For some reason, I was really tired. When I woke up a little after noon, all of her stuff was gone. Her sister, Susan, from Long Island, snuck into the house and helped her. They must have been planning this for awhile. Lucky for her I was asleep. If I had been awake, she never would have gotten past the front door; I would have stopped her and forced some sense into her."

I leave our session in a daze. As if the wall of a dam has just opened to release an internal flood, hundreds of conflicting emotions churn. The profound truth sinks in. After all of these years, Gerald is finally free! Now he has a genuine opportunity to choose one of us to be his woman. We have all been waiting patiently for so long. In an instant, forgetting all of the abuse I have sustained at his hands, I am propelled by a force much stronger than my own will or common sense, back to the frustrated desires I experienced for Gerald originally, and I desperately want it to be me. This sensation is a hundred times stronger than any crush I ever experienced as a schoolgirl, and it afflicts me for forty-eight hours straight. In fact, the electrical impulses which require me to fulfill them are so intense that I almost can't stand it, but from them, there is no escape. Despite these enslaving internal demands which contradict and smother my true feelings, I know that something is wrong. I couldn't possibly desire Gerald as my lover. I truly despise him!! So, I endure without acting on my feelings or sharing them with anyone, praying for relief. Then, all of a sudden, as quickly as this tornado has come, it disappears without explanation, and I am released from my unrequited love for Gerald forever, a thousand tons lifted instantaneously from my back. The episode concluded, I realize that I have been following an appalling, self-destructive lie, a seduction which manifested spontaneously for no reason, but always felt real and valid. Now finally, after almost twenty years, I have woken up, and shaking my head, I wonder how I could have ever been interested in him at all! Never again will I fantasize, as I have thousands of times, about earning a relationship with him for myself.

Several months later Gerald informs the rest of The Group about Doris' departure. No one has suspected anything and interestingly, they have no reaction either. They do not question why she left him or bring up his previously contradictory assertions about their marital relationship. Somehow what he has always told us repeatedly, and with certainty, has been magically erased from their memories. "No matter what, Doris will never leave me, The Energy would never allow it."

The unexpected loss of his wife of thirty years doesn't seem to fluster Gerald in the least and his mission continues as usual.

"Hey Elizabeth, I have a new gig," he informs me one morning soon thereafter. "Every Wednesday I meet with a group of about twenty inmates at Sing Sing Prison in Ossining, N.Y. They all read my book and are really starting to feel The Energy. I have your mother to thank; it was her idea and she wrote me the letter of recommendation."

My stomach tightens at this news, another group of people who have let him into their lives, who take him at face value, only listening to his words and never seeing the man behind them. I wish they knew him as I do. Perhaps their opinions of him and his philosophy would change radically.

Samantha and Gerald continue to do book signings a few times a month. Their primary motivation is not really to sell books; they sell very few. No, more important, they must spread The Energy. Still constantly competing with them in my head, I feel that I am not doing my part. I decide to organize an event centered around the flash cards and "Quiz Show", a *Jeopardy*-like game, is set for October 11, 1995 at the *Barnes & Noble* in West Paterson. Judy volunteers her keyboard to add sound effects to the presentation. Gerald and Samantha are enraged that I am bringing an outsider rather than using the talents of group members to help me. They insist that her presence will block products sales because "she is my mommy". I won't be able to act like an adult in her presence and attract customers. Nevertheless, I want her to come and I ignore them.

On Thursday afternoon, several hours before the quiz show is to go on, Gerald warns me again in his den. "You will see tonight that because you insist on bringing your mommy, you will fail."

His warnings trigger self-doubt. Fear lives in my heart as the hour of the event approaches. That night my Quiz Show draws a crowd of forty or so students, teachers and family members. The store manager is happy with the response generated from the activity, but no one comes up after the event to purchase a box of flash cards. My heart sinks. Gerald was right. Judy's presence and my defiance of his orders must have somehow spiritually stopped the people from wanting to buy the product. Inside I recede, anticipating Gerald's inevitable "I told you so" the following day. As I predicted, the next afternoon, he attacks me for ignoring him and Samantha in favor of "Mommy Judy". He accuses me of thus preventing Samantha from having the free path to make a large sale for the company. I squirm in anguish, not wanting to believe him and yet feeling sucked in by his familiar logic at the same time.

Suddenly, I catch a glimpse of his profile. Instead of the man I have revered and feared, I see a pouting hurt child and for the first time I fight back.

"You look like a miserable spoiled little boy."

I inject energy to raise my voice, to push away the wave of receding and choking self-doubt, my normal response to his accusations and attacks. Gerald goes crazy, instantly beginning to babble. Frantically he connects disjointed phrases of irrelevant but rational sounding concepts in order to build a ladder of logic which he uses to escape the truth about himself I have just exposed.

November 1995

These days, I keep my asthma inhaler within reach twenty-four hours a day. When I sleep, it is clenched tightly in my palm. One night I wake violently at 3:00 A.M. feeling as if someone is choking me, squeezing the breath out of my lungs with a powerful grip. Desperately, I reach for the rescue inhaler. About to expire, I place it in my mouth and squeeze the trigger. Almost instantly, my lungs relax and I can breathe. The medicine is miraculous. *My God*, I exclaim to myself, *I wouldn't have even been able to pick up the phone to call for help. Without my inhaler, I would have died of suffocation this night.*

I think of how Gerald has always discouraged us from visiting a doctor . . . Life and death. I have visited the edge, even if only for a brief moment. *What would Gerald have said if I had died?* Unfortunately, I know the answer. He would have concluded that I had defied The Energy and had earned this fate as my payment.

The next day Judy begs, "Honey, I think you should go to a doctor for your asthma."

She has been trying to convince me for several months now and I have always resisted her, using Gerald's excuses that I must find the way to push past my physical symptoms, and not wanting to pay the doctor's bill; I have no medical insurance. However, after last night's episode of terror, I finally give in. I do not want to die. She makes an appointment at her own doctor's office for the next day. The doctor finds my lungs to be severely swollen. After an x-ray, he informs me that there are spots on my lungs from tissue damage. In addition, after years of struggling to breathe, my lungs are 20% larger than they should be. The acute asthma I am experiencing requires immediate and daily attention. He prescribes three different inhalers to control my condition. After a trip to the *CVS* pharmacy, I return home, take the medicines, and fall into a deep sleep. A huge burden lifts from my back; I know I have done the right thing.

The following day, Thursday, November 17, I enter Gerald's den at 2:00 P.M. for my regular two-hour session. He is sitting with Pauline chatting. They face each other at opposite ends of the couch with their feet up. It is the kind of comfort two people settle into after they've just had sex, and I wonder if they have. When Gerald sees me, he stops his conversation abruptly to address me,

"How are you doing?"

"Fine. Nothing's new," I return, my voice flat.

He seems to want to probe me about something but I don't know why. Finally he comes out with it, "I heard you went to a doctor."

I haven't mentioned this appointment to anyone. However, I do write things on my desk calendar and Samantha, the snoop, must have reported to her father. "Yes, for my asthma," I respond.

Sensing that his territory (my mind) has been invaded behind his back, the demon that possesses Gerald growls and dons his battle armor. A violated dragon, he stokes the flames in his belly, ready to spit fire, intent on repossessing his stolen property.

"You know that doctors are all liars and we don't need anyone in our group going to one," he shouts wrathfully.

I don't argue with him. I simply say nothing. However, he continues voicing his displeasure until he has worked himself into a frenzy, finally sputtering out,

"Admit that you and Judy are playing a game."

I am incapable of agreeing with him; his accusation is simply not true. My lack of cooperation fuels him and he rises from his seat to stand, almost touching my body, violating my personal space. He glares down at me. Despite his willful insistence, I am unable to give him the response he seeks so anxiously, to invalidate my relationship with my best friend, Judy. Instead I stammer an impotent defense.

"No, Judy and I genuinely love and respect each other."

Pauline sucks in her breath as if I have just stated the worst possible blasphemy. I don't understand what is happening. I have done nothing to provoke Gerald, yet now he towers, glaring, focusing his overpowering will upon me. He commands me to admit that he is right, that I am playing a game with Judy, a game with one sole purpose, to provoke him to react. But I cannot lie, even though now my survival seems to demand it. Fortitude and determination I never knew I had wells up from the depths of my being to oppose this mental and spiritual force-feeding, to refuse to give him what he wants. In these moments revelation comes. *Oh my God! This is what has been happening all along. He has been shoving his will down my throat to control me. All the things I have been believing and feeling has been inserted by him specifically to serve him!*

In the next moment, he shoves me onto the love seat. Towering over me still, he commands, "Admit you are playing a game; admit it!"

I am frozen and can make no move to defend myself against this powerful man, twice my weight and a former Karate Black Belt. Now, in addition, I am mute from terror. Pauline sits in silence, emotionless, but I read her silent message and discern her betrayal. She believes I deserve this treatment for insubordination.

"Admit you are playing a game," Gerald repeats again.

Then his rage to control me moves his hand to strike me in the face. He has lost it, but I still can't move, neither to defend myself nor to leave the room, and I can't force the words out of my mouth which will subdue him.

"Admit you are playing a game with Judy," he says as he slaps me again, and then again.

I am so numb from emotional shock that the blows don't even hurt. Then, all of a sudden, in the midst of his tirade, Gerald stops dead. As if yanked by some invisible string attached to the middle of his spine, he staggers backwards several feet and falls into the white swivel chair. He appears dazed, as if someone has just struck him, and mumbles in confusion,

"I can't do this anymore."

I have no idea what has just stopped him from outright killing me in his violent fury. I have never seen anything like this before. Hurt feelings flood my chest. What makes him think he has the right to treat me like this? I start talking fast in an attempt to shift myself emotionally.

"All I ever wanted to do was help with your mission. I never meant you any harm; I care about you."

I try to convince him of my pure intentions and my genuine spirit, as if emphasizing my own goodness will drown out the reality of the dreadful event which has just taken place. Gerald continues to stare blankly and at one point, weakly affirms what I am saying,

"Well that's good. We need people to help out, not oppose each other."

Ten minutes later my pager beeps. It is Judy. I can tell that Gerald knows who it is and he is jealous, but he doesn't say anything. At 4:00 P.M., when my scheduled time is up, I rise and leave, handing him his $80 fee on the way out. The concept of filing charges against him for unprofessional conduct or assault does not even enter my thoughts, a mind where Gerald is permitted to make his own laws, and his rights come before mine. He has convinced us that the things which happen in his den occur for a higher reason, that the lessons we gain from our fights and reactions will pave the way to our enlightened futures. As if a divine plan exists, beyond all of our comprehension, the way it is, is the way it must be.

I call Judy from my office. She sounds concerned and asks I'm all right. I tell her I'm OK and try to shift the conversation. I can't tell her the truth now. I am too weak from shock to deal with her inevitable enraged reaction. I know she will want to rip his head off and will suffer over not being able to satisfy her urge.

I realize that my process of separation has its own road-map and I must yield to its direction. Each event is a necessary lesson. There will be no maneuvering here, no premature actions taken from thought, personality or reaction, neither mine nor hers. This procedure is as delicate as brain surgery and my emotional well-being is at stake.

Two days later, when I finally do tell Judy, my distress has mostly passed and she is able to accept that as much as she would like to, she cannot retaliate for me. That Thursday evening, only three hours after the incident, I return to Gerald's den for The Group. I don't know how I even get my feet through the door, my hurt is so huge. I am still hoping that after these extreme events, he will finally reveal what I still believe must be buried somewhere inside — that he cares about my feelings, about how traumatized I must have felt to have him attack me like that. However, there is nothing like that coming from him.

Instead, he informs us scientifically, "The Energy sent me a message today while Elizabeth and I were together. This will benefit us all. We can't fight anymore. We have to do things a different way."

I sit in silence, containing my raging feelings. There is no hope of explaining my side. I will never convince him of my rights. It is all beyond that now anyway. I finally face the facts; Gerald has been tested enough; he truly has no conscience.

A few days after the attack, in the middle of a conversation, I sense a motor kick into gear inside of him which I know will drive him to attack me all over again. This time, I figure out the necessary dialogue to pacify and distract him until he calms down. I have changed; I will never let him touch me again.

It is Tuesday afternoon, about a week after my visit to the doctor. Samantha leaves at 2:00 P.M. as she usually does, to head over to her father's den. However, at 3:00 P.M. she returns unexpectedly, informing me that she wants to talk. She commands me to drop what I'm doing immediately and my stomach sinks from anticipation. I sense in her tone that what I am about to hear will not be pleasant.

"Elizabeth, I have just rented an apartment. I am moving in on the first of December."

I stare at her blankly, completely taken off guard. I had no idea she was even looking and I can't handle the sudden upheaval of all that is familiar.

"Samantha, how can you do this? We have had a home together for four years. Why would you want to leave? How long have you been planning this?"

Her reply is whimsical and disconcerting, "I just got the feeling to look in the paper last Sunday. One listing sounded interesting so I went to see it. It felt right when I walked in, so I decided to go for it."

Reality sinks in. I have only two weeks to find my own place and the last time I attempted to rent a decent affordable apartment in Bergen County it took several months. On top of that it is our busiest season of the year. Most important, I am worse than broke. Moving is costly. Nevertheless, Samantha is set; in fact she has already signed a lease.

An hour later I enter her father's den. Ignoring my inevitable turmoil over his daughter's decision, he says nothing to me, but of course he knows all about it; he and Samantha are thick as thieves. Finally I whine and whimper,

"Why did she do it?"

His voice is cold and adamant. "Because this is good for her growth."

"But how will I find a place in two weeks? I can't afford to stay in that house and pay the rent all by myself."

He doesn't respond, but my emotions are running out of control and now I throw a fit.

"I hate her. She doesn't care about me. Why? Why? Why? What will I do?" I work myself into a frenzy.

Expressionless, he observes me. Finally he responds, irritated at my scene, "You had better calm down. You are raising your blood pressure and your veins are popping out of your forehead. You'll give yourself a stroke."

Enough said. He starts shaking his head . . .

That night I call Judy in tears.

"What's the matter, Honey?" she asks, and I recount the day's events. Softly she reassures me that maybe it's for the best, although I am too upset to understand how this could possibly be true.

At that moment her husband comes home from work. She excuses herself from the phone and then calls me back about an hour later.

"Michael wants you to come and stay with us if you can't find a place."

"Really?" I can't believe it. The idea of someone offering help when I am in distress is unfamiliar. "Why does he want me to stay with you?"

"He is really angry about what Samantha did to you. It was selfish and inconsiderate. He wants to call her and Gerald up and give them a piece of his mind. I wouldn't do that to anyone, let alone my business partner and supposed friend of eighteen years."

"Tell him not to call," I request, "I have to handle this myself. I don't want you guys getting involved but I feel really . . . touched." A strange new emotion.

The next day I cannot suppress my intense feelings of hurt from Samantha's abandonment, and I throw them in her face,

"I hate you, you stupid cold insensitive bitch. What will I do now? This is the absolute worst time for me to move. How could you just get up one day and leave without telling me?"

I fling four letter words at her, making my throat hoarse from screaming out of control, but she is unresponsive and instead stares blankly at me in the same manner as her father the day before. I want to go for her throat, to hurt her back for the pain she is causing me, so I grab my pager and throw it at her chair, wishing I had more courage to aim higher and smash her skull. It breaks, costing me $89 to replace it. Samantha continues to say nothing. I am so frustrated by her indifference that I turn spiteful, throwing out the most hurtful secret I have, a terrible reality I have spared her in consideration of her feelings,

"You used me and then dumped me just like your father. That son-of-a-bitch seduced me, my mother and every other women in there. He assembled his own personal harem behind your mother's back. Every day for ten years there was a fuck-fest established for his pleasure alone and he laughed all the way to the bank!"

The arrow hits the bull's-eye. This new information about her precious father drives her into a state of shock and high anxiety. Suddenly I feel ashamed at my childish retaliation. The guilt is so overwhelming that I flee the studio to escape further confrontation.

Sitting in my office, the phone rings. I glance at the caller-ID which displays *Expressions Photography*. Eagerly, I pick up the phone to greet Elizabeth.

"Hi, Liz."

"Hi, Judy. It's Samantha."

Surprised, I slip into a state of suspicion and question why she is calling.

"What's up?"

"I need to talk. Elizabeth and I just had a fight."

She sounds upset and humble. Sympathetic, I ask what happened. When she gives me the details, I wonder whether her distress might create an opening to finally reach her about her father's hidden, corrupt agenda.

"I know this was hard for you to hear, but you are an adult now and maybe it's time for you to understand your father's true nature. He has taken advantage of many people for his own selfish purposes."

"No, you don't understand my father; he means well," she answers automatically.

"You look up to your father, but he is a human being, and human beings don't always do things for the right reasons. If you could only step outside of your relationship and see him for the person he truly is."

"I <u>do</u> see him for who he is," she states matter-of-factly.

Her stubborn intention to defend her father cuts off my hopefulness with the speed of a falling ax. My previous empathy is replaced with frustrated outrage at her denial and I lose my temper.

"How can you continue to defend your father after knowing this? What a self-centered bastard! He claims to be a professional therapist and then exploits his position of authority to convince a roomful of paying, female customers that they must intimately explore his body for their personal growth, when in reality he simply wants to satisfy his perverted obsessions! According to Elizabeth, your father teaches that a man doesn't need to touch his partner at all, that the so-called energy which emanates from his motionless, naked body is all that is necessary to bring sexual fulfillment to any woman! Furthermore, when his victims fail to feel aroused, he blames and humiliates them for holding themselves back. He accuses them of being sexually inadequate when in reality he has set them up for failure. What a sadistic, psychological manipulation! It is obvious that he despises women and punishes them by stealing anything he can for himself while denying them any gratification whatsoever."

After my passionate speech, Samantha remains unaffected and I realize that there is nothing more to say, so I quickly end the conversation.

That night I return home. Everything feels the same as before she gave me the news. Maybe it was all a dream; maybe this isn't really going to happen, or maybe Samantha will change her mind as she often has. Then I notice that some knick-knacks from her bedroom are missing; she is starting to move already.

Each evening for next week, I find something else has been removed. With the help of Martin and her father, Samantha is moving out little by little. First, her collection of numerous posters which have graced almost every wall in the house, then some small pieces of furniture, then some dishes. As each item disappears, I experience emotional withdrawal. It feels as if Band-Aids are covering my entire body and she is ripping them off slowly, one by one. I keep praying that this isn't real until, finally, one day a week later, her bed is gone.

The next day I find the strength to open the newspaper. I circle a couple of places, specifically in Bergenfield, where Judy owns her house. I want to be close to her. A day later I walk through a three-room apartment for $750 a month. The place is disgusting. It smells and needs repainting, an insult to a potential tenant at any price, but this doesn't seem to bother the landlord. $750 is more than I have been paying to share the house with Samantha and I can't afford it anyway. Two days later, I try another listing, $50 less, just a few blocks from the first one. Disheartened, I expect more of the same. I meet the landlord at 1:00 P.M. on a Sunday and we do a walk though. It is small but OK, not at all luxurious, but clean enough for me and my two cats, Flash and Ophelia. On the spot, I tell him I'll take it. As if he intuitively but unconsciously knows the truth, how significant this transition is to my well-being, he shakes my hand and congratulates me.

Mitchell Stavos, who knows many local people, refers me to a young man with a truck who can move my furniture for about $300. I drive over the rest in my car. It takes about three evenings to bring everything to the new apartment. Friday night, the day before the mover will come, Judy helps me with the last load.

As we walk into her new living room I observe,

"You know Liz, it is very strange, at the house in Closter I felt turmoil, and when I walk into this apartment I feel peace."

"You know, you are right," she replies and then sits down among the boxes

Ophelia (left) and Flash

containing her meager possessions and begins to sob.

"Judy, what have I done to myself? Look at me. In four years I'll be forty. I've wasted twenty years of my life. All of that time I could have been saving for my retirement. I'm all alone. I've missed the chance to date and perhaps marry. Soon I'll be too old to have children. I've allowed myself to be abused and exploited. The scars are all over me . . ."

Then, as if she has forgotten that she is a woman in her mid-thirties, she climbs into my lab and throws her arms around my neck. She clings to me so tightly and I realize that I am the only person she has in the whole world, her only support. I hold her tight, rocking her like a baby, reassuring her, loving and accepting her in the way her mother should have but never did.

"At least you are discovering all of this now. Just thank God that you are not those other poor women, Nora, Bess and Laura, who are ten years older than you. Think about the regret they'll feel if someday they wake up at more than fifty years of age and discover they have given away their entire adult lives. You have plenty of time left to live and you don't know what God has in store for you. I know one thing, from now on, it will only be good things."

I know that the concept of a "good thing" is still beyond her understanding, but I continue,

"Let yourself cry. It is OK. You are realizing that a horrible mistake has been made, that your lack of experience and hopefulness allowed it to happen. After this you will learn to let it go. Passing out of any important stage in your life feels like a death, and when the burden becomes too heavy to bear, you must learn to give it up to God. A new, happier life will be there for you after you leave the old one behind. You've made mistakes, but through this pain, you've learned from them. You have been pressure treated and your character has been tempered like steel in a hot furnace. You have undergone baptism by fire. Those trials have made you strong and courageous. This is the person that I know and respect."

I look up at her face. Struck by the depth of empathy in her eyes, I can't hold back my feelings,

"Of all the eyes I have ever seen, yours are the most beautiful."

"Really?" she responds, not used to such a sincere and heartfelt compliment, "Why do you say that?"

"Because you came out of the darkness when I was drowning and had no hope. You reached out your hand and you pulled me to safety. You saved my life. You taught me about God's grace and love. I will always be thankful."

I hug her even more tightly, sobbing into her chest for quite some time.

December 1995

One Thursday night, instead of gathering in Gerald's den, we take a field trip, joining a group which meets at the New Age Center in Nyack, New York. It is led by the center's director, Dr. Pollinger, a Ph.D. in philosophy. We all sit in a circle and I choose the seat directly to Gerald's right on purpose; I want to be as close as possible. I need to experience him as much as I can; the only way out is through. To open the meeting their group of approximately eight explains what they do — experiment with various New Age techniques such as Yoga, Reiki, and crystals. Then Gerald explains what we do. He shakes his head and tells them all about The Energy. The center's members look uncomfortable and skeptical as Gerald speaks, and the director asks our group to each explain in turn why we are so dedicated to Gerald and his philosophies. My mother speaks first, then Jane, Pauline, Beatrice and Mitchell. A year ago, my friends' testimonies would have been terribly significant to me. I would have nodded my head in silent agreement, so grateful to be blessed with my precious membership in our exclusive circle, excitedly awaiting my turn to experience my own self-importance as I expounded on my personal ordeals and the wisdom I had thus obtained. But tonight, none of it makes any sense. It sounds like empty double-talk and generalizations. I feel alien, an imposter in my own family. Mercifully, I am not asked to speak. However, after Gerald shakes his head, the director asks me what I am feeling and with difficulty I squeeze out a few words.

"I feel powerful surges of energy in my entire body. I am shaking from the intensity."

And for some unknown reason, revelation occurs in this moment. An answer appears in my mind like handwriting on a blackboard which had been blank before. This overpowering sensation is my own adrenalin surging through my bloodstream, triggered by fear, because I have always been terrified of Gerald. It is not The Energy!

The director comments after I do. "I see something that distresses me; I see immense dependency in this room."

This undeniable truth blasts in my ears and I silently thank God for his gift, yet another piece to the puzzle. Gerald becomes nervous immediately. He resembles a child making excuses to his teacher after being caught cheating on a test. This is one of those occasions which he always attempts to avoid, an outsider intelligently criticizing our group. He begins to babble logical sounding statements. His speech flows faster and faster, distracting the listeners until they have completely forgotten what was originally said. He stops only when he feels that he has pushed himself past this moment of possible exposure and into the clear.

To end the evening, we stand in a circle and hold hands. I notice that Gerald doesn't seem very comfortable with the physical contact between us; his palm is sweaty.

After it is over, I ride back in silence. Sandwiched in the back seat of Beatrice's car between Mitchell and Pauline, I am a stranger in these familiar surroundings. When the cars of the various group members return to the front of Gerald's house, he waves everyone inside for a powwow, to discuss what we have learned this evening. My comrades file into the house obediently, but I, in contrast, without even hesitating, as if navigated by some unseen director, enter my car and drive home quickly. I feel exuberant in my independence and I know my absence will not go unnoticed by Gerald . . .

The following evening Bess has an engagement with her bluegrass band in a Long Island café. I drive out to see her on that chilly Friday night, offering a ride to Nora and Pauline. Bess and Pauline spend the evening singing, leaving Nora and me at the table. In that dark café, away from the watchful eyes of The Group, the two us begin to genuinely relate, probably for the very first time in all of the years we have spent in such close contact. I make the acquaintance of a warm and decent human being, a person I really like.

Entering Gerald's den the following morning, I look right into Nora's eyes. Remembering the connection we shared only a few short hours ago, I smile warmly. Already mesmerized by the atmosphere of Gerald's aura, she returns my gaze blankly. Sadly, the wonderful person with whom I spent the previous evening has disappeared completely. Nora has fallen into the ranks of The Group once more, an obedient soulless soldier, as quickly as a lamp can be turned off. As I continue to observe her sitting there holding rocks and staring at Ben, I realize that she has no idea at all that two completely opposite people live inside of her body. If only she could choose that person I enjoyed for those few brief moments last night. If only she would push this other freeloading zombie the hell out of her mind!

Still considering bankruptcy, I finally decide to contact a second lawyer. The man points out that I am the president of two small corporations and a bankruptcy would most assuredly come back to bite me. In addition, the credit card companies which carry my debt will not just forgive the loan and go away. They will work at finding the means to seize assets, take a portion of my salary and in general make my life miserable in ways I cannot even anticipate. The undeniable truth comes through his lips and verifies the subconscious fears which prevented me from declaring bankruptcy six months ago. As I drive away from his office,

I know that I will have to solve my financial problems another way. Now, there is only one thing left to do, something I dread more than anything, something I will postpone as long as I possibly can . . . I will have to cut back even further on my hours with Gerald . . .

It has become clear that Louis Gavin has chosen to commit himself to helping *Flash Blasters Inc.* and *Exambusters Study Cards.* Although there is no formal agreement, no written contract, no promised compensation, Louis throws himself in with fervor. He requests all the details of the company's history, especially the sales figures. He appoints himself "Sales Manager" and has me fax a memo to *Cliff's Notes*, notifying them that he will act as liaison from now on. Based on his analysis of our product's sales potential and their company's size, he concludes that sales are way under par and he wants to know why. It is not easy to get a straight answer out of a member of a corporate hierarchy. The higher up you go, the harder it becomes, and Louis goes all the way up to the vice president. He endures two hours on the phone wrestling with the man's evasion, but finally uncovers the truth; they hate my "budget" packaging, which has significantly lowered the consumers' perceived value of the product. In fact it looks as if it was made in someone's garage, which indeed it practically was! That day, the operations of *Flash Blasters Inc.* come to an abrupt halt. We instruct *Cliff's* to return all of the remaining inventory. Now they have nothing to sell and I must start from scratch, my fifth attempt at a marketable, affordable package design, but this time, *Cliff's Notes* will approve the layout before we go to press. You would think Louis had invented the product with the attention and time he commits to helping me.

The next afternoon I find myself, Samantha and Louis meeting at our office to determine the next step. Louis is adamant on one point. We must have a professionally designed box.

"Books will be judged by their covers."

Louis agrees to arrange the art work and negotiate with printers, and we reach a preliminary agreement regarding his fee. Our meeting ends and it is time to give Louis a deposit. I am seated next to Samantha on the black leather couch in our photography gallery and Louis faces us across a small coffee table. Unexpectedly, a powerful resolve rises within me and my mouth moves before my mind can debate.

"Of course Samantha and I will split the cost."

I know I have just betrayed my original agreement with Samantha, the one where I foot all of the bills. I have said something unpardonable, even sinful. I begin to shake, almost uncontrollably, and my face turns bright red. My partner senses my lack of confidence and turns to shoot me an evil ugly look, so poisonous that I feel as if sulfuric acid has just been thrown in my face. Then, as she turns her head back in the direction of Louis's field of vision, she erases that look as quickly as closing a Venetian blind. When their eyes finally meet, all evidence of rage is gone, and she smiles sweetly. He, noticing only the pause in the conversation queries,

"Why wouldn't you want to invest? It is half your company and this new course of action will turn it around. You have told me many times how much you believe in it . . ."

He isn't yet aware that I have paid all of the bills up until this moment. Samantha is trapped. In front of a third party who has not been trained to worship her, she must give in. My emotions throw streams of confetti as I celebrate inside myself. *Yes! Victory! I have found a way to extricate this leech from my being. From now on, I must expose the injustice in front of a third non-Group person. There, she can't maintain what she gets away with behind the closed doors of Daddy's den.*

After Louis leaves, I anticipate a physical attack from her. I brace myself, but none comes. She simply walks into the office and goes back to work. About ten minutes later she approaches me. Her eyes appear soft and kind and her face is saccharine.

"Elizabeth, I was going to offer to pay for half anyway. You didn't have to say that in front of him and embarrass me."

I am amazed and impressed at her chameleon-like skill of mood switching. Nevertheless, I know she is lying . . .

In keeping with my eighteen-year program, I buy Gerald a holiday gift, a CD of Beethoven's First Symphony. I know that Gerald sometimes likes to shake his head to classical music. When I enter the den, I discover that I almost can't bring myself to hand it to him. I have no steam left to interact. He nods his head perfunctorily in acceptance, without thanking me, and returns immediately to the focusing he has been doing with Martin. These days, Gerald doesn't seem to want to relate either. In fact, he rarely talks to me at all. Whenever I show up, he glances at me quickly, throws out a mechanical "What's doing?" and then turns to someone else, anyone else, before I even have a chance to answer. Frequently, he looks upset, on the verge of exploding. I don't understand what is driving him so crazy, but for my part it is increasingly difficult to even remain in the room; his presence repels me. Today, as usual, I force myself to focus on a spot on the wall until it is time to go.

January 1996

My days are filled with a whirl of activity as Louis and I brainstorm about the new packaging. Samantha offers very little input except to frequently ask how much it will cost. It is a strange sensation, but I feel the train moving again to another, unknown station . . .

Naturally, there will be several thousand dollars in start-up costs to develop the new packaging and Louis's consultation fees as well. Each day the figures change. One day the projected costs are $1000, the next, $5000. Although she never shows it, I sense that Samantha is squirming for the first time since we embarked on the grand flash card adventure. I don't care that it will cost a little more. I have invested so much already and this time, for the first time, I can see my path out of the woods. Meanwhile, Louis is concerned with putting together a partnership agreement like the one we have just signed for *Expressions Photography*, before we move forward. Samantha and I must define our individual duties and responsibilities in this new phase of our business. If we can supply our existing excellent *Cliff's Notes* sales force with a decent product to sell, then there will be profit left over for the officers of the corporation to compensate themselves. In order to construct an equitable agreement, Louis requests a written synopsis from each partner, listing her personal input over the previous four years. He wants to know who has made sales and how much they were for. Who has put in the development time? How much capital has each invested? He assigns us this homework for the weekend.

Sunday morning, my notebook computer on my lap, a carafe of strong coffee at my side, I spend six hours writing the entire history of the company. My final document exposes unequivocally that despite Samantha and her father's inexhaustible efforts to convince me otherwise, my partner has supplied very little of value. The onus has always been on me. Viewing these facts on paper gives me permission to accept them as truth. I can't wait to see what she will write as she strives to convince him that we are and always have been "equal partners". In my five page synopsis, in an effort to be complete and accurate, I even include a list of Samantha's contributions!

At our meeting we turn in our lists to Louis. From mine it is obvious that I have financed the entire venture for my brainchild and invested countless hours toward research and development. Her list includes all of the places we have traveled (at my expense) and the fact that she has handed out over five thousand flyers at conventions and trade shows. It also mentions the various celebrities into whose hands she has managed to push a box of flash cards. They include Oprah Winfrey, Leslie Nielsen, Margaret Thatcher, our contacts from *United We Stand America*: Ross Perot, Governor Jim Florio, Governor Christie Whitman, Representatives Marge Roukema and Robert Torricelli, Senators Bill Bradley and Frank Lautenberg and of course, Barbara Bush's secretary. There are other celebrities she has met at the "Hudson River-Keepers" charity benefits, Robert Kennedy Jr., actors Christopher Reeve, Marlee Matlin and Robbie Benson, rap singer L.L. Cool J. and the son of Mohammed Ali. As she puts it, *We're well known by some very important people!*

Louis responds to her resume, formulated to impress him.

"That's all fine and good Samantha, but I need to know about sales. How many dollars in sales did you make last year? We want to get the company out of debt."

Instead of answering, she changes the subject, again referring to the thousands of flyers she has handed out, evidence of her true dedication to the business. Louis is beginning to get the message. The officers of this company have certainly had many exciting adventures. Their product flyers and catalogs are beautifully photographed and designed. There is a potentially profitable product waiting on the shelf, but aside from the current *Cliff's Notes* sales force, there have been few other sales, despite the fact that Samantha keeps insisting that she has always been the sales manager. Louis doesn't say anything, but he seriously questions how Samantha ever obtained the right to own half of this company and to share half of the profits. For our next meeting, Louis asks us each to write down what we will contribute in the next leg of the company's journey and fair compensation.

Thanks to Louis's in-depth analysis, I am beginning to evaluate myself through the neutral eyes of a third party, rather than through the twisted thinking of The Group. Going forward I know that Samantha and I can equally share the daily administration requirements. From future profits, we will structure a plan to repay my loan of $165,000. I have only one other stipulation — I am entitled to a royalty for developing/authoring the fifteen titles of flash cards. At our next meeting with Louis I present my proposal — loan repayment plan, 15% royalty, and the remainder split between us. Samantha agrees to the loan repayment but refuses the royalty. I can't believe her. How can she deny the obvious fact that I have a right to be compensated for my substantial contributions? With Louis looking on and saying very little, we fight for more than five hours without a break. Neither of us will bend. Finally, she agrees to a 10% royalty on half of the titles, but I will not accept less than what I have requested. Conviction courses through every fiber of my body. Deadlocked, we "agree to disagree" and postpone the contract for future resolution. Right now priority presses to create new packaging for *Cliff's Notes*.

Elizabeth and Samantha have been at each other's throats for days and one evening Elizabeth asks me to help her try to smooth things over. On separate extensions in her apartment, we telephone her partner. It has always been difficult to talk to Samantha. She never validates any observation, no matter how obvious, regarding herself, her father or The Group. Remembering my last visit to Gerald's den a few months ago, I bring up the issue of how he treats his "clients". Since that evening, I have been outraged at the humiliation I witnessed.

"Samantha, there is a better way to reach people than by glaring, intimidating and insulting them. What your father does to everyone, especially Grace, is cruel and inhumane. I feel sorry for her. He has no respect for the people in his room. Anyone outside of your circle can see that. What gives him the right to treat people like that and then charge them for it?"

"No, you don't understand what he's trying to do."

"No, I do understand. He has harvested a group of weak-willed women with low self-esteem that he can get over on."

"No, you don't understand . . . "

This fruitless loop of arguing continues for three hours. When we finally end the conversation due to sheer exhaustion, we have accomplished nothing. Samantha never admits that anything her father does is unjust or unkind. However, within the next week, Elizabeth reports a change in Gerald's behavior. Not only has he stopped attacking Grace, he is now treating her with the utmost respect, assigning her as leader in the daily group sessions. As if she is a wise sage, he instructs others, such as Nora, Bess and Pauline, who are having trouble in their lives, to seek her advice and direction. Grace is more than pleased to fill this new, assigned role and eloquently quotes passages from Deepak Chopra's writings and *The Celestine Prophesy* to satisfy the women's needs for leadership and solutions. Content to finally feel special, she doesn't ever seem to question the reason for Gerald's 180-degree turn in attitude toward her.

At the office, Samantha changes her behavior too. She stops attacking Elizabeth and even puts a sign on the wall which reads "No Fighting Allowed". All of a sudden, in The Group, all hostile and provoking behavior is subdued in favor of the outward expression of kindness, sweetness and feigned empathy. The words "love" and "caring" now appear frequently in their dialogue. In other words, to deliver their doctrine, they have created a perfect imitation of spirit-filled Christian behavior. Clearly, Gerald heard about our conversation from his daughter and must have concluded that I was correct. However, not for the right reasons, not because he really cares about how he treats others.

Instead, I made him realize that his dysfunctional personality leaks out to an unbrainwashed public through his behavior, creating a red flag to the true evil intentions he is trying to conceal. If he doesn't clean up his act, he will never be able to circulate in a broader arena, beyond his personal den, which he is clearly reaching for through his book signings and other lectures. Instead of waking him up to his moral transgressions, we have instead helped him refine his lie with even more sophistication, to further camouflage his aim into a more socially acceptable package so that he can continue his mission to exploit new people in the larger world outside of his inner circle!

Unable to obtain Samantha's accord, Louis and I decide to put together our own proposal which will compensate us justly for our respective contributions, both past and future. Naturally, these earnings will be far from equal. Going forward, her salary will be entirely based on real performance, not on her ability to manipulate me with fear tactics or "talk a good talk". Louis contacts her himself to schedule another meeting. In Samantha's presence, he has never appeared to take sides. Therefore, she views him as an unbiased problem solver and phones him frequently with questions. Unbeknownst to her, behind the scenes, Louis continues to insist that Samantha has "got to go". He stresses that she contributes practically nothing, and has no legal right to her shares of either corporation. Through the fog of my habitual thinking, I still only half understand what he means . . .

The meeting is scheduled for a Tuesday afternoon. Louis is actually excited about exposing her and putting her in her place, and so am I. However, the behavior of both of us toward her is intentionally neutral. I visit Gerald's den for a session a few hours before the scheduled meeting. We always do this to get the extra Energy necessary for increased success. When I enter, Samantha is lying on the couch. She appears pale and sick. After I settle in, next to Beatrice on the love seat, my partner declares,

"Elizabeth, I'm not going to the meeting and I don't want to continue working on this agreement with Louis."

"Why?"

"It doesn't matter why." She cuts me off from further questions.

The opportunity for restitution was so close that I could taste it. I have waited so long, and it has just been swept away before my helpless eyes. Rising out of my seat I begin yelling at Gerald in frustration.

"What is going on? We have been working with this man for several weeks. Now she just backs out for no reason, throwing our time and money into the garbage! What gives her the right to do this without explanation?"

As Gerald stares at me with no response, no recognition, the wave of oppression thickens and I feel a giant unseen hand squashing the life out of me. I gasp for breath as I impotently try to fight through this invisible wall — to freedom, to justice, to common decency.

"What does she think? Just because she is a Sharkman she doesn't have to play fair? I hate the Sharkmans. You are all selfish, secretive assholes."

Beatrice sucks in her breath at this blasphemy and glares like a parent scolding a defiant teenager,

"Sit down and shut up. You have no respect for Gerald and Samantha and all they have done for you. You wouldn't even <u>have</u> a business if it weren't for them. Look at how ungrateful you are."

I can't win. There is no support, no opening. All three dispassionately observe me raging helplessly without leverage, begging to be heard, a person who has just fallen off a cliff grasping at thin air in a vain effort to stop the descent. I will probably give myself a stroke from frustration if I do not stop yelling, so I force myself to calm down, sit, shut my mouth and throw in the towel.

Although I have never learned how to pray to God by name, my heart cries out fiercely and plaintively to some higher power for assistance. The injustices born from Samantha's presence in my life are becoming an insupportable burden, although in my mind she is a permanent fixture, an institution which I would never even allow myself to consider eliminating. In the past year, Samantha and I have grown apart to a point of almost complete separation. She still owns half of *Flash Blasters Inc.* and yet, her contributions have become practically nonexistent. Regardless of her participation, I am more determined than ever to make this one last ditch effort to save the company and my investment.

These days I am the only one doing any work; regardless, if I succeed she possesses legal right to half. I continue obtaining quotes for our new package prototypes. Like a balloon inflating, the figures keep mounting. By the first week in February, Louis and I present Samantha with an estimated figure of about $6000. We don't have much time to spare either. *Cliff's Notes* needs something to sell fast.

The next day Samantha pulls me aside at the office for a private meeting. "I have something I need to talk with you about."

An impulse of fear shoots through me. I have no idea what she wants, but I instantly drop what I am doing and give her my full attention. Strange, but after all the hours we have spent together, today she looks like a stranger.

"I am leaving *Flash Blasters*," my partner informs me bluntly.

Never in a million years would I have believed that this might come to pass. After all of her injustice, my initial reaction surprises me; I am profoundly upset and I truly don't want her to leave.

"Samantha, why can't we work things out? I want to and we can do it with Louis. We are about to turn the company around. Why would you want to leave now anyway?"

In my mind, if she would only be willing to correct her unreasonable personality and the injustices in our financial arrangements, we could remain friends and partners. In this moment, I envision how it would be possible for us to change everything and do business together fairly for the first time, but I am struck with the realization that Samantha is blind to this alternative.

Samantha continues, "I just feel it's time to move on. My books are demanding more of my attention and I want to focus on them and the photography business."

At the same time that I am sincerely protesting her decision to exit, the sensation of a thousand pounds of bricks being lifted off of my back comes all in one moment; I almost cry out from relief.

Our discussion ended, she calls Louis and asks him to draw up corporate dissolution papers, and one week later, February 13, they are signed. With the company in debt, there is nothing to split, and Samantha walks away empty-handed.

Samantha has always acted as if she really cared about the flash cards. In fact, several potential investors we courted have commented on the incredible dedication they witnessed in both of us. Therefore, I do not recognize the person who inhabits Samantha's body on the day following our corporate divorce. First, it is clear that after a five-year investment, she is suffering absolutely no separation anxiety. In fact, her nonverbal attitude seems to be a matter of fact, *Oh well, that was interesting, but now it's over. Next.* She shows less emotion than she might if she had just discovered that her movie of choice at the local ten-plex cinema was sold out and she must select another. Like a slap in the face, I wake up to the reality that she has merely played an Oscar-winning role as the dedicated vice-president of *Flash Blasters Inc.* Her behavior was merely a facade hiding a total vacuum behind it. The Wizard of Oz has finally emerged from behind the curtain.

"Samantha," I inquire, "What if I had asked you to leave a week ago?"

"I wouldn't have," she replies with certainty.

"Why is your decision different now?"

"I just changed."

With no obvious conflict over this empty logic, she sets about making the necessary changes in our office to accommodate our new arrangement with each other. Like a woodsman wielding an ax, she begins.

"You will take all of the flyers and samples off the shelves. This furniture is the property of *Expressions Photography*, so you must store them somewhere else. Put the company records in your personal drawer in the filing cabinet. If you store any cartons of flash cards in the studio, you must pay $12 per square foot in rent every month to *Expressions*. The files for *Flash Blasters Inc.* are taking up room on the computer database and they must either be removed, or you will pay a small rent each month for computer usage. You may store anything you like under your desk."

Considering that I originally purchased all of the furnishings in the studio myself, the injustice of her attitude is doubled. I am a fugitive in my own premises. I can't believe what I am hearing and feeling from this girl who, only one month ago, was the loudest spokeswoman for the business and our partnership. As tears of hurt and betrayal well up in my eyes, I push them back, because technically, as far as I understand the law, she is correct. She is legal half owner of *Expressions*, which pays the rent, and *Flash Blasters* is now solely mine. The company no longer has the right to make use of any of *Expressions'* resources. Quickly, I begin to take the necessary steps to fulfill her demands. My partner observes me, and when she is satisfied that I made sufficient progress, she moves to her desk to commence her work for *Expressions Photography*. After a long intimate intense collaboration together over our joint publishing project — the aspirations, brainstorming and adventures — she has severed her connection with a guillotine blade . . .

It is Friday evening, just a week after my split from Samantha. Still unsettled about the event, there is another, more pressing matter I can put off no longer. I drive aimlessly on Route 4 in Paramus, seeking to distract myself from the inevitable. I must tell Gerald that I am cutting back on my hours, that I can't afford his fees; I must do it tomorrow. I experience a terrible emptiness. I feel like Swiss cheese. There are holes inside of me, all over, as if a vacuum cleaner is sucking the life out of all that is familiar, only to propel me into outer space where I'll drift forever, disconnected from anything I have ever called home. It is weird and eerie. Later, lying on my back in bed, I telephone Judy. Magically, she seems to understand what I am feeling and finishes my sentences for me. At one point in the conversation I blurt out,

"I can't just cut back on my hours; I have to leave The Group completely."

Where did that come from? The thought never entered my mind before! I dream restlessly and get up late, filled with uncertainty and not wanting to leave the security of my bed. I arrive at my office at 2:00 P.M. to find that Samantha has already left to go and sit with her father. The fog of my emotions is so thick that I can barely see to put one foot in front of the other. I only know one thing, I must go through with my plan. I sit at my desk staring at the wall, unable to do any work. Everything around me seems pointless except the one decision that I must put into effect. Pushing against my resistance, I pull out an index card and write down my new schedule, two hours a week, and the Thursday night group. This still amounts to an unaffordable $5200 a year, but this is the least amount of time I feel I can commit to and still remain connected . . . and sane. Fears seize me regarding my future mental stability. What if I can't make it without the frequent contact with him that I am dependent on? What if I crack up and can't afford extra time with him to fix myself?

I postpone as long as I possibly can. Finally, I can hold back no longer. I leave my office, and make the five-minute commute to Gerald's house. As my feet lead me down the driveway, my fear increases. *No, I don't want to. I can't.* A tantrum of emotions rages within. *I wish this weren't happening. Why did this happen to me? I tried to repair my circumstances, to stop the avalanche of impending poverty. I did everything I could do and it happened anyway. Why me? Why? Why? Why?* More than anything in the world, I want to turn around and run away.

However, I cannot. An invisible hand in the middle of my back pushes me firmly and steadily onward, despite my conflict. It propels me through some hidden, predetermined plan which only reveals itself moment by moment. It doesn't matter what I feel, think or want. Something else is calling the shots — my destiny — and I have no say in the matter.

February 24, 4:00 P.M.

I enter the room, just as I have nearly three thousand times before over the past nineteen years. Gerald sits in his chair with the dog carcass. Everyone around him is engaged in "focusing", serious and pious. The regulars, Nora, Samantha, Martin, Pauline, Bess and my mother, are all present. The rocking chair facing Gerald's chair is free, and I sink into it. Gerald looks asinine to me, a grown man worshiping a disgusting rotting eighteen-month-old dog's carcass, like a child clinging to his blankie and talking to an imaginary friend. The others appear ridiculous too. Mature college-educated women emptying their bank accounts to participate in this stupid charade. I know that many of them have been sitting in the den since 9:00 A.M. They have spent all of these hours imagining that the dog's hair is growing, his skin is glowing, his spine is changing and his body is transforming into a god. They have fed him bagels at lunchtime, morsels which have disappeared mysteriously because the dead dog "ate" them when for a moment, they were out of the room. I am sick of the whole thing. I want to blow up a bomb in the middle of the den and wake them up. I want to slap them in the face to make them realize how childish and horrible this whole thing is. Over the past year I have evolved into a state of complete alienation. It feels like revisiting my third grade classroom and trying to fit my body back into my old chair and desk. I can no longer even begin to feel at home here. Participation in this absurd drama has been impossible for quite some time, no matter how hard I have tried.

After a moment Gerald pauses from his intense concentration on his spiritual interaction with the carcass. He looks up toward me. Nodding to acknowledge my presence, he throws out his trademark phrase.

"What's doing?"

I can tell that he prefers not to interact with me. Perhaps he even wishes I wasn't there. I look at him soberly, my internal conflict written all over my face and body posture.

I stammer out, "Nnnothing really."

I hope that he will see I don't really mean it and will probe me further, inviting me into a loop of interaction with him so that I can gain momentum to push past my internal hurdle of conflict. I sense that he knows I am not telling the truth, that I am silently asking for help. However, in the next moment, he makes a choice to cut our connection and returns to his focus on Ben. Like so many times before when I was in real trouble, he dumps me. I sit immersed in my private feelings, focusing alternately on a knot in his paneling and the corner of a picture frame. I desire fervently to be someone else, or somewhere else, that this nightmare is not my life . . . It is the longest hour I have ever lived through. Not one of my other comrades, even my mother, so absorbed in their focus on the mission, has any sensitivity toward my distress.

Once again, I see how totally alone and completely dependent on myself I have always been. However, I have my plan and there is no turning back. I must hand him my new schedule. As I hold that tightly folded index card in my sweating palm, I think of how much I want to be able to tell him to his face instead. *I can't afford it. I must reduce my hours. I have tried to find solutions and all the doors have closed. I will have to cut back until something changes.* I pray desperately for the strength to confront him like an adult who has the right to make choices in their own best interest. I want to be able to deal with his response face to face, and stand my ground. I pray that magically, this strength will enter me sometime before the end of the session. As the clock approaches 5:00 P.M., I sense impending doom and begin to recede even more than I could have ever imagined was possible. Finally, it is quitting time. Gerald pulls himself out of his self-imposed trance, checks his watch and says softly, comfortingly, familiarly,

"OK everybody. It's time to go."

I sit frozen in my chair, watching the rest file out slowly. Some throw him a warm smile, rub his back with affection, slip him a check, or wish him a nice weekend. He returns these pleasantries to his students with the gaze of the kind and knowing professor of successful living which he believes himself to be. Finally, they are all gone except my mother, who is using the bathroom. Gerald and Samantha remain in the room. During this ten minute exodus of his followers I have not moved an inch. He glances over my way, picking up my hesitation, but pretends to ignore me. I can hear his thoughts. *Whatever's wrong with her is not my problem.* Finally I can hold back no longer. I rise slowly and approach the door. By this point, what little resolve I had before has drained completely, and my heart flutters in my chest. My face is white with fear and I shake uncontrollably. The twelve-foot trip across his carpet feels like a mile. Near the door, I intersect with him and turn toward him. Staring at the floor, I extend my hand and offer the index card.

"Here."

"What's this?" he questions.

"That's my new schedule."

I don't even look at him, but race toward the door, too afraid to wait for his response. I exit quickly, right after my mother who has just emerged from the bathroom. Just before I close the den door and step down to the deck, I glance over my shoulder to see him opening the card and staring at it with confusion. My step is lighter as I stride rapidly down the driveway, toward the welcome sanctuary of my car, grateful that it is finally over. I catch up with Grace and invite her to dinner. My mother never turns down an invitation for food, so the date is set. We settle into my car, parked right in front of Gerald's house. Suddenly I look up to behold Gerald positioned in his front entrance. A menacing figure, he glowers at me from across his twenty-foot yard, his face portraying a combination of hurt and anger.

"Elizabeth," he roars like a general commanding a private, "just don't bother coming back at all."

I had not expected this in my wildest dreams! I look back at him with no expression on my face, simply nodding in acknowledgment. I have received his dictum and I will comply. I am actually surprised that I don't have a comeback, for I usually do, but there is none present inside of me. He disappears inside while I remain motionless in my seat. My mother finally asks me why I am not moving the car. In her characteristic oblivious insensitive fog, she has no clue to what has just transpired or its significance in her daughter's life. Staring in disbelief at the steering wheel, I reply,

"Gerald just threw me out."

"Well, that won't affect my relationship with you." Her response is cut and dry.

"I'm really glad to hear that," I reply, having feared I would lose her too, "Let's go eat."

As I drive down his block and turn onto the main road, the implications of this turn of events begin to sink in. I have just been freed from an eighteen-year term in a mental concentration camp. I am in too much shock to feel excited or exuberant, to throw my arms in the air and scream "Yeah!" However, I do feel a deep sense of relief and peace. My head is empty of any possible conflicted thoughts. Unquestionably, I have been navigated through the entire journey by a force and intelligence much greater than my own. I know instinctively that today's outcome is the only possible one, the right and healthy one, and I will be able to deal with the consequences. Experiencing profound gratitude, I would drop to my knees to thank God, right now in the car, if I could . . .

We grab a bite at a local diner. When I have positioned us at the table and placed our order, I excuse myself and head for the pay phone to call Judy. The sound of her familiar voice on the other end of the line is a welcome comfort.

"Jude, guess what? He threw me out of The Group!" I tell her with excitement and a decent measure of awe.

"How do you feel?"

"Great! I mean, OK." I tell her how it all happened. "My only regret is that I wasn't able to speak to him directly about reducing my hours of therapy. The index card was cowardly."

"That was the only way you could tell him," she reassures me, "The important thing is that you accomplished what you set out to do. Your method doesn't matter."

I hadn't thought of that and she relieves my burden. "What do you think about it, Jude?"

"I think it's good. This is what we have been working toward for more than two years. It's graduation day!"

We chat a while longer, and then I return to the table, promising I'll call later after I drop my mother off in Manhattan. Dinner is uneventful. Grace, totally focused on tasting the array of foods set before her, is completely disconnected from me. It feels as if I am taking a preschooler out for an ice cream sundae, a child who understands nothing of adult feelings and responsibilities. Crisis usually brings out the true inner person. At this monumental, critical event in my life, she displays not even the slightest interest in, or understanding about what I must be going through this evening. She clearly has no idea of the depth and destructiveness of my connection to Gerald and the degree of courage and intelligence it has taken to disconnect myself. In this restaurant, I experience my mother at a deeper level. Despite our biological tie, she is no different from the rest of The Group. She is no friend of mine . . . For her, the most significant issue during our meal is whether or not she will have room enough to order the chocolate cake for dessert. I realize that I cannot make my mother understand, any more than an infantryman who has risked his life on the battlefields of some distant land can communicate his experience to his five-year-old son. So after our meal I drive Grace into the city. Kissing her on the cheek, I wave as I watch her enter her apartment building, the place where Gerald's cursed groups began so many years ago. With my mother safely inside the lobby, I dial Judy from my car phone and recount every minute detail of the day's events as I drive up the Henry Hudson Parkway and over the George Washington Bridge toward home. Reality sinks in ever more deeply. Handing that index card to Gerald today was the hardest thing I have ever made myself do. Now it is over and I have survived.

Sunday, the day following, I rise close to noon. My mind is murky, an emotional dream-state I have developed to protect me from overwhelming anxiety. I think of what happened yesterday. It's really true! I am free from bondage. Then I remember that I will have to face Samantha at the office tomorrow, a prospect which terrifies me. I must occupy my mind or I will drive myself crazy. A few days ago I purchased a copy of Thomas Monteleone's *The Blood of the Lamb* and now I pick it up, for it offers the perfect distraction. I spend the entire day in my recliner, reading cover to cover. The next day I force myself out of bed, into the car and up the stairs toward my office door. I have committed an unpardonable sin in the eyes of The Group. Gerald has thrown me out, and I have allowed it, rather than begging him to permit me to return. No one has ever done this before. Although I know that I couldn't have made any other choice, I still harbor doubt and conflict. This will surely be magnified in the presence of another devotee to the doctrine. Although I have lost Gerald, I am still stuck with Samantha. She is my business partner. We must continue to work together, for my survival depends on that income.

On this first morning I discover that Samantha has arrived before me. I want to avoid her, but this is not possible. I anticipate an attack, but to my relief, she looks weak, pale and confused. I certainly can't pretend that this is a normal day and just say, "Hi. How are you doing?" What can I say to her? After all, what is there really to say? At a total loss for words, I approach her and shove *The Blood of the Lamb* into her hands, telling her,

"You've got to read this book."

"Oh yeah? Thanks," she responds, taken by surprise.

My unexpected gesture breaks the wall and shifts us both into a more comfortable place where at least we can get our work done. After that day, we stay out of each other's way and begin splitting the office hours between us. On the rare occasions that we find ourselves together, the only words exchanged are directly about business. We both work at adjusting ourselves to the change, neither able discuss her feelings and reach some kind of understanding . . .

After four days, I begin to wonder what Gerald is thinking. I hope against hope that he is beginning to realize that I mean business, that I have finally grown up and will not compromise my dignity by begging him to take me back, that I refuse to cover for his mistakes anymore — he must acknowledge them and make restitution if he is to have me in his life. I pray that he will finally wake up and see what I mean to him, that my absence will cause him to examine his behavior, and force him to be humble and drop his rigid ego in order to get me back. On the other hand, perhaps he is assuming that my return is inevitable and he is just biding his time. Maybe that is why he has not contacted me to try to resolve the conflict. I want to show him my position definitively, to push him to act. I am too afraid to speak with him on the phone, so I decide to write my feelings in a letter. I will show him the kind of person I truly am, that I appreciate all that I have learned from him and our relationship, but I have matured from the needy young woman he met so many years ago. Now I want respect as an equal; I deserve it. In the past couple of years I have come to understand that I am a quality person. He is not the only one with something to offer. I will show Gerald that I have done my part to relate with him fairly, and now it is his turn. I am willing to forgive and forget if he agrees to make amends for his mistakes. Truly, I would like to be friends . . . My letter reads,

Dear Gerald,

So many unspoken thoughts and feelings. What a shame we can't communicate. Maybe someday we'll be able to. I hope so. I have learned so much from you. I could fill several books! I thank you for that. No matter how you react or think about me I have and always do see the GOD in you. I see that it is the same as me. I wish I could share with you what I have learned, I have tried many times but there was no opening. I'm sorry it turned out the way it did. Take care.

> *Love, Elizabeth*

I mail it, but receive no response.

The worst day is Thursday — Group night. This night has always been the highlight of my week. I know that all my other "friends" will be there without me. Now, I am ostracized and can't attend. I wonder if they will even care that I am gone . . .

The following Monday, Samantha's facade finally dissolves.

"Why did you do it? Why did you make him throw you out?" she cries at me.

I truly have no answer for her. If she is still on her father's side, blind to the injustice I have suffered at his hands, I will never make her understand.

I reply simply, "I had to do it," and return to my work.

Each day I continue to dig myself out of a dark tunnel, one spoonful at a time. I do not know how long this task will last, I cannot see the light, but I know it is out there somewhere in front of me. At the office I begin to ask Samantha questions — questions to which I know I don't want to hear the answers.

"What did your father say when he got my letter?"

I am hoping that he was distressed, that he realized I was serious and that he was really going to lose me if he didn't come to some emotional compromise. After all, I have given him the message that I am willing to meet him half way.

Samantha answers matter-of-factly, "He said that it looked like you were saying good-bye. He wasn't upset."

So, the truth is that Gerald indeed has no conflict over my action; I have tested him for the hundredth time and he has failed as always; there is no longer any basis for me to hope that I was wrong about him, that he will change. It doesn't make any difference to him if he never sees me again. He is not pretending or covering up his true feelings; there simply aren't any there. I never had any emotional leverage over him because he never valued me. To him, I am like a cigarette, to be used until its contents are depleted, and then flicked away, never to be thought of again. Knowing that someone in whom you have invested so much doesn't care about you is one thing, accepting it and getting over the hurt is quite another.

But there are more questions to ask, even as I am recovering from the answer to this one . . .

"Samantha, what did your father tell the rest of The Group about me?"

"He said that you decided to leave."

"Did he tell them why, that I was having money problems?"

"No, he didn't mention that. He said that you had become miserable because you weren't following the direction of The Energy. You preferred to do it on your own. You were blaming your misery on him because you didn't want to admit that you were making a mistake with Judy and let him help you separate from her. He told them that you were no loss, and they should just move on and forget you. You weren't committed to the mission and didn't appreciate him. You were always a know-it-all with no experience."

"Did your father mention that he threw me out?"

"No . . ."

Every night these first weeks, alone in my apartment, I wait for the phone to ring. Every other person who has left The Group has been chased, first by Gerald and then by the others, in an effort to convince them to return. I wonder what my friends are thinking, especially Pauline, Nora and Bess to whom I have felt closest. I wait for the phone to ring and yet, at the same time, I know in my heart that it never will. While driving back and forth to work, I look for their cars on the road. Every time I pass a white Toyota (Laura), burgundy Honda Accord sedan (Gerald), blue Honda Civic (Bess), white, silver or blue Acura (Marty, Mitchell, Samantha, Nora) I peer inside to see if one of them is the driver. I am going crazy, obsessed with thoughts of all of them. How could they all just walk out on me like that? I feel like an American Indian who has broken tribal rules and is now abandoned on a hillside to die. Even though Gerald's street is on my way to work, I can't bring myself to drive past it. Instead, I take the long way around to avoid it. I wouldn't be able to stand seeing their cars all lined up in front of his house, knowing that it is all still going on just fine, without me.

I can't believe that the people Elizabeth has known for all these years would tolerate her unexplained disappearance without calling to find out if she was OK! Even her own mother doesn't check up on her.

I try to make excuses for this incomprehensible behavior. Maybe they are all afraid to contact her because Gerald would perceive this as betrayal and throw them out in punishment. I know that their addiction is even worse than Elizabeth's ever was, but in my heart, I still can't justify their decisions. How shocking for Elizabeth to realize that those she considered family never really cared!! Holding Elizabeth's hand through every moment of the experience, I suffer almost as much as she does from this awful reality.

So, I live through that first week with the terrible truth that they will, indeed, just let me go. Each and every one of them. Gerald will never call to negotiate. If I do not do things 100 percent his way, he has no use for me. The only way I will ever be able to relate to any of them again is if I crawl back and apologize, and I can never do that. My entire former life, including my thought process, has just fallen into a deep dark well, out of sight. I have no friends, no family, only Judy and her husband Michael. The second week passes, and the third. No calls from anyone, not even my mother. My worst fears are realized. Not one of those people really values me, and if somewhere inside they do, I am not important enough to step forward for. Instead, they choose to hang onto the comfortable familiarity of the doctrine and their allegiance to Gerald. These are the people to whom I have dedicated the past two decades of my life. Worse, I realize I would have continued, if debt and physical exhaustion hadn't forced me to withdraw.

The reality of the giant mistake I have made is sinking in more and more. Rage against my tormentors runs through me like stampeding buffalo, murderously painful, as if the blood in my veins has been replaced by caustic acid. My head screams with violent thoughts of revenge and I want to act on them. I think of — calling the *Barnes & Noble* stores on Gerald's lecture circuit and revealing his true nature to the managers, alerting Doris of the secret crimes he has committed against her and their children, informing Nora's and Beatrice's husbands that they have financed their adulterous wives' sex sessions, calling Nora's school and exposing her dog- carcass-worship hobby to her colleagues and her students' parents. I realize she could lose her job. It would serve them right, all of them.

I caution her to consider her actions very carefully. "Don't forget, Elizabeth, you are dealing with someone's greed. If Gerald or the others sense that you might affect their pocketbooks, they could retaliate. This enemy is too big for you to fight. After all that we have been through I don't want to see you hurt. As painful as it is, for now, you must accept that you made a mistake and try to move on with your life. You are not the one to discipline him for his wrongdoing. Do not worry. His days are numbered. God does not like what is going on in that den. In his own time, Gerald will get his."

My fury intensifies so much that I fear Gerald is picking it up in the spiritual airwaves. Leaving my office at night, I terrify myself with images of Martin hiding in the shadows. I picture him choking me in the dark parking lot behind my building, just to make sure that I will keep my mouth shut. Yet, I can do nothing to vent my devastating reactions.

I comfort her through her anger. Migraine headaches plague her frequently and one evening she collapses from emotional exhaustion, vomiting into the toilet with hopeless tears of sadness. I hold her head and rub her back to calm the violent retching, and when the fit has passed, I put her to bed. The pain she must be enduring is incomprehensible to me . . . I phone her several times during the work day to make sure she is OK (Samantha doesn't seem to forbid my calls to their office phone anymore.) I invite her to sleep at my house when she is lonely. The worst part is that, six days a week, she has to work with Samantha. Despite everything that has happened, not one person in that group believes that Gerald exploited Elizabeth.

From the first day that he threw me out I have wondered what I would feel after being released from such a long confinement in P.O.W. camp. Now I am aware that a tiny light bulb has turned on deep inside of me, as if my self-confidence is emerging after years of imprisonment in a dark attic trunk. What a strange new sensation! As the weeks pass, this light burns brighter, completely on its own; the glint in my eye and the life in my smile begins to return. I know that Gerald is completely responsible for its absence for all of those lost years. How did he ever accomplish this unforgivable crime against me?

Periodically I experience a strange sensation — huge waves of oppression lifting from my back. Pressure begins deep inside and rises upwards, finally releasing itself from my body as if a resident ghost has just vacated, a specter which has crushed my spirit and soul for so long that I had forgotten it could ever be any other way. These events occur spontaneously for a few weeks. I am an observer, watching my rebirth . . . Yet even in the midst of this extraordinary transformation my mood often turns melancholy. My thoughts drift back to the security of membership — the daily comfort in reporting for duty, the role I played for The Group, so long and so masterfully. The big questions begin to invade my thoughts: Who am I? What is the meaning of life? Do I have a special purpose, a destiny? And for each question, where once a ready answer was supplied by the doctrine of The Energy, there now exists a terrifying vacuum. And I feel the loss of my friends' energy in my stream of existence. I miss them all poignantly; I cannot help it . . .

I call my mother from Judy's. Hearing her familiar voice for the first time since the breakup, I feel like a resident of the twilight zone, in a world I don't understand. Grace expresses no concern over my emotional state. She doesn't seem to care that after such a major change, I might be upset. I confront her on the issues which bother me the most.

"Mom, I was really in trouble for the past few years. For several months, I felt like I was on the edge of dying. I was terrified and lost. I really needed you. Why weren't you there for me?"

She changes the subject, but I insist again, until she gets annoyed, attacking me for cornering her "like a lawyer". I can't hold myself back, and I vent all of my pent up hurt and frustration onto her, almost shaking the walls of Judy's house with the power of my voice.

"You are not my mother. You are not my family. I can't rely on you. I hate you for abandoning me."

She allows me to verbalize, and then without responding to my agitation, she ends the phone call.

Grace has revealed her true allegiance. How could Gerald turn Grace against her only daughter, her flesh and blood? I remember that recently, Gerald has been praising Grace for "new discoveries" and assigning her as co-pilot, raising her above the others to emulate. What's wrong with this picture? Of course!

Gerald must have been sensing Elizabeth's separation from him for several months now. He knew it was only a matter of time before she would leave, and he didn't want her mother to follow her. Therefore, he decided to feed Grace what she always wanted, praise and acceptance. He filled her deepest wants to tie her to him, knowing that her need for those things was greater than her need for Elizabeth. By succeeding at breaking Grace's connection to her daughter, he has scored a major victory for his doctrine — his goals of complete self-sufficiency, isolation and the defiance of love. It doesn't matter to him that he has turned blood against blood to accomplish this.

A couple of weeks later I attend a *Barnes & Noble* lecture about soul mates. The lecturer tells us that sometimes you travel with the same souls during different lifetimes. She also introduces her belief in reincarnation. I don't know what I believe, but I listen with interest, wondering, *If there is reincarnation, did I know Gerald in another life? Is that why our relationship has been fraught with so much rivalry?*

After the lecture, I approach her,

"What if you really love someone and everything you try doesn't work? What if you can't get them to return your feelings?"

"That may be a message that you must learn to let go."

Let go. Let go. I have to let go. I repeat these words over and over in my mind. *She's right. It all happened the way it did, and now it's over. I have to disengage myself. My job now is to let go and build a brand-new life.*

New life, that's exactly what it is. Like Alice stepping through the looking glass, at the age of thirty-six, strange as it seems, I am starting over, from nothing. Scared and frequently depressed, I shift myself out of my low moods by counting my blessings. *I have two cats. I have a good photography business. I have two friends, Judy and Michael. I am a good and loving person with goals and ambition. Things may feel really bad now but they will get better every day. Have patience . . .* I learn to coach myself with this reminder and you know what? Things really do start to get better, and my episodes of depression begin to subside. Corny as it sounds, I begin to appreciate small things I never noticed before — the pleasantness of a warm day, the feeling of driving my *Acura* down a smooth road, the moonlight through the clouds.

Every night, before going to bed, I drop to my knees and pray. Holding onto my ruby-inlaid gold cross, a gift from Judy that I wear around my neck always, I speak to God, reminding myself that I will never forget what He has done for me.

"Dear God, thank you for your bounty and your grace. Thank you for protecting me. Please help me heal. Please lead me where I need to go, and please, I would never ask you for anything, but . . . , I lost my father and Joe, please don't ever take my Judy from me, anything but that . . ."

Every morning when I wake up, a realization fills my head, renewing me, strengthening me. *No one is watching me anymore. No one will hurt me anymore.* I experience a sense of peace that I have never known.

But there is so much work to do, and these days I consciously push against the wall of privacy I have respected for so long which protected the internal hidden activities of The Group. I seek opportunities to expose the true facts to people who have known both Samantha and me. I must reestablish contacts with other people, "the outsiders". I must convince myself that they are not worthless fools, as Gerald has taught us, people who will destroy me and themselves unless I use The Energy for protection. Deliberately, I take out my Rolodex and force myself to make calls. I want to see what will happen and what I will feel, to challenge Gerald's assertions which are still lodged in my mind. I know that if he is wrong, the truth will rise like cream to the top, through no manipulation of my own. I feel guilty, talking behind Samantha's back, usually on our office phone after she has left for the day. I become paranoid that they have bugged it and I imagine Martin in his father's basement, listening to my conversations as I reveal the ugly details of sex, money, shoplifting, assault and dog carcasses. Tom Perrone from SCORE, Peter, Dave — Lisa's ex-boyfriend, Christina — the editor of our Sign Language flash cards, the staff at my photography lab, first cousins in Pennsylvania . . . Over the next several weeks, they all hear the story. Each time I tell it, I tighten in genuine fear, believing that something inexplicably horrendous will happen to me because I have exposed The Group's sacred secrets. I cringe in anticipation of their inevitable damnation for breaking the rules, the vow of secrecy I have shared with them. Yet, I will not allow myself any alternative. I must push at the envelope of my fear until the membrane breaks and flies away. Amazingly, the people I share my story with always respond in the same way. They never liked Samantha. They sensed that I was in trouble and wanted to help, but they didn't know what was really wrong and were too polite to ask questions. As I portray some of the more extreme details, anger and outrage rise naturally in them. They throw solutions at me in a vain attempt to help me obtain retribution.

"Can't you take the son-of-a-bitch to court and sue him? Tell me where he lives, I'll go over to his house right now and knock his head off. He should have a chance to feel the pain that he has caused to innocent people."

Tom Perrone reassures me, "Gee, I wish I had an Uncle Guido. I would send him over to pick up Gerald and deposit him in the Dumpster behind the Closter *K-Mart*!"

Their empathy warms my heart, welcome evidence that good souls really do exist. Slowly, I am coming to realize that from now on, I will always have people on my side.

A memory returns to me, of David Arkenstone (the New Age musician whose concert Samantha and Bess staged five years ago) speeding out of Gerald's den into the dark Westwood night. Suddenly others just like him parade before my mind's eye. Pauline's mother, visiting from Roanoke, Virginia, could only stand a half hour in the den. She spent the remainder of the four hour session on Gerald's deck, defiantly reading a novel while waiting for her daughter to emerge and drive her home. Bess once brought her niece, age ten, to participate on a Saturday morning. After several minutes the child bolted out of her chair and toward the exit. Despite Bess's sincere efforts to coerce her back into the room, the little girl refused and chose instead to remain in her aunt's car for an additional two hours, with nothing to do, until Gerald finally let everyone go. Another time Bess brought a co-worker to a Thursday night Group. The following day she raved to Bess about "bad energy" and Gerald's "evil". We all had a good laugh when Bess told us how crazy the woman was; how she had reversed the "good" in the room and misinterpreted it as "bad". Now I know her co-worker was right. The "outsiders" knew the truth; they were on to Gerald all along.

On a breezy Wednesday evening in the middle of the month, I wander past the *Dunkin' Donuts* at the end of Judy's block and spot a familiar man seated on a stool by the window. Rich, Mitchell Stavos' friend, had left The Group in 1984 and it's been years since we've spoken. He appears terribly pleased to see me and gives me a big bear hug. Naturally, our conversation falls to the topic we share in common, Gerald, and I ask him why he left.

"I didn't like how negative the people were, especially Samantha. You could feel evil coming out of her even when she wasn't saying anything."

I summarize The Group's history for the last twelve years and Rich has to scrape his jaw off the table. A furious fire ignites in his eyes. Like everyone else, he is incensed at Gerald's ability to take advantage of people and destroy them.

"You know," he confides, "last September I saw you walking up the block here and you looked awful, like the walking dead. I always liked you and I was very concerned that there was something wrong."

"Rich, that was probably just about my lowest point."

"Well, you look great now!"

"Thanks. I feel much better to be out of there."

As I am about to leave, we embrace. Suddenly, a powerful surge of electricity passes through both of us triggered by our shared emotions, a tremendous sense of relief that I have finally come home after a long and dangerous journey. Now I have reconnected with a former comrade who has shared part of the nightmare with me. I have another ally . . .

The following Sunday I decide to call my mother and invite myself over. I have not seen her for a month, since that fateful day when Gerald threw me out of his life forever. I ring the bell, and when she answers the door, I feel a rush of betrayal and wish I had never decided to come. She invites me to sit in the living room and offers me a cup of tea. Facing Grace today, I am confused and distraught. Nonetheless, the invisible hand, my friend and coach, pushes firmly at my back again, reminding me that I am making this visit for an important reason, commanding me to ask the essential questions to which I am afraid to hear the answers. I am far from resolving my hurt over the previous month's events and the fact that she never telephoned me to make sure I was OK. Small talk is impossible as I plunge right into the issue that will not stop torturing me. Already in tears, I demand her to explain why Gerald threw me out. Her callous response comes quickly and automatically,

"Because you were rude to him. You didn't have enough respect to discuss reducing your hours with him, to ask his opinion. He decided he'd had enough of your selfish attitude. You were always interfering with his group. He doesn't need a co-pilot you know."

It feels as if she has just spit on me, declaring me worthless. How unfair, to be judged and rejected for my outward behavior, while ignoring the struggle I was confronting.

"What do you mean rude? Doesn't he care about me? I was there for nineteen years; what about my side?"

"You know how you behaved on your last day there. I don't need to remind you of your bad manners. Gerald is special. We need him to show us the way. He doesn't need us."

"What about me? I thought I was special too. I am your daughter. Don't you think I am special?"

"Yes, Liz, you are special to me. I love you, but Gerald is not like us. He is beyond. He certainly doesn't need you when you are uncooperative."

"But doesn't he care about me after all we've been through together?"

"He doesn't have to care about anyone. His only responsibility is to his mission."

"What about his children? He must care about them."

"No, Martin and Samantha are like us. They are responsible for their own lives and must follow him to get the guidance they need. Right now, his only concern is learning from Ben, because he believes that Ben is God and will help us to be God too."

"What the hell is wrong with you? Are you totally stupid?" My eyes bug out threateningly. I would like to choke her for her lack of common sense. "Why doesn't that bother you? That means he doesn't give a damn about you either."

"That's OK; I don't care about him either. All my life I have been looking for a man like Gerald, and all I want is his Energy so that I can grow. Anyway, everyone in that room is completely self-centered. They all hate each other and that makes them no different from anyone else in this world. I find that <u>all people</u> are basically phony; they just present you with nice behavior so they can get what they want out of you. They'll turn against you at a moment's notice if you inconvenience them. Bess and Pauline are like that, just ass-kissers, two wives competing to please him. They make me sick!"

As my mother grimaces, repulsed by the image of her two female competitors for Gerald's approval, a picture pops into my head. I imagine all of Gerald's women sitting in adult-sized, highchairs. They beat their spoons on the tray screaming, *Daddy, pay attention to me*. Suddenly, I realize that beneath the intellectual talk, that is all that is really going on there.

"But Mom, he took all my father's inheritance from me. I have $190,000 in canceled checks in my safe deposit box from the past ten years. Don't you care what he did to me? He stole from me. All he sold me were lies. He is a con man. Why aren't you angry at him? I'm your flesh and blood."

At the end of my statements, I am literally screaming from frustrated infuriation which runs through me in giant surges. I'm out of control, like a lunatic, and continue raving about how Gerald victimized and betrayed me. My mother observes me with genuine lack of comprehension. There is no empathy, no attempt to soothe me or rescue me from this dreadful emotional trap. She merely cautions flatly that I'd better calm down.

"It's not a good idea to be so angry. You are raising your blood pressure and it's not healthy."

I continue screaming, demanding that she validate my concerns until I exasperate her. In retaliation to my annoying tantrum, her lips form a snarl as she defends her position,

"Look, I did my job raising you and you always defied me and never appreciated me. You are more than twenty-one, so <u>you are on your own, kid</u>. I wish you well, but it is not my problem what happens to you. I am only responsible for myself. Remember what Gerald says, that we all have to look after ourselves, not waste our time in distractions by mothering each other. We are adults, not babies. We don't need to play Mother Theresa with each other."

I finally succeed in calming myself, despite her heartless rebuttal, and try to explain intelligently.

"I didn't defy you. I just couldn't follow you because I didn't like where you were leading . . . and what about love, Mom? If you love me like you say you do, then why don't you care when I get hurt?"

"I prefer that you don't get hurt, but it is not my job to step in and save you. That is your responsibility. Everyone is responsible for everything that happens to them, good and bad."

This conversation isn't going the way I had planned. I thought I had some serious ammunition with all the things I have figured out about Gerald this past year, but the person in this living-room is a stranger to me. For the first time my mother is informing me in no uncertain terms that I don't mean anything to her, unless it's convenient. My hurt and anger battle inside of me; I could never adequately describe in words what I am feeling; it is awful . . . A maze of tangled emotions swells my chest — hurt, anger, frustration at not being seen, betrayal. I wish this wasn't happening to me, but I am here and I must stick it out to the end, whenever that will be, so holding back my tears, I push on,

"But Mom, love is what helps two people grow together, learn from each other and share. It feels wonderful. It fills you with joy."

"Oh would you just shut up with that Valentine's Day crap! Who needs that? Besides, how can you speak like such an expert about love when you are the one who killed your pet squirrel Rocky? Love is a big fantasy. All you need is yourself. That is what Gerald is helping me to do, find myself, then I won't need anyone else. You are just immature. You want to defy Gerald's wisdom and do it on your own, even though you know he has the only answers. That is why you think you need other people, like that Judy person." She practically hisses as she states Judy's name.

"But Mom, I love Judy. She is my friend and helped me when I was in trouble, when I couldn't help myself."

"Bullshit on Judy. She is just an exploiter. She wants to use you because she is an uneducated blue-collar bitch in an empty marriage, who screws her husband for a paycheck. You are smarter than her, and she only wants to suck off of you because she is bored. Anyway, she's probably a lesbian who's only hanging onto you so that she can get a piece of your ass. She'll turn on you someday when you stop kowtowing to her and giving her everything she wants."

In my heart I know she is wrong about Judy, wrong about everything. My mother is hostile and prejudiced and I hate her for her allegiance to Gerald and not to me. It is not fair; she is _my_ mother, not his, but she has made it very clear that whenever I am in trouble she will abandon me. I thought a mother was supposed to love you, to feel connected. That connection doesn't end when you reach age twenty-one.

"Mom, he placed his daughter in my business and then convinced me that she was valuable and that I was nothing without her. Do you believe that about me too?"

"Absolutely not. You are more talented. Samantha is a dud. I can't stand her. She is not very bright either. You are much smarter than she is."

Wow, she actually has something positive to say about me, maybe I can reach her after all? I have to keep trying.

"Then why did Gerald lie, and why don't you care that he lied to me?"

Her response comes quickly and cuts deep, crushing my hope,

"I told you not to go into business with Samantha and you ignored me, so you deserve what you got."

Her comment is so unfair and I don't even remember her ever telling me that. "Mom, how could I have even listened to you anyway? Did you realize that Gerald was manipulating me and I was blind to it? Did you alert me to his hidden intention to use me to supply his lazy, selfish and untalented daughter with a free ride? Did you realize that I couldn't refuse any of his commands without risking physical or intolerable emotion abuse? Did you try to help me escape my trap?"

My mother shakes her head and ignores what I have just said. In my mind I imagine her advising a Jew, imprisoned in Hitler's concentration camp, that if he doesn't like the conditions he should stop complaining, get off his lazy ass and walk out, that if he doesn't take her advice his ultimate demise is his own fault.

"Mom, what about the money? Don't you hate that you give him more than $20,000 a year?"

"Sure. I don't want to pay him, but Gerald is the best bargain in town. He only charges $40 an hour. A psychiatrist in the city charges $100 or more and you know that they don't know what they're talking about either. Because Gerald cares that we come along with him, he has remained reasonably priced."

"But Mom, where he is going in the new spiritual place beyond, we aren't supposed to need money, and he says that place is all he cares about. He hardly ever spends anything in this society, but stays home all the time, shaking his head. All that money is just sitting in a bank doing nothing, so why does he want to take so much from the people he claims to care about, that he is trying to help? He knows you and many of the others have a hard time paying your bills because of your involvement."

She snaps at me, "He has a right to make a living! Do you want him to exploit himself and give away his knowledge and talent for free?"

"What living? Doesn't any one of those stupid people know how to use a calculator? What do you think he makes with those big groups of people? It's got to be at least one and a half million over the past three years!!"

"That's none of my business. All I care about it that I am making progress."

"Yeah, and what about his temper? If he is so spiritual, then why does he glare at people and physically bully them? He attacked me three different times. You obviously don't care that he abused me, and that really hurts."

Referring to these painful moments with Gerald brings back my profound feelings of hatred toward him. My head feels as if it's about to burst from the frustration of watching my mother consistently choose the side of my tormentor instead of rising up to defend me.

To my surprise, she hesitates for a moment and then murmurs,

"Well . . . I wasn't in the room during the occasions you are referring to, so I'll have to take your word for it, but I don't really feel very comfortable, in fact it's kind of scary, when he threatens Laura or Bess . . . I really don't think it's a good idea for him to do that."

Hope rushes through me. *Maybe I've finally found a hook, my mother's sense of right and wrong . . . Maybe now that I've exposed her buried feelings, her inner sense of justice, those feelings will take the reins and she will wake up to Gerald's injustice; she will finally stand up for what is right. This could be the beginning!*

But in the next moment the illusion is smashed as she throws this revealed truth into the trash and returns to her usual position,

"Gerald is not yet perfect although he is really close. He has told us that there is still five percent he needs to work on in himself. That temper is part of his five percent."

Her response really pisses me off. My mother is willing to accept what she acknowledges is injustice until Gerald is ready to change, even if that day never comes . . . I have no idea how to corner her, to discredit him enough to make her see the light, but my frustration fuels a relentless drive, I must keep trying.

"Mom, he contradicts himself too. He tells us not to go to a doctor and then he sends Martin to the eye doctor. He tells us not to buy health insurance because The Energy will take care of us, but *he* buys it. What about that?"

"That is part of his five percent."

I guess she won't get off that excuse. Obviously he can do anything he wants and she'll attribute it to his remaining flawed five percent . . .

"If his energy is so great then why are all the women like Bess, Pauline, and Laura broke from giving all of their money to him? Why doesn't The Energy make them wealthy? Gerald has failed to help them."

"Their failure is their fault. They don't listen to him, so they lag behind. They defy him and The Energy. They are stupid."

I should have known she would blame it on the girls. Gerald is so great and can perform miracles, but when things don't go well, it's always the other person's fault, never his. How convenient for him! She is so hostile to them too, as if they are garbage. I don't feel that way about Pauline, Bess and the rest. I care about them. We have shared a lot together and it breaks my heart to see them continuing to suffer under the whip he cracks over their backs. I wish I could help them free themselves; I would do anything for them if they would only be willing to reach out for help . . .

"But Mom, when is the graduation? When does everyone grow up enough not to need Gerald?"

"There is no graduation because he is always changing and growing and we will always be behind him, needing to learn from him."

"Right, so I guess you'll be with him for the rest of your life. Nice set-up for him, permanent income."

I am hostile, sarcastic and fed up at her refusal to face the facts, but I decide to shelve my emotions and try to explain from an intellectual point of view. Maybe that will work . . .

"Look Mom, I know I was emotionally needy and I realize now that several things kept me harnessed to Gerald — my want for a sense of family and belonging, my search for guidance and a confident role model, my attraction to his charisma which inappropriately developed into unrequited love, and a compelling hunger for spiritual knowledge, which I believed he possessed. When you are needy, you are willing to compromise your well-being and common sense because those needs are screaming. They are lies, but louder and more demanding than your true gut feelings. I made mistakes, starting from the day Gerald suggested I take my blouse off in Dr. Rogers' office, the beginning of my seduction. In that moment something inside of me should have risen up and declared, *This man has no right to ask me to do this; he is sick*; I should have walked out and reported him to Dr. Rogers, but I didn't. It has taken me all of this time to figure out why. The link which should have connected my innate sense of right and wrong to conscious thought had never been formed, probably because I spent my first eighteen years observing you, my own mother, my only role model, allow, no, invite people to take advantage of her."

I can't avoid it; I have worked myself into a rage again. I really want to stick it to her, to expose her lack of morals and make her feel ashamed. However, Grace seems to possess protective skills which I didn't know about, and she neither responds nor reacts; it's almost as if I were talking about someone else. Frustrated even more, I jump out of my seat, put my hands on my hips and look directly into her cold eyes, trying to force the truth into her, to make her wake up.

"You know Mom, I behaved just like you did with all your nutritionist gurus; I believed that Gerald had all the answers. He was so charming and good-looking; he made me feel like it would be so easy, just follow him and he will blaze the trail. I had no idea that all he really wanted to do was take my money and get sex for free, behind Doris' back. I always assumed that everyone was like me, that they wanted to be fair. I thought the world was like school — work hard and fulfill the teachers' instructions and you will be rewarded, ignore the assignments and you will receive a failing grade. You introduced Gerald as the authority, like a teacher or doctor, so I automatically believed that he knew more than me. I was always insecure, and he had confidence. I followed him without even realizing it. You never taught me that I could be cheated by people in life, or how to handle it. That was part of your job, and you let me down. I had no survival skills, but you threw me into the water anyway, a turtle without a shell, and watched me get attacked. Then you blamed me for losing the battle. I hate you for that, you stupid bitch."

I run toward her, wanting to shake her, even punch her, but I stop myself in time. My mother couldn't care less about my unhappiness, about my loss and my wounds. I resume my frustrated attempt to beat some sense into her.

"You told me today that my failure was my fault, that I am responsible for everything that happens to me, but you are totally wrong. I always opposed Gerald, from the moment I met him, but I didn't have the strength to stand up to him and spit in his face, which is all he deserves. That bastard found a way to trap me; he used my insecurities and ignorance against me. He victimized me, because he is so insecure that he can't live in the real world and needs to surround himself with trained Barbie dolls who won't upset 'The King'. I refuse to share responsibility with him for my downfall because as soon as I met Judy and she started feeding me information, I wouldn't let her go. I could never explain to anyone what it feels like to give up your entire familiar world, including all of your thoughts, but I was willing to do whatever was necessary to free myself from Gerald's grasp; I didn't care how hard it was. I hate that I have lost almost twenty years of my life, but I am not going to lose the rest of it. A man like Gerald will never get over on me again. I am on to him. I want you to understand why he is evil. I don't want you to keep hurting yourself. This can't go on. He must be stopped and I pray to God to show me how to do it. Why do you push me away? I want to help you. Don't I have any validity as your daughter? Won't you even consider my information?"

My mother turns her head away stubbornly. She refuses to respond and I realize I can't reach her. Most people do not like to be lied to or stolen from, but Grace obviously doesn't care. I realize that she is caught in the same trap of brainwashing and lies that I was in, but for her it is different. She wants to live in Gerald's fantasy world! She skillfully and purposefully blocks any information which will expose his hypocrisy. I can't understand how she can diminish her own value and lift another human being above her in worship. Where is her self-respect and dignity?

For some reason, I decide to ask the ultimate question.

"Mom, how would you feel if I died?"

Pensive, hesitating for a moment, she stammers without any conviction, "Well, I don't know. I guess I'd be upset. I'd have to wait until it happened to see what I'd feel."

I imagine her standing before my coffin and in this moment, I know what she would be feeling inside, almost nothing, just anxiety from change, similar to what she might experience starting a new job. If I hadn't made sure to anchor myself before asking the question, right now I would be throwing furniture, pulling my hair out and shaking her violently in a desperate attempt to somehow force her to love me. But I don't lose it. I embrace the truth, knowing I will have to accept it no matter what. This woman doesn't love me, not in the way God meant for us to love one another, with compassion and connection. She is another species with different alien values. Someone I can't really understand.

"But Mom, you must have real feelings for me somewhere. You must have loved me at some time when I was your baby. You spent twenty-four hours in labor to give birth to me. You helped me survive colic. You watched me take my first step, speak my first word. You held my hand on my first day of school. For Christ's sake, you used to write down things that I said as a toddler because you were amazed by my insight. Even though I protested from embarrassment, you insisted on keeping it all in a special book, one of your most treasured possessions. You sat proudly in the front row when I played *Anne of Green Gables* — the lead in my eighth grade play. I colored my hair red with *Henna Rinse* and sang seven solos totally off key, but you recorded the entire play on a portable cassette recorder. Don't you remember? And only six months later you sat in the same auditorium to watch me give my valedictorian speech with a tear in your eye because my father couldn't be there, because you knew how much I missed him only one short year after his death. What happened to that? Where is all of that now?"

My willful persistence finally pays off and she snaps out a response.

"I did love you, when you were small, because you were so smart. I was fascinated by you."

Before my eyes, the window to her concealed feelings closes as quickly as it has opened. It slams on my hopeful fingers which have just eagerly reached in to grasp her exposed heart and drag it out into the light. In the next moment I realize that it was only by virtue of my powerful will that she revealed these feelings at all. Otherwise, she would have never wanted to tell me. Obviously, she has chosen to disconnect herself from any maternal feelings and I stand before her, an acquaintance she feels no obligation or commitment to, not in any capacity. This is her choice, and I must accept it. It has nothing to do with me or anything I have ever done. It is no reflection on my value as a human being. For her, I guess that love is too much work and cutting herself off from it eliminates any possible conflict. I cannot understand how any human being would make this choice; I certainly never could . . .

Our confrontation lasts for more than four hours, until I am spent. At one level, I feel relieved. Having the truth shoved down your throat hurts, but after it is over, you feel better. Except for the biological fact that she carried my fetus for nine months, and passed me through her loins thirty-six years ago, I have no mother. Right now, I am too exhausted to keep hating her, but a terrible sadness fills me. I have been deprived of a relationship with her. I know she has lost too; she will never feel the joy of my spirit in her life, never have me as a friend. Now I realize why I have endured such conflict as long as I have known her. I have spent my entire life trying to convince my mother to love me, and she has always opposed me.

April to May 1996

So freshly out of The Group, I fear running into any of my former comrades. Even so, while Judy, Rich and I share coffee in *Dunkin' Donuts* one spring evening, Mitchell Stavos enters, forcing me to confront feelings of abandonment and betrayal once again. Rich beckons him to join us and he accepts, soon seating himself next to me at our table in the back.

"How have you been?" I ask tentatively, at a loss for words.

"Oh great, I've been going with Gerald to visit Sing Sing Prison and the inmates are really getting The Energy; it's fantastic!"

Mitchell, the eternal blow-hard, puffs his chest like a proud peacock and continues.

"You know," he leans in closer, confidentially, "there were about five suicides at the prison last year; they've never had that many all at once. Of course they kept it hushed up, but Governor Pataki was looking into it. Now, you people know why that happened — some of the guys couldn't handle Gerald's Energy and they had to kill themselves to run away from it. That's how powerful he's getting!!"

Mitchell, who has nothing else to talk about, continues by authoritatively spouting Gerald's philosophy.

"Have you noticed that there are disasters happening all over the world: wars overseas, floods, earthquakes, shootings in schools and post-offices? Did you ever think that in this area, nothing bad is happening? Well, where do you think our protection is coming from? Gerald's Energy, that's where!"

Mitchell's audience sighs, collectively aware that challenging him would be useless, and the lecture goes on,

"You know that the planets are held together with resistance."

"You mean gravity?" I query.

"Whatever . . . The scientists don't know what they're talking about with that gravity nonsense. Anyway, there's going to be a change very soon. The resistance will break all at once. All of our thoughts and programming will be removed in one instant and the planets will fly away."

"Then what will happen to us?"

"There will be a giant void which no one will be equipped to handle. Unless you are prepared, you will be toast."

"How do you prepare?"

"I have found my way to prepare. Everyone must do the same or they won't survive. You know what you're supposed to do," he states condescendingly

"Oh, you mean The Energy will fill in the void?"

"That's right. It's the only way." He shoots me a disapproving parental look. "Boy, you really ruined your life, Liz. You treated Gerald like shit. You pushed him over the limit until he had no other choice but to let you go. I feel sorry for you. You know you're not going to make it without Gerald. You're down the toilet now."

Judy responds, "Well, that's Gerald's side of it, but what about Elizabeth? She has a story to tell too. You haven't heard her side."

"Elizabeth has no side," Mitchell retorts defiantly, then continues pontificating about The Energy and God. Repeating one of Gerald's favorite phrases, "We are all God".

He points to each of us in turn. "Elizabeth is God. Rich is God. Judy is God."

Rich, who has been absorbing this in silence suddenly interrupts, "If Elizabeth is God, then why does she need Gerald?"

Mitchell's face turns beet red at this unexpected challenge for which he has no comeback. His body shakes as he rises quickly, mumbling, "I have to go." With that, he races toward the *Dunkin' Donuts* exit, leaving his coffee on the table, barely touched.

It sounds like Gerald is predicting the Armageddon or the Rapture, prophesied in the Bible with the second coming of Christ. However, instead of the survivors being filled with God's love, they must seek to be filled with Gerald's Energy. Mitchell and the other followers seem to be in a desperate race to accumulate this Energy, like squirrels storing nuts for the winter, to protect themselves from being destroyed. As ridiculous as their behavior may seem to us, Gerald's predictions are right in line with many New Age thinking patterns which anticipate the year 2000 and the possibly cataclysmic spiritual changes it will bring.

The following week Samantha brings a copy of The Group's new bible, *Conversations with God,* to the office. She offers to read me a few excerpts, sure that I'll be impressed. The author's assertions sound logical, yet there is something about God's attitude in this book which just doesn't feel right to me. He seems to be an impersonal God, lacking compassion and empathy. Samantha informs me that my mother, still a leader in The Group, is reading from the book to help Beatrice and Bess with their problems. Wanting more insight into their current activities, missing the familiarity of contact with them, I ask,

"Is Ben walking yet?"

This is a hard question for me. Although I know in my heart that it is all a ridiculous lie, their ability to influence me emotionally, even against my common sense, is still powerful. All of The Group members are completely convinced that Ben will be resurrected, and their unified belief forms a powerful mental energy field, still strong enough to seduce me to join them. Resisting this pull with all of my resolve, I still half fear she will tell me that he has been revived.

"No . . . But he is getting closer. We see changes in him every day."

"Is anything new with everybody?" I ask next, suddenly feeling like a sad puppy whining outside his owner's door on a dark rainy night.

"Well, this week Hollywood caught onto my father's information again. You really should go to the new John Travolta movie, *Phenomenon*. We've all seen it, and it's no coincidence that the lead character has the same name as my father. They finally got the message and made a movie that talks about energy and the unlimited potential of your brain, things he has been trying to teach everyone for years!"

Understanding . . . , my conflicted mind starves for knowledge, to put together the pieces of the puzzle, to solve the mystery, to figure out what is really happening in that den, how I got trapped and why. My answers seem to come from everywhere, and everyone, one revelation after another . . .

One Sunday afternoon I open the Bible; I don't know why. Fascinated with *The Book of Revelations*, I read the entire section. Judy soon shares my new interest with me, and together we visit local churches, listen to Christian radio and purchase teaching cassettes about the "End Times". We have an insatiable appetite for spiritual truth, good and evil, God and Satan, demons and angels, and the expected return of the Messiah. Everywhere we collect bits and pieces of information, and with each discovery I come to understand more about my journey with Gerald. In my heart I have probably always known good and evil, but in my mind, I have never identified either. From a biblical perspective I can now classify Gerald's innate character. His lies and manipulations to fulfill a self-benefitting hidden plan at the expense of others' well-being remind me of the qualities possessed by Satan.

At the office I play a teaching cassette recorded by a local preacher. Samantha looks uncomfortable and inquires,

"What? Are you turning religious?"

"No. I am just trying to learn spiritual truth. That was what attracted me to your father. From the way he talked, I thought he knew a lot about it . . ."

On the tape the preacher explains, "Satan knows the Bible. He knows the truth. He will con you by quoting the Bible, but twisting just one word. That twist, should you follow it, will destroy you."

Now I know how Gerald got over on the spiritually ignorant, such as me. His theories sound good because there is truth mixed in. However, a deadly agenda lurks behind an impressive verbal display — a fancy show of smoke and mirrors with no foundation in truth. I know what Gerald is now; he is a spiritual con man!

I have thought a lot about Gerald's overall strategies and the choices he has made — the sex, the shoplifting, his goal to resurrect. He is actually claiming to be the messiah, yet he has none of the godly qualities of Jesus Christ. God instilled a conscience in us so that we could discern right from wrong. He gave us some of his rules in the Ten Commandments. Gerald challenges these very rules. Instead of validating them as a frame of reference, our anchor, he claims that they are part of an oppressive 'Program' whose only goal is to keep man small. Therefore, he asserts, in order to grow, we must break each of these inborn intentions to follow God's will, except that he labels them as 'barriers blocking us from our freedom'. He has no respect for the institution of marriage, no misgivings about stealing another's property. He invalidates the physical laws of nature, claiming that he can alter them by reversing life and death, controlling the weather or communicating with the sun. He has purposely stolen his followers' inheritance from God, gifts of conscience, rage at injustice, discernment, curiosity, love . . . and when his job is complete, he inserts his own intention and therefore becomes their new and only god. This is precisely what Christians believe that Satan is trying to accomplish, to win people's allegiance away from God and to him, with deceit and injustice.

Most nights, restless sleep tosses me with anxiety, my body translating my shredded emotions into pain — TMJ, allergies, sinus headaches. Judy knows that these afflictions are psychosomatic and sends me to her chiropractor for relief. During my interview, I add chronic fatigue to my list of complaints. After a battery of questions and a few tests, he concludes that my adrenal glands are functioning at 70% below normal. With so little adrenalin in my system I will never experience adequate energy levels. He prescribes mega-doses of vitamin B and an array of other vitamins and minerals.

"I think you have hypoglycemia too," he adds, "Your eating habits are poor and irregular; you have abused your body and thrown your sugar metabolism completely out of whack; you need a high protein, low carbohydrate diet."

Consulting a manual from his shelf, he reads me a list of fifty-two symptoms of "Low Blood Sugar" disorder. I have experienced forty-eight in the last several years, many such as exhaustion, depression, allergies and asthma, to the extreme.

"How has this happened?" I ask.

"Probably from stress. Do you have a lot of stress in your life?"

"Yes, I have had more than my share of stress. Could this come from fear as well?"

"Yes, adrenalin gets released when you are afraid. It is called the Fight or Flight Reaction."

The realization cuts through me like a knife. The very concept which Gerald introduced me to on that first day has turned out to be my downfall! I think of all the hours I spent with Gerald "feeling The Energy" in my body and that session with the Nyack, N.Y. New Age group, only a few months ago, when I discovered that this physical sensation was from my own terror and not his "Energy". Gerald created an environment which forced me into perpetual survival mode, an unavoidable biological response to his personality which severely debilitated my body's chemistry. Now, he has slipped away like a thief in the night, leaving me to repair the damage. Still, I am grateful that it is not too late . . .

One Saturday afternoon, not too long after our meeting with Mitchell, Judy runs into Gerald at *Pergament's*. She decides not to avoid him so she approaches and shakes his hand,

"I saw him from across an aisle. He seemed to be in a daze; his eyes were blank and he looked lost. After I said hello, I introduced him to Michael. Michael was really not impressed. He said that when he shook his hand, it was like being handed a wet fish. As a man, he is a joke. There is no power in him at all; he's just a bully who can act big to his people because he's convinced them that he's a big shot."

"Really?" I reply, grateful that someone is finally telling me what I needed to hear about nineteen years ago . . .

A few evenings later, while channel surfing, a TV show about serial killers such as Jeffrey Dahmer grabs my interest. I watch with morbid fascination. These murderers show no remorse for their crimes, even after years of incarceration. The show describes the activities of one man who, after he had done away with his victims, dressed up the cadavers and carried them around the house as if they were life-sized dolls. He conversed and even slept with them!

How is Gerald any different? Look at Bess and Pauline. Thanks to his manipulations, they are broke, have no future, and spend all of their spare time pursuing the hopeless resurrection of Ben. Gerald has completely taken over their lives, forcing them to play out specific roles. They are certainly dolls to him, existing solely for his pleasure.

Fascinated by the description of "evil" people outlined in the show, I purchase a copy of *Speaking with the Devil — a Dialogue with Evil*. The author, Dr. Carl Goldberg, a psychologist, specializes in the malevolent personality. By the end of the first page, I realize that this is a book about Gerald. According to the author, a malevolent person creates undeserved suffering. He treats people as objects, without consideration for their humanity, and justifies any destructive action against his chosen victims. The malevolent person also displays "magical thinking". Finally I have a textbook definition for The Energy and Gerald's claims that "he alone can lead us out of this crazy lousy stinking world to a wonderful life." In addition, the malevolent person is contemptuous, paranoid, deceitful and unwilling to examine himself. When confronted, he will deny, change the subject, intimidate and confuse; whatever it takes to get you off his back. How many times have I observed Gerald do that!? Now I have verification; I know how Gerald thinks and why. He is not a uniquely gifted spiritual leader, but merely a case study in a psychology book; he is clinically insane.

I skip to Chapter 11, *Courage and Fanaticism,* and I can't stop underlining. The chapter describes the Jim Jones cult, but my own life jumps off the pages! Our group has exactly the same dynamics as the Guyana group. Like Gerald, Jones convinced his followers that if they follow him without question, they will be rewarded with immortality and control over the rest of the human race, but once they leave, they are doomed to lose the shield which protects them from misfortune and illness — "Father's aura", just like The Energy! Once, only a few years ago, I told Gerald that I would be willing to die for him, reasoning that the loss of my life would be a minor casualty compared to his, since he was destined to save humanity . . .

Dr. Goldberg also describes how the Jones' cult members constantly re-indoctrinated their leader by reinforcing his role of superiority. A memory returns of Laura telling Gerald they should name a wing of the *Columbia Presbyterian Hospital* after him.

"You could just stand in the lobby and shake your head. All of the patients in the building would be cured at once."

He had replied to her, "Yes, I could cure them, but they would just get sick again as soon as I left. They really don't want to get better because it's more important to use their illnesses to play sympathy games with their families for recognition."

Bess' soft upturned eyes and sweet stroking voice drift back into my mind's eye, "I am so grateful that I found you; you are the highest spiritual being on the planet." And then the sudden shift to brazen confidence as she added,

"I know I could fuck my way from here to China and never get AIDS, not with The Energy protecting me."

I phone Judy and read her the entire chapter over the phone.

"Gerald's group is a cult." I declare with elation. Another puzzle piece in place. Each piece releases me from darkness, exonerates me . . .

Apparently my studies have been preparing me for an important confrontation, because one Tuesday morning, while sitting on my couch killing time before my afternoon shift at *Expressions*, the phone rings. Gerald's voice floats over the wire, as casually as if we have just had a pleasant lunch together yesterday. Caught off guard, I immediately dive for internal support to protect my vulnerability. He addresses me enthusiastically,

"Hello there; how are you doing?"

Hesitantly I answer, "Fine."

His voice caresses me with classic little-boy sweetness. "Why don't you start to try to come back slowly?"

"Why?"

"Just trust me. You don't need to know anything else." He sounds a little annoyed.

"Yes, but you must have a reason. You are a human being just like me and human beings have reasons for doing things."

Inside I think of the possible reasons I'd like to throw in his face. *Do you want my money? Is it too much of a blow to your ego to lose one of your Barbie dolls? Are you looking for another set of buttocks to fill the seats in your den?*

"Stop intellectualizing and being a know-it-all." He tries to intimidate me with the domineering voice which had always subdued me in the past.

But again I press him, "Yes, but I want to know the reason you are asking me to come back. I know you have one."

In the next moment the line goes dead as he hangs up on me . . .

A week later I confront Samantha at the office.

"Why did your father hang up on me? Why can't he hold a conversation like a normal human being for more than three sentences?"

"I don't know. I'll call him and you can ask."

She gets him on the line and hands me the phone. I am anxious. It is more than difficult to talk to him. Praying that he will not press any of my buttons and cause me to fall apart, I push through my hesitation.

"Gerald, what did you feel when you hung up the phone on me last week?"

"Nothing," he says flatly.

I know he is lying. Gerald has lost much of his former hold on me. I see now that what Michael said is true. He is a coward who only operates in an arena where he has full control, where everyone responds in the way he commands them. He cannot deal with a person who possesses even the slightest amount of self-confidence, who might request that he explain himself. I am proud that I was able to make the bully run away from me.

Having survived my showdown with Gerald, I realize that I have climbed over a high fence. I see a whole other side to life, and now I have many more questions. I must come to understand The Group from an outsider's perspective.

My days at the office are filled with confrontation as I take every possible opportunity to question Samantha. Like a lawyer interviewing a witness, I am gathering data. Sometimes her responses are painful; they grate on the emotional wounds which still remain, leaving me raw and bruised . . .

"Samantha, did your father ever hit you?"

"No, never."

"Then why did he hit me and some of the others when he claimed we were going the wrong way? He always <u>insisted</u> that he treated you and Marty the same as us."

"I don't know," she answers, not the least bit interested in examining the contradiction between her father's talk and his actions, not the least bit distressed at the reference to his violent attacks on women who were defenseless against his imposing stature.

I press on, "Well, what did you feel the day Rocky had a seizure and he pulled me off the floor by my hair?"

"I felt like you deserved it."

I realize at a deeper level that in his daughter's eyes, Gerald can do no wrong. She believes every excuse that his mind implements to rationalize his behavior. There is no hope of ever separating her mind from his and she will never question his decisions.

"Elizabeth, I know you think that I spend so much time with my father because he is my parent and familiar to me. I know you think that he forced me to be involved with the things that he does. That is not true. I am an adult now and I am making my own choice. I <u>want</u> to be there and I always have. I believe that somehow, before we were born, we chose our parents, and I chose my father on purpose."

My eyes widen at her confident direct statement. In regard to her father, unlike myself, I have never perceived any conflict in her. Her allegiance to him is always absolute. Without conflict, there is no hope of change. I have always felt sorry for Samantha, assuming that she had been trapped and brainwashed when she was too small to know any better. But now, after all the events which have passed, I am not so sure that this is sufficient excuse or explanation for the choices she makes.

"Samantha, do you remember the light bulb getting longer in The Group last year?"

"Yes."

"How do you know that it was really getting longer?"

"Because I saw it."

"But what if your eyes were playing tricks on you?"

"No, it was real."

"How can you be so sure?"

"Because I felt it."

"But that doesn't prove anything; your feelings could be wrong."

"No, they're not."

"How do you know?"

"I just know . . ."

"If you're so sure you're right, then prove it to me."

"I don't have to; as long as I know, that's all that's important. If you don't agree with me, that's your opinion and your problem. I don't owe you any explanations."

"Why aren't you interested in knowing the truth?"

"I do know the truth because I feel it."

"But there are facts that are indisputable; not everything is an opinion. Two plus two always equals four; that is not my opinion. The sciences of physics and mathematics are built on a foundation of accepted facts."

"Come on, scientists don't know what the hell they are talking about. They think small and rigid; they are insecure and cling to their theories like children clinging to teddy bears. You know that all of the men who are scientists are still babies; they never gave up The Program; they don't know what we know . . . Have they ever been in my father's room? Have they ever felt The Energy? They are still controlled by their mothers, wives and society. How could they discover anything real when their own lives are a wreak?"

Her eyes bug out self-righteously, as if to say, *What are you, a total stupid idiot? Haven't you ever listened to what my father says?*

Despite her opposition, I continue.

"But what if I took a ruler and measured the light bulb before and after your father held it? What if the ruler measurement didn't change? Then would you admit that your father is not able to change the shape of the light bulb and you were all imagining it because you wanted it to be so?"

Samantha doesn't even hesitate for a moment, but states with absolute assurance,

"No, I wouldn't have to admit that, because the ruler could change length too."

Son of a bitch, I think, *Where did this young woman learn to slip out of a logical contradiction so skillfully and so quickly? Her flat out denial of reality is more than frustrating, it is actually terrifying. How can I ever reach her if there is no common basis for agreement anywhere?*

"Do you mean that there is no frame of reference for anything?"

"No, there is none, because everything is constantly changing. Choices that are good for me today may be bad for me tomorrow because we are always getting new information."

"Do you have any rules about the way you treat people?"

"No, because I am always changing."

"Then how do you stop yourself from hurting people?"

"When you make the intention to move ahead, to grow, you can treat them any way you need to. Any decision will be correct, as long as you focus on your goal and don't let yourself get off track."

This is her father speaking, but obviously it is her too . . .

"Do you believe in evil?"

"No, evil is just an illusion."

"What about murder, isn't that evil?"

"No, because the person who is killed is always asking for it."

I am awed at her thinking process, so irrational, so self-serving, so defiant of the rules of logic, common sense and human decency. It all feels so impossibly wrong. How did I ever survive with all of them for so long . . . ?

My emotions surge for several hours after we have parted, and my distressed mind protests,

"I wish I didn't have to be in business with her."

"What choice do I have?" the other side of my brain counters.

"None, I guess . . ."

And with no possible resolve in sight, I push away the conflict and move on to other things.

During the following weeks, I decide to add a new title to my list of flash card sets, "GMAT study cards", and serendipity, my faithful friend, pays me another call. I make a trip to *Barnes & Noble* to research the exam where I flip through Barron's *How to Prepare for the GMAT — Graduate Management Admission Test*. Skimming a section on logic and reasoning, I happen across the concept of faulty logic. As I read the details, a bell goes off in my head. Here, in front of me, in a book read by millions of people each year, is the fundamental tool Gerald used to mislead us and reshape our minds. It is called a "causal fallacy" and put simply — just because event "b" follows event "a" doesn't mean that "a" <u>caused</u> "b" to happen.

My thoughts travel back to the day Bess informed us that *Loreal Cosmetics* had just announced they would no longer test their products on animals. "And it's amazing," she added, "I just sent them a donation yesterday!" "There you go!" Gerald responded, "The company felt The Energy from touching your check and that changed everything." With Gerald's magic wand sweeping through our minds, Abracadabra — a coincidence was transformed into "cause and effect". The link between the events was imaginary, created only to serve the Sharkman's needs, and a creatively constructed sequence of assertions always led exactly where they wanted them to go, although their final conclusions were rarely accurate.

Now I understand precisely how Gerald's brainwashing was accomplished. Those false connections between incidents, after hundreds of repetitions, came to

<u>feel</u> so familiar that they were <u>assumed to be true</u>. Amazing, that after investing only ten minutes to peruse this workbook, I have completely revealed how Gerald manipulated me and the rest for so many years, how he justified the power of The Energy and made it seem real, how he reinforced his own validity. Once again, I can't believe that I repeatedly fell for such a simple ruse. Furthermore, I can't understand how my mother could ever refer proudly to her Master's Degree in Sociology when she has allowed the framework of her mind to become completely restructured with faulty logic. Why isn't she ashamed of herself for throwing away her higher intelligence?

For some reason, thinking of my mother reminds me of a will I wrote with her when I was twenty-one and had something to bequeath. I haven't looked at it for years and when I dig it out of my files, I discover to my horror that, should my mother predecease me, Gerald has not only been assigned as executor, but is also entitled to 20% of my estate! I drop everything and call a lawyer. Within a week, a new will is drawn up, and Gerald and Grace have been officially disinherited.

I am constantly complaining to Samantha that not one of my friends, including my college roommate, Pauline, has called me to find out how I am doing.

"If they were my friends, why aren't they still my friends? Why must I go to Gerald in order for them to like me? Don't they like me for me, separate from The Group?"

I get out of her that Gerald never mentions me at all. Since the day he dismissed me, he has only informed them of one thing, that I was not coming back. That was it — no explanations or analysis, no plans for a series of phone calls, no chasing, no discussions of what a jerk I am for denying The Energy. I do not get the treatment Lisa and Caroline received. Still hurting from their collective indifference, I yell out,

"They don't care about me. Why? The people in The Group keep saying they're friends with each other, but they aren't; they're lying."

Samantha's eyes turn soft and sincere,

"But we do care, that is why I tried to help you with your relationship with Judy. We all did, but you didn't want to listen, so we had to give up and let you make your own mistakes."

"Tried to help me! You mean that you tried to help me to not think for myself; you tried to help me do things your way!"

"No, we really do care; you just don't appreciate us."

"What kind of bull is that? You people toss the word 'care' around like salad, but you don't know how to do it. You were the reason I went down in the first place and Judy was there to help, not to mislead me as you are dead set on convincing me. Without her, I don't know what would have happened to me; I would probably be dead now, and I'm not being overly dramatic when I say that."

The next day Samantha tells me that she talked to her father and he has invited me back to The Group tonight, Thursday, as a guest. I don't even have to pay the session fee. I immediately accept. Not that I want to go anywhere near them, but I must. There are still emotional bonds which must be broken, probably many more than I even realize.

At 7:30 P.M. I turn down his block. Seeing all the familiar cars throws me back in time; it feels as if I have never left. The rest are already inside except Bess, who has just parked. She notices me, and without warning or conscious intent, runs into my arms and hugs me hard. The same connection I felt when Rich and I hugged a few months ago, a fusion of emotion and soul. Does her heart have real feeling for me which her mind denies? Has her higher self emerged for one precious moment, hurling her into my arms to deliver the message that she too is trapped like I was? Is she asking for help? And if this is true, where would I begin? As quickly as the connection began, it ends, and I wonder if she is even aware of the feeling she has just released. We turn together to walk down the driveway as we have so many times before . . . Still afraid of Gerald, I am shaking enough that walking is difficult. I still have a lot of healing to do. After all, it has been less than four months. I force myself up his deck stairs and through the den door.

The Group wasn't told I was coming, but when I enter, no one seems surprised. It is too eerie. After all that has transpired, they treat me as if I had just been there this morning. There are no hellos or "how are you doings", no smiling faces or warm looks. In fact, they barely acknowledge my entrance and I wonder if my former associates have fallen prey to the "Body Snatchers". The only source of light comes from a solitary end table lamp. Gerald is hidden in the shadows at the back of the room. Focusing straight ahead, catatonic, he ignores me completely. The Group members speak in low murmurs with intense faces. I sit down slowly, greeting everyone, and they pause momentarily to look up with mild curiosity. A wave of nostalgic familiarity strikes, deep sadness for times gone by, an enormous piece of my life which I must find the strength to bury.

"Just a moment, I want to look at all of you," I request aloud and slowly scan the room, pausing on each of the ten or so faces. Their countenances bring memories of shared experiences and my own personal investment. In each I see a special soul, a person whose absence in my life still aches. If there is any desire on their part to return their feelings to me, it is hidden out of sight, forbidden in this den. My body still trembles from nervousness, but since for some reason they seem to be looking for me to lead the conversation, and Gerald is already busy shaking his head, I ask the only question I can think of, what they feel about my decision not to return. Instantly, the ten people unite and begin to poke at me from all directions, using intimidation and inaccuracies to condemn me, a systematic attempt to trigger my self-doubt. They have studied my insecurities for many years; they have weapons against me. What really strikes me is that I recognize the behavior of each person to be an aspect of Gerald's personality and not their own. Undulating like the snakes on *Medusa's* head, they are not individuals; they have no self. I thank God again that I have escaped this fraternity infested with lies and oppression . . . Jane, the eighth-grade special education teacher from Manhattan, employing same patronizing voice she uses on her students, begins ever so sweetly,

"Come on, Elizabeth, you know that you really want to come back to The Group. You are just in denial. Why don't you relax and you will experience the real truth in a few moments."

Why doesn't she just wave a spoonful of arsenic mixed with honey under my nose and describe its delicious taste in order to convince me to swallow it? Others accuse me of being a misdirected fool, ungrateful and stupid to have thrown away Gerald's energy; they fire judgments and criticisms at me from their collective arsenal, and not one person ever asks me about my own life. I manage to hold my ground despite my feelings of betrayal, now intensified in the face of their solidarity against me. At the same time, I am amazed at how astute I have become in the past few months. I discover that I have developed the ability to identify most of their tactics as they deliver them, tactics I was totally blind to several short months ago. Matter-of-factly, doing my best to hold my voice steady, I feed their techniques back to them.

"You are trying to intimidate me by talking fast; you are trying to trigger my doubt. You are only telling your side; I have a side too, which you haven't inquired about; you can't understand the whole picture until you have all the facts in front of you. You are making assumptions without proof; your logic is faulty."

Finally, after about an hour, Gerald realizes that his army is failing at their assignment to browbeat me into submission, into admitting that I was wrong to leave, so he drags himself out of his head shaking to challenge me. An expert at intimidation and confusion, he employs his favorite confrontational technique of yelling so quickly and loudly that any possible response is drowned out. He tells me that I look wretched, that I am lost, nowhere, on my way to failure, or worse. Although I was once so terrified of his rage and so bent on pleasing him, today I face him with new strength, albeit unstable, and some measure of confidence. I oppose him, even as his roaring denouncements monopolize the floor, and my voice remains steady and firm.

"Your voice is louder than mine, but yelling at me does not make you right. You can keep going, but it's not going to work, your loudness will not convince me."

Inside, I hold onto my anchor, while outside, emotions explode. The anchor I cling to is composed of many things. For one, I know that only one mile away, Judy is in her office. She is rooting for me now. She loves me and believes in me. Also, I have survived four months without The Group. When I first arrived an hour ago, reality had slapped me in the face as I perceived a room occupied by Gerald Senior and ten Gerald Juniors, all resident slaves with one sole function, to deliver the intent of their leader's will. I would rather perish than rejoin that team! Tonight, Gerald gains no ground with me. As terrified as I still am of his bullying techniques which have always worked before, I promise myself that he will not win. Gerald soon becomes frustrated over his failed attempts to control me and he works himself into an ego frenzy, roaring,

"Elizabeth, you are too stupid to see this, but someday all people will <u>have</u> to come this way to me, because of The Energy. They will. They <u>must</u>. I have the answer. I am God."

His mighty storm of personality and willpower rages, and I imagine that I am hanging onto a lamp post in the middle of a tornado. I hold on for dear life!

Finally, the gale subsides. Exhausted from his tirade, he inquires impotently, "Why do you want to lead the people away from here?"

"I don't," I reply, "I just want them to be able to experience their own empowerment instead of relying on you . . ."

Naturally, he has no response and immediately dismisses me.

Later, as I am leaving, Nora — a woman I spent many weekend hours with, sharing our mutual interest in photography — a woman I house-sat for, taking care of her cats — approaches me as if I am a casual acquaintance she has just met once or twice before.

"It's nice to see you again, Liz."

Her denial of our past friendship together hurts, but I push beyond these feelings too as I move toward the exit. At the door I slip Gerald $25. He balks.

"That's not necessary."

"No, you earned it," I return. I am willing to pay for my education; I don't want any favors from him. He hands me a small booklet, his latest creation entitled, *The Ezra Commandments, Discover the Splendor of Life.*

Inside are his eleven commandments, replacements for God's ten. They read:

1) You always feel good.
2) You succeed at everything you do.
3) You are never sick.
4) You respect all living things.
5) You are great.
6) <u>B</u>e <u>E</u>verywhere <u>N</u>ow.
7) You know everything.
8) You keep everything simple.
9) You are forever.
10) You are relentless.
11) You already know.

So self focused, I think, *so different from the commandments God entrusted to Moses on the mountain* . . . For the next two days, I recover from the exhaustion of the ordeal. For some reason, after that, another aching layer lifts from my psyche.

My new apartment is only two blocks from Lisa, my former college roommate who disappeared from Gerald's group in early 1993. Since February I have driven by her house several times. I have been afraid, however, to ring the bell. After all, I played my part in The Group's endeavor to convince her to come back. I remember believing, along with the rest of her "friends", that she was a stupid jerk. Now, I can't recall if I employed Gerald's tactics of abusive verbal persecution, but I fear that I might have. I know I couldn't handle it if she snubbed me for this past mistake. Yet, I really do want to see her. On Saturday morning, two days after my return to The Group, I finally find the courage to try.

To my relief, Lisa is genuinely pleased to see me. When she left three years ago, her last words to me had been,

"I hope we can still be friends . . . ", but I had replied with conviction, "No. If you are not in The Group, then I don't think that's possible."

Now I understand why she said that to me . . . Lisa gives me a tour of her house and introduces me to her new husband of eighteen months. Finally, after about half an hour of superficial chatting, she asks me if I still go to Gerald. I tell her all the details of my exodus and her eyes light up with surprise and joy.

"I never thought you had any chance of escape. You were more carefully guarded and deeply buried than anyone else."

"Lisa, I never could have escaped on my own. I had help."

I tell her about Judy and we spend the next hour comparing notes. On her own, Lisa has come to understand the mechanics of Gerald's control, strategies I am still in the process of discovering, and today for the first time, I learn of the circumstances which drove her to wake up and leave.

"Lisa," I ask, "Why did we do all of those terrible things we didn't want to do?"

"Because we were so desperate for his approval," she replies, "Because to refuse him and suffer his wrath and castigation would have been the equivalent of committing emotional suicide."

With Lisa's permission, I contact Dave, her ex-boyfriend, to let him know I am out of The Group. I invite him to a celebration-reunion dinner with Lisa and Judy. He, like Lisa, is elated and informs me that he never liked Gerald, that he picked up his ugly intentions immediately. On the evening of our dinner, after Dave arrives at my apartment, I pull out the videotape I made on the first night Dave came to The Group, back in 1992. Expecting to laugh over this reminder of times gone by, I am shocked at what I see. There I am, on film, sitting next to Gerald, in the precise posture of the "little girl" Judy warned me about that November evening at her kitchen table, now almost three years ago. I imitate Gerald, shaking my head, injecting incredible willful energy into my desperate attempt to force him to pay attention to me and laugh at my antics. Seeing this for the first time since it's filming, I am appalled as I view the deplorable behavior which kept me trapped in that deadly "daddy-child" interaction loop with Gerald. I am disgusted with myself for all of the years I have thrown away for this ridiculous drama. I am sad too. If only I had seen my mistake sooner, I would have changed myself immediately . . .

A week later, my apartment phone rings. The woman's voice at the other end is so familiar — Pauline, my former roommate and Lisa's too. Based on her attitude during my return visit to The Group a few weeks ago, I am sure that this is not a pleasant social call to catch up on old times because she misses me from her life. My frequent complaints to Samantha at the office, that none of my "friends" have called me, must have spurred her to act, a change in behavior to conceal their hypocrisy. Subjected to her lame attempts at superficial chatter, my hurt feelings rise and I deliver them to her. Why hasn't she called me before? We were college roommates for three years! Why did she dump me when I left? Why wasn't she concerned with how I was doing? Pauline is nervous immediately. She is not as skilled as Samantha and Gerald in verbal combat. She does not have a bunch of logical sounding comebacks she can quickly pull out of her hat to fend off my questions, so she changes the subject, speaking of Gerald's wisdom, her personal growth, and how he is still helping everyone. When she refers to the equality they all experience, I shoot a question at her.

"Does he ever give himself to you?"

"I don't know what you mean by that," she stammers, deterred from her stream of Gerald propaganda.

I explain, "That is what you do when you genuinely care about someone; you extend your spirit, sincerity, humility . . . , and the other person gives these things back to you in return, forming a circuit of shared relating."

"I don't understand," Pauline repeats, revealing that their "equality" is all a farce. She is unable to handle my confrontational attitude and soon begins to sob. Her weakness is pathetic and yet, I pity her and feel guilty for upsetting her. I back off and apologize, attempting to shift her so we can continue our conversation.

Suddenly, as if propelled in spiritual space, my awareness shifts from my outer physical surroundings to deep inside of her, where her soul lives. There I experience the horror of her state of being. I see a trapped gerbil running on a wheel, faster and faster — a wheel which never takes her anywhere, but just serves to occupy her energies until the time when she will inevitably expire from the exhaustion of a wasted life. This revelation explodes like thunder in my brain. Pauline has no independent identity, no personal rights of individuality, no self! In The Group, having a self is not permitted and she has traded her most prized possession, the expression of her individual soul, for a ticket to Gerald's amusement park. From that terrifying vision of this helpless animal, I experience at a very deep level what you must give up to worship and follow another human being. I know how precious my own reemerging sense of self is to me. It means more than wealth, accomplishments or recognition. I know that in my lifetime, I will never jeopardize its safety again, not for anything. Our conversation doesn't last much longer; we really have nothing in common anymore.

Sadly replacing the phone in its cradle, I remember how Pauline once told me that her stomach twists when she walks up Gerald's driveway, that she often hates being there. I wonder if these feelings are the seeds of the same conflict I have experienced with him. I hope that someday she will want to leave. I worry about Pauline and the others who still remain faithful to their leader; I am so sorry I encouraged her to join. Today I would do anything to take it back . . . The other day I passed Pauline on my way to work; she was riding home on a bicycle after another all-day session at Gerald's. My first thought was that she had developed a concern for her health, but after questioning Samantha at the office, I uncovered the wretched truth. Exercise is not the motivation here, it is saving money. Her car has deteriorated and is marginally serviceable, available just for emergency, and I know only too well where all of her available means, funds she should be applying toward her personal needs, are channeled. Rapidly approaching forty years old, does she ever think of her future? I can imagine her thirty-five years from now, a gaunt septuagenarian, alone and penniless, trying to stretch a can of tuna across three meals. I know she has no "rich uncle" with a fortune to leave and her active years will have been squandered in Gerald's den; whatever resources this world might have had to offer were never cultivated. Gerald would be in his mid-nineties, his precious carcass abandoned for a walker or a cane, if he is even alive at all. He certainly won't be doing too much head shaking! The dreams of our exclusive nirvana are long forgotten. The magic carpet he chauffeured us on each day is moth-eaten and incapable of flight, despite the fact that he always made us feel nothing would ever change, that youth and vitality were guaranteed forever and we needn't concern ourselves to "make hay while the sun shines". I want more than anything for my former comrades to free themselves. Knowing how difficult my journey was and how each passing month brings them an additional suffocating layer of lies and control, I fear that it may already be too late. Often I pray to God to save their souls, especially my mother, even if not in this lifetime . . .

Reconnecting with Lisa excites me and I think of how Gerald told her she would die within a year of leaving The Group. Well, she is very much alive, pregnant with her first son in fact, and I feel that I have finally found a way to prove to Samantha that her father is a fraud. So, the following Monday, I confront Samantha once again at the office . . . We seem to devote more time to these sessions than to the business!

"Samantha," I begin, certain that I possess the means to trap her, "Your father told Lisa, Caroline and me that we would die if we ever left The Group. Well it has been three years and Lisa is certainly not dead. I don't look dead to you, do I? Your father lied to us."

Samantha doesn't even blink an eye, "Oh, he didn't mean physically dead, he meant spiritually dead."

My hopes are dashed and I realize in this moment that I will never be able to get them to admit to anything. No matter how compelling the evidence against them, they will always find an excuse to cover their duplicity, an escape hatch. She has won this round, however, I want to continue our discourse, there is always something more to learn, so I open a new line of discussion.

"What do you people do in that den anyway these days?"

My partner is more than happy to explain. "We are preparing for the big change that will happen soon. You must transform your whole system, your thoughts, dramas and programmed behavior into the electrical field. You will be in danger if you don't start now, or else, when this sudden incredible surge of energy occurs, you won't be in condition to tolerate the intensity. Your body will instantaneously disintegrate as if struck by lightening."

She states this as truth, proven and accepted, just as Mitchell Stavos did at *Dunkin' Donuts* a few months ago,

"I should make your father a new business card which says *Apocalypse Preparation Skills Workshop*", I quip in an attempt at lightheartedness, requiring a moment of relief from the ugliness of our discourse. I pause, realizing how strange it feels to rejoin the rest of the population. After twenty years, I have once again become an insignificant civilian, no longer a member of the specially chosen spiritual Navy Seals on whose backs the fate of humanity rests. I decide to switch back to my original intent,

"You know, your father and The Group almost destroyed my life and I hate them for that."

As if what I have just said is insignificant, she responds with a soft reassuring tone, "Everything has always really been OK My father is just floundering on the road to the truth and he doesn't always have all the answers, but he gets there in the end."

My God, I think once more, still unable to accept that Samantha is truly this dense, *she really believes that he has never done anything wrong!*

Her voice caresses and her denial of truth creates a powerful charismatic field of energy, intent on convincing me that I have imagined all of the abuse, that Gerald always meant well, that none of ugliness I felt ever really happened. In response to her posture and attitude, in this moment, I experience a sort of dream state taking me over. As if Samantha has cast a spell, as if I am being sucked into a deep hypnotic trance, doubt arises, and my mind submits involuntarily, commencing to follow her train of thought. *Maybe I really only imagined it all?* I tighten my body to force this wave of amnesia and confusion away, to retrieve my senses . . .

That night I realize I must write about my experiences. I must remember it all, make myself believe that I really was abused, betrayed, lied to and robbed. I must come to terms with my past. If I do not figure out what really happened and resolve my feelings, I will carry baggage from the experience for the rest of my life. My synopsis of the past nineteen years takes about four weeks to write and I struggle through a veil of emotional denial and unfounded guilt that I am betraying them. I rely only on my mental power of recall to blast through the overwhelming sensation that the past events I remember so clearly were simply a fantasy! Nonetheless, as I force myself to write, I begin to be able to believe that it is all indeed true, and I have the right to stand up and declare it. I communicate with myself until finally, my conclusions feel valid.

About a week later, Samantha informs me that Pauline has just declared bankruptcy.

"My father said that it is a good move because now she can make a fresh start."

For a brief moment I am seduced to follow this logic, but then I grab myself.

"Hey wait a minute!" I challenge, "Did she analyze and correct the mistakes she made which got her into jeopardy so that it doesn't happen over again? What about the fact that other people will now have to pay for her mistakes? Why doesn't she feel responsible for correcting them herself?"

Somehow I doubt that she has done this type of soul searching, and Samantha has no response to my valid questions, irritating me further.

"Pauline went broke because your father manipulated her into that position for the sake of his own greed. I know your father has more than $1,000,000."

"No, he doesn't."

"Samantha, I am not stupid. I can do simple arithmetic. In fact, he probably has much more than that."

"No, he lost a lot of his money."

"Don't lie to me. I know he never buys anything, not even his groceries. How could he have lost it?"

"Well, that's none of your business."

Lies . . . Always lies and evasion . . . It is all so sickening; I can't stand it. Once again I wish we weren't partners, that I didn't have to spend every day with this woman. But she is legally united with me; I can't throw her out and I certainly can't leave myself.

That night I call Lisa with the news, but she already knows. Before she and Pauline parted, they had purchased their Queens co-op apartment. This bankruptcy releases Pauline from the responsibility of paying her half of the mortgage, leaving Lisa stuck for the entire sum by herself. In addition, she informs me that Pauline ran up $50,000 on credit cards. This information was included on the lawyer's report.

Despite Pauline's current injustices to Lisa, I am still concerned for her future.

"At least Pauline has that retirement fund from her old job."

"No, she doesn't, when she left her job, she liquidated it to pay Gerald."

"Wow! When will she ever wake up? Now the taxpayers are responsible for financing her addiction and you are screwed too. Pauline can't even afford to buy a new muffler for that rusted out 1983 *Honda Civic* she bought from you when the two of you split, and Gerald is sitting on top of the whole pile of cash, laughing at us . . ."

About a week later, Samantha, tired of my constant grilling and questioning, makes an attempt to patch things up.

"Elizabeth, I know that we are always fighting and I want to find a way to be friends. Why don't we go out to dinner and just try to be nice to each other?"

I grit my teeth, repelled by the idea. However, as usual, I go along with her plans, there is always something to learn when I allow her to be herself. After an uncomfortable meal at a local diner with little conversation, I suggest that we go to Judy's office for coffee. Samantha is willing. She continually forgets the fact that Judy and I are both outraged at her and her father, and that her presence triggers us to vent our anger. Her attitude seems to be that if Judy and I would just let bygones be bygones, all three of us could let go of the past, move on and become friends.

We arrive and after some minimal social formalities are exchanged, Judy and I turn the conversation toward my unresolved feelings for Gerald and The Group.

"You know, your father never came clean about the abuse he forced on me. He hides from me and I can't even tell him what I feel to get it off my chest."

"My father didn't abuse you."

"Really, what about when he hit me?"

"You drove him to it."

My eyes light up with fire. I can't hold back and give her a piece of my mind, raising my voice and ramming her with the truth.

"Your father just gets over on people with no self-confidence. Elizabeth's mother raised her with no survival skills; she never knew how to identify a person who wanted to cheat her until she met me. I have been teaching her street smarts and that is why Elizabeth has finally been able to stand up to you and your father. He feels that he has the right to abuse people, to treat them like dirt. You want to know what I think of your father? He is a sadistic, lazy, manipulative bastard who doesn't have the courage to confront his hurt from a bad relationship with his mother, so instead, he spends his life persecuting innocent women, projecting his hostility onto specifically selected females to get even for his mother's abuse. He is too dysfunctional to do an honest day's work so he robs them as well. Your father has passed on a legacy of Gestapo skills to you, but I will never, ever let him or you hurt Elizabeth again. If I have to protect her with my own physical body, I will. I would go right into your father's face and beat the crap out of him before he would ever touch Elizabeth again. You people have taken enough from her already; you will not get any more. Mark my words. She has people on her side now, watching out for her. You can't fool us, no matter how you change your behavior like a chameleon. When it comes to exploitation, there isn't a fly that goes past my nose whose name I don't know."

Samantha sits stunned, pale. No one has ever threatened her family of bullies and meant it. This friendly meeting isn't turning out the way she had planned.

"You don't understand. My father is different now. He doesn't do that anymore. We are all trying to start fresh and get along, to be nice to each other, to let the past go."

"Oh, so we should just forget what has happened and move on? Did he come clean for his sins? Did he make restitution with Elizabeth? Does he feel regret? I don't think so."

From the look on Samantha's face, you would think I was speaking ancient Greek. She can't make sense of what I am telling her, and she doesn't want to either. Instead she tries to change the subject, but I won't let her slip out. I bring her back to my point, my voice shaking the walls of my tiny office with the passion of my conviction.

"Why should I have a tea party with you when you refuse to admit that there are dead bodies in your basement? Do you want me to ignore your crimes and pretend that they never happened? I can't do this. I believe in truth and honesty, not secrets and lies. I believe in admitting mistakes, apologizing and trying to make it right, not denying them and pointing the finger to blame an innocent person. Until you and your father come clean, Elizabeth can never be friends with you."

Samantha suddenly decides that she needs to go home. She bids us goodbye hastily and heads out of the door. The next day, at our office, she informs me,

"I would never socialize with the two of you again. You are rude; you don't know how to treat people. Talking with the two of you together is like being hit by a Mack truck and I don't want to be hurt anymore."

She is hurt! What about me . . . ?

Every day I battle with the reality of the loss of so many years of my life. *I want to punish the bastard*, fights for supremacy over *I should just let it go, forget it and move on.* I am convinced that there must be a way to get Gerald arrested or legally get part of my money back, so I decide to visit Hackensack, our county seat, and turn my completed synopsis document in at the Bergen County Prosecutor's office. Approaching my destination, half of me digs my heels into the ground in hesitation while the other half firmly pushes me down the corridors of the court house like a teacher shoving a child with incapacitating stage fright out in front of the audience. With The Group's brainwashing still in my head, I feel that I don't have the right to tell on them, that something terrible will happen to me if I report Gerald to the authorities . . .

The officer who interviews me focuses on the details of the sexual encounters, planting seeds of hope,

"Perhaps we can go after Mr. Sharkman as a sex offender. Leave your information here, and give me a call in four weeks."

I leave the building shaky, fearing that Gerald is omnipresent and must already know what I have done. Right now he is planning my punishment. On the other hand, perhaps something good will come, because I was willing to step forward.

In a month I dutifully call back. The man I had spoken to barely remembers me and has no time for me either. Hurriedly, he explains that I wasn't a minor and Gerald didn't employ physical force. On the surface it appears that I complied under my own volition. There was no legal offense committed. The law is set up to handle overt crimes, such as rape or passing fraudulent checks, which leave visible physical scars. Gerald's crime is intangible, invisibly performed and the damage is emotional and spiritual. In addition, I realize that he has been careful to basically stay within the bounds of the law. The illegal events, shoplifting and adultery, are petty crimes which I can't convict him for. Their gravity in the eyes of the law is far from representative of his true sabotage to my life. My hopes are dashed momentarily, but I will try again . . .

Although Peter moved out of our building two years ago, we are still in touch. I decide to ask him for advice and he refers me to a friend, an accomplished lawyer and former judge in Englewood Cliffs. Peter is optimistic,

"Maybe my friend will feel passionate about your case and will want to help you find justice."

I mail the lawyer my synopsis and within twenty-four hours he pages me. On the phone he sounds very excited, encouraging me once more.

"I think you have something here. I'd like to meet."

Judy and I visit his office a few days later. I am nervous but hopeful. He extends a warm welcome and invites us to sit. I plop a plastic Baggie on his desk with the $190,000 in canceled checks to Gerald inside. He winces at this evidence, and then reassures me,

"You definitely have a case."

"What do I need to do now?" I respond, feeling an immediate lift from anticipation.

"Just give me a $3000 retainer and I'll start working on it," he states with confidence, as if my writing this check would be an insignificant but necessary detail, requiring a minor decision on my part.

But I hesitate, "How much will it cost in total?" I query, reaching for a sense of my future obligations.

He hesitates, not seeming to want to give an estimate. I continue to look at him, waiting for his response, so, finally he volunteers,

"Well I don't really know. It could be as much as $50,000."

I tighten at the figure. This is not going well at all. I request another significant detail,

"And how long will it take?"

At this point, it is clear that the lawyer is not comfortable with my direct questions. He had hoped to sweep me away in a cloud of hope, which, it is becoming clear, might very well have left me trapped in mounting debt to him on top of all of my other problems.

"The aspects of your case are complicated, so it probably would take some time, perhaps three to five years."

Judy intervenes, "And on what grounds will you bring him down?"

Now the lawyer began to babble and skate. He tries to present a strategy which sounds legal, but this doesn't appeal to Judy's and my common sense. It is obvious
he has no specific plan of attack, that he is preying on my legitimate desire for justice in a legal system where this case would be far from clear cut.

Finally, I interject passionately. "I told you I was broke. Where would I get $50,000 for your fee? I could never hire you knowing that I might not be able to pay . . . !"

I can't stand another moment of watching yet another person try to take advantage of Elizabeth. The rules of social decorum can't hold back my feelings, and they erupt into words,

"What is wrong with you? I just gave this woman two years of my life. I saw that she was in a desperate position, so I put aside my relationship with my husband and my business to help another human being in distress. It is clear that there is no hard evidence against Mr. Sharkman; you would have to prove intention and that is very hard to do. Elizabeth is just a dollar sign to you.

Where is your sense of decency? She is broke and in debt. You would just be leading her on a wild goose chase, putting her even further into debt and cultivating false hopes in her. I can't stand to be in this office anymore."

I jump from my seat and run out of the door, breathing heavily from emotion. After my explosive exodus, Elizabeth remains behind for a few more minutes, trying to find a polite way to end the meeting. Finally, she rises from her seat, extends her hand, thanks him for his input and exits.

Outside, I remain calm but inside my emotions swell. I had hoped this man would feel the same outrage that many others have upon reading my story, and would take the case on contingency. I wouldn't have minded giving him a good portion of the lawsuit's proceeds; he would have been entitled. However, he is clearly not the man for the job. As much as I want to go after Gerald, I would never put my financial well-being at risk. Judy and I leave the lawyer's office reeling. Another dead end.

Fall to Winter 1996

A new coffee house, the *Coffee Dog Café*, opens for business about five minutes from my office. A coffee lover since high school, I stop by to sample their brew. Waiting for my change, I discover a flyer next to the register announcing that Bess and her country-western group, *Stone Pulse*, (named after Gerald's rocks no doubt), will be performing this Saturday night. Most of The Group will surely show up; I think I should go. I will need support, so I organize my own group, Judy and Michael, Lisa and her husband, and Rich. As the gig approaches my anxiety increases. Samantha and I speak at the office every day, but she never mentions the evening. A year ago, I would have been involved in promoting the event; I would have handed out flyers, sent invitations, taken pictures of Bess as official photographer on the big night . . . Now they don't even let me know it is taking place.

Saturday evening I postpone until the last possible minute. When I finally arrive, my party of five is already seated at a large table. The café is crammed full of people and as I predicted, almost the entire Group, with the exception of my mother, is there. I make a beeline for Judy's side. She looks up and smiles warmly,
throwing a supportive arm around my waist, grasping me even more tightly when moments later, my knees buckle from intense anxiety.

Samantha, who seems to bear no grudge toward Judy for "hurting" her at our last meeting, is seated at our table, casually chatting. Her eyes turn to mine and she shoots me an ugly look, born from her hurt feelings. As she perceives it, I have betrayed her by organizing this group to crash their little party. In half of a blink of an eye, she turns toward Judy once again, switching back to her charming, social facade. I survey the crowd and spot Nora, Beatrice, Pauline, Bess and Gerald. Beatrice looks at me with a hateful parental attitude. I can read her thoughts, *You were a very naughty child to leave The Group and never come back.* Pauline avoids my gaze entirely; she is clearly uncomfortable. I sense Gerald's intense irritation over our invasion. However, he wants to hide this, so he strides over, extending his hand like a politician.

"How are you doing Elizabeth?" he queries, a phony smile covering the identical rage and hurt I have just perceived in his daughter.

Without giving me a chance to respond, he retreats as quickly as he has approached.

I have been living on the other side of the fence for several months now, and an entirely new picture of The Group comes into view. I see Gerald with his army keeping close rank behind him, always focused on the general, ready to jump and fulfill his every command. Their world appears immeasurably small and ludicrous.

Bess begins the performance, and soon Gerald is shaking his head purposefully. It is all so familiar. He has done this at each of Samantha and Bess's concerts in the past. I think back to the David Arkenstone concert where, according to him, his shaking made the musicians play better. By releasing his energy tonight, he is trying to help Bess connect with her true inner talent. Observing him run through his routine, unexpectedly, I begin to laugh. Gerald looks so ridiculous that it is actually funny! Of course, the non-Group customers of the café seem uncomfortable as people always do when he shakes. However, I am having great difficulty preventing myself from chuckling out loud and noticeably at his inane display. I hold my hand in front of my face to hide my expression. I laugh too, from relief, knowing that I am no longer inside the cage looking out; I laugh because what he is doing doesn't make sense to me anymore. Suddenly, I notice that he has stopped. It doesn't take me long to figure out why. This is the first time there have been people in the room who are on to his game and aren't afraid to expose him. My entire table of six knows what he is doing and why . . .

As we sit facing The Group, the atmosphere is heavy with opposition, an unresolvable feud like Mark Twain's Hatfields vs. McCoys. Several times during the evening, after Gerald shakes his head, I feel myself getting drowsy, as if someone just "slipped me a mickey", and I struggle to stay awake. I don't understand it, but it is obvious that when Gerald does this, there is some kind of energy shift which forces people in his presence into a mesmerized submissive state. So this is the floor plan of Gerald's strategy, how he has controlled Elizabeth and the rest; I have finally figured it out! With the power of a skilled hypnotist, he puts his ignorant victims under. Once they are susceptible, he inserts his self-serving suggestions into them. <u>This man is dangerous</u>. From what I have just experienced, I conclude that he does, indeed, possess a concealed energy of willpower against which most people would be ignorant and defenseless.

After the concert, I walk around dazed and disoriented. I know there is something I must do before I leave, but I don't know what it is . . . In the next moment, I intersect with Gerald, seated in the middle of the room. Before I even have time to think, I reach out and grab his hand. Hanging on, I look straight into his eyes, directly at the source of all of my current pain and anger, all of my past longings and fantasies. I drink him in and a powerful wave of sensation passes through me, as if I am experiencing every single emotion I ever had for him all in one instant; my body can barely tolerate the intensity. His eyes are vacant stones, two black marbles; his hand is limp and lifeless, as if he is under some supernatural spell, as if he doesn't even know that I am there, touching him. In this moment, I realize that it has always been me, all along. My relationship with him existed only in my mind, a projection of my desires for love and friendship onto him, an illusion. He never participated in my fantasy. Gerald never knew who I really was and he never cared to . . . In a little while, Michael, aware that I appear frozen, walks over and nudges me gently.

"Come on Lizzy. It's time to go."

I see that he is protecting me in this enemy territory and I release Gerald's hand. Gerald says nothing and makes no motion to acknowledge that I was ever there. I say goodbye softly, with a caress. Tonight, I feel as if I am letting go of an entire piece of my life. There is sweet sentiment in saying farewell to the person I once was, immersed in Gerald's existence. I turn from him, from all of it, and walk out into the chilly September night, my emotions still churning turbulently.

The fall progresses. In November, Samantha informs me that Bess will play at the *Coffee Dog Café* again. This time I am invited to join . . . A few hours before the gig, Samantha and I dine at a local restaurant. As we sit across from each other struggling to make small talk, I realize how separate we truly are. We still share a commitment to our photography business and yet, I know she leads another life outside of the office which influences her every thought and decision, a life that is abhorrent to me. At work we interact with increasing superficiality. In the last nine months, since her father threw me out, I have evolved into a completely different person and I have absolutely nothing in common with this woman anymore; I can't even fake it. These days, almost every moment, I experience her as an enemy, even though most of the time her behavior is perfectly acceptable . . .

During our aimless conversation a spontaneous question pops into my head. I decide to write it down on an index card and hand it to her. The card reads, "What is The Energy?" *Strange*, I think to myself, *I knew for years what The Energy was, it was very real to me. Now in this moment, I realize that I can't understand it at all.* It is spooky to listen to Samantha's explanation of the special force Group members share, as if I was a person she had only just met at one of her book signings rather than a former card-carrying member of The Group who helped give birth to the concept.

"The Energy is a force that helps you get ahead in life. It gives you success. If you listen to it and let it direct you, it will bring you anything your heart desires."

As I absorb her words, I realize that they make no sense at all. In fact, their belief system sounds like a story about finding a genie's lamp and rubbing it to get three wishes, still I can't think of a single good or real thing that The Energy has brought to any of them. In contrast, I reflect on my own life and the blessings I have been rewarded with — my friendships with Judy, Michael, Rich and Lisa, a renewed sense of self- worth and confidence, the self-actualization I experience in my profession as photographer. These things were brought by struggle, hard work and solid moral character, certainly not by a magical force which demands my absolute allegiance in order to deliver the goodies. In this moment we are galaxies apart, even though we sit separated by only a small round table in that dark restaurant. I can never conceive of going back to their way of thinking and living. Samantha and I are like oil and water . . .

A little while later we arrive at the café. Gerald and the rest are expecting me. They greet me with shiny smiling faces as if I am an old dear friend. Stronger this time, I go solo, without Lisa's or Judy's support. Right away, I spot my mother sitting at a table in the back. I have neither seen nor spoken to her for several months, since my meeting with The Group this past June. She appears to be in a deep stupor and as I approach her, she looks up listlessly and murmurs,

"Oh hi Liz."

Grace is distant, as if she barely knows me. The knife fashioned by Gerald's handiwork finds its mark once again and I choke back my tears. Even though I know the truth, it seems as if I will never get used to the fact that my mother simply doesn't love me. I stand next to her the whole time, wanting to savor this rare moment close to her, to project my genuine feelings, even though she does not return them.

At one point I turn from watching Bess' singing to glance at Samantha. She is in the process of focusing on a little girl of about five, a customer of the café. I know her intentions only too well, to get The Energy into that child with her hypnotic stare. The child returns her gaze, already half mesmerized. Outraged, I call out something to Samantha to interfere with her objective. Temporarily distracted, the child snaps out of their connection and walks away. I want to go over and shake the child, to warn her,

"Don't ever let anyone do that to you again. Stay away from that woman. She is dangerous."

About half an hour later Judy pages me and I call her.

"Get out of there," she entreats me, "You've seen what you have to see. There is nothing and no one there for you anymore."

She is right. I stand next to my mother for another five minutes, drinking in the activities and energies of my former family, treasuring these few stolen moments with Grace, although I know she is oblivious to my feelings. Then I gently kiss her on the cheek and depart, driving directly to Judy's house. Her husband answers the door.

"Judy is down the block at *Dunkin' Donuts*." He winks at me with genuine affection.

A minute later I am at her side. She senses my distress and reaches to hug me. I draw strength from her compassion. Yet, when our eyes connect, I can't hold back my tears.

"My mother acted like she doesn't even know me," I sob.

Judy returns my gaze with empathy. Her voice comforts me as she shares my pain,

"I know this is really hard . . ."

A few days later, Judy has a brainstorm. "I'm going to invite your mother to my house for Thanksgiving."

"OK," I reply, not really wanting to deal with it, yet permitting her to make this decision for me anyway. Presently, she picks up the phone and dials. My mother, enthusiastically accepts; she loves food! I offer to pick her up from her apartment, but apparently, she has other plans.

"Liz, that's great, but you'll have to pick me up from Gerald's. He's having sessions from 9:00 A.M. to 1:00 P.M. on Thanksgiving morning and I want to go."

I hang up the phone numb with rage. I hate him. He just has to suck every moment, every dollar from our lives, even on a holiday. The reminder of Gerald's selfishness sends me into a frenzy and I appeal to Judy,

"I just can't do it. I can't go to that block and see all of those people coming out of his place knowing what's going on in there. Less than a year ago I would have been in there with them!"

"Don't worry, Michael will pick her up," she reassures me.

So, on Thanksgiving day, Michael and my mother arrive at 1:30 P.M. In addition, Judy has invited Rich. Grace enters the house and heads straight for the kitchen, solely concerned with drinking in the enticing smells and sights destined to pleasure her palate later this afternoon. She doesn't attempt to socialize, but appears to be in a sort of trance, as if she is still in Gerald's den focusing on the dog carcass. She falls asleep on the couch, in a sitting position, several times during the next few hours . . .

After dinner we play Bingo. The Energy from the competition makes us all giddy. For the first time my mother seems to be alive and genuinely enjoying herself, making silly jokes and betting quarters and dollars. Watching her come out of her shell and have fun like this, I hope that maybe she might appreciate the joy I feel in my new surroundings and want some of it for herself, that she might appreciate my new friends and maybe even compare the wonderful feelings in this room to the ugly ones in Gerald's den. I want to announce to her that I have a new family now, a real family with people who care about me, people I trust; I want to force her to admit that I am happy now, away from Gerald's group, and that she made a mistake to encourage me to join in the first place. This past year she has made it obvious that she chooses to strengthen her allegiance to the same group that abused me, a group from which I had to strive so hard to escape, and I can't stop hating her for her choice. I want to ram these things down her throat until she breaks her stubborn wall of denial. I want her to feel guilty for jeopardizing my well-being. I want to . . . As conflict plagues my mind, despite the fact that this social setting is inappropriate, I find myself no longer able to hold back. Besides, perhaps my friends will help her see the light.

"Mom, I'm very concerned about you. You are seventy-five years old and still working. You give all of your extra money to Gerald. What will you retire on?"

My mother's defenses rise immediately. "It's none of your business," she snaps, "I am an adult and I can take care of myself."

"But mom, you are my family and it is my business, because I care about you."

"No, I don't need anyone, just myself. You just deal with your own problems, of which you have plenty," she adds sarcastically, "and leave me alone."

Michael cuts in. Grabbing my hand and holding it up for her to see, he explains with genuine sincerity, "But Grace, everyone needs this."

"What's this?" she sneers.

"Touch, connection, love, kindness."

"Well, I don't. I'm fine. Maybe you people do." Her face twists in condescending self-righteousness.

"But Mom," I add, "Why can't you see the joy that having people love you brings? Don't you realize that nothing you could do by yourself, alone, could ever compare to the feeling of being loved and loving in return, of sharing your life with other people? Why don't you understand this?"

Dropping her defensiveness for a moment, she responds almost pensively.

"Maybe you're expecting too much of me. Maybe what you see is all that there is to me."

I grasp the profundity of what she has just said and my eyes fill with water because in these moments, I have faced the deepest desire of my soul, that my mother would want to share the things Michael refers to with me. This can't really be true. If it is, then it would be eternally hopeless to ever try to share love with her. This is my mother, the only one I will ever have. Somewhere inside of her, she just has to value love. She just has to be able to go beyond her small world. She just has to want to jump the restrictive fence that encloses her in emotional dysfunction. She must be just really hard to reach right now. I have to try harder to break her wall. Noticing my tears, she inquires with what feels like concern,

"Liz, are you crying?"

"Yes," I respond, "because I so desperately want you to understand me and I can't reach you."

But my mother can't understand my pain.

Michael, Rich and I can't believe what we are witnessing, the coldness, the flat out denial of family ties and emotional obligations, the unshakable determination to hold onto her dogma at all costs. We experience Elizabeth's frustration right beside her, of trying to reach a person who refuses to be reached, even with love, kindness and truth. The brainwashing, resulting from Gerald's tactics, has separated mother from daughter inexorably. I see the enemy. The confrontation lasts another two hours. As hard as Elizabeth tries, her mother remains separate. Near the end, Grace makes an unthinkable statement.

"Liz, you seem to be in an awful lot of conflict. Even though I know you won't agree with me, I think you were better off when you were in The Group."

That does it. Elizabeth loses control. Screaming at her with all she's got, she strains her throat, making herself hoarse.

"Why don't you just get out the poison now and give it to me to drink, because that is exactly what would have happened to me if I had stayed there!"

Hysterical, pounding the walls of my living room with her fists, barely restraining herself from throwing things, she shrieks over and over,

"I hate you, Mom. I despise you with every cell in my body."

Her mother sits unmoved, cold, with no response to her daughter's rage. She just stares, offended by her antisocial behavior, annoyed at her for embarrassing her in front of strangers.

During the next few weeks I send Christmas cards to several members of The Group — Laura, Bess, Pauline, Harriet, Nora . . . I include my home phone number prominently. The sole response to my heartfelt gesture is fearful silence, only adding to my hopeless sense of isolation and estranged abandonment. No one calls me. No one sends me a card in return . . .

It is Christmas day and I make the twenty-minute drive from my apartment to Manhattan's Upper West Side. My mother meets me in her lobby. As we ride up in the elevator, she refers to *Conversations with God*, still their current bible.

"There are so many wonderful things in that book. I realize more and more every day that I am God, but I just don't want to accept it."

A question pops into my head. "Mom, I don't understand something. If you believe that you are God and God is all-powerful, then did you create the universe?"

"No."

"Well, then who did?"

Quickly, nervously, she mutters, "I don't know." and changes the subject. She puts up a wall immediately which lets me know that there will be no further discussion.

Once inside her apartment, I notice that she is wearing a tee-shirt covered with images of rocks advertising *The Ezra Touchstone*. Across her belly The Group's slogans are blazoned, *One God Fits All* and *Be Everywhere Now*. Her apartment is a monument to Gerald, with propaganda strewn everywhere. Books are stacked on the marble coffee table in piles threatening to topple; this is the same table where cocktails once rested on expensive coasters, as my parents' well-heeled guests at the hub of the 1950's Upper East Side intellectual circle exchanged opinions on the latest psychological or political theories. *What a shame*, I think to myself.

My parents at a fifties cocktail party

I recognize several items from The Group's reading list, Gerald's book — *Biofeedback Without Machines*, Samantha's *Dark Chronicles* trilogy, *The Celestine Prophecy*, *Way of the Peaceful Warrior*, *Ageless Body — Timeless Mind*, *Conversations with God* and *The Seven Habits of Highly Effective People*, volumes from which they derive new spiritual truth. I now understand that the excitement and sense of control derived from absorbing new mental concepts compose the fuel which drives them through another day. Experiencing an emotional lift from mental stimulation and a sense of wisdom and control supplies the evidence that they are paving the way to a glorious future, complete with everything their hearts might desire. Relating to the written word, they feel so terribly significant, a temporary self-esteem fix which distracts them from their genuinely empty lives. I sense their frenzy to collect this new information, and the profound fear that if they don't constantly fill up with truth, like the cow which must spend the entire day eating grass in order to maintain her basic life functions, they will not be prepared for the inevitable spiritual shift, predicted by Gerald to happen at any moment. Over the past three years I have shed the fears I used to share with them, and I no longer feel empty. I do not need to inflate my mind with mental concepts in order to feel alive and significant.

Several small black velvet pouches containing Gerald's energy rocks, *The Ezra Touchstone*, are scattered around. Of course my mother has purchased this paraphernalia from Gerald. *More to line his pocket with,* I think angrily, *as if he hasn't already stolen enough from us already.* She informs me that he is selling the rocks on his own web-site, apparently believing that his worldwide exposure and subsequent omnipotence are just a step away from realization.

"Gerald has given us new information this week," she tells me, "He says our programming has taught us to hold back our feelings. We must all pay attention to what we feel in the moment and give it validity even though our minds will try to dismiss it."

"Mom, he said that exact thing ten years ago," I reply with disgust, "I can hear it in my head as if it was yesterday. This is not new information at all. It just sounds new because you didn't hear it in a long time."

"Oh yes, it may sound the same, but now we are at a higher level," she retorts confidently.

They always have a comeback to avoid the truth . . .

An outright non sequitur, she inquires if I still feel The Energy. The scientist in me bursts forth, eager to deliver the full and honest truth as I have painstakingly unearthed it.

"You know, Mom, I have a powerful drive to figure out specifically how Gerald controlled me. I have been doing a lot of research; I've read over forty books on cults, the psychology of mind-control, brainwashing and evil, hypnosis, abusive therapists and religious leaders, and even demonic possession. The mechanics of his manipulation are really quite simple once you identify his tricks of the trade."

My mother cuts in. "Research," she smirks, "Why do you waste your time with that crap? Why don't you just live your life and quit thinking about him?"

"But Mom, isn't research your profession? I thought you've been working as a research economist for the past twenty years . . . Anyway, this is what I have learned . . . First, do you remember the night we all stared at a lightbulb in The Group and Gerald claimed it was getting longer?"

She nods her head in accord.

"Well, Bess was the first to notice the change and then everyone else jumped on the bandwagon. I started to see it also when suddenly, a profound realization interrupted my concentration and I remembered the concept of 'the power of suggestion' from a college psychology course. My head split open in that moment as I recalled another day where I had called Gerald on my car phone and asked him to shake his head at his end of the line to break up the traffic jam I was caught in. As my body calmed from his Energy, I stared up the road and believed that he was indeed influencing the traffic flow. There were so many times we stared out of his den window at the rain or snow and connected its intensity to his shaking. I realize now that I made myself feel what Gerald told me I should feel, because I had put my faith in him and concluded he had superior knowledge. I fooled myself with the power of my own mind while he manipulated an age-old trick — painting the bull's eye around the arrow!"

My mother nods her head as if my logic makes sense, and I continue,

"I do believe that there is a spiritual energy field separate from physical energy; I have felt it, especially in crisis, but its source is not Gerald as I used to presume. He may have tapped into it, but anyone can and many who have never met him do. He has no position of exclusivity except in his own fantasies. Now that I am able to consider information from sources other than him, I have a much more enlarged perspective. Also, Gerald makes The Energy out to be a sort of invisible friend, an intelligence that will get you a raise on your job, improve your health, direct others to give you gifts, etc. I have discovered this to be nothing more than faulty logic, erroneously associating two unrelated events in order to prove your point. This is a powerful tool he has used to manipulate the Group members' thinking and actions."

My mother actually does not oppose my heretical explanation. I realize that the presence of indisputable truth is too profound and she can't find a justification to contradict me. On the other hand, my conversation doesn't seem to phase her, the merciless exposure of the mechanics of her mentor's lies, exhaustively examined under a microscope. She simply continues to nod her head as I proceed.

"I know that even new people usually feel some type of energy field in his presence. This has been the hardest for me to figure out but I finally have. Every living being has a magnetic field around them. Gerald's field must be very strong; after all, he is able to drain batteries by holding them in his pocket. He is a phenomenon, but only in the realm of physical energy. There are many people with super-normal abilities in this area; I've seen them on TV documentaries. A physicist recently did research on the effects of magnetic fields on the human brain. He discovered that with certain strong applied fields the subject feels dissociated from his body and sincerely believes he is having a profound spiritual experience. But he isn't!! People <u>do</u> feel something from George's body, but then he creates a story to explain the implications and origin of this feeling and that's where the lie begins. It's just plain and simple physics misinterpreted to benefit him!!

Lastly, and most important, a lot of times when I thought I was feeling The Energy, I was actually experiencing an adrenalin rush, triggered by my absolute fear of him."

Suddenly, she cuts in,

"Yes, I know what you mean, I am afraid of him too."

"Why? He never hit you. I really had something to be afraid of."

Her response horrifies me. "Oh yes he did."

My natural protectiveness awakens.

"What! Why? When?" I exclaim with genuine outrage.

"Awhile ago. He didn't strike me, but he did grab my collar and shake me forcefully. It was very scary."

She refuses to be specific and appears uncomfortable as if protecting something.

"He decided I had to change my attitude for my own good. I wasn't committed enough to the mission and he wanted to shake me out of my fog. The first time it actually worked. I can understand why they developed shock therapy for mental patients. The second time . . ."

"The second time! You mean he did it again!"

"Yes and it was different; I didn't like it one bit. I felt scared and overpowered. The next day I told him in no uncertain terms to never do it again."

She imitates her stance during the encounter, a mother correcting a naughty child.

"And he listened?" I inquire.

"Yes."

"Well, it upsets me even more that he shook you than that he hit me. You are seventy-five years old! How the hell does he believe that he has the right to do that? To someone who is paying him no less!!"

My mother, in the face of my genuine passion, becomes defensive,

"Don't worry. I can take care of myself?"

"Did he realize that he was wrong after you told him to stop, or just obeyed your command?"

"No. He didn't realize he was wrong; he still feels free to assault the others."

All of a sudden she stops. Looking at me intensely she demands, "You're not going to tell Judy about this are you?"

"Why not? Are you ashamed?"

She is immediately irritated and lashes out at me, "It's none of her business; that's all. Keep your big trap shut about my private affairs."

I do not want to give her false promises so, taking a deep breath, I decide to be honest.

"Mom, I could lie convincingly and you would believe me, but I am going to be truthful. Judy is my best friend and knows everything about me, especially the things which upset me terribly as this certainly does!"

As if kicking herself mentally she sputters, "I shouldn't have said a word about this. I wish I had never told you."

I remain silent and wait, praying that she will not clam up now and separate herself from me. Gently, I take up the conversation again, hoping she will follow my lead. It works.

"Well that's how a bully works. He takes advantage of others' weaknesses, but as soon as his victim asserts himself with confidence, the bully turns coward and takes a hike, fleeing to search out another weakling, never to return. I'm glad you stood your ground."

She nods her head in agreement and I continue, "Are you absolutely positive that this violence won't recur? **I don't want him to touch you!**"

"Don't worry, I've taken care of it."

The tone of her voice communicates that this discussion is at an end. I believe her and realize I can't do anything anyway. Although I am ready to file a report with the Westwood police tonight, to hire a lawyer and sue Gerald for assault, I realize that it would be up to her to press charges, not me, and she never would.

"Elizabeth, I know he has problems, but won't you admit that he has valuable information?"

I sigh deeply, "Yes, I did learn a lot from him, enough to fill several volumes, and I was very grateful for those lessons. I told him so in a letter I wrote after he threw me out."

I do not explain that he set up circumstances which almost destroyed me, that this state of emergency forced me to reach inside of myself, to uncover strengths I never knew I had in order to survive. It was the challenge of the enemy in a life or death struggle which compelled me to evolve, not Gerald's counterfeit benevolent facade of teacher and coach. I can never explain this to my mother, and I observe that she seems satisfied with my affirmative response. She appears to believe that we are in agreement on this point and continues analytically, making it all seem so cozy and productive,

"All the years that you were with him, he was dominated by his personality, by his bad temper. I think this is the reason that you had such an unfortunate experience with him. Since he has become occupied with Ben and the rocks, he has changed; he has separated himself from his former involvement in other people's lives. He is much more placid most of the time. Now it's like teamwork.

He is working on his project and when you come in, you are working on your own growth. There is simply an exchange of information. Kind of like a creative art class with each person at his own individual easel."

Grateful for the opportunity her candid evaluation has afforded me, I seek to slip more truth into her brain, hoping the seeds will someday take root and flourish. I begin to describe how I came to spend so much money on Gerald.

"You know, Mom, after Samantha and I rented the house together, she set it up so that we would drive in her car to her father's office in Manhattan. Of course she didn't have to pay, so the hours got longer and longer. It got to the point where I was giving him a check for over $2000 every couple of weeks. I hated it but I was held captive. Defying her and taking my own car was not an option because, as you know, Gerald backs up all of his daughter's decisions, and once the pattern was set in place, I could not break it without incurring his wrath and vengeance."

She grimaces noticeably and volunteers, "Yes I know what you mean. He is very motivated by money. He has his methods of getting more out of you. On a particular day he might tell you that you're doing really well and then add, 'You should stay an extra hour so we can keep going. It will be good for you.' The following week it's expected that you'll continue this new schedule. Whenever you try to reduce your hours, he accuses you of losing interest in The Energy. He lets you know that if you choose to weaken your commitment to it, then he'll lose interest in you. He threatens to withdraw the attention he would normally give you during the time you are there, as a punishment."

But even in the midst of her unsolicited disclosure of Gerald's brazen manipulations an unspoken message is transmitted, intent on smothering my outrage over his crimes. In these moments, an unholy spiritual peace emanates from her, a soporific energy field which virtually drugs me into denying what I know in my heart to be true. The gaze she focuses communicates silently and indisputably, *Acknowledging the facts about Gerald is sufficient, taking action to put a stop to the crimes, or seeking retribution, is unmerited and a waste of precious time and energy. Your passions against him are motivated by childish emotions.* This feeling is shockingly familiar, the same hypnotic sensation I have experienced in Samantha's presence many times, the absolute disavowal of my natural human reactions to Gerald's treatment. I now realize that my mother is remarkably aware of the negative aspects of Gerald's environment, particulars which took my naive mind years to figure out; still, she welcomes the opportunity to continue swimming in these poisonous waters. Why?

Without explanation, she pops a small black rock into her mouth. I withhold comment. This bizarre behavior of Group members is familiar to me. Nonetheless, she mentions it herself.

"I bet you're wondering why I'm sucking on the rock!"

"Why?"

"A month ago I went to the dentist and she said I would need a root canal for my two front teeth; the enamel is literally peeling away."

She pulls her bottom lip forward to reveal a horrible gap between the two rotting teeth. I wince at the sight. Then she continues,

"I told Gerald about it and he advised me to suck on a rock to help my teeth. I do it as much as I can: at work, at home watching TV . . . and I know you won't believe this, but the enamel is actually growing back!"

I wonder if this miraculous change is in her imagination or the build-up of plaque, but I button my lip, simply inquiring if she has returned to the dentist for a second visit to verify this magical healing.

"No, but I have an appointment next week. I can't wait to see what she says!"

Like a gullible child, she appears enamored with Gerald's concocted

My mother at my parents' Park Ave. apartment

fantasies. I pity her, knowing there is nothing I can say to sway her, convinced that a root canal is inevitable.

She picks up a typed sheet from a pile of books on her table and begins reading an essay Samantha has just written entitled *Female Manipulation — Rules of the Female Program.* Rule number three reads, *You think you can manipulate and control every male because you think they are a piece of shit for they cannot have babies.* Rule number eleven reads, *You want to destroy everything for if you do then you can create and destroy giving you all powers thus making you God.* Typical Samantha, terrible grammar, parroting her father's hatred of women, saying nothing in as many words as possible.

"You know, I told Gerald that I wasn't sure I agreed with her writing," my mother tells me, "But, he told me to just keep reading it and it will sink in as the truth if I let it. He was right, after a few days of reading what Samantha wrote, I am beginning to see in me the Female Program as she described it. Now I know I have to do more work on myself."

It all sickens me. Gerald threw me out ten months ago and I have discovered so much more to life than the limited thinking process he breeds in his den. I feel as if I am looking at Grace from high on a mountain top. Her world now seems so limited, ridiculous and fruitless. Nonetheless, despite my desire to have it be different, it is finally sinking in that this is the life she has chosen. The lies Gerald concocts feed a profound need in her, in fact, she appears to thrive on them and to reject the truth with equal commitment. There is nothing I can do about this, and it dawns on me that my mother seems to lack some significant qualities — compassion, rage at injustice, respect for the truth, a drive to perfect herself and a desire to connect with and love others. I am coming to realize that no amount of screaming, reasoning, begging or wilfulness on my part will alter her position. As much as I disagree with her decisions, as much as I hate the rift between us, I am helpless to convince her that there is a better way. A memory flashes through my mind and I acknowledge the sad irony of Grace's letter of reference, included in the back of Gerald's book, *Biofeedback Without Machines*, written many years ago when we all first met. In an attempt to communicate to the reader all that her new advisor had done for her life with his brilliant, innovative methods of self-exploration, she ended her letter with this statement — *Thanks to his enlightenment, my daughter and I are friends.*

Today, I sense that I have changed profoundly since our emotional confrontation in this same living room, one month after Gerald first evicted me from the kingdom. It is as if the rubber band which had previously bound me to an insatiable need to convince her to see Gerald from my perspective has now finally broken. I realize that my drive to reprimand her has been replaced with determination to accept her for who she is, even if only for my own peace of mind. I sit quietly next to her on the couch, willing to chat superficially, about nothing. She comments that I look nice and thin; she wishes she could lose weight. I tell her about my experience on the diet roller-coaster during my twenties. I had developed an insatiable appetite for sweets while in college and put on more than twenty pounds, quickly reaching size 13. I hated myself, but my willpower was not strong enough to overcome the impulses which were controlling me and keeping me fat. For more than eight years I struggled without success. Unexpectedly and for no reason, in my late twenties, something changed inside of me. As if my silent prayers had finally been answered, the ugly intention to keep me overweight and miserable finally released me. I began to lose my appetite for short periods of time and after a few years, arrived at my current size 6. I have never gone back up. My mother looks at me, and for an instant I see the light of truth in her face as she responds to this story about me which she never knew,

"Liz, you are lucky. You have a presence inside of you that cares about your well-being. I don't have anything like that inside of me."

She seems to have no idea how profound this statement is. As for me, I am in awe, as if God has just used her lips to send me a personal message, to help me comprehend and accept the abyss between us . . .

We chat some more and I tell her that I have finally developed a marketable packaging for the flash cards, that the sales have been strong for the first time these past six months and I have put the company into the black.

"I feel like I'm finally out of the woods after a long and exhausting journey." She seems genuinely pleased with this good news.

"Liz," she reflects, "your persistence has led to success. You were always passionate and dedicated to anything you ever committed yourself to. All of your life you were reaching for the light."

"What about you, Mom?" I respond, wishing she'd say the same about herself, that for once, I would find us on the same side.

However, her answer disappoints me as all her others have, although I suppose I have really always known the truth — "Not really."

These moments illuminate the foundation of a lifetime of internal struggle. She has revealed the nature of my highest self, my soul, the hidden drive deep inside of me toward my destiny. Maybe there is more to our story, my mother's and mine, than "Grace met an evil man and got sucked in by his manipulative strategies." Perhaps this is her way of confirming that she has never known a desire or ability to love and share with others. She has never possessed the God-given gifts of natural intelligence and common sense, qualities which have lifted and protected me on the spiritual battlefield all of my life. Maybe we really are two very unlike types of people — different species, opposite seeds of the soul. In a way, these two insights which she has shared about me this day are the best Christmas presents I have ever received . . .   When I am about to leave, she presents me with my wrapped Christmas gift. It contains a set of six pairs of cheap slouch socks in tasteless colors. They must have cost no more than $8 at a local bargain store. I smile weakly in an effort to thank her, quelling my hurt. I realize now that she is not purposely trying to insult me or comment on my value to her, she really doesn't know any better. I recognize the accompanying card. It is more than twenty years old, given to us as one of several free samples by a family acquaintance in the stationery business. After the corny canned verse my mother has written, in true Gerald fashion, *To Liz, Wishing you growth that grows and grows!*

January 1 to February 6, 1997

Our business holiday rush passes. Without the demands of continuous work to force us together, Samantha and I drift apart, having less and less to say to each other. Over the past year, we have had numerous verbal confrontations, often continuing for several hours. As I was not truly ready to disconnect when Gerald threw me out almost twelve months ago, Samantha has served as the necessary liaison to the rest. Unable to confront her father directly, I have delivered my outrage to her instead, in an attempt to achieve closure. Thank God she was willing to sit through my attacks and interrogations! For Samantha's part, I believe that she is finally getting the message that I am not coming back. Furthermore, I am not falling apart and my life is not going down the tubes without The Energy as Gerald had predicted. I have friends who support me and as Rich phrases it, I am "growing like a weed". My former oppressed state is rapidly being replaced with new-found self-confidence. Daily I apply my efforts toward clearing out the cobwebs in my mind, products of The Group's detrimental influences. It is strange to realize for the first time, at the age of thirty-seven, that I am an adult. I often wonder where exactly I have been all of those years since high school . . . Samantha has given up bullying me with accusations of such false crimes as, "You are trying to stop the business from succeeding" or "You want to fail". She pretty much just stays out of my way. In fact, more and more, she appears truly uncomfortable in my presence. Over the past year she has rescheduled our hours so that we split each day completely in half. Six days per week she works the mornings, and I work the afternoons. Like an estranged husband and wife with separate bedrooms, we barely cross paths. A quiet alienation settles over the studio. Yet inside, I am anything but quiet. I experience intermittent bouts of internal rage. Although I have tolerated her presence and tried to convince myself to make the best of it, in my heart I have never accepted that she deserves half of the business' profits. It's not that I want her to leave; I simply need to work out a new arrangement between us which will be fair to both. However, I know this can never happen.

As the days pass we fight again and again over nothing in particular. The tide of unrest rises, tossing us helplessly in turbulence until we are exhausted; it falls, allowing us only a short recovery before rising once more. One day, in the heat of an unusually severe conflict, Samantha blurts out a proposal which she has never been willing to consider before.

"Elizabeth, I'll leave the business for $40,000 or $50,000. I don't want to be here anymore if I'm not going to be appreciated."

That night, she tells Gerald that we are fighting hopelessly, that resolution is impossible. He suggests she invite me to his book signing at the West Paterson *Barnes & Noble* the following evening. He explains that I have been away from The Energy too long, that the exposure to his power will calm me down and resolve the rift between us . . .

When Samantha proposes his plan the following day, I accept without hesitation. I must ride this out to its natural conclusion, through whatever is destined to take place. Besides, every time I make contact with them, I learn something valuable, I grow. Still, I decide to ask Rich to accompany me for support.

We arrive after Gerald has started. He is in the middle of explaining to the audience that they think small and this keeps them from achieving their true potential.

"You people only use 3% of half your brains."

How many hundreds of times have I heard that before! He continues with an analogy that the world is a personal mail-order catalog, if only we could find the courage to claim our merchandise.

"I know that most of you are not big enough to accept this; it is too scary for you, but you are God, I am God, this rock is God, (he reaches into his pocket and withdraws the familiar white Ben soul-rock, holding it up for all to see) everything is God. Only small thinking keeps us from claiming our inheritance, from owning the universe and having anything we want, from creating a wonderful life for ourselves."

Samantha, who still serves as her father's manager, nods hello as we seat ourselves next to her in the back of the audience. Still the ambitious student of spiritual truth I have always been, I focus intently on his every word. However, this evening for the first time, I discover that I can anticipate much of what he is going to say. Even though his lectures are unrehearsed and unmemorized, I know him like a book. Where before I was convinced that he was constantly changing — he was so fascinating to me, now he is equally boring. When a "truth" pops out of his mouth, I can easily identify which volume in his vast library he has plagiarized it from. From his lips, there is nothing original or new. I watch him babble and yet observe how very skilled he is at making his explanations appear very important and significant indeed. I notice that the audience seems divided in two. Several have obviously seen his lectures before and are fascinated. Others appear unimpressed, uncomfortable, even disturbed. In one profound moment, I flash back to a memory of my former self. I re-enter the body of that hopeful trusting little girl, completely entranced by that six-foot handsome man who stole her heart with his confidence and charisma so many years ago. I realize that I couldn't have helped what happened, that if sent back in time, I would make the same mistakes all over again. I was young and desperate for passion and assurance and I responded to his personality. I paid him to help me. Naively, I offered myself to him and he took what I gave, and then found a way to grab more, to get it all. This evening the painful lessons I have learned over those ravaged lost years parade before my mind's eye. I watch myself evolve until I reach my current state of wisdom and maturity. No, I am not afraid of this man anymore. I could put myself right in his face and listen to all of his rhetoric and he wouldn't be able to pull me off of my position, not one inch. Today, I study him as he manipulates his faulty logic, confusing and seducing some of the members of the audience. However, I can figure out his strategy as easily as I can solve an eighth grade algebra problem.

After the lecture he approaches and sits down to face me.

"How are you doing?" he demands with authority, ready to twist my response with enough willpower that my confidence will be shaken. From there, he plans to intimidate or con me into believing that I am not doing well without him.

"You know."

I refuse to fall into his waiting trap by extending any information which he can use against me.

"I want to hear it from you," he commands.

"I'm doing fine, but I wanted you to tell me what thoughts were in your head."

I know he will withhold the information I request, and I am right.

"There's nothing in my head; I don't think," he informs me as if I am stupid not to realize the obvious.

Gerald has always made this claim, to prove that he is spiritually above all of us, the poor slobs in The Program. I know he is lying; I have seen him think, but I let it go.

He looks into my eyes, to focus his Energy on me, to try to control me, and I willingly return his stare. Then he hands me Ben's soul-rock. Gerald wants me to feel how powerful he and the rock have become, to understand from its vibrations how imminent Ben's resurrection is. The rock is hot and charged from Gerald's body energy. I am not imagining the jolting sensations in the palm of my hand as I hold Ben's rock. The ability Gerald has to electrify an inanimate object is powerful and scary.

Locked in his gaze, I seek a deeper spiritual experience with this member of the opposite species. I possess a drive to understand everything that I can about good and evil.

"What is evil?" I ask him.

"It is a lie; an illusion created by the mind," he answers with authority and certainty.

The wrongness of his position impacts me deeply. How can Gerald and I ever communicate if he doesn't believe that anything is evil? According to him, every action must be acceptable, even torture, child abuse and cold-blooded murder. With words and attitude, I feel him trying to pull me into his spiritual field. His powerful will reaches out, groping and shoving, trying to uproot me. But inside I am immovable. A resolve rises to support and protect me; I will never back down again; he no longer has any piece of me.

"Is love an emotion?" I continue.

"No, love is everything. Love is God. You are God."

I ask him the same question I asked my mother just one short month ago.

"How could I be God? I didn't make the universe, neither did you. Everyone knows that God made it. Therefore, He must be outside of us, larger than his creation."

"Don't intellectualize," he snaps and then lectures his defiant student parentally, "You must work at pursuing The Energy every day or else you won't be prepared when the spiritual change comes. You will be lost."

This is his Armageddon speech. It is all too familiar to me and I am not impressed. He can't make me feel like I need him to survive. I know he doesn't possess the answers for my spiritual future. He isn't my savior anymore. In his face I see nothingness — profound infinite coldness. I look beyond his physical eyes and see the span of his life, an entire eternal universe without love or hope, without kindness, conscience or God. I experience an eerie suction, as if a giant vacuum exists behind those eyes, endless outer space with no hope of life ever. I hold onto my internal anchor desperately, not to protect my body, but to protect my soul. What I see in him must be the true Hell — interminable frigid emptiness, and I want no part of it. I know that I would die in a world like that with nothing to feed my soul. I yearn to feel the warmth of Judy's smile, to be reassured that I am loved, to forget I ever had knowledge of a realm such as this. However, I know I never will forget, and in a way I am grateful to have been shown this vision, to have been blessed with the opportunity to stand at the precipice of the eternal abyss, to know the truth. To quote Judy, "You cannot truly know God without knowing his enemy." Beyond what little he has left of his personality, beyond my past projections, needs and hopes, I see who Gerald Ezra Sharkman truly is, and I understand what he stands for . . .

We focus in silence for a time but then he abruptly breaks the connection; in a heartbeat he is on his feet. I watch him turn from me and stride away. He doesn't even say good-bye. I understand why. He has played all of the cards in his hand and lost. He has failed and he knows it. I have reclaimed my life.

A little while later, Rich and I approach two former members of the audience, a man and a woman, seated at a table. I ask them what they think of Gerald. The man says he has seen Gerald lecture a few times at this *Barnes & Noble*.

"His ideas are wonderful and they really work!"

He is all pumped up with excitement and exhibits that Rah, Rah, end of the AMWAY meeting attitude, a temporary emotional high based on conceived fantasies of future success which will in reality never come to pass. This state of mind is familiar from many years in the Group watching the others pursue failing business enterprises. I know only too well, from painful personal experience, how misleading these feelings of exhilaration are, how they never culminate in anything fruitful but instead escort you right into the pit. Regardless, I can say nothing to this man, drowning in the seduction of his imaginary enlightenment.

Thankfully, the woman has the opposite view. She doesn't feel comfortable with Gerald's spiritual bill of goods, but she can't figure out why. Almost magically, the perfect question to pose comes to my mind.

"Did you see any humility in him?"

"No. He seems selfish, with a big ego."

"Do you have humility in you?"

"Yes. That is a gift from God; I would never give it up, not for anything!"

I respond gently, in awe of what I have just discovered and am about to explain,

"I believe that is the reason you didn't like him. If you have the potential to 'be your own God', and 'become the architect of your own life', then Mr. Sharkman is telling you that you have the power to create and control your destiny. In order to do this, you must give up the very thing most precious to you — your humility, your willingness to yield to God's plan — in short, your allegiance to God."

However, after speaking with both people this evening, I now realize that as Gerald goes out into the world he will find his followers; not everyone will feel about him as this woman and I do . . .

Friday morning, January 17

It has been a week since I attended Gerald's lecture, and I have finally reached my breaking point. Feelings of injustice explode like fireworks in my chest; this sensation is almost unbearable. Impulses to close the bank account, change the locks, grab Samantha and physically evict her from the premises, torment me relentlessly. All week long I have been unable to speak to or even look at her. I can find no comfortable place to communicate. Waves of rage pass through me frequently, and violent desires to yell at her, attack her and abuse her, refuse to cease. Despite the power of these feelings, I do not want to act on them and I restrain their expression with all of my willpower. However, I fear that I won't last much longer.

At 1:00 P.M. Samantha leaves for the day. Unexpectedly, an hour later she returns. That's when she breaks the news.

"Elizabeth, I have decided to leave Expressions. We can't get along. I don't want to be here anymore. I am going to sell my half of the business for the $40,000 value that Louis Gavin included in our official partnership agreement." I stare at her with dumb relief. Unlike the day, eleven short months ago, she withdrew from *Flash Blasters Inc.*, I do not tell her that I want to work things out. I simply murmur weakly,

"OK, if that's what you want to do."

I add that I don't know how to handle this legally, but I will consult a lawyer. She agrees. God had finally answered my prayers. Before leaving, she adds,

"Our relationship has been the deepest rivalry I have ever known . . ."

Saturday morning, January 18

I arrive and notice that the wall above her desk is bare. Only yesterday it was filled with several black and white photographs of herself and her two cats. I think back wistfully to the laughs we shared when her white cat shed all over her black outfit the day I took those pictures, and my pain of separation commences . . . Several Disney posters with which she had adorned our walls are missing also. My partner summons me to her.

"Elizabeth, I am leaving because you are mean to me."

I realize that I don't want us to split in a fight; it will only make things more complicated, and she might plan some type of retaliation. For my own protection, I must shift her to a neutral position. I throw myself out of my natural character for a moment, betraying my true feelings I flatter her, using the logic I learned in The Group, her natural language.

"You are such a talented author, Samantha. Now is the time to be courageous, reach higher and follow your future. Pursue the writing career meant for you. Don't hold back and stagnate in the security of your job here. This business was my passion, not yours," I state boldly and gloriously.

Samantha, a legend in her own mind, drinks in my words and instantly forgets that her books have never done anything but lose money. High on the fantasy of becoming the next Stephen King, the fact that she is giving up a $40,000-a-year twenty-hour-a-week job eludes her for the moment. Feeding her ego to manipulate her is child's play. The "mean to her" concept evaporates, and she looks upon me with new vision, as a supportive mentor and friend. Later that day she borrows my reasoning, telling family and friends she's leaving *Expressions Photography* so that she can devote herself to her books, so that she can become "more of who she really is".

Tuesday, January 21

I consult the same lawyer who was decent enough to warn me against declaring bankruptcy last year. Initially he assumes that I need help on a quite standard corporate partnership dissolution, but when I pour out my heart for over an hour he is more than a little surprised. In fact, he appears considerably upset. I can see that he understands my entrapment and genuinely wants to help. I recount the story of how we came to sign the fifty-fifty corporate agreement at the offices of the Sharkman's family lawyer and he explains that I signed under duress, at psychological gunpoint. According to him a combination of fraud, extortion and conspiracy have been involved. As he outlines our plan, I know I have come to the right person for help.

"This is what will happen next. I am scheduling a partnership meeting to be held at my offices. Ms. Sharkman will bring her own lawyer. A court stenographer will be present to take down all conversation. In front of this group of people she will not be able to deny the true facts."

The meeting is scheduled for the following Friday, January 31. I gladly give him a retainer of $1000. This is it, the beginning of the end. The train is moving again . . .

Although inside I am jumping for joy, I play it cool the next day at the office. Concealing my emotions, I tell Samantha only two things — she must hire a lawyer, and the official partnership meeting is scheduled for the end of next week. A couple of days later Samantha retains a lawyer and we all exchange phone numbers. Now we are ready for stage two of the "corporate divorce". I continue to act like nothing is out of the ordinary, as if I am committed to Samantha obtaining compensation as per Mr. Gavin's agreement. I only make it clear that, due to my personal debt, I am in no position to purchase her shares myself.

Wednesday, January 22

Samantha is maintaining the position that she has every right to sell her shares of *Expressions Photography* to a third party. It is getting ugly and there is perpetual tension between Elizabeth and her. I know something has to be done, but I'm not quite sure what. On my way to visit Elizabeth at her studio, at an intersection just minutes from my destination, I find myself taking an unexpected detour. Immediately, I instinctively know where I am going, but, as if invisible hands have just grabbed the wheel, this navigation is not coming from my mind. I feel upset and frightened about what I am about to do.

A few minutes later I pull up in front of Samantha's mother's gift shop and shut the engine. I sit behind the wheel, my mouth dry from anxiety. Pacing in front of the building, I hesitate before gaining the courage to open the door and enter. I remember seeing Doris at Gerald's house three years ago when Christie Whitman visited the *UWSA* core group members there, but I know she will not recognize me. I browse through the gifts aimlessly as my mind races, searching desperately for an opening statement. Finally, I decide to purchase a small stuffed bear. I approach the counter to pay for it, and as she removes the price tag from the item, I take the bold step.

"Hi, are you Doris?"

"Do I know you?" she inquires hesitantly.

"I don't think you would remember me. My name is Judy. I was at your house when Governor Whitman visited and I remembered you as Samantha and Martin's mother."

She smiles and looks pleased as I comment on how handsome and charming her son, Martin, is. I add,

"I'm good friends with Elizabeth and I know Samantha very well from *United We Stand America.*"

Then, I take a deep breath and plunge into the unknown territory. "You know Elizabeth doesn't see Gerald anymore."

Doris doesn't seem upset at the mention of her estranged husband and I am relieved.

"Yes, and neither do I," she responds.

We both smile and I know she can feel my sincerity. I exit the store, confident that an opening has been created to connect with her in the future if I want to. As I drive away, I realize why I have visited her so spontaneously. Now, I head for Elizabeth's office to give her the stuffed bear I purchased from Doris. We intentionally position the bag, labeled prominently with her mother's store name, where Samantha can see it. I want her to know that I have seen her mother and leave her wondering what was discussed. I know she will be terrified at the possibility that I might reveal her father's secret infidelities. When Samantha arrives and spots the bag I notice her tighten, although she clearly tries to hide her reaction.

Saturday, January 25

Samantha confronts me. "I know all about how Judy visited my mother," she spits out, trying to intimidate me. However, her facade is transparent and underneath I see her tension.

"Oh yeah? So what's the big deal? She went to look for a gift for her niece," I retort, making light of it.

"She was asking her personal questions," Samantha accuses.

"No, she wasn't. She was just talking about Christie Whitman's visit to your father's house."

However my eyes are daggers, piercing her. Disgusted with the entire charade, they tell another story, *If you don't get your ass out of here, your mother will know all about how your father committed adultery on her ten times over, and that he has convinced you and Martin, <u>her children too,</u> to spend at least thirty hours a week staring at a dog's carcass and willing it to walk again. This information might help her immeasurably in divorce court. In addition, don't think that I won't back up my threats by stepping onto a witness stand and declaring these things under oath!*

Sunday, January 26

With the intention of presenting my lawyer with full written details, I write an outline of Gerald's behavior concerning my business. His techniques of manipulation and abuse compose a ten-item list. I describe his temper and physical bullying, his assertions that The Energy is solely responsible for any business success. Judy, Lisa and Rich sign the document as witnesses who would be willing, if necessary, to testify in court.

Gerald Sharkman's techniques for
making you feel invalid and isolated from the outside world

1. Glare at you with rage
2. Threaten to throw you out, claiming that if you push him to that point, you will die in a year, friendless and poverty stricken.
3. Yell the same phrase repeatedly to drown out anything you are trying to say.
4. Ignore any opinion which contradicts his belief system. Give you no validity.
5. Grab you and throw you out of the door or slam you against the wall for disagreeing with him.
6. Randomly select a daily scapegoat and engage the rest of The Group to verbally attack and humiliate them.
7. Tell you repeatedly that you are a valueless failure without his Energy.
8. Tell you repeatedly that non-group members are dead robots, assholes who will eventually be destroyed by their own stupidity.
9. Organize social activities solely with other group members. Forbid outside relationships.
10. Praise members who spend the most hours (and money) with him. Threaten and humiliate anyone who tries to cut back on their hours.

Monday, January 27

I think it will be over soon. My lawyer received the fax about Gerald's intimidation tactics and he is even more outraged than before. I can't take much more. To Samantha, I continue to act like there is nothing out of the ordinary, as if I fully expect her to receive the $40,000 from some investor, but I am sick and drawn; I can't eat or sleep. I am afraid that she will vandalize the studio if she discovers that I have given my lawyer details about her father's precious Group. I want to change the locks on the door to protect my property but I can't make any moves which would raise suspicion. Now I must wait. I have done all I can do. It is out of my hands. I must have faith. I am scared. Judy's going to come to work with me tomorrow . . .

Tuesday, January 28

My lawyer calls Samantha's lawyer and tells her that Samantha must leave the corporation with no compensation due to her. Her lawyer, however, doesn't understand why I am so rigid and unreasonable, so my lawyer faxes her my synopsis of The Group's history. A few hours later she calls him back, asserting that she has no idea what is going on, and she doesn't want to get involved.

The following morning Samantha informs me that her lawyer has withdrawn from the case, without telling her why.

"Anyway," she adds whimsically, as if this transaction is no more significant than planning the menu for a dinner party, "I have good news for you, we can do this without lawyers! You can cancel that meeting in your lawyer's office that you scheduled for this Friday. I called Louis Gavin and he says we can just make a new document up and then I can sell my shares of the corporation privately."

I bite my lip. She is trying to slip out. I remember the day Louis and I had planned to expose her, right before she withdrew from *Flash Blasters Inc.* She had canceled that meeting too. Although I have given her no facts to go by, she seems to possess some type of ESP which informs her when she is on the brink of being unmasked. I know that I will never, ever allow her to sell the shares she has not rightfully earned to a third party so that a new person can perpetuate the injustice by owning half of <u>my</u> business. I imagine her inviting innocent prospective buyers to examine the studio. I visualize myself shaking their hands and then brazenly handing them the synopsis of my history with Gerald's group. I prove to them on paper that she has no right to sell them those shares. I throw in the bizarre details of orgies, shoplifting, head shaking and the dead dog. I picture their faces turning ashen as they hurriedly bid Samantha a polite but nervous goodbye, all the while sprinting with much momentum, toward the exit. Still, I need something more to push her out of the door . . .

Wednesday, January 29

I am almost too afraid to be alone anywhere and Judy accompanies me to the office again. With my friend by my side, Samantha doesn't dare start conflict, and instead, in an almost surreal moment of reprieve from the hostile clouds which have been smothering us, the three of us reminisce about our history together — *UWSA*, the flash cards, the people we know from The Group . . . Curious about Samantha's response, I ask her a question.

"Your father is not like anyone else we know. What drives him to do such strange and antisocial things?"

"I don't know. He just feels like it I guess."

"But why? Many of his experiments fail. What is he trying to prove?"

"Nothing to anyone else. He just has to find the answers to free us. He is driven."

"Driven by what, or whom?"

Suddenly my perception is propelled higher, beyond Gerald's personality to the spiritual mass of humanity we are all a part of, and revelation comes . . . my mouth moves automatically without thought and these words come forth,

"My God, it is not Gerald, the man, who is directing his actions. There is a more powerful spiritual force behind him calling the shots. There is a man behind the man."

Samantha observes with intensity, appearing to acknowledge I have just stated something profound and true. She too seems to agree that her father is being navigated by some higher force, but who exactly is this "man behind the man"?

Several minutes later Samantha announces she must leave. For some reason, as if she unconsciously knows what I will soon discover, that this moment is goodbye, she requests a hug from both of us. She approaches me first, but I am uncomfortable and pull back as she advances. However, Judy throws herself in, projecting her natural personality into her arms as she envelops Samantha with genuine warmth. Samantha, only going through the motions, is incapable of returning Judy's affection. Her soul is a wasteland in which no real feelings seem to have ever existed. When confronted with Judy's sincere offer of sentiment, she remains pale and stiff, corpse-like.

"Come on Samantha," Judy requests, "Give me something real. There is no feeling in you at all. Are you a robot? Are you dead? I would get more feeling out of hugging my ironing board!"

Samantha doesn't appear to be in the least bit offended. It is as if the concept of true affection is a foreign language to her. The personal exchange of love between two humans is a vast resource of joy which she neither knows exists, nor has any desire or need to discover. A few minutes later Samantha exits, and that is the last time I ever see her.

Thursday, January 30

Louis Gavin calls me around 10:00 A.M.

"Samantha wants a settlement for her five years of input into *Expressions*."

Pacing the floor of my living room in consternation, I deliver to him verbally what I had only shown her in my eyes the previous Saturday.

"I have given her everything she is ever going to get. She will never, ever get one more cent out of me. I will expose their dirty secrets if I have to, to make sure."

Inside I am a brick wall; I will accept no negotiation and I feel this in every fiber of my being. Louis gets the message. Considering that he was the very person who spent considerable energy the previous year drumming the facts into my head that, *Shares of a New Jersey corporation cannot be gifted, and therefore Samantha has never had any right to them*, he knows only too well that I have the truth on my side to back up my position. How ironic that she chooses to contact Louis for help, the person who forcefully impressed into my mind that *Samantha has got to go*! After an hour on the phone he assures me that he'll talk to Samantha, that "she trusts him". With that he ends our call and phones her, communicating my frame of mind, telling her that if she wants any money out of me she will have to take me to court. Gerald would never allow this to happen. Information exposed during the legal battle for his daughter's half of *Expressions Photography* would surely adversely affect his divorce negotiations with Doris. He has much more to lose than his daughter's measly $40,000.

Not knowing what to expect, I arrive at my office at 2:00 P.M. for the afternoon shift. An eerie sense of emptiness strikes me immediately. I look around, but nothing is amiss. I sit down at my desk and begin some paperwork. About ten minutes later the phone rings. It is Louis.

"The keys are there on your desk. Didn't you see them?"

I suppose this is his way of asking why I haven't called yet to thank him. I glance down and sure enough, they are there, a few inches from me; I hadn't even noticed!

Samantha is finally gone. Apparently, at the conclusion of her conversation with Mr. Gavin, she left abruptly. After a six-year business relationship and a more than fifteen-year "friendship", there is no goodbye, no note, no message on the answering machine, just her keys lying in the middle of my desk. Her father, like a general commanding a private, must have given her the evacuation command to protect his own hide. The entire process has taken a little more than two weeks and she has left with nothing, absolutely nothing . . .

I look around the office, my office now, and I can't believe it. They are gone, truly, really gone, all of them, out of my life forever! I drop to my knees. More humble than I have ever felt in my entire life, tears fill my eyes as I put my hands together and look up toward the Man responsible for my rescue.

"Thank you, God. Thank you so much!"

I call Judy with the news and she comes right over. I throw my arms around her, thanking her for supporting me selflessly for so long. We page Michael at his office. Into his alphanumeric pager we type, _The demon is out!_ He is in a meeting with his boss, Tim, when he receives the message. He reads it and can't help blurting out,

"Yes!"

His boss looks up with curiosity. "What's going on?"

"Oh, Tim, it's a really long story. Maybe some other time I'll explain . . ."

For some reason, in the days following, I feel far from elated, free or even comfortable. An unholy rage hangs in the air. It follows me everywhere like a dark cloud. In my mind I sense departing demons shrieking in fury, as if heaven has just opened, extending a celestial hand to drag them off my back against their will, to pluck these evil ones from my life, back to the Hell which gave birth to them. The casualties on my side have been high, but Gerald and his comrades have lost the war and been evicted from the territory they used to possess — me. I sense how much they despise this.

Saturday, February 1
Bess is playing with her band at the café again and Michael and I decide to pay a brief visit during the gig to check things out. Gerald is clearly agitated when he discovers us standing there. As if desperate to deny our presence, he appears incapable of even looking anywhere near us. Nora and Bess are friendly. Obviously Gerald and Samantha have kept their failure a secret from the rest.

Tuesday, February 4
I run into Martin unexpectedly at the Closter Diner down the block. He looks right through me as if he doesn't recognize me. Hurt is written all over his face and I assume that he is enraged at me because according to the three Sharkmans (the unholy trinity) I screwed Samantha out of her half of the business, more than $40,000.

Thursday, February 6
The corporate dissolution papers are completed and Louis brings them to my office for signatures. All ties are broken. Legally, I owe the Sharkmans nothing more, not now, never . . .

Michael and I, visiting some relatives in Hoboken, decide to grab a coffee at the *Starbuck's Café* in the local *Barnes and Noble.* Coincidentally, we discover that Gerald is in the middle of a book signing lecture. Standing at the back of a group of approximately forty people who compose the audience, I nervously scan the room and spot Samantha in the crowd. I also notice that the front row is occupied by several middle-aged women who appear to dote on Gerald's every word and movement. Not recognizing them as members of The Group, I conclude that they must have heard him lecture here before. Gerald, unaware of our presence, states decisively,

"The Energy will prevent you from aging if you follow it with commitment."

Michael raises his hand. Gerald recognizes him and tightens, but has to allow him the floor.

"Excuse me. Can I ask you a question? You mean to tell me that for the last twenty years you haven't aged?"

"That's correct," Gerald contends.

"I find it hard to believe that you are exactly the same now as you were twenty years ago. How old are you?"

"That's irrelevant," he snaps, glaring at Michael with the same intimidation he uses to suppress his female Group members. However, these tactics will not work tonight. Michael loves to debate and is relentless in getting his point across.

"No, it's not. If you are exactly the same as you were twenty years ago, do you have a picture of yourself to prove it? I'd like to see it. You mean you had the same gray hair twenty years ago?"

Now visibly upset, and not wanting to lose credibility in front of his audience, Gerald attempts to slip out by shifting the focus away from Michael's as yet unanswered question. Raising his voice threateningly, trying to browbeat him into silence, he challenges,

"What gives you the right to question me?"

"I give me the right, and I'd still like to see the picture . . ."

At this point, the audience reacts to the conflict, and one of the front row groupies turns around to throw Michael a nasty look.

"Why don't you stop harassing him? It's impolite and disrespectful."

"I'm not; I'm simply asking him to prove his theories, and he can't. That's the reason he got upset and tried to change the subject."

At this point, several other people in the audience begin to groan in disgust. Samantha turns around, a puzzled look written across her face, as if to say, *Why are you doing this to my father?*

"Well, that's enough out of you," Gerald spits out, cutting us off abruptly, diverting his gaze and dismissing us like naughty school children.

"I've seen enough," Michael comments, fed up, as he and I turn to exit, accompanied by approximately one third of the audience.

A man shuffles past us and I hear him mumble, "This guy is a fraud."

Judy and Michael's confrontation with Gerald spurs me to call my mother; I am curious about her reaction to Samantha's exit. After a few moments of empty small talk, I get to the point.

"Did you hear that Samantha left my business?"

"Yes, and she has decided to reach higher. She is running for state assembly on the Independent ticket; Mitchell Stavos is running also, for state senator. There is even talk of billboards to promote Samantha!" she adds with genuine excitement.

It figures Samantha would come up with a scheme like this to puff up her ego. Why is my mother so gullible? It never ceases to infuriate me.

"But Mom, how will they get votes? They have no following, no experience and no campaign funds. Besides, what do they have to offer the public?"

"Well, you know that all the other politicians are just standard programmed robots. Samantha and Mitchell can think creatively. Even you have to admit that they are intelligent."

This statement is uttered by a woman who has told me repeatedly, as recently as a year ago, that she hates both of them, that they were ordinary, unimpressive and stupid. What has happened to her's brain?

"You know," I continue, "Michael and Judy saw Gerald at a book signing last week. Gerald claimed that The Energy will stop you from aging. That is an outright lie."

Not that I expect Grace to validate this fact . . .

"I heard something from Samantha . . . Michael was really rude to disrupt Gerald's lecture."

Her response is true to her form and I change the subject.

"What will Samantha do now that she doesn't have a free ride in my business? She will never make that kind of salary again."

"Samantha is going to make it," my mother states resolutely, clearly trying to convince herself. "How are you doing?"

I answer honestly. "I am shaky, but OK. It is strange running the two businesses all by myself; it is a lot of work!!"

But she has her own solutions for me.

"You really want to come back to The Group. I know you do, but you are just in denial."

I do not respond to her statement; what can I say? We continue to chat about this and that, but ten minutes later, she repeats her previous assertion. Before we hang up, she has stated it for a third time . . .

At the office, feeling empty and alone, I cling to the familiarity of the daily patterns which Samantha and I have established over a six-year period. Slowly, I begin to inform my customers of my partner's departure, and the evidence of Samantha's real influence on the business immediately rolls in. One woman tells me that she and several of her friends, conscious of the intensity of our relationship, had concluded that we were a lesbian couple. I am horrified.

"You wouldn't believe how far from the truth that is!" I proclaim, not yet ready, however, to expose the real story.

Others, also too polite to have commented while she was still my partner, tell me they didn't like her. Many are passionate about their feelings — Samantha was pushy, demanding, selfish, greedy or worse. Some even sensed an evil fume from her, so noxious that they found contact with her practically intolerable. They admit they would have never returned for repeat business if it wasn't for my presence, that when they called on the phone, they avoided her and requested me. I realize sadly that unbeknownst to me, during the years she was my partner, I have lost many good customers because of her. This is the real reason the business experienced stunted growth. Gerald and Samantha projected her destructive actions onto me and blamed me for them. Everything they accused me of doing — stopping the business, wanting to fail — was in reality what she was doing. On a daily basis, not only did I have to fulfill the regular demands of running the office, but I had to expend extra energy to try to oppose the negative destructive force she was continually exerting, a force which drove customers away. No wonder I always felt so exhausted and alone! Thus released from their oppression and lies I now sense myself soaring upwards, a little more each day, regaining my old talents, my abilities to relate and my desire to excel. However, self-doubt, so well planted by the Sharkmans, still plagues me and frequently, especially on slow days, I return to my former fears, *Without Samantha, the business will surely fail.* Judy is enraged at this conclusion and she fights my mind's decree with her will.

"That is a lie, Liz. They just taught you that so they could use you for their own gain."

Regardless, it takes me several months to let it go . . .

My customers' supportive responses give me courage, and I realize there is another mistake I must try to correct.

I telephone Judy G., Brigette's mother. I haven't seen her since that fateful day in early 1994 when, because of my stupid planning, her daughter rejoined Gerald's group. Now that I have left I feel guilty and partially responsible. I hope that if I can get her mother on my side, together we may be able to pull Brigette and her two kids out. Judy G. hints that she is afraid her daughter is in a cult and she has a bad feeling about Gerald. I fill her in on some of the details, but I do not want to go too far and shock her. Instead, Judy (Carlone) and I plan a visit Long Island. I know I must reveal the truth, but I haven't figured out how to begin. Judy G. is distressed over how much money Brigette is spending on Gerald. She knows that as a single parent, her daughter can scarcely afford this expense. She also senses her daughter's powerful allegiance to Gerald and it scares her. When we sit down to dinner, I decide to tell her a story from my own experience. I take her back to Dr. Rogers' office, to the day when Gerald first asked me to take off my shirt. Judy G.'s eyes pop out. In one dramatic moment she gets the message and instantly reacts. I assure her that Brigette is not involved sexually with him, but that many other things happen there which are equally unwholesome.

"We must get Brigette away from Gerald. I am sure she will want to leave when she hears what you have told me," Judy G. states with urgency as we immediately pile into her car and head for Brigette's Jericho home . . .

My heart sinks and my hope fades when I discover her house filled with Samantha's posters and knick-knacks, obviously gifts Samantha distributed when she moved from our large Closter house to a smaller apartment. In the bedroom, black rocks are spread across her pillows, — a bizarre display. Even more distressing, Brigette's personality and body language have altered severely since our last visit together. She has evolved into a perfect Groupie clone; she reminds me of the "Moonies" I have seen so frequently on the streets of Manhattan. In fact, she resembles Samantha and the rest almost completely in speech, attitude and thought. We gather in the living-room and her mother informs her soberly,

"Liz has told me some very disturbing things about Gerald which I think you should know."

She frantically relates the details of the sexual incidents, but Brigette doesn't blink an eye. In fact, when her mother has finished, she displays no reaction whatsoever. His blatant lack of morality and audacious intention to mercilessly exploit those patients who have put their trust in him does not phase her in the least.

"Oh that doesn't matter. Gerald doesn't do that anymore; it is all in the past and he has changed. Besides, Liz is very angry with him because she can't control him. She wants to punish him, so she talks behind his back to try to get other people against him. That is why she is telling you this."

Coming up against the brick wall of Brigette's brainwashing, her mother's hopes are dashed instantaneously. Personally, I hadn't expected any other response; the loyalty of Group members to Gerald is supernatural, powerful and ugly. Now Judy G. is beginning to comprehend the vise grip in which Gerald holds his followers. Brigette goes on to praise her guru, describing all of the things she has learned from him. Fed up with her lack of common sense and morality, I ask her how she can justify the violence, sex and financial exploitation which have occurred, but faithful devotee responds with confidence,

"Oh I can see that Gerald used you all to learn from, but it doesn't matter. His ends are worth your sacrifice . . . Liz, I know you think this is a cult, but you are wrong. Gerald told us last week that our group is definitely not a cult because in cults they sacrifice animals; we love animals."

Her words carry so much conviction that they sway me momentarily and I doubt myself . . . Meanwhile, her cold shark's eyes fill in the rest of her opinion of me, *You are a frustrated disgruntled upstart who wants revenge, a spoiled child throwing a tantrum to get her way.* I feel sick at this injustice. Exactly like Samantha, I do not sense anything inside of her that is even willing to examine Gerald from another perspective. There is nothing but rigid finality in her personal convictions. Her mother wants to know how Brigette can justify paying Gerald so much while she is struggling with her finances, but Brigette replies assertively,

"Paying Gerald is more important than paying my electric bill. Besides, whatever I give now will come back to me later."

Gerald's familiar "Law of Reciprocity" strikes again . . .

Judy G., disheartened by her daughter's responses, asks how Gerald has helped her, and Brigette credits him with better health and more stable emotions. Whenever she is in trouble, she can always go to him for answers . . . Brigette has just betrayed one of God's central truths and her mother's eyes light up with fire,

"Brigette, you can't rely on another human being to tell you how to live. You can only do your best every day, hold onto God's hand, and ask him to help you."

These wise words, straight from her heart, are lost on her daughter. She responds to her mother's distress in the same way my mother responds to mine, with cold eyes and no emotion, only a slight shake of the head as she wonders to herself, *What is wrong with these people? Why are they wasting their time fighting when it is so obvious that Gerald is right? Why don't they just give in? When will they ever learn?*

While dissension storms in the living room, I slip into her children's bedroom. Craig and Lacey, now aged seven and six, third-year veterans of The Group, are playing on the floor with dolls and trucks. I ask them what they think of Gerald, hoping they have held onto their original feelings, but my hopes are dashed.

"Gerald is great. He loves everyone. We trust him to help us," they reply like little robots. "We like going to New Jersey".

My heart breaks. They have lost their ability to discern. Those innocent children; I would kidnap them tonight if I could . . .

When we finally leave, Judy G. is in terrible conflict. She has confronted the unconquerable monster, Gerald's hold on her daughter's mind, and she realizes that she has no weapons to bring it down. Deflated, she shares her innermost feelings,

"I will pray now, and every day, that someday God will open Brigette's eyes and she will want to leave The Group like you did, Liz."

I will pray also, and ask God for forgiveness that I ever brought Brigette and her children there in the first place.

A couple of weeks later, Judy G. receives an unexpected phone call from my mother. After they hang up, Judy phones me at my office.

"Your mother just called me; she hasn't done that in years. I guess Brigette told The Group about your visit. She seemed to be fishing around to see what I knew and finally, I confronted her, 'Grace, how could you do this to us? Jeannie and Liz met in the sandbox in Central Park when they were three years old. We have all been friends ever since. We spent holidays and summer vacations together. I trusted you. We were like family. How could you send us to such a sick man for therapy when he was having sex with both you and your daughter at the same time?! You betrayed us. How could you?'"

I pick up a copy of *Cult Mind Control* at a local bookstore. The author, Steven Hassan, a former "Moonie", has brilliantly outlined the specific distinguishing characteristics of a cult.

He defines mind control: "changing a person's belief system without their consent or awareness and making them dependent on an outside authority — creating an addiction to the leader."

He describes the in-depth personality of a cult, identical to The Group. "Going to a doctor proves their faithlessness — Members are taught that the world is a hostile evil place and they must depend on cult doctrine to understand reality — They live in a fantasy world created by the power of The Group's collective consciousness — Spiritual weakness is the cause of their medical problems — Members are taught to be phobic about ever leaving the group — Most cult leaders believe that they are the Messiah . . ."

The author relates that the methods used to indoctrinate members generally include a form of hypnosis, accompanied by sensory and emotional overload. I think of the countless hours we spent in terror of Gerald's temper or focusing on his shaking head, afraid to get up to go to the bathroom. (We would have been accused of interrupting the flow or seeking a distraction.) How very similar his head movements were to the classic picture of the swinging hypnotist's pocket watch! Despising Gerald's deception, I remember how he would chuckle when, not too infrequently, a member of his *Barnes & Noble* audience would ask, "Is this hypnosis?" and he would reply patronizingly, "You can never understand; your thinking is too small; so why don't you just be patient and experience the good stuff that's coming out of me . . ."

The book goes on to explain the mechanics of manipulation. The charismatic leader begins with "nominalization", ie. speaking in broad generalization. In essence, he supplies the paint and blank canvas and invites the listener to create his own scene. He encourages a utopian fantasy where all needs will be filled and problems solved, provided specific requirements (outlined and controlled by him) are met. Gerald's assertion drifts into my mind, "Just follow The Energy and you will live forever in total happiness and prosperity." The con-artist has mastered the art of creating an air of expectation, and he knows how to dangle the carrot indefinitely. In addition covert hypnosis is effected through repetitive visual or auditory vibrations at specific frequencies to which the human brain is responsive. Even verbal modulation (speaking slowly, softly or rhythmically) can encourage relaxation. Hypnosis, a place where we are more suggestible, occurs when brainwaves slip from the waking, critical thinking, "beta" state into the slower "alpha" state. Since this happens to all of us naturally several times a day (daydreaming or "spacing out"), given the appropriate conditions, anyone is vulnerable. A deep trace may also be induced if the subject accepts the hypnotist as an authority. Suggestions made to the subconscious will be retained by the mind upon waking, or triggers may be inserted to elicit specific behaviors at will. The exploiter is free to insert new mental software (brainwashing) to serve his interests. (I remember those sessions where the entire group would fall into a profoundly deep sleep for a few hours and awaken more dedicated than ever to our mission.) In addition, cult members soon learn self-hypnosis. They maintain a dissociative state of semi-trance by chanting (Hare Krishna members) or constant mental repetition of doctrine ("thought-stopping") to drown out any conflicting information. How often I repeated Gerald's logic for hours to repress my anxiety over the inordinate sums of money I was giving him! And then there was Judy's description of The Group members' mesmerized eyes, "cold, empty, remote, like the *Children of the Damned*".

Finally, most cult victims are approached at an emotionally vulnerable time in their lives. I think back to Joe's death . . .

At the back of the book, Cult Information Services, a N.J. cult awareness group, is listed, and I contact them. The secretary explains that similar organizations are present in many states — a source of information, counseling and legal advice. I warn them about Gerald, submitting his name and address for their database, and they offer to refer me to a lawyer who specializes in cult cases. In fact, I can meet him at their yearly gathering, coming up in just a few weeks.

At the meeting, a former "Moonie" and a woman who escaped a small religious cult in Upstate New York the previous year, speak during the morning lectures. If I ever questioned what The Group really was, after hearing their similar testimonies of abuse, brainwashing and emotional manipulation, my doubts are put to rest once and for all.

Just a few weeks earlier, the "Heaven's Gate" cult committed mass suicide in California and the two courageous parents of Gail Maeder who lost their only daughter to one man's perverted insanity arrive at lunchtime amid scores of TV cameras. They speak for a few minutes and I stand just three feet from them, absorbing the grief-stricken incomprehension in their faces. If you have never been inside, how can you truly understand how a normal intelligent person can follow a raving madman to such extremes? I wish I could say something to ease their suffering, but nothing will ever bring back their daughter, and they will probably never be able to truly fathom how and why they lost her.

After lunch, we return to the lecture hall. As I walk through the entrance doors a man approaches me, shoves his hand at me, and introduces himself as Herbert Rosedale, the very lawyer for whom I have been looking. Supposedly the most sought after cult lawyer in the country, he currently represents Reverend Moon's daughter-in-law who is filing charges against the Unification Church. I offer him a copy of my synopsis of The Group's events, and he invites me to telephone him the following week. If anyone can help me, he can . . .

A week later I phone, hopeful for the last time. He explains the legal reality to me. Gerald can lawfully operate as a therapist, without a Bachelor's degree or any other type of certification. I, an adult not a minor, have <u>agreed</u> to pay him for his services, regardless of the fact that Gerald was the primary source of coercion. No matter how ridiculous and pointless his activities might appear to someone else, in the absence of actual physical force, Gerald has done nothing illegal. Again Mr. Rosedale repeats what I have read in a few books about cults. The law is set up to deal with tangible crimes, such as guns and embezzlement, not psychological intimidation and wrong intentions. Gerald has been clever enough to select invisible emotional crimes against the spirit, permissible within the bounds of the existing law. Because he has induced his victims to commit the crime against themselves, like driving someone to commit suicide rather than killing them yourself, there is no blood on his hands. It would be virtually impossible to convict him on anything concrete. Unless I have a bottomless pit of money which I can afford to invest in the hope that my case will set a new legal precedent, I must let it go. Gerald's only recognized offense is assault. However, there is a statute of limitation in New Jersey of one year and I am well over the time limit. Unfortunately, it is too late. In conclusion, I have no solid case against him and Mr. Rosedale sympathizes with my feelings but reiterates that I have no options open to prosecute. He sincerely recommends that I try to accept the past and get on with my life.

The Rest of 1997

Thankfully, it has been several months since I have set eyes on Samantha or any other Sharkman. Surprising, since they only live five minutes from me and we shop in the same stores, eat in the same restaurants. I dread the day when I will round the corner of a *K-Mart* or *Shoprite* aisle and run into one of them. I do not know if I will be capable of controlling my emotions; I fear that my hurt and loathing will erupt like a volcano, that I will scream of their crimes at the top of my lungs, breaking all rules of social propriety. After my tantrum passes, I will find myself trembling, sweating, hyperventilating and embarrassed beyond description. I know that someday I will be put to the test and I pray that day is far in the distant future . . .

It happens in October at Bergenfield's *Colonial Diner* on Washington Ave. Not a place I would expect to run into Samantha, not part of her regular circuit and yet, as the waiter shows me to my table I glance up and discover her, seated at a booth in the back corner. My heart skips and I grit my teeth, but she smiles encouragingly, appearing excited to see me, although I can't imagine why. After all, I am the ungrateful selfish bitch who screwed her out of her half of the business; regardless, she acts as if there were never any harsh words between us, as if our history was never anything but pleasant and superficial, and I hate her all that much more for denying the truth. I would prefer it if she were angry at me, at least that would be more human, but she seems to be have joined the "Stepford Wives", a "moving on" and "living in the moment" kind of a robot, forever a student of her father's logic. In this frame of reference, the realities of our emotional traumas appear to have never existed in her mind at all, as if they were a file she dutifully erased from her computer's hard-drive the moment she walked out of our office for the last time.

I do not play by the same rules and the sight her face triggers acute anxiety, a sensation of being propelled backwards instantaneously into my former miserable oppression and terror. I try to push past this reaction and force myself to approach her.

"It's really good to see you, Elizabeth," Samantha smiles with apparent sincerity while rising from her seat immediately to give me a hug. I recoil at her touch; a cobra has more warmth.

"How are you?" I respond nervously, trying to calm my quaking limbs, hoping she won't notice.

"Oh, really busy. I've been flying all over the place; just got back from Orlando on business," she declares with self-importance.

"What kind of business?" I probe, observing her eyes shift as her mind switches gears immediately in response to a direct question and searches for a diversionary statement. I can see that nothing has changed. She is still manufacturing justifications to pretend to be in business just as surely as she dragged us to Toronto, Florida, St. Louis and all over the tri-state area in fruitless pursuit of the ultimate flash card deal.

"You lost a lot of weight." I observe

"Yes, well you know we are all vegetarian now. We don't want to kill animals to eat. How are your cats?"

"Oh, just fine."

"Magic died, you know," she states matter-of-factly.

When we shared the house in Closter, Samantha had two cats which kept company with mine, Magic and Taz. Magic was an orange-striped male. I am genuinely surprised and saddened, he couldn't have been more than seven.

"What happened?" I ask, distressed.

"It was his kidneys, something genetic. I tried several vets, here and in the city, and a lot of other things, (I know this means Gerald shaking his head over the poor animal) but he didn't have the courage to fight the negativity. He actually died in my arms, just last month."

"Oh, that's terrible, I am so sorry."

"Yes, it was really hard . . ."

She pauses for a moment as if considering something and then focuses directly at me, two cold marbles mounted on a plastic mask of facial features,

"I had him freeze-dried," she reveals, and I perceive that she is actually repressing an almost whimsical giggle.

"What!?" I exclaim, horrified, repulsed, "Why? How? What is that? I never heard of such a thing!?"

As if discussing a new flavor of ice cream she is about to order, Samantha continues, "I heard about it on TV, so I decided to try it."

"But, I mean, what do you do with him? Is it like taxidermy?"

"No, he's not stuffed, just all the moisture taken out."

I imagine what Magic must look like now, a flattened mat of orange fur with a tragically sunken face, like road-kill. *Why, why, why, would you want to do that to an animal who used to sleep with you, a constant companion? How could you stand to look at this grotesque monstrosity and remember that he was once your friend?*

"Samantha, that's so morbid; what does it look like?" I continue, struggling to grasp the reality of what she is describing, "Like beef jerky with fur?"

She smirks and then actually begins to grin with what seems like pride, self-recognition of the unconventional choice she has made which I suppose serves to define her to herself as a unique human being.

"I mean, what do you do with him now?" I continue.

"Oh, I just keep him," she responds vaguely.

"Why? For what? Where? On your mantle as a decoration?"

"Oh, you know, I just wanted to do it . . . "

I can see that there will be no more details forthcoming and thankfully, our conversation ends in a few more sentences. Before I return to my table she rises to hug me again, placing her hand meaningfully on my shoulder, assuring me of how "really good it is to see me again". She leaves the diner about five minutes later, touching me once more on my back as she passes toward the exit, murmuring softly, sincerely, for me to "take care", and just after she passes my head splits open with the truth — like father, like daughter, a chip off the old block; she means to have a try at the resurrection experiment herself.

Samantha mails a videotape of her father shaking his head to the television program — *Strange Universe*. Thanks to her efforts, Gerald wins a position as one of five semifinalists in their contest entitled, "America's Strangest Person". A video crew gathers footage in the den during a Thursday night group meeting and in November, Gerald makes his debut on national television. He performs for his audience, shaking energetically while supporting a thirty-pound rock on top of his head with both hands and explaining pompously,

"One day my head just started shaking on its own — and —" he adds confidently, "I always speak the truth; it's the only thing that will survive".

That son-of-a-bitch, I think to myself, cursing at the screen as I watch him lying to millions of viewers.

On the three-minute clip, I observe Mitchell seated on the love seat across from Gerald. Recognizing that familiar blue and green plaid couch, my mind drifts into the not-too-distant past . . . If only that innocent-looking piece of furniture could reveal the tragic history of crimes to the human spirit which have taken place upon it — the day Gerald slammed me down there, viciously slapping me in the face for visiting a doctor — the hours he spent sprawled across those ample cushions while his female followers knelt dutifully on the floor delivering sexual favors, paying thousands of dollars for the honor — the group sessions of accusation, humiliation and emotional massacre, devoted to punishing us for spiritual crimes fabricated at the whim of our leader — the water he denied his perpetually thirsty diabetic dying dog because it was too much trouble to carry him outside to pee so often. If only the viewers could be present in just a few short hours when Ben will emerge from his carefully selected hiding place, even now within camera range, and the resurrection process will begin again for the thousandth time as Gerald quakes vigorously in his chair after feeding his "best friend" a morning meal of tiny bagel morsels.

Mitchell speaks to the cameras, glorifying Gerald's mission, and from my television monitor I spot my mother seated on one of those uncomfortable green velveteen folding chairs behind him, on the other side of the universe from me, in a semi-trance as usual. I am offended and appalled. The show capitalizes on Gerald's weird habits, only to benefit their ratings. Disgusted, I think to myself, *It's all a big joke to them, an empty amusement. If only the viewers knew the real truth; if only I could tell them about the lives he has destroyed . . .*

The following week, Judy and I run into Rich at *Dunkin' Donuts.*

"I have news for you guys," he tells us. "I just ran into Mitchell Stavos and he told me a few interesting things. First of all, he is running for State Senator, as an independent against Senator Lautenberg, and Martin is running for Bergen County Sheriff. In addition, Gerald is broadcasting a weekly radio program from his house. He has purchased the equipment and obtained an FCC license. Several out-of-state stations are picking up his show."

To add insult to injury, Rich whips out a copy of an article about Gerald in *The Suburbanite*, our local weekly paper. It refers to Gerald's work with the inmates at Sing Sing Prison in Ossining, N.Y. and describes his radio show, featuring him as a benevolent, gifted citizen.

"By the way," he adds, "I also heard from Mitchell that Gerald and Doris' divorce became official in November."

"She must have gotten half of his money," I reply, "My money, my mother's money, blood money . . . I hope she enjoys it . . ."

That night I sleep restlessly. In a dream, I run into my mother and Pauline a few blocks from my mother's West Side apartment. They are walking quickly, arm in arm, giggling together like girlfriends, on their way to The Group in New Jersey. They barely notice me as I approach them, and Grace greets me lackadaisically, despite the fact that I have not seen her in almost a year.

"Oh, hi Liz."

My rage and hurt escalate once again, choking me with the pain of my mother's indifference. Seeking to strike back at them all I turn to Pauline, threatening her,

"I'm going to call your parents and tell them what you are doing, that you are a member of a cult and destroying your life."

Unimpressed, Pauline retorts,

"Well, they won't believe you. Anyway, it's not a cult. You are just upset because you can't control Gerald."

With that, she shrugs her shoulders and walks away, continuing to chat and joke with my mother, taking her away from me . . . I reach out my hand toward them as they disappear around a corner, chatting in comfortable camaraderie.

"Don't go Mommy, please don't leave me," I cry out to the empty street.

Another night I dream about Bess. Tossing with anxiety and anguish, I implore her to face the truth, to realize that her personal well-being and future are in serious jeopardy. But I can't reach her, and at 3:00 A.M. I jolt out of my sleep to find my body soaked with sweat, my heart crying helplessly for her to wake up and escape from Hell before it is too late . . .

December rolls around and I invite my mother to Christmas dinner but she refuses.

"No, Liz, I don't think so."

"What do you mean?"

"I don't want to see you."

"Why not?"

"Because you can't keep your trap shut about Gerald. You blab to other people about his private affairs when it is none of their business."

"You'll never see me again, forever?"

"Maybe someday I will, but not now."

"But when?"

"I don't owe you any explanations."

I stare at the phone, white with shock, the lump in my throat choking me.

"I bought you a beautiful Christmas gift; I guess I'll UPS it to you."

And then, there is nothing more to say — "Bye Mom."

Is there any hope? Have I lost you forever?

Elizabeth is a joy in my life and the best friend I ever had. I have been more than repaid, with the richness of our friendship, for the sacrifices I made and the terror I experienced to venture into the "Devil's Den" like a fireman, carrying Elizabeth out on my back. God has put me in many places to do many things, but this has been by far the most fulfilling and rewarding assignment I have ever completed. The experience has lifted me to incredible spiritual heights, and I will forever be honored that He selected me for this very special mission. What a wonderful testimony this story is to God's love and power, when you can find Him inside of yourself and follow your heart!

Epilogue - The Year 2000

The oddly-shaped package labeled with my mother's return address arrives at noon. My 40th birthday passed exactly one month ago but I haven't heard from her since mid-November of last year — the day I presented her with a copy of this book. I knew she wouldn't take it well and the butterflies in my stomach almost caused me to change my mind, but I didn't want her to find out from someone else that our sordid past, mine and hers, was now unashamedly exposed for the world to see. I endured nearly three hours of superficial conversation, but it was she who finally pushed me over the edge . . .

"Liz, Gerald is ready for you to come back. He told me to let you know. . . Now I'm not supposed to share this with you," she suddenly lowered her voice as if the walls had ears, "but I overheard him confiding in Bess that he'd realized it might have been a mistake to throw you out."

She stated all of this with a straight face and complete confidence that I might very well take him up on his magnanimous offer.

"Mom," my voice trembled with disbelief and hurt, "I'm Gerald's greatest enemy. How could you or he begin to think otherwise? I am the only person who has no problem exposing him. In fact, I am a time bomb just waiting to blow."

"Enemy? Why? I don't think you really are. I remember you correcting Bess, Pauline and the others many times by declaring 'Be quiet and listen to this man; he's the only one who makes sense.' I know you got a lot out of your sessions with him; you told me so many times . . ."

"Don't you get it at all!!" I stated with force, ineffectively curbing my frustration. "I have changed. That was not Elizabeth speaking, but Gerald's brainwashed puppet."

She gazed at me quizzically, unmoved, so I rose from my seat, finally finding the strength to retrieve my book from its hiding place under my purse. Her pained eyes filled me with instant guilt, and when a few moments later she clutched her chest and moaned, "I'm not feeling very well," a harshly recriminating voice choked my mind, *You should have respected your mother's privacy. Now she might have a heart attack and die from shame, and it will be your fault.* But a moment later she recovered and I realized that despite my abusive thoughts, nothing could have stopped me from telling my story.

"Why did you hurt me like this? For attention from others? You must really hate me. You have always criticized me and put me down, ever since you were a little girl. Why can't you just forget the past and move on?"

Her voice descended like an iron fist and I squirmed in self-doubt. Betraying your own mother by revealing her ugly secrets publicly. What kind of daughter does such a thing? Then I grabbed the response that Judy, in her wisdom and strength, had given me the previous week,

"Mom, every word is the truth, and if you didn't want these things to be revealed then you shouldn't have done them to me. This was my life; I lived it; I have the right to tell anyone I want."

I shed tears of regret that day, seated at my mother's rickety dining room table piled high with manila folders, yellowed newspaper articles and several treasured rocks, my shoes stirring patterns in the dusty red Persian rug below. I told my mother I loved her and that I was so very, very sorry; not sorry that I had written my story, but sorry that it had all ever happened and that she had been a part of the crime; sorry that in this very room Gerald had gotten his start twenty-two years ago and that my mother was still to this day one of his most avid promoters.

The package contains a small wrapped item — an inexpensive scarf imprinted with teddy bears, a card indicating that this is a "happy birthday gift" and a copy of Gerald's latest book. Apparently he is writing prolifically and had added three more titles to his collection over the past few years. *Why did she send it a month late?* I wonder. And then Judy proposes a probable explanation,

"She must have waited until her connection to The Program broke, you know, the obligation to give gifts on holidays. What an atrocity for Gerald to teach that expressing love by remembering someone's birthday hinders personal growth."

Judy hugs me with genuine sadness for the twisted mind of my mother and the relationship I have been deprived of, but I turn to her and try to make the best of it,

"It's OK, Jude. I believe I've learned to accept her for who she is. I can't ruin the rest of my life trying to force her to change. Thank God I have decent loving people to share my life with."

President's Day - Monday, February 21

These days, my life is mundane and uneventful. I attend to the daily demands of business: processing orders for *Exambusters Study Cards*, sorting Bar-Mitzvah proofs and deleting junk E-mail. Sometimes I miss the stimulating excitement we experienced during my escape from The Group, but I truly value my peace of mind. I feel safe now and that is more precious to me than anything. In fact, in my three years of freedom I have never run into Gerald and I find that strange; after all, we are neighbors.

Bob Nicholas specializes in custom framing and I've done business with him for over ten years. I stop in during the early afternoon to pick up some work. Considering it's a holiday and the highways are crammed with retail shoppers, it seems strange that his store filled with gifts, antiques and framed art is completely empty. In fact an eerie silence hovers, and although he's usually speeding from one task to the next, and so am I, today we are both uncharacteristically calm. We fall into light conversation and chat for several minutes, not seeming to be able to break the connection.

The bell jingles on his front door and a shopper enters. We both look up curiously and instantly adrenalin shoots through my system. It is Gerald. Even though he is thirty feet away and his back is to me, I would sense his presence anywhere. I begin to shake. The physical reaction is automatic, a programmed response from years of trained terror, and even though there is no threat today, I cannot stop it. I stare hard at Bob's eyes as he speaks and he seems unaware of the profound change in my emotions; only now my reaction is ringing in my ears and I can't hear a word he is saying. Nonetheless I continue nodding politely, wondering what in the world I will do.

Gerald meanders among the gifts, picking up items at random, inspecting them and putting them back down. He seems to be taking an awfully long time to approach the counter and I know he is here for a reason. Gerald doesn't spend money; material things don't interest him and he is a notorious cheapskate. Perhaps he saw me too. I wonder.

I focus on the surging feelings in my body and apply my will to contradict them. *I must overcome this "Fight or Flight Reaction"*, I tell myself. Gerald poses no threat and this is ridiculous. He will never hurt me again; I would never tolerate it. Judy's lessons have grown deep roots. I take pride in standing up for myself and fending off those who would try to take advantage of me. Besides, Gerald is out of my life for good. It takes about five minutes, but the sensations finally begin to subside and I am grateful. A wave of calm passes over me. The silence in the store, except for Bob's voice, is almost palpable. In the next moment Gerald advances toward us and I must confront him. He acts as if he doesn't know me, obliging me to break the ice.

"Aren't you going to say hello?" I address him with a steady confidence I have never exhibited in all the years we have known each other.

He extends a reluctant hand toward the one I have just offered, but displays no emotion. There is an appreciable lack of interest in our interaction.

"How are you doing?" His familiar little-boy sweetness flows with light caress, but there is no conviction nor impetus to continue the conversation.

"I saw you on Mitchell's show. It was very interesting."

"Yes it was."

"You lost a lot of weight; must be the vegetarian diet."

Actually he looks shriveled, a bit pathetic, and his upper back curves slightly. Perhaps the onset of osteoporosis; overdue reciprocity from his body for years of neglected diet and physical exercise. I can easily project ten years into the future to imagine a withered old man shuffling down the halls of some retirement home, completely drained of his former passion and the terrifying power he once held over us all. The end of his life now seems so near. To me he was such a figure of exaltation, overwhelmingly omniscient and omnipresent all of those years. Now I see how temporary everything really is. What did I ever see in him? I am so angry at myself for being such a silly fool, throwing away my dignity. Like a child, I believed that each moment was eternity, every feeling the only possible reality. I don't see things that way any more. I am no longer looking for a parent to lead me, an authority figure to approve of my decisions. I no longer believe that someone else possesses my answers for life, an escape which allows me to avoid the risk of making mistakes. I suppose I have finally grown up.

There is nothing else to say so I turn and walk away, exiting the store, and neither of us say goodbye. When I reach my car a flood of emotion hits and I grab my cell phone to call Judy. Pouring my heart into the receiver I lament,

"I pushed past my fear and I wasn't angry or hostile. I could have said anything to him, the truth, that I know he is cruel and that he uses hypnosis and brainwashing to exploit people, that he lives in a world of lies and I have done research to figure out how he seduced and conned me, that The Group is a cult and he is a psychopath. Why did I blow the opportunity?"

"What's the point? He'll never change." She counters.

"No, it would just be for me, to be able to say it to his face."

"Well, maybe you'll have your chance someday, but I guess it wasn't meant for today or you would have done it."

Suddenly I realize why he was visiting the store, so I hang up the phone and rush back inside. Gerald, thankfully, has left, but in the middle of the counter lies that familiar velvet pouch on top of his business card, the one where he holds a globe of energy aloft, just like Atlas supporting the world. A creepy shiver runs through me and I look Bob in the eye. I am shaking visibly and Bob shows concern.

"What's the matter? You are pale as a ghost?"

"Oh Bob, you have no idea who that man is . . . ?"

"Do you know him? What's with that guy? He seemed crazy and I felt . . . evil. He offered to buy a small bracelet and I didn't even want to take his money. I just wanted him to leave."

"I'm glad you felt that way. He was trying to sell you his rocks, right? Well do me a favor and throw that thing away, as far away as you can."

Bob seems confused and frozen as I vomit out the details of my relationship with Gerald. I keep glancing at the rock, an ominous reminder of it's master's lingering essence. And after about ten minutes of almost hysterical description Bob finally comments.

"I can't believe you acted so calm. I would have wanted to put my fist through his face if he had done all of that to me."

"I used to feel the same way but I had to overcome the rage. It was too painful and the need for revenge was dominating my life. Although I would give anything to deliver his retribution, I have come to realize that I don't possess sufficient power to defeat this enemy. Declaring war would only cause damage to my limited resources, and it wouldn't put a dent in the momentum of his machine. I have no choice but to let it all go."

One Week Later - 10:00 PM
The phone jangles on my night table and I grab it.

"Hi Liz how are you?" A voice reaches through the wire. I shake my head and exclaim spontaneously,

"Who is this?" Then in the next moment a shred of familiarity reaches my brain and I correct myself quickly, "Oh, hi Mom."

"You mean you don't recognize me?" The voice is slightly defensive, hurt.

"Oh yeah, I do. I'm sorry; it took me a moment . . . "

And that seems to be the way it really is. In my life she is distant but still present. While she chatters my mind drifts. *Yes, Mom, I know you; I've known you all my life, but you don't know me. I know where your thoughts live; I once inhabited that place with you. I remember the geography so precisely that I could draw a map in the finest detail. But I climbed over the fence a long time ago, while you remained behind in your kindergarten world where rocks with names and personalities are your special companions. There you play with your schoolmates, my old friends. All of you share a treasured delusion sustained by perpetual moral dissociation and the mind's extraordinary ability to fantasize — to convince you that what you imagine is the truth — a realm of cotton candy fantasies which appear to possess shape and form and yet when consumed are devoid of substance and sustenance — a loveless life filled only with lies and distractions where dignity, empathy and compassion are completely beyond your reach. Your savior is the "power of suggestion", an enemy I understand intimately and despise absolutely. You and Gerald have discovered and mastered the ultimate escape, the ability to erase and then replace reality. I've ripped myself in half trying to bring you to the safe place where I now dwell, but you've refused every time. I would carry you over the fence myself if you asked, you wouldn't*

even have to climb, but Mother, poor soul, so twisted is your mind that you don't
even know that this fence which separates us exists . . .

I snap back to reality, "Mom, would you like to go to a movie sometime."
"OK, sure."

After everything that has happened, Why do I care to associate with her? I
wonder. But I know the answer. I can't run away and move to another state, wipe
the blackboard clean and start fresh; my home is here. I drive by Gerald's house
every day on the way to work, pass Mitchell's and Marty's cars on the road. They
all remain within the perimeters of my awareness. So, I must resolve my past.
They play by different rules than I do, but for most of them, I believe this is their
chosen life. Perhaps some people just aren't meant to leave a cult. Besides, I
know that to be truly healed I must sit among them and remain at peace within
myself. I must be strong enough to remain anchored to my new life even in enemy
territory. Each meeting is a test and I am getting there. Although familiar feelings
still sway me, they cannot uproot me. As if watching a movie, my memories no
longer trigger flashbacks of emotion. The nightmares are gone. An abandoned
railroad track overgrown with weeds, the once familiar impulses of rage, hurt and
vengeance no longer travel down those well-worn pathways.

And my mother will always be my mother. The seeds of my soul lie with her.
I see my own reflection in the energy of her presence — my true nature,
courageous, humble and passionate — the higher self who loved me enough to
demand my rescue from the arms of Satan.

So I will drive past his house again tomorrow, and instead of averting
tormented, angry eyes as I did three short years ago when he banished me from
the kingdom, I will turn my head and smile at the familiar sight — the cars of my
former comrades clustered around his driveway. I picture The Group gathering
inside Gerald's den — Bess, Nora, Pauline, Beatrice, Laura — doing what I used
to do, feeling what I used to feel, reveling in their seat of evil . . . Finally, I have
overthrown my victim mentality and can raise my head, smile and continue on,
singing to the CD player which blasts my favorite Melissa Ethridge song, proud
with the knowledge that I have cleaned out the cobwebs and overcome, that I
have made a new life despite it all.

> "You looked like father; you felt like mother.
> My mind told my heart, *there is no other.*
> And I gave you my soul, and every ounce of control,
> and I gave you my skin, and my original sin
> . . . ain't that enough?"
> - Melissa Ethridge

Appendix A

Excerpt from Gerald's cable TV interview aired March 2000

Host: Our guest, Reverend Gerald Sharkman, is a unique individual. Author of the book, *Biofeedback Without Machines*, he also hosts a radio show, *BrainTalk* and has been a counselor for the past twenty-five years in stress management and the practice of "The Energy". In fact, he believes that this energy he's discovered may be the salvation of mankind. Welcome, Gerald; tell us how you got started.

Gerald: Many years ago I went into biofeedback, which teaches the patient to listen to themselves and to control their autonomic nervous system. Instead of always running to a doctor to take care of you, you can learn to take control of your life. The nervous system is dominated by our primitive, "Fight or Flight" reactions. We live in a state of constant fear as if we are about to be eaten by a saber-toothed tiger. Our boss, our spouse, our parents — they all trigger us like this. Inappropriate survival reactions overpower us and instead of removing them, we make up stories to justify them. Fear is man-made. We are not made to fear. Now, when you start to relax and slow down to the "speed of life", you will find out that you're made of pure energy, 76 trillion cells all emitting light, and 9 trillion brain chips that we do not use. In reality, if we could activate more of our brains, we would be considered aliens on this planet. Nevertheless, it's time we start reaching for <u>our true potential</u> and become happy.

Host: Psychologists refer to stress as positive; a little stress is sometimes an effective motivator. It sounds like you're saying it's completely unnecessary.

Gerald: Stress is a warning that we are being insensitive to ourselves. Normally, when we have stress we try to do something about it, but this is wrong. We simply need to stop interfering, to get out of the way. Life flows without us doing anything; as soon as you interfere, there's a problem and this creates stress.

Host: How does that affect relationships?

Gerald: Well first of all, there are <u>no</u> relationships, only a relationship with yourself, but you ignore yourself. We're all trained from the day we're born to ignore ourselves. That means we don't care for ourselves, so we can't care for anybody else. That's the way it is. So, when you start training yourself to care about yourself, then you can begin to understand how somebody else feels and then you can care about another person.

Host: What type of problems do people have when they come to you for help?

Gerald: Cancer, heart problems, headaches . . . across the board. I just started treating a woman who has been an alcoholic for twenty years. Within three sessions she was pouring her vodka down the drain. Expensive drain cleaner, hah, hah. Usually people come to see me when there's no place else to go. Then, when we start working and the person finds they can cure it, that's when they get anxious. They're afraid of themselves, of their own greatness.

Host: There are many popular self-help gurus out there today, Deepak Chopra, Tony Roberts etc. Do you differ from what they promote?

Gerald: You have to understand, most everyone can teach someone else, but if they can't teach themselves . . . then it's not working. The human race is on the brink of extinction. We don't take care of the planet. We kill everything around us. Every time we cut down a tree there's less oxygen to breathe. This isn't changing even with all the positive information being taught by people. That's why I became the Reverend of the *Universal Church of Life for People, Plants and Animals.* Everything is alive and we must learn to respect and merge with it all. Scientists say that the molecules in our eyes came from the Big Bang, same as the molecules in rocks and plants.

Host: What did you experience when you were first starting out?

Gerald: I used to use the biofeedback machine myself so I could understand how to help my patients. Then one day my head started shaking on its own, very fast, as fast as light. Now when it stopped, it released an energy, a feeling, radiance. For many years people have been discovering this energy but the problem is that they can show it to everybody else, maybe even heal a disease, but if they don't do it for themselves, it's useless, temporary. They have to go all the way, become who they really are. Like I said before, 76 trillion cells all emitting light, connected to the universe. When you use your brain more than 4% (that's all we use), then you connect to the universe and you KNOW EVERYTHING. The shaking of the head allows me to get past symptoms, problems and anxieties. Beyond all of that we're unity. We belong to everything and everything belongs to us. We are truly GOD inside. No one listens to that inner being because the mind makes so much noise. For thousands of years we've been trying to slow down our minds, but you can't slow it down when you're the one who's creating your thoughts in the first place, so instead of trying to correct the mind, we have to FOCUS beyond the mind. You create a mission, to go for the greatness inside of you. I'm going to demonstrate what happens when a person shakes their head while focusing on a doorknob. Now when you shake, it's like shaking a bottle of seltzer, it expands. Instead of being frightened, just allow it to flow out and you'll feel wonderful. (Camera zooms in as he begins shaking his head back and forth rapidly for about one minute.) Now if everyone watching could start shaking their heads when they feel conflict, they would activate the energy within and shift to a better place; go beyond the problems. That's what it's all about.

Host: Is that shaking natural?

Gerald: When it first started, it was unnatural. It occurred by itself and I was afraid, but then I allowed it so many times that I finally entered in with it, merged my life with its force. We shouldn't be afraid of anything because there's really nothing unknown. If we can just get the brain to work we know everything. We don't need to <u>educate</u>, we need to experience. Education forces information down and interferes with the flow of energy.

Host: Now the whole system is based on education. We've been trained and trained since we were small children. So you're saying that anyone who wants to learn more about what you've discovered would have to un-train themselves? (Gerald nods in agreement.) They'd have to stop, watch and wait — which is what you advise in your book — and to become aware of how they're interfering in their lives so they can open up space for this feeling you're referring to. What you're also saying is that this feeling can expand out into everything, into other people, and they can begin to feel energy and be transmitters for it too.

Gerald: That's right, but the best transmitter I've found so far is a rock. I focus and release the energy in the rock. The rock is alive . . . Everything is alive because it's all made of energy, scientists have proved this in physics labs. I take a rock, shake it up, then it starts to radiate, pulsate and change colors. If you hold the rock it becomes your feedback system while you're growing, a connection to your true spiritual self. When you're nervous or anxious, you hold the rock and feel it pulse. These pulsations are bigger than our heartbeats. We should have our heartbeats regulated to the universe, but we don't. So the rock, which has no interfering thought process and is totally alive, has that universal pulsation and will remind you of who you truly are. Then you'll stop your nonsense — programming, games, lies, dramas, etc.

Host: So really, what you're saying is that the problems we have could be changed by people starting to accept this energy and their potential to feel "god" inside.

Gerald: Yes, and the energy is intelligent, so if we trust it, it will guide us.

Host: And we're all made of energy, so if we integrate, you're saying that we can become a great species.

Gerald: Yes, the energy is white light and everybody thinks of that as a "near death experience". It's not; energy is a "near <u>life</u> experience", but since we're trained <u>not</u> to live, we get frightened and run away. If you walk into the light, you'll feel happy. Energy is happiness; it's pure intelligence; it knows. That's what all of the stars, every planet, every <u>self</u> is made of. We're all connected to that oneness, but we're afraid of getting close because it's so vast and we're not trained to deal with this.

Host: How did your training in martial arts help you?

Gerald: In college I earned a black belt in Karate . . . Martial arts teaches you how to focus but it doesn't get you to your own greatness. However, as long as you remain focused, you will stay out of the way of the bigness, not interfere with the universal life force, then you will be able to finally experience a piece of your own greatness. But you can't take too much. The bigness is much too powerful to handle all at once because our species has been trained for millions of years to think small and feel small. Nonetheless, we're all the same, one big force. You have to trust there's something bigger inside of you than your thinking process. There's something bigger than the U.S. government. There's something bigger than anything man has created and it's inside. But, you have to access it.

Host: Do you believe that people or organizations feel uncomfortable or threatened the first time they experience this energy, that they don't understand and are afraid when they realize that there's a new way, a new direction?

Gerald: First of all, we <u>must</u> follow this new direction if we want to survive as a species. But yes, people feel threatened when they become happier because they're trained to be miserable. A person can only take a few moments of joy and then they'll start to doubt because it's unfamiliar. They react and tighten or contract. That's why people get sick; they're contracting all the time and eventually, their bodies break down. If they could only move out of the way, they would expand and then the disease would <u>have to</u> disappear.

Host: What did you experience many years ago when you first discovered this energy?

Gerald: If you look at history, all the way back to Jesus Christ, anyone who discovers something new is ostracized at first. So when I found this and started talking about it, people didn't want to have anything to do with me. They told me that I was wrong; I was crazy . . . and I had to deal with what they thought. But I believed that there was something more and I didn't care what others said. I used to host biofeedback seminars. I would take the stage, look out over the audience, a roomful of biofeedback practitioner colleagues, and say absolutely nothing for fifteen minutes. The people would get so upset because of their need to be distracted with a speech, to have every moment of their time filled with some type of noise, that they would actually throw chairs at me. They couldn't deal with the quiet, with experiencing themselves. In quiet there's actually an enormous amount of expansion and you can feel and hear it. There's wellness. You're never alone. When people feel lonely that's just their thought process lying to them. If you took a microscope and looked into your body, you'd see billions of living cells and microbes. That means you have a lot of family inside. If you can externalize that and merge with everything on the outside, you're one big force with everything. Not "alone" but "all one"! I can't understand why people feel alone.

Host: You're also the president of the *Bergen County Mineralogy Association*. Tell us about that.

Gerald: Well, people interested in stones love to cut them up. I keep saying, "Don't cut them because they feel as much as we do." The members elected me because I'm a great guy; I talk to stones and they talk back! I can take a rock and put it next to someone and that person starts to lose their symptoms. Most of the members are older and are worried about dying. They get healed while I'm there.

Host: We're hearing a lot about New Age, yoga, Reiki, Chi and healers. Do you differ from all of that?

Gerald: First of all, in meditation they talk about "chakras", centers of energy. I know for a fact that there shouldn't be any points of energy, we are total energy, and we are the whole universe inside. So when I shake my head, the person feels their own totality. They don't need to compartmentalize. Our minds are small and need to classify things in parts, like post office boxes, so we can feel like we have control. Now, we must reinterpret things. For example, arthritis. Remember we are electricity, so imagine that our electric company (the universe) sends 100,000 volts through us. Then we squeeze and tighten from the intensity. The result is pain which we interpret as arthritis or some other disease. What's going through our cells is the total universe and man did not and cannot create this electricity so he tightens. This is because when he loses control, he reacts in fear. We are continuously contracting over this tremendous force we are made of and creating all kinds of diseases. Break the word "disease" into parts and we get "dis" "ease" — stress and anxiety from lack of control.

Host: How should we relate with animals?

Gerald: Animals are energy and intelligence. They don't think as much as we do, so they feel and understand more. We are afraid of them because they know exactly what we're thinking, just like small children. They have a crazy program to kill for food. We see this on the *Discovery Channel*, shows about African lions, but when animals are touched by The Energy, they lose their aggressiveness and they roll over on their backs. Animals are able to be more caring because they don't have a thinking process that instructs them to doubt themselves. We're the only species that doubts ourselves. We were put here to learn from animals so we can guide them to a higher spiritual center, but instead we are making them extinct. We have to take responsibility because we are creating this mess. We're the ones ripping down trees to build another shopping mall and pouring pollution into the oceans and air. If we don't stop, we will destroy our natural world. The animals will have nowhere to live and nothing to eat, and neither will we.

Host: So, can you sum up what we as citizens must do and how this relates to what you're doing with energy?

Gerald: We have to learn to take care of ourselves. My intention is to continue shaking up The Energy. You know scientists have discovered recently that our bodies regenerate all of our cells; the body is really made to live forever. In my opinion it is only the crazy thought process that interferes with this. People don't do anything about their misery and destructiveness because they figure they'll die soon and go to heaven. Everyone's just biding their time. But I have news for them, there is no heaven to escape to. It's all here on the Earth and people are gonna have to deal with their immortality, learn to take responsibility for their negativity and make changes fast or else . . . It'll be too bad for them. Soon this energy I've discovered will finally wake everybody up to see the truth. If they've been practicing to accept the bigness, they'll be able to deal with who they really are, consciously. If they're not in practice, it's gonna be scary. Everybody's wonderful but they ignore this.

Host: Thanks Gerald, for sharing your unique insights with us today.

BIBLIOGRAPHY

1. Ankerberg, John & Weldon, John, *The Encyclopedia of New Age Beliefs*, Harvest House, 1996
2. Arnott, Dave, *Corporate Cults*, AMACOM, 2000
3. Carey, Ken, *The Third Millennium*, Harper Collins, 1991
4. Chopra M.D., Deepak, *Ageless body, Timeless mind*; Crown Publishers, 1993
5. Conway, Flo and Siegelman, Jim, *Snapping*, Stillpoint Press, 1995
6. Covey, Stephen R., *The Seven Habits of Highly Effective People*, Simon and Schuster, 1989
7. Fiore, Dr. Edith, *The Unquiet Dead: A Psychologist Treats Spirit Possession*, Ballantine Books, 1987
8. Forward, Ph.D., Susan, *Emotional Blackmail*, Harper Collins, 1997
9. Fromm, Erich, *The Anatomy of Human Destructiveness*, Henry Holt, 1973
10. Galanter, Marc, *Cults, Faith, Healing and Coercion*, Oxford University Press, 1999
11. Goldberg, Carl, *Speaking with the Devil — A Dialogue with Evil*, Viking, 1996
12. Goleman, Daniel, *Emotional Intelligence*, Bantam, 1994
13. Gomes, Alan W., *Unmasking The Cults*, Zondervan Publishing House — Harper Collins, 1995
14. Goodall, Wayde I., & Trask, Thomas E., *The Battle: Defeating the Enemies of your Soul*, Zondervan, 1997
15. Groothuis, Douglas R., *Unmasking the New Age*, Intervarsity Press, 1986
16. Hassan, Steven, *Combating Cult Mind Control*, Park Street Press, 1988
17. Hassan, Steven, *Releasing the Bonds*, Aitan Publishing, 2000
18. Hoggart and Hutchinson, *Bizarre Beliefs*, Richard Cohen Books, 1995
19. Hoover, William L. Ph.D., *Psychology of Mind Control*, Harcourt Brace, 1995
20. Hunt, June, *Cults* (audio), Hope for the Heart, 1997
21. Hunt, June, *New Age Mentality - a New Mask for an Old Message* (audio), Hope for the Heart, 1997
22. Jaffe and Hilbert, *Barron's How to Prepare for the GMAT*, Barron's, 1996
23. Jeremiah, David, *Invasion of Other Gods* (audio), Turning Point, 1996
24. Jeremiah, David, *What the Bible Says about Angels*, Questar Publishers, 1996
25. Kraft, Charles, *Defeating Dark Angels*, Vine Books, 1992

26. Krimmel, Edward and Patricia, *The Low Blood Sugar Handbook*, Franklin Publishers, 1992

27. Layton, Deborah, *Seductive Poison: A Jonestown Survivor's Story of Life and Death in The People's Temple*, Anchor Books — Doubleday, 1998

28. Lifton, Robert Jay, *Destroying the World to Save It*, Henry Holt, 1999

29. MacLaine, Shirley, *Out on a Limb*, Bantam, 1983

30. MacNutt, Francis, *Deliverance from Evil Spirits: A Practical Manual*, Chosen Books, 1995

31. Marcinko, Richard, *Rogue Warrior*, Simon and Schuster, 1992

32. Martin, Malachi, *Hostage to the Devil*, Harper Collins, 1992

33. Meyer, Joyce, *How to Fight the Devil and Win* (audio), Life in the Word, 1996

34. Milgram, Stanley, *Obedience to Authority,* Harper Collins, 1974

35. Millman, Dan, *The Way of the Peaceful Warrior*, H. J. Kramer Inc., 1990

36. Monteleone, Thomas F., *The Blood of the Lamb*, Tom Doherty Associates, 1992

37. Monteleone, Thomas F., *The Resurrectionist*, Warner Books, 1995

38. Muster, Nori J., *Betrayal of the Spirit*, University of Illinois Press, 1997

39. Norwood, Robin, *Women Who Love Too Much*, Simon and Schuster, 1997

40. Patrick, Ted, *Let Our Children Go,* Ballantine, 1977

41. Peck, M. Scott, *People of the Lie*, Simon and Schuster, 1983

42. Peck, M. Scott, *The Road Less Traveled*, Simon and Schuster, 1978

43. Redfield, James, *The Celestine Prophecy*, Warner Books, 1993

44. Robbins, Anthony, *Unlimited Power*, Ballantine, 1986

45. Sagan, Samuel M.D., *Entity Possession: Freeing the Body of Negative Influences*, Destiny Books, 1997

46. Sargant, William, *Battle for the Mind*, Malor Books, 1997

47. Singer, Margaret Thaler and Lalich, Janja, *"Crazy" Therapies - What are they? Do they work?*, Jossey-Bass Publishers, 1996

48. Sutphen, Dick, *The Battle for your Mind*, Speech delivered to the World Congress of Professional Hypnotists Convention, Las Vegas, NE 1999

49. Unger, Merrill F., *Demons in the World Today*, Living Books, 1971

50. Unger, Merrill F., *What Demons Can Do To Saints*, Moody Press, 1960

51. Walsch, Neale Donald, *Conversations with God*, G. P. Putnam's Sons, 1995

52. Whyte, H. A. Maxwell, *A Manual on Exorcism*, Whitaker House, 1974

53. Williamson, Marianne, *A Return to Love: Reflections on the Principles of A Course in Miracles*, Harper Collins, 1992